CREDO SERIES

Responding to the Call of Jesus Christ

Based on the SL Curriculum Framework Protocol
Option D: Responding to the Call of Jesus Christ

WRITERS
Patrick Manning, MEd, MTS, PhD
and
Daniella Zsupan-Jerome, MA, PhD

GENERAL EDITOR
Thomas H. Groome, EdD
Professor Theology and Religious Education
Boston College

VERITAS

USA Office: Frisco, Texas

www.veritasreligion.com

The Subcommittee on the Catechism, United States Conference of Catholic Bishops, has found that this catechetical high school text, copyright 2018, is in conformity with the Catechism of the Catholic Church *and that it fulfills the requirements of Elective Course D of the* Doctrinal Elements of a Curriculum Framework for the Development of Catechetical Materials for Young People of High School Age.

CREDO SERIES CONSULTANT: Maura Hyland
PUBLISHER, USA AND THEOLOGICAL EDITOR:
Ed DeStefano
CATECHETICAL CONSULTANT: Brendan O'Reilly
COPY EDITOR: Elaine Campion
DESIGN: Lir Mac Cárthaigh
TYPESETTING: Heather Costello
COPYRIGHT RESEARCH: Emma O'Donoghue

INTERNET RESOURCES
There are internet resources available to support this text. Log on to *www.credoseries.com*

NIHIL OBSTAT
Rev. Msgr. Robert M. Coerver, S.T.L.
Censor Librorum

IMPRIMATUR
† Most Reverend Kevin J. Farrell, D.D.
Bishop of Dallas
June 20, 2015

The *Nihil Obstat* and *Imprimatur* are official declarations that the work contains nothing contrary to Faith and Morals. It is not implied thereby that those granting the Nihil Obstat and Imprimatur agree with the contents, statements or opinions expressed.

SEND ALL INQUIRIES TO:
Veritas, Customer Service
4848 N Clark Street
Chicago IL 60640
Tel. 866-844-0582
info@veritasreligion.com
www.veritasreligion.com

ISBN 978 1 84730 830 6 (Student Edition)
ISBN 978 1 84730 831 3 (Teacher Resource Edition)
ISBN 978 1 84730 832 0 (E-book: Student Edition)

Printed in the United States of America
1 2 3 4 5 6 7 / 18 19 20 21 22

CONTENTS

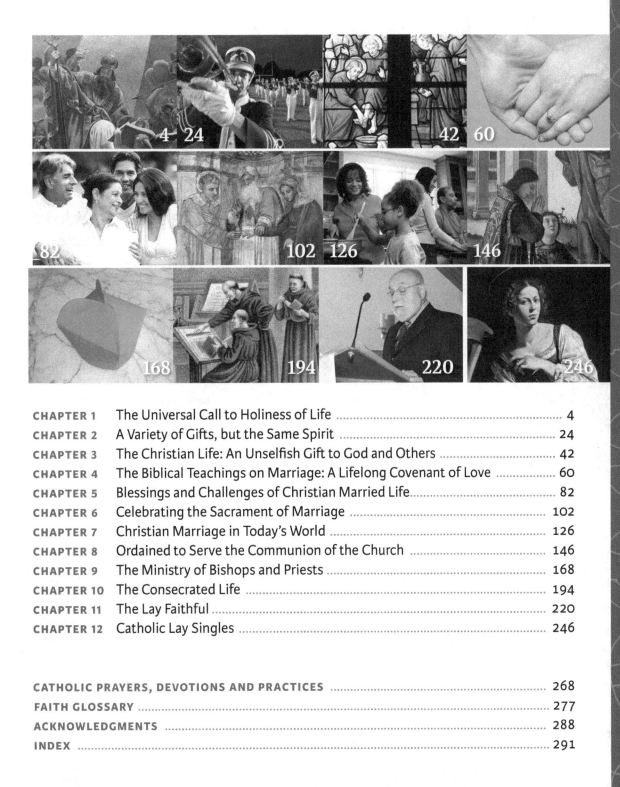

CHAPTER 1

The Universal Call to Holiness of Life

OUR COMMON VOCATION

TO KNOW, LOVE AND SERVE GOD

TO REFLECT GOD IN OUR ATTITUDES, WORDS AND ACTIONS

TO GROW IN HOLINESS OF LIFE

TO LIVE IN LOVING COMMUNION WITH GOD, WITH ONE ANOTHER AND WITH ALL CREATION

TO SHARE IN THE LOVE AND LIFE OF GOD

TO BECOME LIKE GOD

JESUS IS OUR MODEL OF HOLINESS

THERE IS A LONGING WITHIN EACH ONE OF US for God, who has created us in the divine image and made us sharers in his very own life. Through this longing implanted in the human heart, the Blessed Trinity calls all people to know, love and serve God and offers us the grace through Jesus Christ to share God's life and love and grow in holiness of life.

GOD'S GRACE COMES TO US THROUGH:

THE CHURCH

THE SEVEN SACRAMENTS

THE PEOPLE WE ENCOUNTER

THE NATURAL WORLD

OUR INNERMOST THOUGHTS

THE EVENTS AND EXPERIENCES OF OUR LIFE

Faith Focus: These teachings of the Catholic Church are the primary focus of the doctrinal content presented in this chapter:

⊙ There is a longing for God the Creator in the heart of every person.
⊙ God desires that all people would come to know, love and serve him.
⊙ All people share in the common vocation to strive for holiness of life.
⊙ There is an integral connection between one's work, job or career and one's vocation. A vocation is not the same as a job or a career.
⊙ Jesus Christ, in his life and teachings, and in his Passion, Death, Resurrection and Ascension, reveals the way to strive for holiness of life.
⊙ Holiness of life is the pathway to true success and happiness and the ultimate goal in life.
⊙ Holiness of life reflects the life of the Trinity, God the Creator.

Discipleship Formation: As a result of studying this chapter and discovering the meaning of the faith of the Catholic Church for your life, you should be better able to:

⊙ recognize God's personal invitation to come to know, love and serve him;
⊙ make the connection between your life and your God-given vocation to strive for holiness of life;
⊙ value holiness of life as the real measure of human success and happiness;
⊙ live as an image of God by striving to reflect the Trinitarian life in your attitudes, deeds and words;
⊙ imitate the way of life that Jesus preached and lived;
⊙ cooperate with the many graces the Holy Spirit offers you each day.

Scripture References: These Scripture references are quoted or referred to in this chapter:
OLD TESTAMENT: Genesis 1:26a–27; **Deuteronomy** 6:4–5; **Leviticus** 19:8
NEW TESTAMENT: Matthew 5:1–11 and 48, 6:19–24, 13:31–32, 19:21, 22:34–40, 28:20; **Mark** 12:28–34; **Luke** 10:25–28; **John** 14:6 and 25–26, 15:9–19; **1 Corinthians** 12:4–11; **Galatians** 2:20; **Philippians** 2:4–11; **Colossians** 1:15 and 17; **2 Timothy** 6:19; **Titus** 3:6; **1 Peter** 2:9; **2 Peter** 1:4; **1 John** 4:7–12, 16b and 19

Faith Glossary: Familiarize yourself with or recall the meaning of these key terms. Definitions are found in the Glossary: **covenant, grace, holiness, image of God, Incarnation, Kingdom of God, sacrament, sanctifying grace, Trinity, vocation**

Faith Word: vocation
Learn by Heart: 1 John 4:12
Learn by Example: Jesuit Volunteer Corps

What do all people most long for?

The human person longs to be loved and to give love in return. This longing is at the root of just about everything we do and desire—it determines the people we hang out with, how we dress, the activities we choose and so on. We try to get people to like and accept us in various ways, such as by being funny or athletic or smart. This longing for love is so much a part of our nature that we are always seeking to fulfill it.

OPENING REFLECTION

◉ Do you identify with this description of the human desire for love? Do you agree that it is a universal desire? Why or why not?

◉ What do you imagine the ideal of a truly loving relationship to be like?

◉ How many people do you think find this sort of true love in their lives, and where do they usually find it?

◉ What helps a person attain such love? What hinders them?

GOD: SOURCE OF OUR HUMAN LONGING

Many wise people who initially thought they had found "true love" will tell you that they still long for more. No other person or career, no fame or fortune ever fully satisfies our longing. And so we keep searching.

Blaise Pascal, a seventeenth-century French Christian philosopher, physicist, mathematician and inventor (he invented an early form of the calculator, the Pascaline), summed up this truth

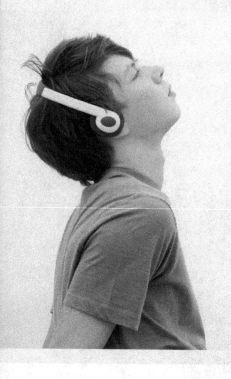

Fall in Love

Nothing is more practical than
finding God, than
falling in Love
in a quite absolute, final way.
What you are in love with,
what seizes your imagination, will affect
   everything.
It will decide
what will get you out of bed in the morning,
what you do with your evenings,
how you spend your weekends,
what you read, whom you know,
what breaks your heart,
and what amazes you with joy and gratitude.
Fall in Love, stay in love,
and it will decide everything.
   —Pedro Arrupe, SJ (1907–91), 28th Superior
      General of the Society of the Jesuits

St. Augustine's life was one long search for the relationship that would satisfy the longings of his mind and heart

ST. AUGUSTINE | BERGAMO, ITALY

about humanity and proffered an argument for why this is so. Pascal, in his *Pensées*, wrote: "There's a God-shaped vacuum in the heart of every man which cannot be filled by any created thing, but only by God, the Creator, made known through Jesus."

The Catholic Church today teaches the same truth in this way: "The desire for God is written in the human heart, because man is created by God and for God; and God never ceases to draw man to himself. Only in God will he find the truth and happiness he never stops searching for" (*Catechism of the Catholic Church* [CCC], no. 27).

OVER TO YOU

- ⊙ Compare Pascal's words with the words of Father Arrupe in his reflection "Fall in Love." How are they similar?
- ⊙ Do you agree with their reasoning? Why or why not?

THE COVENANT: THE GREATEST LOVE RELATIONSHIP OF ALL TIME

The life of the great St. Augustine of Hippo (354–430) is testament to the truth that no created person or created object, not even the purest human love, can fulfill the deepest longing of our mind and heart to be loved and to love. Augustine's life was one long search for the relationship that would satisfy the longings of his mind and heart. Augustine's often-quoted words describe his own searching and the conclusion he reached: "You have made us for yourself, O Lord, and our hearts are restless until they rest in you" (*Confessions*, Book 1, Chapter 1, 1).

Why is this the case? God has revealed that he freely created the human person out of love; and, above all else, God desires that all people would share in his love and live in intimate communion with him. Sacred Scripture names this divine–human relationship the **covenant**.

This covenant began at creation and was most fully revealed and fulfilled through the redemptive life, Passion, Death, Resurrection and Ascension of Jesus Christ, the Incarnate Son of God. Even the most dramatic and intense human love relationships are only subplots in the reality of this bigger and universal love story. All created love points to the unfathomable generosity and mystery of divine love. The beloved disciple, the Apostle John, put it this way:

Beloved, let us love one another, because love is from God; everyone who loves is born of God and knows God. Whoever does not love does not know God, for God is love. God's love was revealed among us in this way: God sent his only Son into the world so that we might live through him. In this is love, not that we loved God but that he loved us and sent his Son to be the atoning sacrifice for our sins. Beloved, since God loved us so much, we also ought to love one another. No one has ever seen God; if we love one another, God lives in us, and his love is perfected in us. . . .

God is love, and those who abide in love abide in God, and God abides in them. . . . We love because he first loved us.

—1 John 4:7–12, 16b, 19

- ⊙ Why do you think no person can ever fulfill another's longing for love?
- ⊙ Do Augustine's conclusions about human longing ring true for you? Why or why not?

THE CHOICE TO RESPOND IS OURS

We love and crave love because God, who is love, first loved us and invites us to respond to that love. The Triune God created us in the image and likeness of that divine love. To put it another way, by creating us in the divine image and likeness the Creator has infused into our very nature and being a longing for love—to love and to be loved.

We can follow our divinely implanted internal compass that points us to God, to our one true source and fulfillment, or we can wander in other directions. Blaise Pascal is said to have put it this way:

There are only three types of people: those who have found God and serve him; those who have not found God and seek him; and those who live not seeking or finding him. The first are rational and happy; the second unhappy and rational, and the third foolish and unhappy.

Friendship and love must be freely chosen; neither can be compelled. God's love for us is revealed in the fact that God created us with a mind to come to know and believe in him and a will to freely choose to love and serve him. We show our love for God and for others when we make a gift of our self to God and to others, as Jesus did. God gives us the inner compass and grace to orient us to our ultimate fulfillment in a life of intimate communion with him. The choice to follow that compass is ours to make—such is the mystery of the depth of God's love. We can choose a path, as Pascal pointed out, that will lead to happiness or unhappiness.

OVER TO YOU

- ⊙ How do you feel when you are with someone who really cares about you, as opposed to being with someone who just wants something from you?
- ⊙ What does it say to you that God orients us to share in his love but gives us the freedom to choose to accept or turn our back on that love?

A LIFE OF INTIMATE COMMUNION, OR LOVE, WITH GOD

God has created the human person to know, love and serve him. The fulfillment of this fundamental drive implanted in the very nature of the human person is the universal human **vocation**. The word "vocation" comes from the Latin verb *vocare*, meaning "to call." Typically we first "hear" this call in the form of the inner yearning we have been talking about. It is subtle but persistent.

We exist to love. As Jesus made amply clear, our vocation as human beings is most

FAITH WORD

Vocation

The term given to the call to each person from God; everyone has been called to holiness and eternal life, especially in Baptism. Each person can also be called more specifically to the priesthood or to religious life, to married life, and to single life, as well as to a particular profession or service.

—*United States Catholic Catechism for Adults* (USCCA), Glossary, 531

The Giving Up of Self

Until you have given up yourself to Him [Christ] you will not have a real self. Sameness is to be found among the most "natural" men, not among those who surrender to Christ. How monotonously alike all the great tyrants and conquerors have been: how gloriously different are the saints.

But there must be a real giving up of the self. You must throw it away "blindly" so to speak. . . . Give up yourself and you will find your real self. . . . Keep back nothing.

—C. S. Lewis, *Mere Christianity*

ICONS OF THE SAINTS, CHURCH OF OUR SAVIOR, ST. PETERSBURG, RUSSIA

fundamentally our response to the call to love God, ourselves and one another. Personal satisfaction in life, as the Great Commandment teaches, finds a firm foundation in our relationship with the Lord and in our relationships with other people. Recall Jesus' teaching about the Great Commandment. (Check out Matthew 22:36–40; Mark 12:28–34; Luke 10:25–28; see also Deuteronomy 6:4–5; Leviticus 19:18.) As we will see later, living out this vocation takes many different forms and each of us responds in different ways, but every dimension of human life has this common goal.

GOD CALLS EVERY PERSON TO HOLINESS OF LIFE

When we respond positively to our vocation to love God, neighbor and self, we are seeking holiness of life. We are striving to reflect the life of the Trinity in our own life. The term "holiness" is understood in many ways. Often people equate being holy with going to church, praying and little else; but holiness means so much more than these and other practices. Take a moment and review the Catholic Church's understanding of holiness.

Holiness is a "state of goodness in which a person—with the help of God's grace, the action of the Holy Spirit, and a life of prayer—is freed from sin and evil. Such a person, when gifted with holiness, must still resist temptation, repent of sins that may be committed, and realize that remaining holy is a lifelong pilgrimage with many spiritual and moral challenges. The struggles evident in the lives of the saints are instructive when trying to explain and describe holiness."

—USCCA, Glossary, "Holiness," 514

Our regular participation in Mass and reception of Holy Communion is the foundation and heart of our seeking and growing in holiness of life. Our Church teaches and reminds us: "The Sunday celebration of the Lord's Day and his Eucharist is at the heart of the Church's life" (CCC, no. 2177). "The Sunday Eucharist is the foundation and confirmation of all Christian practice" (CCC, no. 2181). Regular participation in Mass and receiving Holy Communion nourishes and strengthens all our other practices and efforts to live our life in Christ.

Holiness of life is sharing or participating in the life and love of God and making a gift of oneself for others

Holiness of life means realizing our full potential as human beings. St. Catherine of Siena (1347–80), who was known for her care of the poor and the sick and for working for peaceful solutions to conflicts within the Church, is reputed to have written these words: "Be who God meant you to be and you will set the world on fire."

At its root, holiness of life is sharing or participating in the life and love of God and learning to make a gift of oneself for others, as Jesus did. It is living in communion with God and witnessing to that holiness in one's words and deeds, which include a diversity of religious practices. It means responding to the circumstances of life with joy and love, and enjoying the fulfillment that comes with such joy and love here on earth and, hereafter, eternally in heaven. Jesus taught the blueprint for this life of happiness and holiness in the Beatitudes.

Holiness of life is real success in life. It is the hallmark of "the life that really is life" (2 Timothy 6:19). Striving for such holiness of life is a "lifelong pilgrimage with many spiritual and moral challenges." It is a task that God both calls us to and supports us in undertaking so that we may transform ourselves and the world.

LET'S PROBE DEEPER: A SCRIPTURE ACTIVITY

- Revisit Jesus' teachings on the Beatitudes in Matthew 5:1–11.
- What do the Beatitudes teach about finding happiness in our life?
- How are people who live the Beatitudes giving witness to holiness of life?
- Share your responses as a class.

OVER TO YOU

- Have you come to think about happiness and holiness differently? What might a life of happiness and holiness look like for you personally?
- How can you embrace that vocation?

Called to be images of God

OPENING REFLECTION

- Think about how you are an image of God. What is it about you that reflects God?
- Think about how your classmates are images of God. What is it about them that reflects God?
- Share your reflections if you feel comfortable in so doing.

THE VOCATION TO BE AN IMAGE OF GOD

The Book of Genesis reveals:

God said, "Let us make humankind in our image, according to our likeness"; . . .
   So God created humankind in his image,
      in the image of God he created them;
      male and female he created them.
                              —Genesis 1:26a–27

The human vocation and challenge is to be **images of God**—to reflect God in our attitudes, words and actions. God the Creator has revealed himself to be a Holy **Trinity**, that is, one God in Three Persons—Father, Son and Holy Spirit. The Three Persons of the Trinity share one divine nature and are inseparable in who they are and in what they do. The Trinity is a divine communion of love.

As beings made in God's image, we live our vocation and become who and what God created us to be only when we strive to live in loving communion with God, with one another and with all creation. At the Last Supper Jesus told his disciples:

"As the Father has loved me, so I have loved you; abide in my love. If you keep my commandments, you will abide in my love, just as I have kept my Father's commandments and abide in his love. I have said these things to you so that my joy may

RUSSIAN FRESCO DEPICTING THE HOLY TRINITY AS THREE PERSONS

be in you, and that your joy may be complete.
   This is my commandment, that you love one another as I have loved you."
                              —John 15:9–12

The standard for our ultimate success in life is to reflect the love of God the Holy Trinity, who is a communion of love. Therefore, it is important for us to ask: How do we learn to live out our vocation to reflect the Trinitarian life and love here and now? Jesus, of course, shows us the way. Our success in life depends on how we accept and respond to our vocation.

THINK, PAIR AND SHARE

- What does the Revelation that God creates every person in the divine image and likeness say about the human person?
- What obstacles and distractions in life can impede us from being images of the life and love of our Creator, the Triune God?
- What can young people who are disciples of Jesus Christ do in order to live out that vocation? Share specific examples.

WHAT ABOUT YOU PERSONALLY?

⦿ How will your striving to live as a reflection of the Trinity contribute to your success and happiness?

JESUS CHRIST, THE IMAGE OF THE LIVING GOD

How can we best respond to God's call? Christians believe and trust that we are not alone in striving to fulfill our vocation. First and foremost, Jesus Christ, the Incarnate Son of God, is our teacher who is with us "always, to the end of the age" (Matthew 28:20). He is there to guide us through all the ups and downs that we will encounter.

St. Paul wrote: "[Jesus Christ] is the image of the invisible God, the firstborn of all creation; . . . He himself is before all things, and in him all things hold together" (Colossians 1:15, 17). Jesus Christ is the Second Person of the Trinity made flesh. Through his words and deeds the Incarnate Son of God, who is fully divine and fully human, made God visible. Jesus is the fullest and clearest Revelation of who God is and of the kind of person God calls each of us to be.

"The Word became flesh *to be our model of holiness*" (CCC, no. 459). Through the mystery of the **Incarnation** the Son of God took on a human nature and, without giving up being God, lived among us. Our vocation is not simply to imitate the divine love manifested in Jesus Christ. God calls us to actually *become like God*. "The Word became flesh to make us '*partakers of the divine nature*' (2 Peter 1:4)" (CCC, no. 460). St. Athanasius (296–373) wrote: "For the Son of God became man so that we might become God" (*On the Incarnation*, 54, 3; quoted in CCC, no. 460).

God calls us to participate in and share with others the life and love of God by uniting ourselves to Christ. St. Paul, who responded to this vocation, wrote, "it is no longer I who live, but it is Christ who lives in me" (Galatians 2:20). Our union with Christ, the source of life and love, is the source of all holiness. Our lifelong vocation is to respond to God by striving to join with Christ and make our self a gift of self-sacrificing love to God and to others.

The more we love, the closer we abide in God and God in us. In the words of the beloved disciple, "[I]f we love one another, God lives in us, and his love is perfected in us" (1 John 4:12). Such intimate union requires nothing less than the complete gift of our full personhood. It requires holding nothing back, just as Jesus held nothing back in his own life and Death.

Responding to our Christian vocation is not simply a matter of adding one more thing to our to-do list. It means doing everything with great love, from contributing to our family life, to being with friends, to sharing with others in the wider community. This is how Jesus lived and it is the life he commanded his disciples to live. Holiness is wholeness, and God wants nothing less than our whole selves.

OVER TO YOU

⦿ How do you show by your words and actions that you are like God, or God-like?
⦿ How and where do you find the knowledge and strength to do so?

JESUS CHRIST, "GOD-WITH-US"

Jesus was like us in all ways except sin. He lived a full human life just like we do. He enjoyed sharing meals and spending time with family and friends just as we do. He also endured the unpleasantness of human conflict, pain, hunger and temptation. Where we might sometimes act out of hurt or selfishness in seeking success, Jesus responded out of love to every person and every situation he encountered. His love was without limits. He loved the people whom society ignored, especially the least, the lost and the last. He loved those who deserted him in his time of greatest need before his Death, even those who conspired to kill him.

Thanks to Jesus we do not have to wonder what it means for humans to strive for holiness of life by loving as God loves. God is always with us, empowering us to meet that challenge. At the Last Supper Jesus promised that he and the Father would send the Holy Spirit, the Third Person of the Trinity, to be our ever-present companion, advocate and teacher. (Check out John 14:16 and 25–26.) Perhaps it was through reflecting on this promise and teaching of Jesus that St. Paul would write that God's Spirit, the Advocate, dwells within us and is "poured out on us richly through Jesus Christ our Savior" (Titus 3:6).

LET'S PROBE DEEPER: A SCRIPTURE ACTIVITY

◉ Work in small groups. Look up, read and reflect on a gospel passage in which Jesus reveals the way of love that he commands us to live.

◉ Discuss:
 – How do Jesus' actions in this passage reveal the divine love of the Trinity?
 – How does Jesus reveal and model for us the human vocation to make a gift of oneself out of love?

OVER TO YOU

◉ What impact have our discussions had on your thinking about the purpose of human life?

◉ What connection do you see between your striving for success in your life and your striving for holiness of life?

◉ What concrete steps can you take to live out your call to holiness of life more fully?

Jesus loved those who deserted him in his time of greatest need; he even loved those who conspired to kill him

LONGINUS PIERCES JESUS' SIDE | FRA ANGELICO

Growing in holiness with God's grace

ST. THOMAS AQUINAS | STAINED GLASS FROM THE 1920S

Is it really possible for us to become *like God*?

God is infinite and we are finite. God is perfect and we are imperfect. God is all-holy, the Holy One, and we are sinners striving for holiness of life. So how can we even dream of becoming like God? There is always infinitely more difference than there is similarity between God and us. St. Thomas Aquinas (1225–74) responded to our question this way: "The only-begotten Son of God, wanting to make us sharers in his divinity, assumed our nature, so that he, made man, might make us gods" (*Little Treatises*, or *Opuscula*, 57:1–4). We become *like God, not God*, because God desires to make us partakers in his life and love and that we will live in communion with him.

At some time or another most of us dream dreams that seem to be unreachable stars. It can be daunting to seek to reflect the life and the love of the Trinity by following Jesus, who declared, "I am the way, and the truth, and the life" (John 14:6). We can only reflect God's life and love in an imperfect way and only when we respond to God's grace.

OPENING REFLECTION

- ◉ Do you know or have you learned about anyone who has reached for what seemed to be an impossible dream? Who?
- ◉ Are you striving to attain what might seem like an impossible dream? What is that dream? Why are you pursuing it?
- ◉ Do you sometimes feel that God is calling you to strive toward impossible goals?
- ◉ Share your thoughts and feelings with God.

BECOMING LIKE GOD: AN IMPOSSIBLE DREAM?

Recall what St. Athanasius wrote about why the Son of God became one of us: "For the Son of God became man so that we might become [like] God."

GRACE: A HELPING HAND TOWARD HOLINESS

Fortunately, God always desires to help us live in communion with him. God's desire for us is not an impossible dream. The Triune God actively gives us the assistance we need. God abides in us and assists us in attaining the reachable goal of becoming *like God*. The Church names this effective presence of the Trinity with us grace.

God's grace sanctifies us (sanctifying grace), or makes us holy, and supports us in living a holy life. In addition to sanctifying grace, God offers us other graces. The Church names these graces actual graces. They are gifts for specific circumstances we face in our life. Actual graces include "sacramental graces (gifts proper to each sacrament), special graces or charisms (gifts that are intended for the common good of the Church), among which are the graces of state that accompany the exercise of ecclesial ministries and the responsibilities of life" (*Compendium of the Catechism of the Catholic Church*, no. 424).

So how do we recognize and respond to grace? The primary medium of God's grace is the Church, through her teachings and ministries and the Seven Sacraments—Baptism, Confirmation, Eucharist, Penance and Reconciliation, Anointing of the Sick, Holy Orders, and Marriage. The mysteries of Jesus' life and the Paschal Mystery of his Passion, Death, Resurrection and Ascension are the foundation of the sacraments. In these Seven Sacraments we encounter Christ and receive his saving and sanctifying graces in the most effective way.

The Triune God offers everyone—not just a select few—the graces to strive for and reach a state of sanctification. The faithful whom the Church has canonized, or named saints, were not born saints. They cooperated with God's grace and strove for what many non-believers might call "an impossible dream," an "unreachable star." We can be confident that God's grace is always guiding and supporting us in this work of sanctification.

GOD'S GRACE IS EVERYWHERE

While we tend to look for and expect to receive God's grace in churches, shrines and other holy places, God's active presence in our life is not bound to such places. God offers us his grace in many and diverse ways. For example, God offers us grace through the people we encounter in our life—Christians and non-Christians—through whom God invites and challenges us to love more fully. The Triune God reveals himself to us through the natural things in our lives—the sights we see and sounds we hear, and in our own innermost thoughts. The events and experiences of our life—personal triumphs, traumatic losses, long-term labors—are also among the many ways God reaches out to us.

The Principle of Sacramentality

God's presence permeates creation. Catholics describe this presence as the sacramentality of life in the world. When we look at the world through sacramental eyes, we can recognize God's grace pouring forth from every seam, crevice and corner. The Seven Sacraments are the most effective expression of this sacramentality.

THE SEVEN SACRAMENTS | ROGIER VAN DER WEYDEN

THE CONVERSION OF ST. PAUL | PIETER BRUEGEL THE ELDER

We cannot travel the path to holiness on our own and through our own efforts. It is a journey we can make only with the grace of God and the Church

God's grace is everywhere, surprising us and inviting us to respond to his call to strive for holiness and wholeness of life. God offers us the many graces we need to become the holy People of God, everywhere and at all times. Most of all, it is in the Seven Sacraments that God offers us his many graces. It is there that we assuredly encounter Christ and are offered the graces to live as "a royal priesthood, a holy nation, God's own people, in order that [we] may proclaim the mighty acts of him who called [us] out of darkness into his marvelous light" (1 Peter 2:9).

The Triune God leaves it up to us whether we will accept the grace God offers. But we cannot travel the path to holiness on our own and through our own efforts. It is a journey we can make only with the grace of God and the Church that Christ established to guide us. Our refusal to answer God's call may result in a more difficult road to eternal life, or it may even jeopardize our salvation.

When we consider that God only desires what will make us holy and whole, happy and free, we see clearly that refusing the abundance of grace is like refusing to breathe the air that keeps us alive.

THINK, PAIR AND SHARE

- What do you think holds people back from accepting God's grace to strive for holiness of life?
- Share your thoughts with a partner.

JOURNAL EXERCISE

- Where and when have you been surprised by the offer of God's grace?
- Recall the situation. Did you respond or not respond? What difference did your response or lack of response make?
- In what people, things or events that you overlooked before can you now recognize God at work in your life?

MAKING A GIFT OF OURSELVES

To be sure, everyone has their own reasons for keeping God at a distance, for turning their back on God and on his grace and love. Most often, though, the root of this resistance is a reluctance to relinquish control over our own lives. It can be a frightening thing to put our lives in another's hands. Yet this is exactly the example Jesus set for us—he placed his life in his Father's hands. (Check out Philippians 2:4–11.)

Accepting God's love and grace means opening ourselves to the fullness of life that God wills for all people. This includes making a gift of ourselves to others as Jesus did; it means opening ourselves to others and sharing with them God's love. It is precisely in making a loving gift of ourselves to others that we find true happiness and freedom. That is the paradox of human life. This paradox, which the saints discovered, is that "it is in giving that we receive." This was the way of Jesus, who served his Father and all people. Out of love for his Father and humanity Jesus freely gave his life, therefore "God also highly exalted him." This is the way of life that Jesus calls us, his disciples, to live. We are to use our gifts to give glory to God by serving others in Christ-like love for the love of God.

Happiness in this life and in our life after death can and will only be found in giving glory to God by striving faithfully to fulfill the Great Commandment. (See the response of Jesus to a scholar of the Jewish law in Matthew 22:34–40.) Our relationship with the Lord our God is inseparable from our relationships with other people. (See Matthew 19:21.)

Our search for true happiness "is fulfilled in [our] vocation to divine beatitude" (CCC, no. 1700) "in the glory of heaven" (CCC, no. 1715). It is seeking to be perfect as our heavenly Father is perfect (see Matthew 5:48). "This perfect life with the Most Holy Trinity—this communion of life and love with the Trinity, with the Virgin Mary, the angels and all the blessed—is called 'heaven.' Heaven is the ultimate end and fulfillment of the deepest human longings, the state of supreme, definitive happiness" (CCC, no. 1024).

OVER TO YOU

- Prayerfully read Philippians 2:4–11.
- Recall these words of Jesus to his disciples: "No one has greater love than this, to lay down one's life for one's friends" (John 15:13).
- What concrete things can you do to make a loving gift of yourself to others today?

The Way of Jesus, the Way of God

Let each of you look not to your own interests,
but to the interests of others. Let the same mind
be in you that was in Christ Jesus,
  who, though he was in the form of God,
    did not regard equality with God
    as something to be exploited,
  but emptied himself,
    taking the form of a slave,
    being born in human likeness.
And being found in human form,
  he humbled himself
  and became obedient to the point of
    death—
  even death on a cross.

Therefore God also highly exalted him
  and gave him the name
  that is above every name,

so that at the name of Jesus
  every knee should bend,
  in heaven and on earth and under the
    earth,
and every tongue should confess
  that Jesus Christ is Lord,
  to the glory of God the Father.

—Philippians 2:4–11

ECCE HOMO (DETAIL) | MATEO CEREZO

Our personal vocation

ST. CATHERINE OF SIENA

St. Catherine of Siena, as we have seen in the "Attend and Reflect" section of this chapter, wrote: "Be who God meant you to be and you will set the world on fire." St. Catherine counsels us on the necessity of our cooperating with God's gift of grace and setting the world on fire by coming to know and use the gifts with which God has blessed us. The *Catechism of the Catholic Church* states this truth in this way: "Man's vocation is to make God manifest by acting in conformity with his creation 'in the image and likeness of God' " (CCC, no. 2085). God invites every person to fulfill that vocation. He gives every person a personal vocation and the graces to fulfill that vocation. Discerning, accepting and living out, with the grace of God, one's personal vocation is at the heart of our journey to holiness of life.

We will explore the discernment process in the "Attend and Reflect" section of the next chapter of this text.

OPENING REFLECTION

- ⊙ From what you have been learning, what do you think of St. Catherine's description of the journey toward holiness of life?
- ⊙ What role does using one's gifts play in striving for holiness?
- ⊙ Take a moment to write down a list of the key attitudes and behaviors necessary to reach the goal of personal holiness and happiness of life.
- ⊙ Take a second look and prioritize the items on your list. If you think two or more items are equal in importance, then give them the same rank order.

A VOCATION OF YOUR OWN

Up until now we have focused mostly on the universal call, or vocation, to holiness: to share in and reflect the life and love of the Trinity in all we say and do. Though this vocation is universal, there is no one predetermined path in life by which each person responds to that vocation. God creates no two people exactly the same. Just as every person has their own inimitable DNA, every person has unique gifts and personalities. Every person is a finite reflection of the Creator. For this reason, we deny our very identity and cheat ourselves, the Church and the world when we imitate others, such as celebrities. Often our culture gives us the mistaken idea that we have to become someone other than our true selves in order to achieve success and happiness. However, the truth is that real success and happiness lie in responding to our fundamental vocation to grow in holiness and wholeness, and so embrace the unique person God created us to be.

God calls every person to make a unique contribution to building his kingdom in the world. In other words, God calls every person to a *personal vocation*, which we live out in the work we perform or the actions we undertake. The form one's personal vocation takes varies not only from one person to the next, but even for the same person at different times in their life. The living out of our vocation includes even the small and seemingly ordinary choices we face each day, such as responding to a parent's request, doing one's homework, praying, and the bigger choices such as joining with others to work to alleviate world hunger. By working with the talents and opportunities God gives us, we constantly seek ways of responding with faith, hope and love to the ever-changing circumstances of our life.

The Christian vocation is unique. Joined to Christ in Baptism we use our gifts and talents to work with God to bring about the **Kingdom of God**, little by little, day by day. That kingdom, you will recall, is the bringing about of God's will and desire for humanity—"a community of justice, peace, mercy, and love, the seed of which is the Church on earth, and the fulfillment of which is in eternity" (USCCA, Glossary, "Kingdom of God,"

517). Every job or career, every form of work, big or small, is an opportunity to bring God's "justice, peace, mercy and love" into the world as we use our gifts to serve God and others.

TALK IT OVER

- ⊙ As a class, share your unique ways of contributing to God's work of bringing about the "justice, peace, mercy and love" that he desires for humanity.
- ⊙ Create a class profile of your unique contributions.
- ⊙ Discuss: What difference would it make if we all endeavored to use our gifts and talents to contribute to God's work?

OVER TO YOU

- ⊙ Read the parable of the mustard seed in Matthew 13:31–32.
- ⊙ Reflect on your talents and gifts.
- ⊙ How can you use them to serve God and others? How will this contribute to the bringing about of the Kingdom, or Reign, of God?

"Put on Christ": Pope Francis Speaks to the Youth of the World

Jesus brings God to us and us to God. "Put on Christ!" in your life, and you will find a friend in whom you can always trust; "put on Christ" and you will see the wings of hope spreading and letting you journey with joy towards the future; "put on Christ" and your life will be full of his love; it will be a fruitful life. . . .

Jesus offers us something bigger than the World Cup! He offers us the possibility of a fulfilled and fruitful life. He also offers us a future with him, an endless future, eternal life. But he asks us to train, "to get in shape," so that we can face every situation in life undaunted, bearing witness to our faith. How do we get in shape? By talking with him: by prayer, which is our daily conversation with God, who always listens to us. By the sacraments, which make his life grow within us and conform us to Christ. By loving one another, learning to listen, to understand, to forgive, to be accepting

and to help others, everybody, with no one excluded or ostracized. Dear young people, be true "athletes of Christ"!

God calls you to make definitive choices, and he has a plan for each of you: to discover that plan and to respond to your vocation is to move toward personal fulfillment.

—World Youth Day, Rio de Janeiro, 2013

POPE FRANCIS AT WORLD YOUTH DAY, RIO DE JANEIRO, 2013

ONE'S VOCATION IS FAR MORE THAN A CAREER

Our personal vocation concerns the way God calls us to be in every aspect of our life. The work we perform, "what we do for a living," is but one part of the way we fulfill our vocation to a life lived in communion with God and others— whether one's work is in the home or outside the home; in corporate America or in public service; in education or business or medicine or technology or whatever.

One reason it is important to distinguish vocation from career is that the vocation to which God calls us leads to a fulfillment and happiness that no job or career can provide. We have all heard stories of midlife crises. After spending their whole adult lives working for a college education for their children, or for a home in a "respectable neighborhood," or for a comfortable retirement, workers realize that they still feel unfulfilled. Often at the root of such midlife crises is the mistaken assumption that the key to happiness is having the right job and achieving financial success and material comforts. Jesus warned:

"Do not store up for yourselves treasures on earth, where moth and rust consume and where thieves break in and steal; but store up for yourselves treasures in heaven, where neither moth nor rust consumes and where thieves do not break in and steal. For where your treasure is, there your heart will be also.

The eye is the lamp of the body. So, if your eye is healthy, your whole body will be full of light; but if your eye is unhealthy, your whole body will be full of darkness. If then the light in you is darkness, how great is the darkness!

No one can serve two masters; for a slave will either hate the one and love the other, or be devoted to the one and despise the other. You cannot serve God and wealth."

—Matthew 6:19–24

The treasures of this world are easily lost. Besides, all the money and material comfort the world has to offer would never fully satisfy us. We are created for something more. If any enduring happiness is to be found in this life, we find it in right and loving relationships with God and with our family and other people.

TALK IT OVER

- ◉ Brainstorm as many forms of work, careers, professions and so on as you can name.
- ◉ Discuss ways a person can fulfill the universal human vocation to holiness by using their gifts and talents in each of the forms of work you identified.

OVER TO YOU

- ◉ How might a deeper understanding of your personal vocation enrich your life now?
- ◉ What indicators might help you measure whether you are pursuing holiness or a false notion of success?

We will continue our discussion of one's personal vocation and the discernment of that call in the next chapter.

Look back over this chapter and reflect on what you have learned about the universal human vocation and one's personal vocation. Share the teachings of the Catholic Church on these statements:

⊙ There is a longing for God the Creator implanted in the heart of every person.

⊙ God desires that every person would come to know, love and serve him.

⊙ God gives every person the vocation to strive for holiness of life and to reflect the Trinitarian life.

⊙ The ultimate goal in life should be holiness and communion with the Holy Trinity; this is where true success lies.

⊙ Personal satisfaction in life finds a firm foundation in our relationship with the Lord and in our relationships with other people.

⊙ A key to happiness is using one's gifts fully for God by serving others in Christian love.

⊙ The members of the Church live out their vocation to a life of holiness and justice as members of the ordained ministry, the consecrated life or the laity.

⊙ Jesus Christ, by his teachings and his life, Passion, Death and Resurrection, shows us the way to fulfill our vocation.

OVER TO YOU

⊙ What do you see as the most important work you do right now?

⊙ Does that work contribute to your coming to know, love and serve God? To your coming to know, love and serve other people?

Jesuit Volunteer Corps

There are many paths to using our knowledge and skills in living our vocation. The Jesuit Volunteer Corps (JVC) offers women and men (known as JVs) the opportunity to bring energy and hope to the individuals and organizations they serve and to gain valuable life skills, insights and connections.

Jesuit Volunteer Corps supports organizations that provide direct service to people who are poor and marginalized by placing volunteers at schools, non-profits and other sites around the world. The volunteers have a passionate commitment to social justice and come from diverse educational and professional backgrounds, bringing with them their unique experiences, perspectives and skills. During their service, JVs immerse in and reflect on four Catholic values central to the Jesuit way of life: (1) spiritual growth, (2) simple living, (3) community with other JVs and those whom they serve, and (4) the pursuit of social justice. Integrated into every part of their lives, these values work in harmony to support faith formation and create a transformative experience that prepares JVs for a lifetime of putting faith into action.

Jesuit Volunteers are working for justice in thirty-nine U.S. cities and six countries abroad with and for people who are disenfranchised, marginalized or vulnerable, such as children with limited educational opportunities, people who are homeless, patients diagnosed with AIDS, survivors of domestic abuse, low-wage earners, former gang members, refugees, or the elderly. Almost three hundred schools, non-profit agencies and grassroots organizations across the world count on JVs to provide essential services.

—Adapted from Jesuit Volunteer Corps website

TALK IT OVER

⊙ How does the work of the JVC give witness to the true meaning of success?

⊙ God calls us to gather *everyone* into right and loving community. Look around your community and your society. Who is being left out, ignored or treated in a non-loving and unjust way?

⊙ What can *you* do about this now?

SHARE FAITH WITH FAMILY AND FRIENDS

⊙ What aspects of the surrounding culture influence your understanding of success and happiness?

⊙ What can you do to promote an understanding of holiness as the true path to success in your school or local community?

HOW WOULD YOU RESPOND?

⊙ Work with a partner or in groups of three or four.

⊙ You are preparing for your future education and career. How would you respond to these messages about success and happiness that are so prevalent in society:

– Having the right vocation, job or career is essential for a person's happiness.

– The real measure of success in life is the degree of one's financial security and material comfort.

⊙ Take turns sharing responses to each statement.

REFLECT AND DECIDE

⊙ How have this chapter's discussions about vocation affected your outlook on the way you are living your life?

⊙ What changes can you make in your life in order to pursue your vocation to love more deeply and faithfully?

JOURNAL EXERCISE

⊙ Reflect: Deep within every human heart is a longing that can only be satisfied by responding to divine love. Describe how you are responding to that love right now. (If you do not know exactly what your personal vocation is yet, you are in good company. We will explore discerning one's personal vocation in the next chapter.)

LEARN BY HEART

No one has ever seen God; if we love one another, God lives in us, and his love is perfected in us.

1 JOHN 4:12

Note: *Each student should bring to class an object that represents a personal gift, talent or passion, for use in the concluding Prayer Reflection.*

Note: *Each student should have an object that represents a personal gift, talent or passion.*

All sit in a circle on the floor around a large candle (if fire regulations permit). After a moment of silent reflection, all pray the Sign of the Cross together.

Opening Prayer

LEADER
Loving God, Father and Creator,
you are the source of all life and love;
you alone are the fulfillment for which we long.
Deepen our awareness of your presence with
and within us as we gather in prayer in your Son's name.
Send your Spirit to help us recognize and acknowledge the gifts with which you have blessed each one of us,
and to guide and strengthen us to become a more loving community
so that we may come to know, love and serve you and one another.
Through our Lord Jesus Christ, your Son,
who lives and reigns with you in the unity of the Holy Spirit,
one God, for ever and ever.

ALL
Amen.

Proclamation of the Word of God

READER
A reading from the First Letter to the Corinthians.
Proclaim 1 Corinthians 12:4–11.
The word of the Lord.

ALL
Thanks be to God.

LEADER
Let us reflect on what God's own word says to each of us personally. (*Pause*)
I invite all who wish to do so to share their reflections.

Students share their reflections.

Presentation of Gifts

LEADER
God is love, and he has called us to be his reflections and images. Each of us has gifts, talents and passions through which we can share God's love with the world. Together we will now come to the candle and touch it as we place our gifts at the service of God and one another. Remain standing around the candle until everyone has finished.

Students present their gifts.

Concluding Prayer

LEADER
God, Father, Son and Holy Spirit, thank you for these our gifts.
Strengthen us so that we may use these gifts to show our love for you,
and for the good of others and all your creation.

ALL
Amen.

Conclude by praying the Glory be to the Father.

CHAPTER 2

A Variety of Gifts, but the Same Spirit

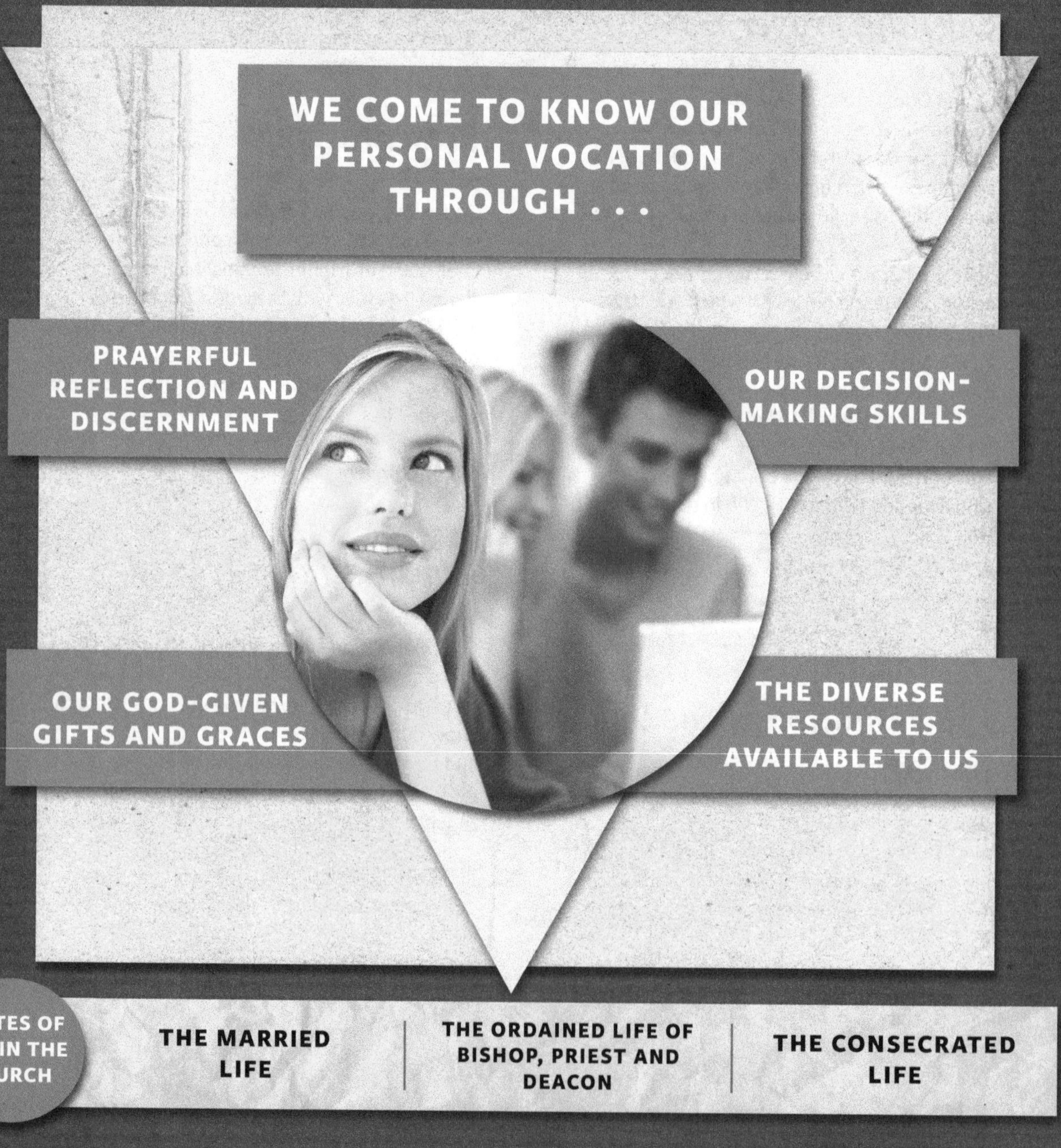

WE COME TO KNOW OUR PERSONAL VOCATION THROUGH . . .

PRAYERFUL REFLECTION AND DISCERNMENT

OUR DECISION-MAKING SKILLS

OUR GOD-GIVEN GIFTS AND GRACES

THE DIVERSE RESOURCES AVAILABLE TO US

STATES OF LIFE IN THE CHURCH

THE MARRIED LIFE

THE ORDAINED LIFE OF BISHOP, PRIEST AND DEACON

THE CONSECRATED LIFE

THE SPIRITUAL DISCIPLINE OF DISCERNMENT ENABLES US TO come to know the gifts with which the Holy Spirit has blessed us and the personal vocation to which God calls us to use those gifts in service to him, the Church and others. The Catholic Church has traditionally recognized three states of life to which Christ calls the faithful to work with him to bring about the Reign of God. These states of life are: the married life; the ordained life of bishop, priest and deacon; and the consecrated life. No matter what our personal calling may be, no one lives out their Baptism in isolation. All the faithful, whether they are members of the laity, or have a vocation to ordained life, consecrated life, or married life, strive for holiness of life as members of the community of Jesus' disciples, the Church.

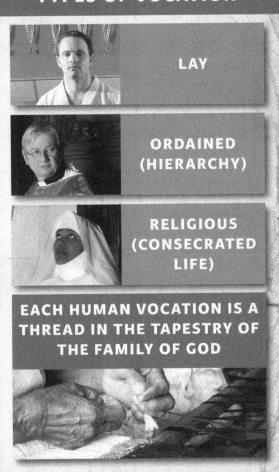

TYPES OF VOCATION

LAY

ORDAINED (HIERARCHY)

RELIGIOUS (CONSECRATED LIFE)

EACH HUMAN VOCATION IS A THREAD IN THE TAPESTRY OF THE FAMILY OF GOD

Faith Focus: These teachings of the Catholic Church are the primary focus of the doctrinal content presented in this chapter:

- ⊙ We can come to know our personal vocation through prayerful reflection and discernment.
- ⊙ God continually shows his loving care and concern for us through the events of our life.
- ⊙ God gives each of the faithful gifts and graces to exercise the responsibilities of the Christian life in a unique way.
- ⊙ The Catholic Church recognizes three states of life in which the faithful can live out their vocation: the married life; the ordained life of a bishop, priest or deacon; and the consecrated life.
- ⊙ The baptismal call to the laity to holiness of life can be lived out in a diversity of ways.
- ⊙ No vocation is lived in isolation; human beings exist in relationship with others.

Discipleship Formation: As a result of studying this chapter and discovering the meaning of the faith of the Catholic Church for your life, you should be better able to:

- ⊙ practice prayerful reflection and discernment to come know your personal vocation to the Christian life;
- ⊙ recognize the many ways through which you can live out your vocation;
- ⊙ recognize and use the many resources for discernment that God provides;
- ⊙ appreciate the common purpose of all vocations: to serve God and others;
- ⊙ value the interconnectedness and interdependence of all vocations.

Scripture References: These Scripture references are quoted or referred to in this chapter:
OLD TESTAMENT: **1 Samuel** 3:1—4:1
NEW TESTAMENT: **Matthew** 3:9, 5:13–16, 6:25–34, 8:20, 10:29–31; **Luke** 9:58, 10:25–28; **John** 17:21; **Acts of the Apostles** 6:1–7; **Romans** 5:5, 12:3–8; **1 Corinthians** 12:4–6, 11–13, 27–37; **Galatians** 5:12; **Philippians** 2:8; **Colossians** 1:24

Faith Glossary: Familiarize yourself with or recall the meaning of these key terms. Definitions are found in the Glossary: *agape*, **Christian discernment, divine providence, laity, ministerial priesthood, prayer, priesthood of Christ, priesthood of the faithful, states of life, vocation**

Faith Words: Christian discernment; states of life
Learn by Heart: 1 Corinthians 12:4–5
Learn by Example: Frank Duff, founder of the Legion of Mary

How do I come to know my personal vocation?

OPENING REFLECTION

⊙ Are you a member of a school organization, for example, a band or an athletic team, a drama club or debating team, a peer ministry or community service group?
⊙ How did you make your decision to join that group?
⊙ List the steps you took, ranking them in order of importance.

ALL OF US MUST MAKE BIG DECISIONS!

As the high school years near completion, graduating students will be making many "big" decisions. They will search for answers to such questions as: Will I go to college or to a trade institute? What will be my major or area of specialty? Will I join the workforce right after high school? Will I join the military? The questions are numerous and deeply personal. The answers will impact one's future, for better or for worse.

In order to make good decisions and choices about our future path in life, good decision-making skills are vital. Using those skills to discern the vocation and path through life that God in his providence and wisdom desires for a person is the surest route to happiness and to a fulfilled life. (Check out Matthew 6:25–34, 10:29–31.)

Divine love is such that God is always present with us during our life. God did not create us, abandon us and leave us to our own doing or undoing. God is always showing his loving care and concern for humanity and for all of his creation. In his wisdom, God is continuously guiding, protecting and governing his entire creation toward the perfection he wills it to have. This perfection will come about in its fullness, in God's own time, when the risen and glorified Christ comes again in glory and hands over his kingdom to his Father. "[God] continues to watch over creation, sustaining its existence and presiding over its development and destiny" (*United States Catholic Catechism for Adults* [USCCA], Glossary, "Divine Providence," 510). We name this truth and mystery of faith **divine providence**.

OVER TO YOU

⊙ What might you like to do with your life?
⊙ How might your Christian faith support you in that major life decision?

DISCERNING GOD'S WILL FOR US

Jesus Christ calls every baptized person, individually and by name, to a personal **vocation**. When speaking about their particular, or personal, vocation, people often talk about God's "will" for them. This truth does not mean that God micromanages and controls and determines the outcomes of our use of the gifts of intelligence and free will. God offers us

Christian Discernment

The spiritual practice of looking out for the presence and the workings of the Holy Spirit in our life. It includes trying to understand the promptings of the Holy Spirit in our life and deciding to act in cooperation with the grace of the Holy Spirit. This process includes seeking to know the path to holiness of life as "collaborators and cooperators in continuing the redemptive work of Jesus Christ, which is the Church's essential mission" (USCCA, 452).

the graces that empower us to use these gifts for our spiritual growth as his children, for our taking part in the unfolding of the divine plan for creation, and for the glory of God. God grants human beings "the ability to cooperate freely with his plans" (*Catechism of the Catholic Church* [CCC], no. 323).

The practice of the spiritual discipline of **Christian discernment** is one of the traditional means for our coming to know and understand the role God wills us to have in the divine plan and how we may cooperate freely with God in his work in the world.

All the baptized have the responsibility to look deliberately and diligently at the variety of ways the Church is carrying out her mission today, and to ask, "How might Jesus be inviting me to collaborate and cooperate 'in continuing the redemptive work of Jesus Christ, which is the Church's essential mission' (USCCA, 452)?" Then, through collaboration with others, for example, with a parish priest or a spiritual director, discern and decide on how Jesus might be calling us to join with him in his redemptive work. This call includes striving for holiness of life in loving service to God and the Church and our neighbor.

OVER TO YOU

- ⊙ Have you, in the past, included prayer and dialoguing with parents and family, a parish priest, a spiritual director, or other people in making decisions about your life?
- ⊙ Why is it vital not to make decisions about your life "all by yourself"?
- ⊙ Compare your analysis with the steps in "The Ignatian Discernment Process" outlined on the next page.
- ⊙ How might you include other people of faith in your discerning of the way to which the Holy Spirit is inviting you to live as a disciple of Jesus Christ?

JOURNAL EXERCISE

- ⊙ Reflect: When discerning your vocation, it can be helpful to ask certain questions of yourself. Here is one classic set of questions that takes into account the personal yet service-oriented nature of vocation: (1) What gives you joy? (2) What are you good at? (3) What does the world need?
- ⊙ Reflect quietly on these three questions and write a response to each one in your journal.
- ⊙ What insights into your vocation might your responses be offering you?

RESOURCES FOR DISCERNMENT

Catholics live in a diversity of relationships that support us in discerning and living out our faith. Central to those relationships are the members of our church community. We are surrounded by caring people—family and friends; teachers, coaches and counselors; parish priests and youth ministers; the list goes on.

While we have many resources at our disposal for discerning the personal vocation to which God is calling us, there is still an element of mystery. There is an element of unexplainable attraction that moves us toward deciding upon our personal vocation within the Church. That mystery is the presence and movement of the Holy Spirit, who abides within us. The Holy Spirit prompts and guides us in many different ways, including, among other ways, through:

⊙ the teachings and life of the Church. We need to listen to and reflect on the great wisdom of the Church and be active participants in the life of the Church;

⊙ intimate conversation with God in **prayer**. We are constantly barraged by voices telling us what to do and who to be. It is crucial that we take time to sit in silence, reflect and have a heart to heart with God. We need to pray;

⊙ our innermost thoughts and feelings. We need to listen to our own head and heart, and to our innermost longings;

⊙ other people. We learn from the life and advice of our family and friends, priests and other members of our parish family, mentors

ST. IGNATIUS OF LOYOLA, MONTSERRAT, SPAIN

The Ignatian Discernment Process

St. Ignatius of Loyola (1491–1556), the founder of the Jesuits, developed a clear process for discernment, which can be summarized in these steps:

1. Pray for openness to God's will and freedom from personal biases and unhealthy desires.
2. Identify the decision to be made or the issue to be resolved.
3. Gather all the information you need to make a responsible decision.
4. Formulate the issue as a positive, concrete choice between two alternatives.
5. List all the reasons for and against each alternative.
6. Evaluate all the advantages and disadvantages for each in light of your sense of God's will and your personal values and motivations.
7. While reflecting on the advantages and disadvantages of each possibility, tell God what you desire and fear.
8. Ask God to give you feelings of consolation and peace about the preferred option.
9. Trust in God and make your decision.
10. Confirm the decision by living with it for a while and observing its effects.

and coaches and teachers—and strangers as well. Sometimes we might seek the counsel of a spiritual director

⊙ the events of our life. We can gain insight through local and global tragedies, family celebrations, school and community events that gain our particular interest and attention.

In the everyday of life we need to be present to God. It is important to listen for what God might be communicating to us. As the teenage Samuel responded, "Speak Lord, for your servant is listening" (1 Samuel 3:9). (Check out the complete account of Samuel's calling in 1 Samuel 3:1—4:1.) While the discernment of one's calling is very personal, it is done best in conversation not only with self and God, but also with others and in community.

REFLECT AND DECIDE

⊙ Which of the above resources have you turned to while discerning your personal vocation?
⊙ Which might you make better use of from here on?

JOURNAL EXERCISE

⊙ Choose a decision that you are in the process of making about living your faith in Jesus.
⊙ Take some time in quiet to go through the ten steps of the Ignatian discernment process. Do not rush. It may take several days or longer for you to journey prayerfully through this process.
⊙ As you move through this process, talk with a family member, parish priest or school chaplain, teacher or coach, or another adult whose wisdom you trust.
⊙ Record your thoughts and insights in your journal as you move through your discernment process.

It is important to listen for what God might be communicating to us. As the teenage Samuel responded, "Speak Lord, for your servant is listening" (1 Samuel 3:9)

SAMUEL AND ELI | A.W. WARREN AFTER E. BIRD

States of life recognized by the Church

CALLED TO BE LIGHTS IN THE WORLD

You know well the story of the disciples gathered around Jesus on a mountainside in Galilee. Those disciples came from a variety of professions and backgrounds—there were fishermen and a tax collector, perhaps farmers and craftsmen like Jesus, married and single persons for sure. After his teaching on the Beatitudes, Jesus shared with the disciples the challenges of the work he was calling them to undertake. He said:

"You are the salt of the earth; but if salt has lost its taste, how can its saltiness be restored? It is no longer good for anything, but is thrown out and trampled underfoot.

"You are the light of the world. A city built on a hill cannot be hid. No one after lighting a lamp puts it under the bushel basket, but on the lampstand, and it gives light to all in the house. In the same way, let your light shine before others, so that they may see your good works and give glory to your Father in heaven."

—Matthew 5:13–16

OPENING REFLECTION

◉ What is Jesus asking of his disciples in this passage?

◉ How are you measuring up to Jesus' invitation to be "salt" and "light" in the world?

◉ Where can you and other Christians find the strength, support and guidance to better respond to Jesus?

THE UNIVERSAL VOCATION TO HOLINESS OF LIFE

All the baptized, all the faithful, share one common calling—God's invitation to strive for holiness of life. Lay people, or members of the laity, make up the largest number of the faithful. God gives each of the lay faithful the gifts and graces to seek

FAITH WORD

States of life

The term "states of life" refers to the ordained ministry, the consecrated life, and the married life.

holiness of life through loving service to God, the Church and neighbor. Jesus Christ calls some members of his Church to live out the universal call to holiness in a unique way. He calls them to accept a vocation to one of the three **states of life** recognized by the Catholic Church. The *Catechism* explains:

God has created the human person to love and serve him; the fulfillment of this vocation is eternal happiness. Christ calls the faithful to the perfection of holiness. The vocation of the laity consists in seeking the Kingdom of God by engaging in temporal affairs and directing them according to God's will. Priestly and religious vocations are dedicated to the service of the Church as the universal sacrament of salvation.

—CCC, Glossary, "Vocation"

THE THREE STATES OF LIFE

The Catholic Church recognizes three states of life to which Christ may call the baptized. These states of life are the ordained life, the consecrated life and the married life. God gives special graces to these faithful to fulfill their call to holiness of life, primarily through their service to God and the Church.

The members of the Church who are called to these states of life have a diverse but mutually necessary role in the life and mission of the Church. The married faithful, working and living in the world, often have the opportunity to go and share the Good News of the Gospel in places where the ordained and the members of the consecrated life might not regularly reach. The role of the lay faithful, both married and unmarried, is so necessary for the life and mission of the Church that the pastors of the Church cannot address the mission of the Church fully without their collaboration and cooperation.

Note: We introduce the married life in this section of the chapter. We will introduce the ordained life and the consecrated life in the "Embrace the Vision" section of this chapter. We will explore the laity in detail in chapter 11.

LET'S PROBE DEEPER: A GROUP ACTIVITY
- Work in small groups.
- Each group names as many ways as possible through which the faithful can live out Christ's call to follow him in each of these vocations: Lay Vocation; Priestly Vocation; Religious Vocation.
- Groups share insights as a class.

THE MARRIED LIFE

All vocations to live the Christian life are vital to the life and mission of the Church and to her members as they seek holiness of life. The love between spouses is an image of God's infinite and unending love for us. God has promised to love us, and he does not break his promises. God calls Christian married people to be a sign of Christ's love for the Church, the Bride of Christ. Jesus raised marriage to the dignity of a sacrament. Through the covenant relationship of a sacramental marriage, freely and knowingly entered, a baptized man and woman are united as husband and wife for life.

The Sacrament of Matrimony, or Marriage, along with Holy Orders, is primarily directed toward the salvation of others. Christian married life is above all a vocation to build up the Body of Christ on earth and to foster the good of the human family, society and the Church. It is the Christian married couple's unselfish gift of self to God and others that leads them toward holiness of life.

God always offers married couples the graces to fulfill this vocation. By giving each other the total gift of their lifelong and unselfish love, married couples support each other and contribute to each other's growth in intimacy and love for God. Their self-sacrificing love, their *agape*, for each other is an image of Christ's love for his Church and an image of God's sanctifying and saving love for all people.

We will return to a more detailed study of married life in chapters 4, 5, 6 and 7 of this text. In the next section of this chapter we will continue the introduction to the states of life recognized by the Catholic Church.

THINK, PAIR AND SHARE

⊙ Recall Jesus' teaching on the Great Commandment in Luke 10:25–28.
⊙ Share with a partner some practical ways in which the life of a Christian married couple can be a living sign of the two Great Commandments.

WHAT ABOUT YOU PERSONALLY?

⊙ Where have you seen those men and women who have the vocation to the married life working together with priests or religious for the good of the Church? For the good of society?
⊙ In what ways might the collaboration and cooperation of the ordained, religious, and married be especially beneficial for the Church fulfilling her Christ-given mission of being salt and light in the world?

Where have you seen married men and women using their vocation for the good of the Church or of society?

The ordained life and the consecrated life

FALLING IN LOVE WITH GOD

Bernard Lonergan (1904–84) was a Jesuit priest and renowned theologian who was deeply respected for his insightful reflections. In his *Method in Theology*, Lonergan described our relationship with God as falling in love. He wrote: "It is a total and permanent self-surrender without conditions, qualifications, reservations. . . . It is other-worldly fulfillment, joy, peace, bliss."

OPENING REFLECTION

- ⊙ Does it surprise you that a priest would describe his love for God as "falling in love"? Why or why not?
- ⊙ Do the words "falling in love" describe your relationship with God? Why or why not?
- ⊙ What kinds of things do people say and do to demonstrate their love for God?

COMMITTED TO GOD

In this section of the chapter we explore briefly the unique vocation to the ordained life of bishop, priest and deacon, and to the consecrated life. The faithful called to these states of life accept their vocation and live out vows and promises. Through the profession of vows they give public expression to the fact that their heart belongs to God and to God alone. Although all the faithful are called to love God above all else with a love that is "total and permanent self-surrender without conditions, qualifications, reservations," the faithful called to the ordained life, the consecrated life, or to both of these states of life, commit to a way of life that allows them to keep God's reign and the Gospel of Jesus squarely at the center of their lives.

THE ORDAINED LIFE

In Baptism all the newly baptized are anointed with Sacred Chrism. This anointing signifies their sharing as the baptized in the one priesthood of Jesus Christ (check out 1 Peter 2:9), or the common priesthood of the faithful. In other words, all the baptized commit themselves to worship God; to proclaim the Word of God; and to build a world rooted in justice and love. God also chooses and calls some of the faithful to share in the priesthood of Christ in a unique way. Jesus Christ calls baptized men to the ministerial priesthood to serve the Church as bishops and priests.

A baptized man is ordained to the ministerial priesthood and, in the Sacrament of Holy Orders, receives the graces to live out this state of life

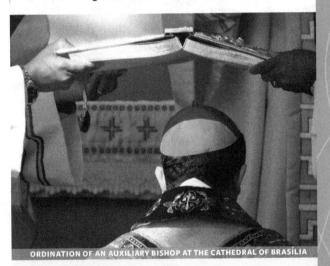

ORDINATION OF AN AUXILIARY BISHOP AT THE CATHEDRAL OF BRASÍLIA

Did you know?

A priest receives ordination a third time when becoming a bishop, but becoming a cardinal or pope does not involve a third ordination. The current church law restricts membership of the college of cardinals to those "who are at least in the order of priesthood" (*Code of Canon Law*, Canon 351).

ST. CLARE OF ASSISI, FOUNDER OF THE POOR CLARES | SIMONE MARTINI

God calls some members of the faithful, non-ordained and ordained, to the consecrated, or religious, life

in the Church. As members of the ministerial priesthood, bishops and priests support all the faithful by celebrating the sacraments with them and by guiding them in living out their Baptism. Christ also calls some men to the ordained ministry of deacon, to assist bishops and priests in their ministry. Deacons also receive the Sacrament of Holy Orders but they are not ordained priests. The vocation to the ordained life is a gift from God. The Church teaches:

No one has a *right* to receive the sacrament of Holy Orders. Indeed no one claims this office for himself; he is called to it by God (see Hebrews 5:4). Anyone who thinks he recognizes the signs of God's call to the ordained ministry must humbly submit his desire to the authority of the Church, who has the responsibility and right to call someone to receive orders. Like every grace this sacrament can be *received* only as an unmerited gift.

—CCC, no. 1578

The ministries conferred by ordination are irreplaceable for the organic structure of the

Church: without the bishop, presbyters, and deacons, one cannot speak of the Church (see St. Ignatius of Antioch [d. c. 110, *To the Trallians*, 3,1)

We will return to a more detailed study of the ordained ministries of a bishop, priest and deacon in chapters 8 and 9 of this text.

THINK, PAIR AND SHARE

⊙ What tasks and responsibilities have you observed bishops, priests and deacons undertaking?

⊙ Check out Acts of the Apostles 6:1–7 for what the assistants to the Apostles were commissioned to do. What might this mean for the vocation of deacons today?

⊙ Why do you think it is beneficial for certain people within the Church to devote themselves to the ordained ministries of bishop, priest or deacon?

THE CONSECRATED LIFE, OR THE RELIGIOUS LIFE

God calls some members of the faithful, non-ordained and ordained, to the consecrated, or religious, life. To "consecrate" something or someone means to devote that person or thing entirely to God. The faithful called to the consecrated life:

bind themselves to the Lord in a special way, following Christ, who chaste and poor (see Matthew 8:20; Luke 9:58) redeemed and sanctified men through obedience even to the death of the Cross (see Philippians 2:8). Driven by love with which the Holy Spirit floods their hearts (see Romans 5:5) they live more and more for Christ and for His body which is the Church (see Colossians 1:24).

—St. John Paul II, *The Adaptation and Renewal of Religious Life (Perfectae Caritatis)*, no. 1

The faithful to whom Jesus gives the vocation to the consecrated state of life most often commit to live their vocation as members of a religious order or congregation approved by the Church. "While not belonging to the hierarchical structure of the church, [the consecrated life] belongs absolutely to its life and holiness" (Vatican II, *Dogmatic Constitution on the Church* [*Lumen Gentium*], no. 44). The *Catechism of the Catholic Church* gives this summary of the consecrated life:

Whether their witness is public, as in the religious state, or less public, or even secret, Christ's coming remains for all those consecrated both the origin and rising sun of their life: 'For the people of God has here no lasting city, . . . [and this state] reveals more clearly to all believers the heavenly goods which are already present in this age, witnessing to the new and eternal life which we have acquired through the redemptive work of Christ and preluding our future resurrection and the glory of the heavenly kingdom' (Vatican II, *Dogmatic Constitution on the Church*, no. 44).

—CCC, no. 933

We will explore the vocation to the consecrated life in greater detail in chapter 10 of this text.

LET'S PROBE DEEPER: A RESEARCH ACTIVITY

- ◉ Work in small groups.
- ◉ Select a religious order or congregation. Prepare a report that includes its:
  - – founder and origins;
  - – unique charism;
  - – current membership;
  - – location and mission in the world today.
- ◉ Present your reports during the study of the consecrated life in chapter 10 of this text.

JOURNAL EXERCISE

- ◉ What new insights have you gained into the ordained life of bishops, priests and deacons? Into the consecrated life?
- ◉ Use the guidelines you learned earlier in this chapter to begin discerning whether Jesus might be calling you to the ordained life of a priest or deacon or to the consecrated life.
- ◉ Spend some time discerning this vocation. Record your thoughts in your journal.

MONT ST MICHEL, FRANCE IS HOME TO MONKS AND NUNS OF THE MONASTIC FRATERNITIES OF JERUSALEM

Personal but not private

⊙ In what sense might this also be true for the Church?

EACH PERSON'S VOCATION IS PERSONAL BUT NOT PRIVATE

There are many levels and types of relationships within the family of God. (Check out 1 Corinthians 12:12–26.) St. Paul wrote:

Now you are the body of Christ and individually members of it. And God has appointed in the church first apostles, second prophets, third teachers; then deeds of power, then gifts of healing, forms of assistance, forms of leadership, various kinds of tongues. Are all apostles? Are all prophets? Are all teachers? Do all work miracles? Do all possess gifts of healing? Do all speak in tongues? Do all interpret? But strive for the greater gifts. And I will show you a still more excellent way.
—1 Corinthians 12:27–37

IT TAKES MORE THAN ONE TO MAKE A SUCCESSFUL TEAM

Are you a member of a sports team? Are you a sports fan? If so, then you know well that for a team to be successful it must have the right combination of talent. A soccer team needs strikers, distributers, defenders and a keeper. A basketball team needs ball handlers, outside shooters, post players and defensive players. If any one of these is missing, the team's chances for success are limited.

OPENING REFLECTION

⊙ Does this description ring true to your experience on a sports team or in any other organization or club? Explain.
⊙ In a group, take turns sharing your talents and passions. Then discuss what you might be able to accomplish as a group that you could not accomplish as individuals.

Obviously, an individual's vocation is a profoundly personal matter. It is that person's life after all! But while an individual's vocation is personal, it is not private. The choices we make and the actions we take and the way we live our life affect many other people. God has created us to live in community. We live in relationship with him and with one another. Our vocation is not solely about ourselves; it is about serving God and others. And this is where we find fulfillment, precisely in loving service to God and neighbor as Jesus modeled.

Each human vocation is like a thread in a beautiful tapestry—the tapestry of the family of God. The tapestry's beauty comes from the artful interweaving of many different threads. Each individual thread contributes to the tapestry. For our part, we typically only see our own thread and those of a few others around ours. Only God, the master weaver, has the vision to stitch all these billions of threads together into the final masterpiece.

St. Paul often taught this about the family of God, the Church, as the Body of Christ. In the Letter to the Romans he wrote: "For as in one body we have many members, and not all the members have the same function, so we, who are many, are one body in Christ" (Romans 12:4–5). Whatever imagery we use, the reality is that all Christians are bound together in their relationship in Jesus Christ, the Head of his body, the Church.

Ultimately all the vocations within the Body of Christ complement one another and serve a common mission—to know, love and serve the Triune God and our neighbor as disciples of Jesus. We do not live out our Christian vocation in isolation. We live it out as *members* of the one Body of Christ. All Christians are to work together as multiple integrated and interrelated parts of the Body of Christ in the world.

OVER TO YOU

⊙ Create your own representation of how God forms the many human gifts and vocations into a beautiful work of art. You might make a painting or a collage or something else of your own invention.

A ROLE FOR ALL THE FAITHFUL

At this point it should be clear that no personal vocation is better than another; nor is any one vocation complete without the others. The Holy Spirit empowers all the faithful "individually just as the Spirit chooses" (1 Corinthians 12:11) for the common good of the Church and the world. By Baptism God calls and offers graces to all the faithful to live the way of Jesus and continue his mission in the world.

God gives the members of his Church a variety of gifts and services to carry on the work of Jesus Christ. St. Paul put it this way: "Now there are varieties of gifts, but the same Spirit; and there are varieties of services, but the same Lord; and there are varieties of activities, but it is the same God who activates all of them in everyone" (1 Corinthians 12:4–6).

Only by joining our efforts together can we succeed in forming the community of love that reflects our Creator, the Holy Trinity. Therefore, when discerning and living our vocation we are to heed St. Paul's advice:

> For by the grace given to me I say to everyone among you not to think of yourself more highly than you ought to think, but to think with sober judgment, each according to the measure of faith that God has assigned. For as in one body we have many members, and not all the members have the same function, so we, who are many, are one body in Christ, and individually we are members one of another. We have gifts that differ according to the grace given to us: prophecy, in proportion to faith; ministry, in ministering; the teacher, in teaching; the exhorter, in exhortation; the giver, in generosity; the leader, in diligence; the compassionate, in cheerfulness.
>
> —Romans 12:3–8

JOURNAL EXERCISE

⊙ What have you learned about the interrelatedness of every member of the Church? About why the vocations of all Christians work together?

⊙ In your experience, what helps people with different vocations to work together? What makes it difficult?

⊙ How might you promote greater cooperation in your own school and parish communities?

REFLECT ON WHAT YOU HAVE LEARNED

Look back over this chapter and reflect on what you have learned about the connection between a person's vocation and their state of life in the Church or work in society. Share the teachings of the Catholic Church on these statements:

- All the baptized are called to service of our brothers and sisters in the Church and the world.
- Though all Christians share a common baptismal vocation, God gives each of the faithful gifts and graces to exercise the responsibilities of the Christian life in a unique way.
- The married life, the ordained life of a bishop, priest and deacon, and the consecrated life are the three states of life traditionally recognized by the Church.

- The vocation of the laity consists in seeking the Kingdom of God by engaging in temporal affairs and directing them according to God's will.
- The Sacrament of Marriage fosters the good of the human family, society and the Church.
- Priestly and religious vocations are dedicated to the service of the Church as the universal sacrament of salvation.
- No vocation is lived in isolation; human beings exist in relationship with others.

OVER TO YOU

- What wisdom for your life have you learned from your study of this chapter?
- To what vocation are you most attracted right now? Why is that? What can you do to discern that call more clearly?

LEARN BY EXAMPLE

Frank Duff (1889–1980), Servant of God and founder of the Legion of Mary

Frank Duff is a shining example of a person who not only lived his own vocation faithfully but also fostered relationships and collaboration among lay and religious people. Frank was born in Dublin, Ireland, on June 7, 1889, the first of seven children. Frank was an avid cyclist and enjoyed tennis and photography. He had an active social life and attended university for a time. When his father died prematurely, the family could no longer afford tuition and Frank left the university and began a civil service career. He devised a system of calculus that was eventually adopted by the Treasury in London.

Frank's life of service took a new direction in October of 1913 when a colleague invited him to join the St. Vincent de Paul Society in its work of serving people who were suffering from and dealing with poverty. Frank became

deeply troubled by both the material poverty and the spiritual poverty he encountered. Several years later, in 1921, Duff, inspired by his reading about the Virgin Mary, founded the Legion of Mary to address these needs.

The Legion of Mary is a lay apostolic association of Catholics who, with the sanction of the Church and under the powerful leadership of Mary Immaculate, Mediatrix of all graces, serve the Church and their neighbor on a voluntary basis in about 170 countries. The first meeting of the Legion of Mary took place in Myra House, Francis Street, Dublin, Ireland, on September 7, 1921.

The Legion grew quickly, spreading around the world and creating a vast network of lay people working together with priests and bishops to support the mission of the Church. Describing the work of the Legion, Frank wrote: "Contemplating the Crucified Lord, who devoted to him his last sigh and the last drop of his Blood, the legionary service must strive to reflect such utter giving of self."

In 1965 Duff was invited to the Second Vatican Council as a lay observer. When his presence was announced, the whole assembly of 2,500 bishops spontaneously broke into applause. Duff later received a private audience with Blessed Pope Paul VI, who thanked him for the services that he and the Legion were rendering to the Church. Duff died on November 7, 1980, and sixteen years later, in July 1996, the Archbishop of Dublin introduced the cause for his beatification and canonization. Fr. Bede McGregor, OP, the Spiritual Director of Concilium, the governing body of the Legion of Mary, captured Duff's life in these words:

> Frank Duff was great in the small things, and heroic in doing the commonplace, and his purpose in all things great and small was his immense desire to love God and to be an instrument with and through Mary and the Holy Spirit in the conversion of sinners and the salvation of souls.

TALK IT OVER

⊙ Frank Duff used his God-given gifts to bring people together for the sake of serving the Triune God and neighbor. How might you do the same?

SHARE FAITH WITH FAMILY AND FRIENDS

⊙ How does God's calling people to different ways of life enrich the whole Church in the world?

⊙ How does it enrich family life?

REFLECT AND DECIDE

⊙ Reflect: Holiness and justice are inseparable. If holiness means loving as God loves, there is no way one can be holy without caring about justice. Whatever our vocational choices, we are all called to live in right relationship with God, with others, with ourselves and with creation. Wherever someone or some group is deprived of the love and respect they deserve, we must work for justice.

⊙ What decision about working for justice might you be called to make now as part of your Christian vocation? How will you respond?

JOURNAL EXERCISE

⊙ Reflect: Vocation is neither a matter of pure choice on our part nor something dictated to us by God. Only in combining our gifts do we achieve the goal of advancing the mission of Christ.

⊙ To which state or states of life do you feel drawn? Why?

⊙ What could you do this week to explore that vocation more seriously?

⊙ In light of this chapter's discussions, what is the best advice you could give to another person for discerning their vocation?

LEARN BY HEART

There are varieties of gifts, but the same Spirit; and there are varieties of services, but the same Lord.

1 CORINTHIANS 12:4—5

PRAYER REFLECTION

Pray the Sign of the Cross together.

LEADER
God, giver of all gifts, send your Spirit upon us today as we gather in prayer.
Bless our reflections so that we may grow in awareness and appreciation of the different gifts and vocations of each member of the community gathered here.
ALL
Amen.

READER
A reading from the First Letter of St. Paul to the Corinthians.
Proclaim 1 Corinthians 12:4–7, 11–13.
The word of the Lord.
ALL
Thanks be to God.

LEADER
Let us pause and reflect on what we have heard from this reading for our own lives and for our discernment of our vocation. When ready, you are welcome to share with the group.

All those who wish to do so share their reflections.

LEADER
God, you are indeed the giver of all good gifts. Grant us now our petitions, knowing that we seek to do your will above all else. (*Pause*)

We pray for all the baptized who are discerning how Christ may be calling them to give generously of themselves and unite themselves to him in all things.
ALL
Lord, hear our prayer.

LEADER
We pray for those who are living the married life, that they may be witnesses of God's love for all the world.
ALL
Lord, hear our prayer.

LEADER
We pray for those living the ordained life, that they may be the face of Christ in their communities and, by their prayer, teaching, guidance and sacramental ministry, that they may guide us in becoming a holier people.
ALL
Lord, hear our prayer.

LEADER
We pray for those living the consecrated life, that their example of radical commitment to Christ may inspire us all to seek greater intimacy with our Lord and Savior.
ALL
Lord, hear our prayer.

LEADER
For what other intentions do you now pray?

All those who wish to do so share their reflections.

LEADER
Trusting in God to lead us to our true vocation, let us pray together this prayer for discernment:
ALL
God our Father,
you have a plan for each one of us,
you hold out to us a future full of hope.
Give us your Spirit of wisdom and understanding
so that we can see the shape of your plan
in the gifts you have given us
and in the circumstances of our daily lives.
Give us your Spirit of counsel and fortitude
to seek you with all our hearts.
Give us your Spirit of knowledge and piety
to choose your will above all else.
Give us your Spirit of wonder and awe
to seek you above all else.
We make this prayer through Christ our Lord.
Amen.

Pray the Sign of the Cross together.

CHAPTER 3

The Christian Life

—An Unselfish Gift to God and Others

THE CHRISTIAN LIFE: A LIFE OF SELFLESS, LOVING SERVICE

TO SERVE IS TO BE FULLY HUMAN

SERVICE IS THE PATH TO TRUE FREEDOM AND JOY

ONLY IN SERVING GOD AND OTHERS WILL WE LIVE IN THE FREEDOM OF THE CHILDREN OF GOD

JESUS IS OUR MODEL OF UNSELFISH SERVICE

JESUS HAS REVEALED THROUGH HIS LIFE, DEATH, Resurrection and teachings that the children of God come to true freedom and fullness of life through their loving service to God and neighbor. The vocations to marriage and the priesthood give witness to this truth in a unique way. The Sacrament of Matrimony gives spouses the graces they need to serve the Church and society and to live in faithful love with each other and with their children. The Sacrament of Holy Orders gives bishops, priests and deacons the graces they need to serve the Church as they strive for holiness of life.

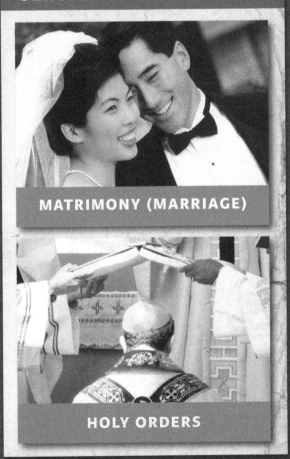

SACRAMENTS AT THE SERVICE OF COMMUNION

MATRIMONY (MARRIAGE)

HOLY ORDERS

Faith Focus: These teachings of the Catholic Church are the primary focus of the doctrinal content presented in this chapter:

- Christians are called to offer their lives as an unselfish gift to God and others, as Jesus did.
- All the faithful have the vocation to strive for holiness of life and to serve others selflessly in the Church and the world.
- Marriage and Holy Orders are the Sacraments at the Service of Communion (the community of the Church).
- The Sacrament of Marriage consecrates a baptized man and woman to foster the good of the human family, society and the Church.
- The Sacrament of Holy Orders consecrates a baptized man to foster the good of the spiritual family, the Church.
- The service of the ministerial priesthood is exercised through the threefold office of sanctifying, teaching and governing.

Discipleship Formation: As a result of studying this chapter and discovering the meaning of the faith of the Catholic Church for your life, you should be better able to:

- serve God and your neighbor selflessly;
- appreciate the vocation of marriage and ordination;
- discern whether God might be calling you to serve the Church in the married life or the ordained life.

Scripture References: These Scripture references are quoted or referred to in this chapter:
OLD TESTAMENT: Genesis 12:2; **Daniel** 7:13
NEW TESTAMENT: Matthew 6:19–21, 25:31–46, 28: 20; **Mark** 10:45, 42–45, 13:26; **Luke** 4:16–21, 16:13; **John** 13:6–9, 35–36; **Romans** 6:16–18, 20–23; **1 Corinthians** 13:4–7; **Galatians** 5:1, 13b–14

Faith Glossary: Familiarize yourself with or recall the meaning of these key terms. Definitions are found in the Glossary: **domestic church, family, freedom, parables, ordination, sacramental graces, Sacraments at the Service of Communion, Son of Man**

Faith Words: freedom; Sacraments at the Service of Communion
Learn by Heart: Galatians 5:13b–14
Learn by Example: Maisie Ward and Frank Sheed, Catholic writers and speakers

How can one be free while being a "servant"?

TO SERVE OR TO BE SERVED? THAT IS THE QUESTION

The Apostles James and John asked Jesus for recognition and a superior place among his disciples. The other Apostles, overhearing their request, became angry with James and John. Jesus' response reveals the essence of being his disciple.

So Jesus called them and said to them, "You know that among the Gentiles those whom they recognize as their rulers lord it over them, and their great ones are tyrants over them. But it is not so among you; but whoever wishes to become great among you must be your servant, and whoever wishes to be first among you must be slave of all. For the Son of Man came not to be served but to serve, and to give his life a ransom for many."

—Mark 10:42–45

OPENING REFLECTION

- How does Jesus challenge James and John's understanding of what it means to be his disciple?
- Who have you learned about or know personally whose greatness in your eyes lies in their serving of other people?
- How willingly and selflessly do you give your time and talents in loving service of God and others?

ST. LUKE, FROM A 12TH-CENTURY GERMAN MANUSCRIPT

The Son of Man

"The title used by our Lord of himself in the Gospel. This title connotes a relationship with the eschatological figure of the 'Son of man appearing in clouds and glory' in the prophecy of Daniel [see Mark 13:26; Daniel 7:13]" (*Catechism of the Catholic Church* [CCC], Glossary, "Son of Man"). The title is used thirty times in Matthew, fourteen times in Mark, twenty-five times in Luke, and twelve times in John.

Freedom

"Freedom characterizes properly human acts. It makes the human being responsible for acts of which he is the voluntary agent. His deliberate acts properly belong to him" (CCC, no. 1745). "The more one does what is good, the freer one becomes. Freedom attains its proper perfection when it is directed toward God, the highest good and our beatitude. Freedom implies also the possibility of choosing between good and evil. The choice of evil is an abuse of freedom and leads to the slavery of sin" (*Compendium of the Catechism of the Catholic Church*, no. 363).

THE CHAINS OF ST. PETER, ROME, ITALY

TO SERVE IS TO BE FULLY HUMAN

Jesus freely came among us "to give his life [as] a ransom for many" (Mark 10:45). Jesus' whole life on earth gave witness to his freely choosing to serve his Father and all humanity. To give one's life for another person is the ultimate form of service. The Cross of Christ is the ultimate witness to this life of unselfish service.

When we imagine success and greatness, or wish for the "good life," we might imagine ourselves with our feet up and with "servants" (or, in today's business parlance, the people who work for us) running about doing our bidding. In such an understanding of greatness we are tempted to cast people aside when they fail to profit our well-being. So prevalent is this practice that Pope Francis, over and over again, has warned us of its evil, and has commanded us to change our ways.

When we look at the life and teachings of Jesus, who lived the perfect human life, we encounter a very different reality. The ambition for honor and power is not a disciple attitude; and certainly not a disciple lifestyle. Such a self-centered lifestyle enslaves oneself and other people. It does not respect the dignity of the human person and works against their living in the **freedom** of the children of God that St. Paul taught: "For freedom Christ has set us free" (Galatians 5:1).

SERVICE—A SOURCE OF TRUE FREEDOM

St. John Paul II, reflecting on his encounters with young people, wrote:

Young people . . . have a profound longing for those genuine values which find their fullness in Christ. Is not Christ the secret of true freedom and profound joy of heart? . . . If Christ is presented to young people as he really is, they experience him as an answer that is convincing and they can accept his message, even when it is demanding and bears the mark of the Cross.

—Apostolic Letter, *On the Close of the Great Jubilee Year 2000*, no. 9

Serving others, especially the poor, the oppressed, the excluded, sinners and all enslaved people, is a source of true freedom. This service is not optional for disciples of Jesus Christ and is indispensable for entering into the life of freedom that Jesus promised and brought about.

In seeking to serve only ourselves, we do not become truly free; we become enslaved and held in bondage to our own selfish and self-serving desires. Only in serving God and others do we discover and live in the freedom of the children of God. Serving others as Jesus did is the only source of freedom for both those who serve and those who are served.

- What examples can you recall of Jesus serving others? (Skim through the Gospel accounts if you need to.) Discuss how Jesus' serving of others freed them.
- Brainstorm how young Christians might serve others in need in ways similar to how Jesus served others. Choose one way of service on your list and put it into practice.

CHOOSE YOUR MASTER WISELY

Jesus' life of loving, unselfish service gives us a profound insight into human nature: *We always serve some master, whether our master be God, one's self, another person, money or any other created object.* Recall Jesus' admonition in the Sermon on the Mount:

"Do not store up for yourselves treasures on earth, where moth and rust consume and where thieves break in and steal; but store up for yourselves treasures in heaven, where neither moth nor rust consumes and where thieves do not break in and steal. For where your treasure is, there your heart will be also."

—Matthew 6:19–21

Consciously or not, the attitudes and habits we develop, the desires we nurture and the things we pursue can absorb us. They contribute significantly to whomever or whatever we seek to serve.

Everyone, believers and non-believers, serves the master they think will set them free. We cannot avoid making a choice between masters. Jesus teaches emphatically, "No slave can serve two masters. . . . You cannot serve God and wealth" (Luke 16:13). Only one master can and will eventually set us free. We must decide who and what to put first in our life.

Freedom itself can become an idol, unless it is properly understood. The choice of God over

"No slave can serve two masters. . . . You cannot serve God and wealth"

LUKE 16:13

everyone and everything else can be a difficult one to make. On the surface it might appear that obedience to God and submission to the rules of a religion involve restricting our choices rather than freeing us to choose.

Following Christ, the Son of Man, results in our growing in the freedom to choose what is good over what is evil, and this leads to happiness and holiness in this life and in eternal life. Making any person or any object our master leads to misery and death. St. Paul taught this truth:

> Do you not know that if you present yourselves to anyone as obedient slaves, you are slaves of the one whom you obey, either of sin, which leads to death, or of obedience, which leads to righteousness? But thanks be to God that you, having once been slaves of sin, have become obedient from the heart to the form of teaching to which you were entrusted, and that you, having been set free from sin, have become slaves of righteousness. . . .
>
> When you were slaves of sin, you were free in regard to righteousness. So what advantage did you then get from the things of which you now are ashamed? The end of those things is death. But now that you have been freed from sin and enslaved to God, the advantage you get is sanctification. The end is eternal life. For the wages of sin is death, but the free gift of God is eternal life in Christ Jesus our Lord.
>
> —Romans 6:16–18, 20–23

St. Paul came to understand that *servitude* to Christ, the Incarnate Son of God, and life in his Church was a source of *liberation*—liberation from slavery and from all that degrades and destroys our humanity.

WHAT ABOUT YOU PERSONALLY?
⊙ Is obedience to Christ a source of freedom for you? Give examples.
⊙ How does your faith empower you to enable others to live in freedom?

THE NEW FREEDOM TO LOVE
After Jesus washed their feet at the Last Supper the Apostles did not at first understand his

JESUS WASHING THE DISCIPLES' FEET | SAINT-PIERRE, NORMANDY, FRANCE

command to them to serve, as Simon Peter's response attests. (Check out John 13:6–9.) Later at that Passover meal Jesus would open up the meaning of the inseparable connection between service and discipleship, saying, "I give you a new commandment, that you love one another. Just as I have loved you, you should also love one another. By this everyone will know that you are my disciples, if you have love for one another" (John 13:35–36). Only after Jesus' dying and rising would they come to understand that by obeying his command and following his example they would become truly free.

Freedom is both a gift and a choice. We have the freedom to serve or not to serve God and others as Jesus did. In the next section of this chapter we will explore how our encounter with Jesus Christ, who came to serve and not to be served, in the sacraments supports and empowers his Church to live his new commandment.

TALK IT OVER
⊙ Does it seem true to you that we find freedom in serving God and our "neighbor"? Why or why not?

JOURNAL EXERCISE
⊙ Are you feeling called to live your faith through a life of service to God and your neighbor? Describe what you think that service might be like.
⊙ What things might dissuade you from living by this standard of discipleship?
⊙ What small acts of loving service and kindness could you undertake this week?

The Sacraments at the Service of Communion

THE JUDGMENT OF NATIONS | AUTUN CATHEDRAL, FRANCE

THE PARABLE OF THE JUDGMENT OF NATIONS

- You have read or listened to the **parable** Jesus told about the judgment of nations when he comes again in glory at the end of time. "Then he will sit on the throne of his glory" and separate the "sheep" from the "goats."
- Recall or read that parable. You will find it in Matthew 25:31–46.

OPENING REFLECTION

- Who did Jesus name "sheep"? Who did Jesus name "goats"?
- Describe and compare the actions of those whom Jesus named "sheep" and those whom Jesus named "goats."
- What does this parable teach you about living as a disciple of Jesus Christ?
- Reflect on how you are living as a disciple of Jesus. Would you place yourself among the "sheep" or the "goats"; or maybe sometimes among the "sheep" and other times among the "goats"?

"COME, YOU THAT ARE BLESSED BY MY FATHER" (MATTHEW 25:34)

Our society tries to convince us, "Feed yourself first! Then feed others!" In other words, "Look out for Number One, first and above all else!" Jesus' life and teaching was contrary to this message. Jesus revealed this paradoxical truth: we find freedom and joy in serving God and others. It is by giving ourselves in selfless, loving service to others—in feeding their bodily and spiritual hungers—that we come to fullness and abundance of life. But why does it work that way? Why does loving service lead to freedom and joy in life?

God creates us in the divine image—in the image and likeness of the one God who is an eternal communion of Three Divine Persons united in infinite love. God creates each one of us to share in that communion of life and love, now and forever after our death. The vocation God gives us is our pathway through life, which guides us to a life of service to God and to others. Cooperating with God's grace and meeting the responsibilities of our vocation are a sure guide to attaining a deeper communion of life and love with God in this life and a "perfect life with the Most Holy Trinity" and "communion of life and love with the Trinity, with the Virgin Mary, the angels and the blessed" in eternal life after death (CCC, no. 1024).

WHAT ABOUT YOU PERSONALLY?

- When have you seen people act selfishly toward others? In loving service of others?
- How are you inclined to act toward others? Why?

JESUS CHRIST: THE SACRAMENT OF GOD

God is always inviting and drawing humanity to live in loving community. Throughout Sacred

Scripture he revealed himself and his divine plan to the Chosen People. God promised to raise up a messiah, an "anointed one," to free and save all people from sin. Jesus, the Incarnate Son of God, announced that he was the Messiah, the Anointed One of God. (Revisit Jesus' description of himself and his mission in Luke 4:16–21.)

The Church describes Jesus as the *sacrament of God*. We most often use the word "sacrament" to refer to the Seven Sacraments. But the root of the word "sacrament" is the Greek word *mysterion*, "which was translated into Latin by two terms: *mysterium* and *sacramentum*" (CCC, no. 774). Jesus Christ instituted the Seven Sacraments by his life, Passion, Death and Resurrection. They make present, in a very unique and concrete way, the *mystery* of the saving love of God at work in our life.

Surely Jesus was God's greatest *sacrament*. By becoming fully and truly human, the Incarnate Son of God made present and brought about God's work of salvation, redemption and liberation in the most concrete and effective way—in bone and flesh, in word and deed. Christ continues this work in, through and with his Church. Through the sacraments of the Church we encounter Jesus Christ and he offers us the grace that makes us sharers in God's life and saving love.

THE CHURCH: THE UNIVERSAL SACRAMENT OF SALVATION

After Jesus ascended to his Father, the risen and glorified Christ and his Father sent the Holy Spirit to be with the disciples and his Church. The Holy Spirit continues God's saving work of salvation through the Church, the Body of Christ. The Second Vatican Council affirmed this truth when it declared the Church to be the *universal sacrament of salvation*. The Council taught: "[The] Church, in Christ, is a sacrament—a sign and instrument, that is, of communion with God and of the unity of the entire human race" (*Dogmatic Constitution on the Church* [*Lumen Gentium*], no. 1).

The Holy Spirit empowers the whole Church through her diversity of ministries to bear God's saving and sanctifying love to the whole world. By the power of the Holy Spirit the members of the Body of Christ are, as St. Teresa of Ávila so eloquently described them, the hands and feet of Jesus Christ here on earth.

THINK, PAIR AND SHARE

⊙ Reflect: Sacred Scripture and Sacred Tradition teach that God works in and with his people to bring about the divine plan of salvation.

⊙ Share with a partner the ways you see the Catholic Church serving the world. Think of people, events and objects that remind you of God's presence and grace in your life.

WHAT ABOUT YOU PERSONALLY?

⊙ What difference does it make to you to know that the Blessed Trinity calls you to be a visible sign of the mystery of God's saving grace to others?

⊙ What attitudes and good habits could you adopt so as to become a clearer sign of God's saving love to your family and friends, classmates and neighbors?

THE HOLY TRINITY | 14TH-CENTURY MANUSCRIPT

SACRAMENTS AT THE SERVICE OF COMMUNION

The Seven Sacraments are at the heart of the Church's work of mediating God's saving grace to the world. The Seven Sacraments are the three Sacraments of Christian Initiation: Baptism, Confirmation and Eucharist; the two Sacraments of Healing: Penance and Reconciliation, and Anointing of the Sick; and the two **Sacraments at the Service of Communion**: Marriage and Holy Orders.

Through the Sacraments of Christian Initiation we receive the grace of God's own life "to live with God and to act by his love" (USCCA, Glossary, "Grace," 514); we are initiated into the Church and are strengthened and nourished to live as children of God and temples of the Holy Spirit. Through the Sacraments of Healing we receive graces in times of spiritual and physical weakness to be restored to the life of God and to be strengthened to live out our baptismal call to holiness of life in loving service to God and others.

God calls, consecrates and strengthens some of the faithful for this loving service through the Sacraments of Holy Orders and Matrimony. It is through this loving service to the community of the Church and to the world that the ordained and married strive for their personal holiness and salvation.

You will get a brief overview of Matrimony and Holy Orders as Sacraments at the Service of Communion in the next two sections of this chapter. In chapters 4 through 9 you will study and discuss in more detail the teachings of the Catholic Church on the vocation to the married and ordained life.

JOURNAL EXERCISE

- ◉ God gives certain members of his Church the vocation to seek holiness of life primarily by serving the community of the Church. How does this reveal the wisdom and love of God?
- ◉ What could you do to discern whether God might be inviting you to the ordained life or to the married life?

THE SEVEN SACRAMENTS: MARRIAGE | NICOLAS POUSSIN

FAITH WORD

Sacraments at the Service of Communion

The term *communion* refers to the Community of the Church. Holy Orders and Matrimony are the Sacraments at the Service of Communion (the community of the Church). This means they are primarily directed toward the salvation of others. If they benefit the personal salvation of the ordained or married person, it is through service to others that this happens.

—*United States Catholic Catechism for Adults* (USCCA), Glossary, 527

Marriage—fostering the good of the family, the Church and society

UNDYING LOVE

Harold and Marion were married for sixty-five years when Harold made the decision to seek the help of others to care for his wife, who was in the advanced stages of Alzheimer's disease. It had been a long time since Marion could either care for herself or recognize her husband. Unable to adequately care for his wife, Harold placed Marion in an Alzheimer's Care Center so that she could receive the care she needed. Harold's decision, far from being a sign of lack of love for his wife or abandonment of his marriage vows, was an expression of his love and commitment to her. In his own words: "The vows that we took were through sickness and through health until death do us part, and there was nothing about 'unless you have Alzheimer's.' "

—Based on a story in *First Coast News*, Jacksonville, Florida

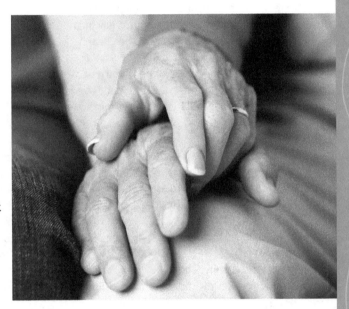

OPENING REFLECTION

- Why was Harold's decision a painful one? A decision to live out his marriage vows?
- Do you think you could make such a decision? Why or why not?

"IN SICKNESS AND IN HEALTH"

The media fill our minds with many portrayals of marriage that are at odds with the kind of commitment Harold showed toward Marion. The media often portray marriage as an *arrangement* that can be easily terminated when either or both spouses no longer satisfy the needs of the other or when things just get too tough to deal with. Comments that refer to spouses as "the old ball-and-chain" and to being "tied down"—as if somehow marriage brings a loss of freedom and is a form of bondage—express this view of marriage.

Fortunately, the real-life marriage of Harold and Marion speaks to the deeper truth of those spouses who honor the sanctity of their vows and the self-sacrificing love that unites them for life through "good times and bad, in sickness and in health." The vocation to married life of a baptized man and woman is, at its heart, a noble call to witness to Christ's love for his Church and to remind the whole Church that Christian life, as was the life of Jesus, is a life of selfless, loving service.

TALK IT OVER

- What do you think are good reasons to marry?
- How do those reasons contribute to a healthy lifelong relationship between spouses?

MARRIAGE: VOCATION TO A LIFE OF SELF-SACRIFICING LOVE AND SERVICE

Jesus raised marriage to the level of a sacrament. The sacramental marriage of a baptized man and woman is primarily a vocation to foster the good of the community of the Church, the family and society. Christian married life is to render this service by being a living witness of the love of God for humanity, which was revealed in the life, Passion, Death and Resurrection of Christ. Scripture, as we have seen, names Jesus' unconditional self-sacrificing love for his Father and for all humanity *agape*.

The married faithful have a unique vocation to reflect this divine love in the many ways they honor each other and join together, day in and day out, in serving the family of the Church, of the home and of society. The sacramental graces of Matrimony strengthen spouses to give of themselves fully and unconditionally to each other. By their faithful love, spouses nurture each other and give light and life to those around them.

OVER TO YOU

⊙ Think of married couples whom you know whose marriages reflect the divine love of the Trinity.

⊙ In what concrete ways do they image that love?

Servants to family: The family is the basic human community; it is the foundational relationship at the heart of human life. The vocation to marriage is realized most immediately in the many small but significant acts of daily living that foster both the spiritual and the bodily well-being of family members. For example, the parents' daily tending to the family's needs and sacrificing their own time and desires contribute to the family's growth in self-emptying love. Serving one's spouse and family also includes challenging one's spouse or children when they fall short of striving to live a virtuous life.

THINK, PAIR AND SHARE

⊙ Read and discuss 1 Corinthians 13:4–7.

⊙ Apply the characteristics of love named by St. Paul to married and family life. Share concrete real-life scenarios.

Servants to the Church: "The family is, so to speak, the domestic church" (*Dogmatic Constitution on the Church*, no. 1). In the selfless support of one's spouse and children, Christian married couples contribute to the building up of the Church, the Body of Christ. In describing the Christian family as the domestic church, or "church of the home," the Catholic Church teaches that it is in the home, under the guidance

DÍA DE LOS MUERTOS ALTAR IN TLAQUEPAQUE JALISCO, MEXICO

Family Love Beyond Death

In some cultures, family members' dedication to serving one another transcends even death. On November 1 and November 2 each year people in Mexico and other Latin American countries celebrate "*el Día de los Muertos*" ("the Day of the Dead"). They decorate the graves of deceased loved ones and construct miniature altars to their memory. In the midst of these celebrations, people pray for the repose of their dearly departed and ask for their intercession with God.

of parents, that children first learn to live the way of love revealed by Christ. Spouses can guide their children to live the Commandments as Christ taught and grow in holiness of life in many ways. They can:

- ⊙ participate in the lay ministries and activities of their parish community;
- ⊙ allow their children to witness them praying together or alone;
- ⊙ make the celebration of the sacraments part of the rhythm of family life;
- ⊙ encourage children to pray daily on their own, to listen for God's call and, if heard, to respond;
- ⊙ talk freely about the presence of God in the joys and sorrows of their life.

—Based on "Tools for Building a Domestic Church," USCCB website

THINK, PAIR AND SHARE

- ⊙ St. John Paul II taught: "To maintain a joyful family requires much from both the parents and the children. Each member of the family has to become, in a special way, the servant of the others" (*Letter to Families*, February 2, 1994).
- ⊙ Think of a number of ways that you can join with your own family and put this vision and teaching into practice.
- ⊙ Share your reflections with a partner.

Servants to society: The service of Christian married couples does not stop with service to their family and to the Church. They are the pillars that support society. St. John Paul II, during his apostolic pilgrimage to Australia, had this to say about the vital role married couples play in society:

[Married couples] exercise more fully that special love and responsibility of the marriage covenant which make them see children as God's special gift to the Church and to society. As the family goes, so goes the nation and so goes the whole world in which we live. With regard to the family, society urgently needs "to recover an awareness of the primacy of moral values, which are the values of the human person as such," thus "recapturing the ultimate meaning of life and its fundamental values."

—Homily, November 30, 1986, no. 4

For most people, it is in the home that they learn the values that enable them to live responsibly in society. There are many ways in which married couples and the home can foster this responsibility. The article "Tools for Building a Domestic Church," on the website of the United States Conference of Catholic Bishops, names these two ways among others:

- ⊙ Teach stewardship and charity to your children, through word and example.
- ⊙ Demonstrate love for your spouse, your children, your neighbors, and the world. Remind [your] children that they are loved by God and have been given gifts to serve others.

TALK IT OVER

- ⊙ What is the image of marriage that you receive from the media?
- ⊙ In light of St. John Paul II's words: "As the family goes, so goes the nation and so goes the whole world in which we live," does the media's message contribute to the health of families and society? Why or why not?

JOURNAL EXERCISE

- ⊙ What would it mean for your family to live out your collective vocation as a domestic church, or church of the home?

Ordained to serve

Did you know?

"Servant of the Servants of God" is one of the titles used to describe the pope. Church tradition passes on that St. Gregory the Great (c. 540–604) first used this title to describe his ministry as pope. There is a story about St. Gregory that illustrates why he might have described himself in this way. Though he was a wealthy Roman prefect (today, in essence, the combined power of a mayor and judge), Gregory gave all his properties over to found seven monasteries, one of which was part of a hospital in which Gregory himself served. It was not unusual, as the story goes, to see Gregory kneel at the feet of those whom he once judged and perform the humble service of caring for them. The story goes on to say that Gregory invited twelve strangers to have dinner with him in order to set in place a tradition for the monasteries he founded of personally cooking meals to feed the poor.

ST. GREGORY THE GREAT | ANTONELLO DA MESSINA

SERVANTS TO ALL

On Holy Thursday Pope Francis washes and kisses the feet of twelve prisoners. In doing so, the Pope demonstrates, in dramatic fashion, what the priesthood calls the ordained to be—servants of all people, especially the vulnerable among us.

OPENING REFLECTION

⊙ In what ways do you see priests serving people?
⊙ How do you support your parish priest or school chaplain in their work?

JESUS: MODEL OF HUMILITY AND SERVICE

Though Pope Francis' actions on Holy Thursday surprise many, their surprise could hardly match the surprise of the Apostles at the Last Supper. On that night their master, the one whom they had come to profess to be their Lord and God, knelt down before them and washed their feet—a task normally reserved for the lowliest household servants. Jesus' washing the Apostles' feet took them by such surprise that, as he came to wash Simon Peter's feet, the Apostle objected:

"Lord, are you going to wash my feet?" Jesus answered, "You do not know now what I am doing, but later you will understand." Peter said to him, "You will never wash my feet." Jesus answered, "Unless I wash you, you have no share with me."

—John 13:6–8

Later on during the meal Jesus told his Apostles that if he, their master, had done this humble service for them, they were to do the same for one another. In this way Jesus made it known to them what it meant to be humble servant leaders of his Church.

TALK IT OVER

⊙ What would be a contemporary equivalent of washing someone's feet?
⊙ Why is it difficult to render this kind of humble service to another person?

FORMS OF PRIESTLY SERVICE

Bishops, their co-workers, priests, and deacons who assist them receive God-given responsibilities and authority to serve the whole communion, or community, of the Church, through their ordination. The ordained are to foster the good of the Church, their spiritual family, through the exercise of the threefold office of sanctifying, teaching and governing the community of Jesus' disciples. All three of these offices serve and build up the whole Church. (*We take a brief look at those offices here, and will explore them in more detail in chapters 8 and 9.*)

Sanctifying: Bishops and priests and deacons serve the People of God, the Church, through their celebration of the sacraments. By the power of the Holy Spirit received in Holy Orders, they mediate God's graces and present the worship of the Church to God. Jesus works through the ordained to unite the Church more deeply to his Father.

Teaching: Jesus, during his earthly life and ministry, by his words and the way he lived, taught how his disciples were to live. He made Simon Peter and the other Apostles and their successors, sharers in his teaching ministry, saying, "Go, therefore, and make disciples of all nations, . . . teaching them to obey everything that I commanded you" (Matthew 28:20). Today the pope and the other bishops and priests carry on Jesus'

teaching ministry in a variety of contexts. They help God's people understand the Gospel, take it to heart and live it out with joy.

Governing: This third office includes the *pastoral* governance of the members of the Church. The word "pastoral" comes from the Latin word *pastor*, meaning "shepherd." By the power of the Spirit of Christ, bishops, their co-workers priests, and their helpers, deacons, continue this work of pastoral guidance of Jesus' flock, first given to Simon Peter. They oversee the ministries and various other activities of the People of God entrusted to their care. (*We will continue our discussion of this threefold office in chapter 9.*)

JOURNAL EXERCISE

⊙ Why is service at the heart of a vocation to the ordained life?
⊙ What aspects of the ordained ministry impress you the most? Why?

PETER RECEIVING THE KEYS | SAINT JOHN NEUMANN CHURCH, SUNBURY, OHIO

REFLECT ON WHAT YOU HAVE LEARNED

Look back over this chapter and reflect on what you have learned about the vocations to the married and ordained life. Share the teachings of the Catholic Church on these statements:

- Christians are called to offer their lives as an unselfish gift to God and others, as Jesus did.
- All the baptized receive the call and grace to serve their brothers and sisters in the Church and the world.
- Marriage and Holy Orders are the Sacraments at the Service of Communion (the community of the Church).
- The Sacrament of Marriage bestows on a baptized man and woman the grace to foster the good of the family, the Church and society.
- The Sacrament of Holy Orders consecrates a baptized man to foster the good of the spiritual family, the Church.
- The service of the ministerial priesthood is exercised through the threefold office of sanctifying, teaching and governing.

OVER TO YOU

- What wisdom for your life right now have you learned from your study of this chapter?
- How can and will you make that part of your life?

LEARN BY EXAMPLE

Maisie Ward (1889–1975) and Frank Sheed (1897–1981), Catholic writers, publishers and speakers

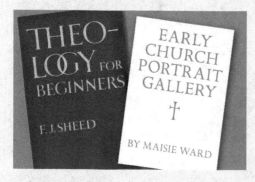

Though often overlooked when the Church's history has been told, married couples have played an indispensable role in the Church's life and work over the centuries. Maisie Ward and Frank Sheed offer one shining example of the loving service married couples render to the Church and the world.

Maisie was no stranger to service, having worked as a nurse during World War I. Frank was raised in the Protestant tradition by his Australian parents, and he surprised them by stating his intention to convert to Catholicism at the age of sixteen. Both Frank and Maisie went on to earn fame as writers and speakers, even preaching the faith in public spaces and at street corners.

Maisie and Frank met at a Catholic Evidence Guild lecture in London, and were soon married. Maisie wrote biographies of notable Catholics and holy people, as well as works in spirituality and New Testament scholarship. Frank, one of the few lay theologians of his time, wrote on a wide range of basic theological issues, offering a rational defense of the Catholic faith. Some years later, in 1926, Maisie and Frank combined their efforts to found Sheed & Ward, which became a prominent Catholic publishing company. Through their research and writing, they rendered a great service to the Catholic Church.

- ⊙ Reflect: Maisie and Frank combined their gifts to better serve the Church.
- ⊙ What married couples do you know personally who are striving to do the same? How are they working together?
- ⊙ Share how their married life inspires you.

SHARE FAITH WITH FAMILY AND FRIENDS

- ⊙ How can you help one another to grow in holiness from day to day?
- ⊙ In what ways could you serve one another better?
- ⊙ What difference would it make to take Jesus' teaching about serving others more seriously?

REFLECT AND DECIDE

- ⊙ Reflect: Marriage and the ordained ministries exist to serve and build up the Church.
- ⊙ Does either married life or the ordained life strike you as a fulfilling way to live out your Christian baptismal vocation? Why?
- ⊙ What acts of service could you engage in to help you discern whether you have a calling to marriage or to the priesthood?
- ⊙ What is the best decision you could make now to help you discern the vocation to which God is calling you?

LEARN BY HEART

Do not use your freedom as an opportunity for self-indulgence, but through love become slaves to one another. For the whole law is summed up in a single commandment, "You shall love your neighbor as yourself."

GALATIANS 5:13B–14

All pray the Sign of the Cross together.

Opening prayer

LEADER

Loving God, you sent us your Son,
who humbled himself to serve us
and, in serving us, saved us.
Send your Spirit of love and humility upon us.
Give us hearts for service and the humility to do
whatever is necessary to help one another grow
in holiness and to serve your Church.
ALL
Amen.

Proclamation of the Word of God

READER

A reading from the Letter to the Galatians.
Proclaim Galatians 5:13–14.
The word of the Lord.
ALL
Thanks be to God.

LEADER

Let us reflect silently on what we have heard from
this reading. (*Pause*)
I invite those who wish to share their reflection
to do so.

Students share reflections.

Lord, unite us, your Church, in the Holy Spirit;
may we serve you with all our hearts
and work together with unselfish love.
Grant this through our Lord Jesus Christ, your
Son,
who lives and reigns with you and the Holy Spirit,
one God, forever and ever.
ALL
Amen.

Concluding Prayer

LEADER

These past days we have reflected on the
meaning of loving service to one another. Take a
few moments to speak with God in silence about
whether you might have a vocation to serve the
People of God in the married life or the ordained
life.

Students pray in silence.

Conclude by praying the Sign of the Cross together.

CHAPTER 4

The Biblical Teachings on Marriage

—A Lifelong Covenant of Love

MARRIAGE . . .

THE FUNDAMENTAL RELATIONSHIP AND FOUNDATION OF THE HUMAN FAMILY

GIVES WITNESS TO THE UNCONDITIONAL LOVE OF GOD FOR HUMANITY

A SIGN OF GOD'S CREATIVE, SAVING AND SANCTIFYING LOVE

REFLECTS THE LOVE OF CHRIST FOR HIS CHURCH

A GOD-GIVEN VOCATION

BENEFITS SPOUSES, FAMILY, SOCIETY AND THE CHURCH

MARRIAGE IS A COVENANT "BY WHICH A MAN AND A women establish between themselves a partnership of the whole of life" (CCC, no. 1601). Marriage is not a purely human institution. God is the author of marriage, which Jesus raised to a sacrament. In God's plan, as the Book of Genesis reveals, marriage is a partnership that "constitutes the first form of communion of persons" (CCC, no. 383). The love of Christian husbands and wives reflects the love of Christ for his Church (see Ephesians 5:25–26, 31–32). The Church promotes the sacramentality of marriage and its vital role in fostering the good of the family, society and the Church.

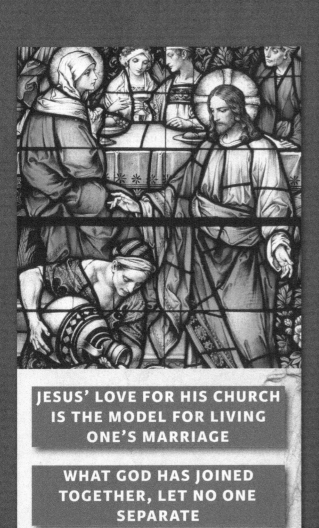

JESUS' LOVE FOR HIS CHURCH IS THE MODEL FOR LIVING ONE'S MARRIAGE

WHAT GOD HAS JOINED TOGETHER, LET NO ONE SEPARATE

Faith Focus: These teachings of the Catholic Church are the primary focus of the doctrinal content presented in this chapter:

⊙ God is the author of marriage; marriage is not a purely human institution.

⊙ God created human beings, male and female, in the divine image, as equal partners in the ongoing work of his creation.

⊙ The attraction between a man and a woman is most intimately fulfilled in the lifelong marriage covenant.

⊙ The covenant of love uniting spouses in marriage gives witness to the committed, unconditional love of God for humanity.

⊙ The marriage of Abraham and Sarah gave birth to the People of God.

⊙ The married love of the baptized reflects the love of Christ for his Church, the bride of Christ.

⊙ The human body is sacred, a temple of the living God, and to be honored and respected.

Discipleship Formation: As a result of studying this chapter and discovering the meaning of the faith of the Catholic Church for your life, you should be better able to:

⊙ deepen your commitment to serve God and other people;

⊙ support your parents and family as they strive to grow in holiness of life through their service to God and people;

⊙ value and respect marriage as a God-given vocation;

⊙ discover the role biblical marriages played in God's plan of salvation for humanity;

⊙ understand that God supports married couples in living their vocation by continually offering them his grace;

⊙ respond to the graces God offers you and your family to live holy lives;

⊙ honor and respect the gift and sacredness of your body and the bodies of others.

Scripture References: These Scripture references are quoted or referred to in this chapter:

OLD TESTAMENT: Genesis 1:26–30, 2:4b–9, 15 and 18–30, 3:1–24 and 20, 12:1–9, 17:15–16,18:1–33; **Leviticus** 19:18; **Deuteronomy** 6:4–5; **1 Kings** 3:1–15, 11:1–15; **Tobit** 6:10–18, 8:1–8

NEW TESTAMENT: Matthew 1:18–25, 7:15–20, 11:29–30, 19:3–6, 8 and 11; **Mark** 8:34; **Luke** 2:40 and 52; **John** 1:14, 2:1–11; **Ephesians** 5:25, 28–33; **1 Corinthians** 3:16, 6:15 and 19–20, 12:27, 15:20; **1 Timothy** 3:16

Faith Glossary: Familiarize yourself with or recall the meaning of these key terms. Definitions are found in the Glossary: **cardinal virtues, celibacy, covenant, divorce, fruits of the Holy Spirit, marriage, miracle, modesty, polygamy, temperance, Theology of the Body, wisdom**

Faith Words: marriage; Theology of the Body
Learn by Heart: Matthew 19:6
Learn by Example: Saints Isidore and Maria Torribia

Why is married life central to God's plan for creation?

The popular novel *The Giver* by Lois Lowry and the three other novels in *The Giver* quartet present a disturbing picture of marriage and family life. The "husband" and "wife" and "children" in a family are determined and controlled by social authority. Marriage is presented as a purely human institution. God is out of the picture. Marriage and family life are products of society's needs alone. The love between spouses is inconsequential.

OPENING REFLECTION

◉ What would society be like if marriage and family life were based solely on social needs?

◉ What would marriage be like if a husband and wife did not freely choose to enter into it based on their love for each other?

◉ What would be the consequences for family life and society?

◉ What is it about marriage that contributes to its positive outcomes for families and for society in general?

A CLOSER LOOK AT MARRIAGE

The human story tells us that **marriage** freely entered, with a commitment of lifelong, faithful **covenant** love, is vital for the spouses, the family and the common good of all. You will recall that a covenant is a solemn agreement involving mutual commitments. In any covenant the relationship between the parties is central, and the word of both parties is its sacred binding force.

In chapter 3 we learned that God calls married people to serve not only each other but also their family, the Church, and society as a whole. In chapters 4 through 7 we explore in more depth the vocation to the covenant of married life. In particular, we examine the teachings of Scripture and the Catholic Church on the sacramental marriage between a baptized man and a baptized woman. Through your study you will gain a better appreciation of the role of marriage in the divine plan of creation and salvation. Your study will also help you begin to discern whether God is calling *you* to the married life.

FAITH WORD

Marriage

The marriage covenant, by which a man and a woman form with each other an intimate communion of life and love. . . . By its very nature it is ordered to the good of the couple, as well as to the generation and education of children. Christ the Lord raised marriage between the baptized to the dignity of a sacrament.

—*Catechism of the Catholic Church* (CCC), no. 1660

Culture Note

In an old multicultural custom, during their wedding ceremony a bride and groom pour salt from separate pouches into a larger common receptacle. Just as it is then impossible to separate the bride's grains of salt from those of the groom, so are their lives inseparable once they are married.

HUMAN BEINGS: UNITED FROM THE START

The biblical stories of God creating humanity (Genesis 1:26–28 and Genesis 2:7–8, 15–25) reveal many important truths about the human person and human society.

- Human beings are made for God and for one another.
- God creates human beings "male and female" (Genesis 1:27); in other words, as gendered people, sexual beings.
- God creates both men and women in the divine image (Genesis 1:27); neither one is any more an image of God than the other. Both are images of God.
- Men and women are to "be fruitful and multiply" (Genesis 1:28); in other words, this is how God intends the propagation of the human family.
- Human beings need other people and are created to live in relationship with one another; they are to be partners in God's divine plan of creation. (Genesis 2:18–25)
- Together in partnership, as one, men and women are given responsibility for all of creation. (Genesis 1:28–30, 2:15)

Thereafter, the whole biblical narrative emphasizes how close the bond is between man and woman. It is stronger than the bond between children and their parents. It is so close that a married man and woman become as "one flesh" (Genesis 2:24). A man and woman in the relationship of marriage have the God-given vocation to work together as loving and equal partners to care for and support each other and propagate the human race. Through their loving union with each other and with God, they discover and enjoy peace and happiness together.

TALK IT OVER

- In your experience, do humans need other people in order to be happy? Why?
- When are you happiest with other people? When do other people most frustrate you?

GOD IS THE AUTHOR OF MARRIAGE

Marriage is not a purely human institution. The Church's Magisterium, reflecting on the Genesis stories and the entirety of God's revealed Word, teaches that "God himself is the author of marriage" (Vatican II, *Pastoral Constitution on the Church in the Modern World [Gaudium et Spes]*, no. 48). God created men and women with a sexual attraction toward each other that is uniquely ordered to their union in marriage. Through the union of Adam and Eve, Eve became "the mother of all who live" (Genesis 3:20). Together they became one and in that union they formed the foundation of the human family.

Beyond simply creating human beings with a desire to become united to one another, God established marriage as a means for people to grow closer to him and to grow in holiness together. The marriage relationship enables spouses to enter more fully into the divine love of the Blessed Trinity. In that sense, any marriage in which either or both spouses focus only on their own wants and needs falls short of the ideal of married love. Married love is always "outward bound," as God's love is toward us.

The Church affirms, "The well-being of the individual person and of both human and christian society is closely bound up with the healthy state of the community of marriage and the family" (*Pastoral Constitution on the Church in the Modern World*, no. 47). In short, marriage epitomizes and protects the loving relationships to which God calls every person. Such love requires putting God and others first. The more we love each other unconditionally, as the Triune God loves us, the more we are able to live happy and fulfilled lives. The covenant of love uniting spouses in marriage gives witness to the committed, unconditional love of God for humanity and to the love on which human relationships are to be built.

TALK IT OVER

⊙ In what ways do you see marriage benefiting spouses? Their family? Society? The Church?
⊙ How unconditional is the love you share in your relationships? How could you improve?

JOURNAL EXERCISE

⊙ Compare how the media commonly present marriage with the Bible's teaching on marriage. Comment on how they are similar or different.

LET'S PROBE DEEPER: A RESEARCH ACTIVITY

⊙ Christians in different cultures have different ways of living and celebrating marriage.
⊙ Research Christian marriage customs in a culture other than your own. How do those customs reflect and celebrate the biblical teachings on marriage as a covenant of love?
⊙ Share your research with the class at the end of your study of this chapter.

Marriage in the Old Testament

NOT YOUR TYPICAL WEDDING DAY

Megan and Marcus celebrated their wedding day a little differently than most. There were no flowers, no limos and no expensive wedding dress. After their wedding, instead of a honeymoon, they made a mission trip to aid victims of the tornado that hit Tuscaloosa–Birmingham in 2011. When the time came to celebrate their anniversary two years later, the couple did not travel to Hawaii or even to a romantic bed-and-breakfast. They headed to Oklahoma where they served the victims of another tornado that had struck in May. For this couple, there is no more fitting way to celebrate marriage than serving others together.

DEVASTATION CAUSED BY THE TORNADO IN OKLAHOMA IN 2013

OPENING REFLECTION

⊙ What do you think of Megan and Marcus's choice of how to celebrate their marriage?

⊙ Given what we have learned about Christian marriage as a Sacrament at the Service of Communion, how do their actions draw out the meaning of their vocation together?

MARRIAGE—A SIGN OF GOD'S CREATIVE, SAVING AND SANCTIFYING LOVE

As the story of Megan and Marcus demonstrates so beautifully, marriage is about fostering the good of others as well as of the married couple. Marriage is a blessing not only to the couple but also to their children, to the Church, to society and to the common good of all. We will now look at some Bible stories to understand better that married life has always played a part in God's creative, saving and sanctifying work among his people. We will also see how marriages can serve as a source of God's saving love in the world and how they can sometimes fall short.

Adam and Eve: The biblical narratives on creation are followed by the narrative of the Fall (Original Sin) of the first couple and the consequences of that first sin for their descendants of ages to come. The tragic events surrounding Adam and Eve illustrate what happens when human beings focus on their own selfish desires rather than on God's plan for them. Genesis 3:1–24 concludes the stories of the creation and fall with the warning that human life, including marriage, procreation and family life, will henceforth be a struggle as a consequence of the sinful choice of Adam and Eve. But the future is not bleak. Genesis 3:15 reveals the good news that God will raise "offspring" of Eve in the future who will heal the brokenness resulting from Adam and Eve's sin.

The biblical account reveals clearly that marriages—indeed, all appropriate human relationships—that do not keep God at their center but focus primarily on achieving their own selfish desires are contrary to the divine plan

ABRAHAM AND LOT TRAVEL TO CANAAN | BARTOLO DI FREDI

of creation. Chapters 3 through 11 of Genesis provide several narratives to illustrate that reality.

THINK, PAIR AND SHARE

◉ What married couples or families have you learned about or know personally who center their lives on God and on serving other people? Share your examples.

◉ How does their relationship with God strengthen their marriage relationship and their family life?

Abraham and Sarah: Chapter 12 of Genesis begins with the story of the call of Abram (Abraham), whose marriage to Sarai (Sarah) would become a blessing on humanity.

Now the LORD said to Abram, "Go from your country and your kindred and your father's house to the land that I will show you. I will make of you a great nation, and I will bless you, and make your name great, so that you will be a blessing. I will bless those who bless you, and the one who curses you I will curse; and in you all the families of the earth shall be blessed."

—Genesis 12:1–3

In the biblical story of Abraham and Sarah we witness the example of one married couple who listened attentively to God's call, responded obediently, and whose offspring became God's own people.

When God called Abram to leave his native land, he and Sarai left their homeland, and they were accompanied by Abram's brother and his brother's son Lot and their servants. They caravanned across the desert and settled in the land of Canaan. (Check out Genesis 12:4–9.) There God entered the covenant with Abram, and changed his name to Abraham and Sarai's name to Sarah. The biblical author writes:

God said to Abraham, "As for Sarai your wife, you shall not call her Sarai, but Sarah shall be her name. I will bless her, and moreover I will give you a son by her. I will bless her, and she shall give rise to nations; kings of people shall come from her."

—Genesis 17:15–16

Because of Abraham and Sarah's steadfast trust in God and his plan for them, their marriage was a blessing for all peoples. Beginning with Isaac's marriage to Rebekah, who would give birth to the twins Esau and Jacob (whose name God changed to Israel), Jacob's twelve sons would give birth to the twelve tribes of Israel, from which would come the awaited Messiah, Jesus Christ. Abraham and Sarah's story exemplifies how the creative, saving and sanctifying work of God the Holy Trinity can enter the world through married people who make faith in God the center of their relationship.

LET'S PROBE DEEPER: A SCRIPTURE ACTIVITY

⊙ Read the story of Abraham and Sarah in Genesis 18:1–15.
⊙ Discuss:
  – How would you describe Abraham and Sarah's treatment of their visitors?
  – What qualities do Abraham and Sarah exhibit in this story that make them fitting "parents" to God's Chosen People?

Solomon: *Read the story of King Solomon in 1 Kings 11:1–15. Reflect: What did God warn Solomon about? Why do you think Solomon ignored God's warning? What wisdom might you learn from this story of Solomon?*
King Solomon was famous for living by the great **wisdom** with which God favored him

to serve the Chosen People. (Check out 1 Kings 3:1–15.) However, later in life this wise king allowed his affection for his wives (**polygamy** was a common practice among peoples of the ancient world) to lead him to act contrary to the wisdom God had given him. Despite God's warnings, Solomon allowed his "love" for his pagan wives to lead him away from fidelity to the God of Abraham and to worship the idols of his neighbors.

Clearly, it is good to love one's spouse—but that love can become a source of temptation to turn away from God. The Torah, God's law of the covenant, was clear: the first and greatest commandment for God's people is to love God above all else, even above one's husband or wife. The love for one's neighbor, which includes one's spouse, is rooted in one's love for God. (Check out Deuteronomy 6:4–5 and Leviticus 19:18.)

The story of King Solomon reveals that the love for God can become a source of conflict in a marriage. We see this conflict play out in the case of Solomon. Yet, in reality, there is no

SOLOMON AND HIS WIVES | PIERRE REYMOND

conflict between loving God and loving others. Our love for God enables us to love others more truly. By contrast, when anything becomes more important than God, everything else falls apart.

Tobias and Sarah: *Read the story of Tobias and Sarah in the Book of Tobit, chapter 6:10–18 and 8:1–8. Reflect: What does Raphael tell Tobias to calm his fears about marrying Sarah? Why did Tobias's marriage to Sarah succeed when so many others had failed? What wisdom do you find here for your own life of faith?*

Last-minute jitters are a common enough experience for couples about to commit to each other for a lifetime. So, imagine if you knew that the last seven people who tried to marry your future spouse had died on their wedding night! As you just read, that was the situation Tobias faced. Yet he had the courage to go through with the marriage because he knew that God had blessed his union with Sarah.

God does not promise that marriage will be easy. Righteous as they were, Tobias's mother and father, Anna and Tobit, met with many misfortunes during their lifetime. What God does promise is that what God has joined together, nothing in this world has the power to separate. Tobias took Sarah because of his sincere and deep love for her. Tobias faced the future bravely because of his trust in God. Tobias and Sarah were blessed with a marriage that brought peace to their parents in their old age.

WHAT ABOUT YOU PERSONALLY?

- ⊙ What wisdom for your life did you learn from the biblical story of Tobias and Sarah?
- ⊙ How might you use that wisdom to build healthy and holy relationships?

TALK IT OVER

- ⊙ Reflect: As you can now appreciate, marriage plays a key role in God's plan for humanity.
- ⊙ Which of the above stories do you find most helpful for your understanding the purpose of marriage? Why?
- ⊙ How might you show your gratitude for the blessing that married people are to the Church and to your community?

THE MARRIAGE OF TOBIAS AND SARAH | 14TH-CENTURY MANUSCRIPT

What wisdom for your life did you learn from the biblical story of Tobias and Sarah?

Marriage in the New Testament

JESUS SAVES THE DAY!

Reread the story of Jesus turning water into wine at the wedding at Cana in John 2:1–11. For fun, let's imagine that Jesus hadn't intervened. The guests would likely have started leaving early or grumbled about the lack of wine. The bride and groom would have been embarrassed in front of all their friends and family. Some biblical scholars suggest that, under the laws of the Ancient Near East of that time, the groom would have been financially liable for failing to provide adequately for the guests. A joyous occasion would have turned into a disaster. Yet, thanks to Jesus, this wedding turned out to be an event so spectacular that it would be remembered for all time.

OPENING CONVERSATION

- Share experiences you have had at weddings.
- Have you ever been to a wedding where the hosts did not make a good job of entertaining the guests? What was it like? What saved the day?
- Did you have a sense that Christ was present on those special days? Why or why not?

MARRIED LOVE: AN EXPRESSION OF GOD'S LOVE

As we saw in our readings from the Old Testament, marriage is far more than a good human custom. It is a gift and an invitation from God for a man and a woman to be a sign of God's love for the People of God and for all humanity. The faithful, lifelong and life-giving love between the couple is an expression of God's own love in the midst of the world.

Jesus revealed this meaning of marriage, which, in their hardness of hearts, God's Chosen People often forgot. Jesus also raised marriage to the level of a sacrament. Jesus transformed marriage into an effective symbol of Christ's unity with humanity. By the power of the Holy Spirit, the Sacrament of Marriage confers the grace that the couple needs to live in faithful married love, ever growing in holiness of life together. We will now explore Jesus' teaching on marriage.

"Marriage is the Icon of God's Love for Us"

Marriage is a precious sign, for "when a man and a woman celebrate the sacrament of marriage, God is, as it were, 'mirrored' in them; he impresses in them his own features and the indelible character of his love. Marriage is the icon of God's love for us" (Catechesis [2 April 2014]: *L'Osservatore Romano*, 3 April 2014, p. 8].
—Pope Francis, *The Joy of Love (Amoris Lætitia)*, no. 121

THE WEDDING AT CANA

The wedding at Cana marked Jesus' first public sign or miracle. It is important to remember that Jesus' miracles were signs of the creative, saving and sanctifying presence of God at work among his people. First, Jesus' miracles "manifest that the kingdom is present in him and attest that he was the promised Messiah" (CCC, no. 547). Second, they "attest that the Father has sent him" (CCC, no. 548) and they "bear witness that he is the Son of God" (CCC, no. 548), Third, Jesus' miracles "invite belief in him" (CCC, no. 548) and in the Father who sent him.

What is the significance of the author of the Fourth Gospel having Jesus perform his first of seven signs at a wedding feast? A crucial clue to help us understand this passage comes from the Old Testament. In Old Testament writings, such as the Book of Isaiah, a wedding is an image of the messianic age when God's definitive act of salvation would come to earth. When Jesus turns the water into wine (a symbol of joy and celebration) at the wedding in Cana, he is effectively giving a sign that he is inaugurating the opening of the messianic age and that the work of God's salvation and sanctification is taking place through him. By inaugurating his ministry at this wedding, Jesus was forever raising marriage to a sacrament of God's loving presence and grace to humanity.

Just as he filled the jars to the brim with choice wine, Jesus calls us to a sacramental and more joyful notion of marriage. A marriage formed by a man and a woman looking out only for their own individual interests is an empty jar. However, a marriage freely entered by a man and a woman who are committed to serving the Triune God and each other overflows with grace. In prohibiting divorce, Jesus challenges us to think of marriage as an effective and enduring means of God's grace at work in the world.

GROUP WORK
⊙ Search the four accounts of the Gospel for other instances where Jesus used wedding language to describe the Reign, or Kingdom, of God.
⊙ Discuss: Why is a wedding an appropriate symbol for the coming of God's reign?

THE MARRIAGE OF MARY AND JOSEPH

Jesus was born into and raised within a family in which the love and care of Mary and Joseph for each other and for him contributed significantly to his growth. We read that he "grew and became strong, filled with wisdom; and the favor of God was upon him" (Luke 2:40; see also Luke 2:52). The *Catechism* states: Jesus "would even have to inquire for himself about what one in the human condition can learn only from experience" (CCC, no. 472).

Of course, it all began with Mary's "yes" when the Angel Gabriel announced to her that she was to give birth to the Son of God, the Savior for whom the People of God had been longing. Then, there was the mysterious announcement to Joseph that his betrothed, Mary, was pregnant. (Check out Matthew 1:18–25.) What a leap it was for him to trust in God, accept that Mary was pregnant by the Holy Spirit, and take her to be his spouse.

THE ESPOUSAL OF MARY AND JOSEPH | 19TH-CENTURY SLOVAKIAN

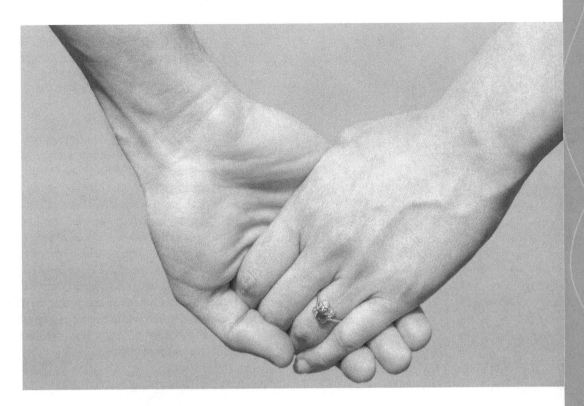

The outcome could have been otherwise were it not for Joseph's love for God and for Mary. Joseph had every right under Jewish law to end his engagement to Mary or even condemn her to death. Instead, Joseph took Mary into his care. For both Joseph and Mary, their marriage represented a radical "yes" to God. Thanks to that "yes," the awaited Messiah entered the world to launch the coming of God's reign.

OVER TO YOU
⊙ Imagine the ways in which Mary and Joseph's family life would have been formative for Jesus.
⊙ In what ways can we encounter the loving presence of God in the world today through loving Christian marriages? Give examples.
⊙ Pray with your family to the Holy Family—Jesus, Mary and Joseph—and ask for their grace as you work to love and serve one another better as a family.

LET NO ONE SEPARATE WHAT GOD HAS JOINED TOGETHER
In the Sermon on the Mount Jesus first reminded his listeners that, in God's plan for creation, marriage is meant to be a lifelong commitment.

Later in Matthew's Gospel Jesus expounded on his teaching, reminding them of the teaching in Genesis. Matthew tells us:

> Some Pharisees came to [Jesus], and to test him they asked, "Is it lawful for a man to divorce his wife for any cause?" He answered, "Have you not read that the one who made them at the beginning 'made them male and female,' and said, 'For this reason a man shall leave his father and mother and be joined to his wife, and the two shall become one flesh'? So they are no longer two, but one flesh. Therefore what God has joined together, let no one separate."
> —Matthew 19:3–6

When the Pharisees objected, saying that the Law of Moses allowed divorce, Jesus made it clear that "at the beginning it was not so" (Matthew 19:8). The Law of Moses *allowed* divorce only because God's people had become "hard-hearted" (Matthew 8). Divorcing one's spouse is not what God desires.

To be sure, Jesus' teaching affirmed an essential aspect of the marriage covenant. The Pharisees taught that divorce was possible under

honor [each other} all the days of [their] life" until they part at the death of one of the spouses.

"NOT EVERYONE CAN ACCEPT THIS TEACHING"

In response to Jesus' teaching on the indissolubility of marriage, the disciples asked, "If such is the case of a man with his wife, it is better not to marry." Jesus replied, saying, in part: "Not everyone can accept this teaching, but only those to whom it is given. For there are eunuchs who have been so from birth, and there are eunuchs who have been made eunuchs by others, and there are eunuchs who have made themselves eunuchs for the sake of the kingdom of heaven. Let anyone accept this who can" (Matthew 19:10–12). The Church has come to understand this teaching to mean that some people are called to marriage, but they choose to live their Baptism by a life of celibacy.

Christ is the center of all Christian life. The bond with him takes precedence over all other bonds, familial or social. From the very beginning of the Church there have been men and women who have renounced the great good of marriage to follow the Lamb wherever he goes, to be intent on the things of the Lord, to seek to please him, and to go out to meet the Bridegroom who is coming. Christ himself has invited certain persons to follow him in this way of life, of which he remains the model.

—CCC, no. 1618

Many Catholics have chosen to live a life of celibacy as members of the ordained or consecrated states of life. Others have chosen to do the same as lay single persons.

MEETING THE CHALLENGES OF MARRIED LIFE

Jesus' teaching on marriage makes it clear that there are many challenges facing those who commit to the lifelong, indissoluble married state of life. We will explore several of those challenges in the next chapter of this text. Whether he calls one to the vocation of the married, ordained or consecrated state of life, Jesus always offers those who accept that vocation the graces to

certain conditions—as do many people today. But Jesus challenged that interpretation of God's law. Jesus went on to teach in Matthew 19:11 that, given the high standards God asks of marriage, marriage is not for everyone.

The *Catechism* teaches: "The matrimonial union of man and woman is indissoluble: God himself has determined it" (CCC, no. 1614). Many today question whether *every* married couple can live by such a high standard.

In chapter 5 of this text we will explore the many challenges that married couples may face in contemporary society. It is important to remember that God offers every married couple the graces to respond to those challenges. God strengthens married couples to face successfully the challenges they might encounter.

Jesus, as we have already explored, raised marriage to a sacrament. In the celebration of the Sacrament of Marriage a baptized man and a baptized woman encounter Christ, who is continuously present with them, offering his grace throughout the good times and bad times. Jesus offers these graces to enable both spouses to fulfill their marriage promise "to love and meet the challenges they will face. The Church reminds us:

This unequivocal insistence on the indissolubility of the marriage bond may have left some perplexed and could seem to be a demand impossible to realize. However, Jesus has not placed on spouses a burden impossible to bear, or too heavy—heavier than the Law of Moses [see Mark 8:34 and Matthew 11:29–30]. By coming to restore the original order of creation disturbed by sin, he himself gives the strength and grace to live marriage in the new dimension of the Reign of God. It is by following Christ, renouncing themselves, and taking up their crosses that spouses will be able to "receive" the original meaning of marriage and live it with the help of Christ (see Matthew 19:11). This grace of Christian marriage is a fruit of Christ's cross, the source of all Christian life.

—CCC, no. 1615

TALK IT OVER
- What wisdom do you see in Jesus' teaching on marriage and divorce?
- Why is this teaching so challenging? What might help married couples to live it?

CHRISTIAN MARRIAGE REFLECTS CHRIST'S LOVE FOR HIS CHURCH
St. Paul reminds Christians that Christian spouses are to love each other as Christ loves his Church. Paul wrote to the early Church:

Husbands, love your wives, just as Christ loved the church and gave himself up for her, . . . He who loves his wife loves himself. For no one ever hates his own body, but he nourishes it and tenderly cares for it, just as Christ does for the church, because we are members of his body. "For this reason a man will leave his father and mother and be joined to his wife, and the two will become one flesh." This is a great mystery, and I am applying it to Christ and the church. Each of you, however, should love his wife as himself, and a wife should respect her husband.

—Ephesians 5:25, 28b–33

Having set out the example of the selfless love of Jesus, St. Paul urged his followers to listen to God the Father's call to spouses to love each other as Jesus loves his community of disciples. Just as Christ has united himself to the Church, so do couples become one in the Sacrament of Marriage. For Christ, to love the Church is to love his own Body. The same applies to spouses in loving each other.

WHAT ABOUT YOU PERSONALLY?
- How have you come to understand marriage in a new light, thanks to Jesus' teaching?
- How can you imitate Jesus' love for the Church in your own parish or faith community?
- How will this prepare you for married life should that be your vocation?

St. Paul reminds Christians that Christian spouses are to love each other as Christ loves his Church

ST. PAUL | ENGRAVING BY LANDRY

The sacredness of the human body

THE FRUITS OF THE HOLY SPIRIT

Toward the conclusion of the Sermon on the Mount Jesus explained, "Thus you will know them by their fruits" (Matthew 7:20). The Tradition of the Catholic Church, building on the list in Galatians 5:35, identifies twelve fruits of the Holy Spirit. They are "love, joy, peace, patience, kindness, goodness, generosity, gentleness, faithfulness, modesty, self-control, and chastity" (CCC, no. 1832). The fruits of the Holy Spirit give witness that the baptized are cooperating with the grace of the Holy Spirit as they strive for holiness of life. They are the first fruits of eternal glory.

OPENING REFLECTION

- Recall what you have learned thus far about the responsibilities of Christian marriage.
- How do the teachings of the Gospel challenge Christian married couples to be a reflection of Christ's love for the Church? Give concrete examples.

- Take a moment and read and reflect on Matthew 7:15–20.
- How do the fruits of the Holy Spirit point to a marriage rooted in the love of Christ and the Gospel?

THE HUMAN BODY: A SACRED GIFT FROM THE CREATOR

"Just go with your instincts" or "Do what feels right." We have all heard advice like that before, and been tempted to follow it. If anything should be clear from our discussions in this chapter, it is that appropriate human relationships, including friendships and romantic relationships, are not firmly built on instinct and feelings. Our relationships should not be based on shallow feelings or emotions or governed by erotic instincts.

In this section of the chapter we examine St. John Paul II's teaching on human relationships and the sacredness of the human body. Pope John Paul II's teachings have become the foundation of what has come to be called his "Theology of the Body." This teaching, as we shall see, helps us to respect our body and our human passions in the development of our human relationships, including marriage. The practice of the human moral virtues is essential in our forming and growing in our relationships with others.

Every person, baptized and non-baptized, has the responsibility to grow in and practice the moral virtues. Modesty and temperance are two of the four cardinal virtues. Modesty is also one of the fruits of the Holy Spirit. "A modest person dresses, speaks, and acts in a manner that supports and encourages purity and chastity and not in a manner that would tempt or encourage sinful sexual behavior" (USCCA, Glossary, 520). Temperance is fundamental to living a life of modesty. The practice of temperance, or self-control, is the moderation of "the desire for the attainment of and pleasure in earthly goods" (USCCA, Glossary, 530).

Catholic Tradition clearly teaches that the human body is a sacred, good and beautiful gift from the Creator. The human person is an integrated unity of body and soul. We have received the gift of an intellect, and we have the free will to use that gift appropriately. The Holy Spirit offers us the graces to know and to choose what is good and to resist what tempts us to abuse our gifts. We have the ability to respond to our passions appropriately.

READ, REFLECT AND SHARE

- Our bishops remind us: "All members of the Church should respond to the immodest aspects of society and culture with a deep and conscious spirituality. The Gospel can renew and purify what is decadent in our culture and gradually can replace the attraction to sin. We must assert Christ's Gospel by word and witness to transform the moral tone of our culture. This approach fosters virtue in the human heart and its development through the grace of the Holy Spirit" (USCCA, 443).
- What can Christians do to promote a sense of the sacredness of human body?
- Share reflections as a class.

WHAT ABOUT YOU PERSONALLY?

- What can you do to promote a sense of the human body as sacred among your friends?

OUR BODIES' GLORIOUS DESTINY

Recognizing the needs and struggles of humanity, the Son of God, in an incomparable act of self-emptying love, became incarnate in order to reveal how we are to live a fully human life. We read in John's account of the Gospel, "And the Word became flesh and lived among us" (John 1:14). The Son of God, the Second Person of the Holy Trinity, assumed a human nature and took on flesh and "became man in order to accomplish

THE RESURRECTION | ST. JACOB'S CHURCH, BRUGES, BELGIUM

our salvation in that same human nature" (CCC, Glossary, "Incarnation.")

God chose to be "revealed in flesh" (1 Timothy 3:16). Throughout his life on earth Jesus showed us how to make proper use of the sacred gift of our bodies. There can be no greater affirmation and revelation of the sacredness and goodness of the human body than the Incarnation of the Son of God.

The Resurrection of the glorified body of Christ revealed to us the destiny that awaits us all—the resurrection of the body. Christians profess in the Apostles' Creed, "I believe in . . . the resurrection of the body." Recognizing Jesus as the "first fruits of those who have died" (1 Corinthians 15:20), we believe that we too will rise with Christ, *body and soul*. Our bodies will rise in glory and be bodily present to God for all eternity.

TEMPLES OF THE HOLY SPIRIT

Despite God's affirmation of the goodness of the body, people, including some Christians, continue to demean their bodies. St. Paul did not mince words when he asked the church at Corinth, "Do you not know that you are God's temple and that God's Spirit dwells in you?" (1 Corinthians 3:16). In chapter 5 the Apostle addresses sexual immorality at Corinth. In chapter 6 Paul addresses the sacredness of the human body, and he teaches:

Do you not know that your bodies are members of Christ? Should I therefore take the members of Christ and make them members of a prostitute? Never! . . . Or do not know that your body is a temple of the Holy Spirit within you which you have from God, and that you are not your own? For you were bought with a price; therefore glorify God in your body.

—1 Corinthians 6:15, 19–20

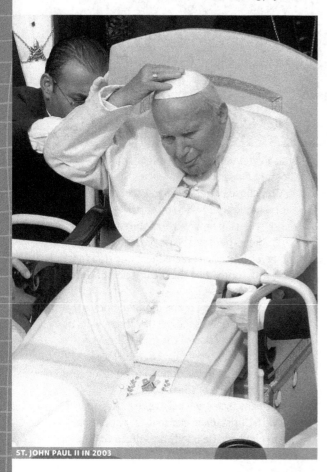

ST. JOHN PAUL II IN 2003

We can reduce the use of our body and our sexuality to its lowest value—as if it were only intended for pleasure. Or we can use our body and our human passions to bring us closer to God, who is love.

St. Paul, in chapter 7, moves on to teach about married life.

When we think about honoring our bodies we must remember that the Son of God took on a human body. Through Baptism we are united to Christ. Through receiving the Body of Christ, the Eucharist in Holy Communion, we become more deeply one with Christ and with the members of his Church, the Body of Christ. As St. Augustine, in commenting on 1 Corinthians 12:27 in his *Sermon 272*, taught, when we receive Holy Communion we become what we receive. When we hear the words "The Body of Christ" and "The Blood of Christ" and say "Amen," we affirm who we are; we are to be true to our word and live as the Body of Christ.

TALK IT OVER

⊙ How does the Incarnation reveal the dignity of the human body?

⊙ How did Jesus teach us how to make respectful and loving use of our bodies?

THEOLOGY OF THE BODY

St. John Paul II, like St. Paul, taught that our sexuality is of God's design and therefore "very good." In his teachings that have become known as Theology of the Body, the Pope affirmed the goodness and sacredness of the human body and its role in our expressing and sharing our truest and most intimate self. Our sexuality exceeds our physical attributes and includes our sexual emotions, feelings and desires. God is the Creator of both spiritual and bodily life. All our desires for what is good, including our sexual desires, are rooted in and connected inseparably with our desire for life with God.

The human body is integral to God's plan for the growth in intimacy and holiness of the human person and for the continuation of the human race. "The procreation and education of children . . . reflects the Father's work of creation" (CCC, no. 2205). The appropriate expression of intimate human love in the divine plan of creation takes place only in marriage. We are to honor and respect the whole human person, body and soul. We are not to reduce the human person to an object, or abuse one's self or another person for our selfish, personal gratification.

Objectification of the human (especially female) body is a major problem in our culture. We support these demeaning abuses of the body when we watch movies, listen to music and buy products made by people who objectify the bodies of others for profit.

The tragedy is that such immoral human conduct is as much a feature of our society today as it was in the time of St. Paul. People still use the bodies of others for personal gain or pleasure, completely neglecting the dignity and sacredness of the people to whom those bodies belong. We often see such hedonistic attitudes and behavior promoted and idealized in film, print, music,

advertising and other social media. It can be very easy to be lured into these ways of treating our own and other people's bodies. What we must always remember is that the human body is a precious gift from God, even if people often misuse it.

TALK IT OVER

⊙ How can you as young people fight against mistreatment and disrespect of the body in our society?

WHAT ABOUT YOU PERSONALLY?

⊙ Has your study of the sacredness of the human body changed your attitude about your own body and other people's bodies? How so?

⊙ What criteria do you now have for the way you are to treat the human person?

FAITH WORD

Theology of the Body

The teachings of St. John Paul II about the goodness and sacredness of the human body and its role in our expressing and sharing our truest and most intimate self. God is the giver of spiritual and bodily life. God creates us body and soul. Our spiritual and immortal soul is the source of our unity as a person. All our desires for what is good, including our sexual desires, are rooted in and connected inseparably with our desire for life with and in God.

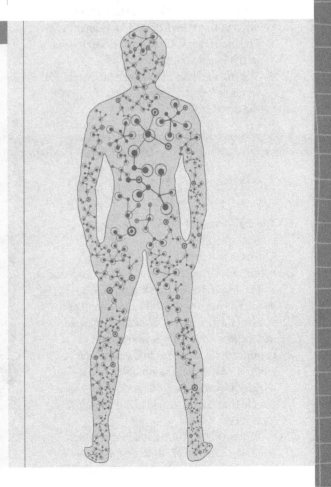

JUDGE AND ACT

REVIEW AND SHARE WHAT YOU HAVE LEARNED

Look back over this chapter and reflect on what you have learned about God's creation of man and woman and their role in God's plan for humanity. Share the teachings of the Catholic Church on these statements:

⊙ The attraction between a man and a woman is most intimately fulfilled in the lifelong marriage covenant.

⊙ The human body is sacred, a temple of the living God, and to be honored and respected.

⊙ God is the author of marriage; it is not a purely human institution.

⊙ The covenant of love uniting spouses in marriage gives witness to the committed, unconditional love of God for humanity.

⊙ The marriage of Abraham and Sarah gave birth to the People of God.

⊙ The married love of baptized husbands and wives reflects the love of Christ for his Church, the bride of Christ.

OVER TO YOU

⊙ What wisdom did you discover for living your life as a disciple of Jesus Christ from your study of this chapter?

⊙ What did you learn about the relationship of men and women in God's plan for creation?

⊙ What did you discover about the sacredness of your body?

MARRIED FOREVER

We can be sure that there have been literally hundreds of millions of married people down through the ages who have helped each other to grow in holiness by living together as disciples of Jesus. Though they will never be officially canonized as saints, they are enjoying eternal love in God's loving presence in heaven. There are a few married couples, however, who have been officially canonized by the Church and whose lives serve as an inspiration and guide for the faithful. St. Isidore and St. Maria Torribia are just one of those couples.

LEARN BY EXAMPLE

Saints Isidore (d. 1130) and Maria Torribia (d. 1175)

The Tradition of the Church, as does the biblical tradition, has many stories of Christian married couples who serve as models for living the married life. St. Isidore and St. Maria Torribia are but one of those examples. Both Maria and Isidore were poor peasants who met, fell in love and married. Isidore was a day laborer who became famous for his kindness to the poor and to animals. Maria kept their humble home, whose door was always open to the hungry people that Isidore would invite to share their food.

Legend has it that their infant son Illan fell down a deep well. With no means of rescuing him, Isidore and Maria turned to

ST. ISIDORE | SAINT ALOYSIUS CHURCH, OHIO

God in prayer. Miraculously, according to the legend, the water suddenly rose up from the bottom of the well so that the parents were able to reach in and recover their child. Sadly, Illan would soon die while still an infant. Deeply saddened, the couple lost neither their faith in God nor their nurturing instincts.

There are many stories about the couple's compassion and generosity toward the poor. Legend tells us that Maria always kept a pot of stew on the fireplace, knowing that her husband was likely to bring home any hungry people he encountered.

These legendary stories about the married life of St. Isidore and St. Maria demonstrate the difference that a married couple can make to the lives of others, especially when they maintain their trust in God and reach out to those in need. The truths about married life revealed through the stories about St. Isidore and St. Maria and other such couples leave a legacy of Christian inspiration and spiritual encouragement to the generations of married couples who come after them.

The Church officially canonized Isidore and Maria, who are considered the patron saints of farmers. Their shared feast day is May 15.

TALK IT OVER

⊙ How did the married life of St. Isidore and St. Maria live up to the ideal of Christian married life as taught in Scripture and the Tradition of the Church?

⊙ Where do you see examples of people living their married life in similar ways today? What difference are those marriages making and who are the beneficiaries?

SHARE FAITH WITH FAMILY AND FRIENDS

⊙ What kinds of attitudes are expressed toward the human body in the media you watch, listen to and read? What influence do these attitudes have on people's outlook and behavior?

⊙ How can you hold one another accountable for respecting your bodies and those of others?

REFLECT AND DECIDE

⊙ Do you believe you would be up to the challenge of living the married vocation as Jesus taught it? Why or why not?

⊙ What habits can you form now that will prepare you for such a commitment?

⊙ What is a wise decision you should make in response to this chapter?

⊙ Write your thoughts in your journal. Revisit your responses often.

WELLCOME LIBRARY

ST. ISIDORE AND ST. MARIA TORRIBIA | D.H.V. UGARTE

LEARN BY HEART

"[T]hey are no longer two, but one flesh. Therefore what God has joined together, let no one separate."

MATTHEW 19:6

All sit in a circle on the floor or around a table on which the teacher has laid out a large sheet of paper with outlines of empty body silhouettes arranged in the form of a church, and some pens or pencils.

Pray the Sign of the Cross together.

Opening Prayer

LEADER
Loving God, you created us for one another and you strengthen us to form holy relationships. Send your Holy Spirit upon us, who gather in the name of your Son today, so that we may be nourished to grow in our love for one another and be responsible with the precious gift of our sexuality.
ALL
Amen.

Proclamation of the Word of God

READER
A reading from the Letter of St. Paul to the Ephesians.
Proclaim Ephesians 5:28–33.
The word of the Lord.
ALL
Thanks be to God.

LEADER
Pause to reflect on how this reading speaks to you. When ready, feel welcome to share with the group. (*Pause*)

Students share reflections.

LEADER
God, who is love,
you have given us a model of perfect love in your Son, Jesus.
Help us love one another as purely and give ourselves to one another as fully as Jesus gave his life for his people, the Church. We ask this through Christ our Lord.
ALL
Amen.

LEADER
Jesus unites himself with us so intimately that each person bears God within. This is why we are all temples of the Holy Spirit. Take a moment to reflect now on how you can use your body to offer spiritual worship to God—as from a temple. When you are ready, come to the middle of the circle and write inside one of the body silhouettes a word or phrase that summarizes your resolution.

Allow some quiet time for reflection and writing on the silhouettes.

Prayers of Petition

READER
Having prayed with Scripture and offered our personal responses, let us now offer our petitions to God.

For all married couples, especially our parents (whether married, widowed, or divorced), that they may be a constant sign of God's love and salvation to the world. We pray to the Lord.
RESPONSE
Lord, hear our prayer.

READER
For all those discerning or preparing for the Sacrament of Marriage, that they may strive to love each other selflessly and to attend to the needs of each other as well as to all others whom they recognize to be in need. We pray to the Lord.
RESPONSE
Lord, hear our prayer.

READER

For the students gathered here, that they may use the gifts God has given them in the service of God and neighbor. We pray to the Lord.

RESPONSE

Lord, hear our prayer.

READER

Any students who wish to do so may now add their own petitions.

Students who wish to do so add petitions.

RESPONSE

Lord, hear our prayer.

Concluding Prayer

LEADER

God, you have loved us with an undying love. Let us never tire of seeking how better to love you and one another. We pray this in the name of Jesus, who with you and the Holy Spirit forms the perfect communion of love.

ALL

Amen.

Pray the Sign of the Cross together.

God, you have loved us with an undying love. Let us never tire of seeking how better to love you and one another.

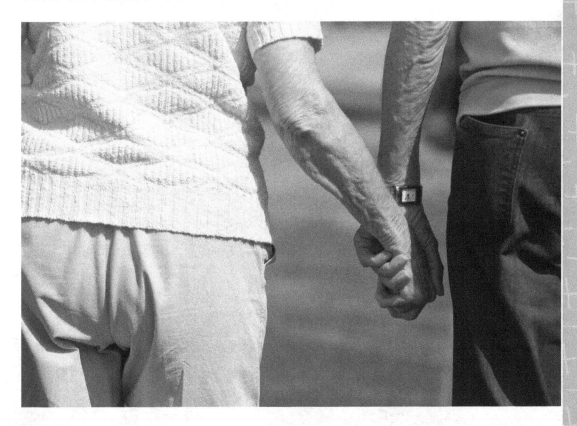

CHAPTER 5

Blessings and Challenges of Christian Married Life

CHRISTIAN MARRIAGE FOSTERS GROWTH IN HEALTHY INTERPERSONAL RELATIONSHIPS AND HOLINESS OF LIFE

CHRISTIAN MARRIED COUPLES CAN BE BEACONS OF FAITH, HOPE AND LOVE

GOD BLESSES THE WORLD THROUGH MARRIAGE

PARENTS ARE INSTRUMENTS OF BODILY AND SPIRITUAL LIFE FOR THEIR CHILDREN

A COMMITTED CHRISTIAN MARRIAGE IS A SOURCE OF TRUE FREEDOM AND JOY

CHRISTIAN MARRIED LIFE BEGINS AND ENDS WITH *AGAPE*

CHRISTIAN MARRIAGE REFLECTS THE UNENDING love of God for his people and Christ's love for his Church. This wonderful sacrament of life and love is an effective sign of God's saving love at work in the world, inviting all people to strive toward bringing about and living in the community of love, the Kingdom of God, that Jesus inaugurated. Through marriage and family life God bestows many blessings on individuals, the Church and society. The vocation to married life also faces many unique challenges in contemporary society.

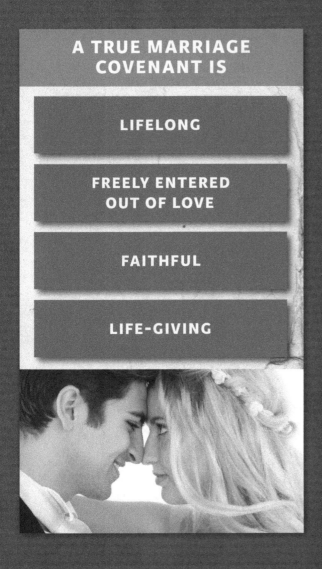

A TRUE MARRIAGE COVENANT IS

LIFELONG

FREELY ENTERED OUT OF LOVE

FAITHFUL

LIFE-GIVING

Faith Focus: These teachings of the Catholic Church are the primary focus of the doctrinal content presented in this chapter:

- Jesus Christ continues his saving and sanctifying work in the world through the marriage and family life of Christians.
- God gives married couples the graces they need to live up to their commitments.
- Christian marriage fosters growth in healthy and respectful interpersonal relationships and holiness of life.
- Christian marriage promotes the dignity of both men and women.
- Same-sex marriages devalue the true meaning of marriage.
- Cohabitation prior to marriage weakens the bond of a couple who intend to marry.
- The witness of faithful couples strengthens the church community and the fabric of society.

Discipleship Formation: As a result of studying this chapter and discovering the meaning of the faith of the Catholic Church for your life, you should be better able to:

- be aware of and respond to the presence and grace of Christ in your home;
- discern the good from the bad messages of the media that influence your attitude toward healthy relationships, marriage and family life;
- grow in those virtues that help you live out your responsibilities within your family;
- respond to your family's efforts to guide you in living as a disciple of Jesus Christ;
- work with your family to build a healthy and cooperative community of love.

Scripture References: These Scripture references are quoted or referred to in this chapter:
OLD TESTAMENT: **Genesis** 1:28, 2:18–24, 19:1–29
NEW TESTAMENT: **Luke** 1:74–75, 2:52; **Romans** 12:4–27; **Ephesians** 5:21—6:4; **1 Corinthians** 6:10, 13:1–8a; **Colossians** 3:18–21; **1 Thessalonians** 4:1–8; **1 Timothy** 1:10; **1 Peter** 3:1–7; **1 John** 4:11–12, 16–18; **Revelation** 19:9

Faith Glossary: Familiarize yourself with or recall the meaning of these key terms. Definitions are found in the Glossary: **cohabitation, concupiscence, covenant, free unions, freedom, joy, theological virtues**

Faith Word: free unions
Learn by Heart: 1 John 4:11
Learn by Example: St. Gianna Beretta Molla, wife, mother and physician

Why is marriage a lifelong giving of oneself?

PUTTING OTHERS FIRST

A table piled high with presents is a typical sight at many weddings. But if you were looking for the gift table on Karen and Gary's wedding day, you would have been out of luck—there was no table. Karen and Gary had asked their guests to make a donation to one of a dozen local charities serving poor and other people in need.

OPENING REFLECTION

⊙ What insight would the action of Karen and Gary have given their guests into how the newly married couple would live out their marriage?

⊙ What does Karen and Gary's action reveal about what they view as the important things in life?

OVER TO YOU

⊙ How would you have reacted if you were one of Karen and Gary's guests? What do you think of their decision?

A LIFELONG COVENANT OF LOVE

Marriage serves to make God's love visible in the world. All who encounter Christian loving married couples encounter Jesus Christ, Christ's love for his Church and God's love for humanity. To reflect the very love of God in one's marriage is a tall order to say the least. It requires serious effort, often heroic, that reaches far beyond the wedding day.

In raising marriage to a sacrament, Jesus made sacramental marriage an instrument of God's saving and sanctifying grace at work in the world. Entering a sacramental marriage, as we explored in chapter 1, is a lifelong and exclusive commitment between a baptized man and a baptized woman. It is a lifelong covenant of fidelity and love. St. John Paul II, in his teaching on married love, wrote:

> Conjugal love involves a totality, in which all the elements of the person enter—appeal of the body and instinct, power of feeling and affectivity, aspiration of the spirit and of will. It aims at a deeply personal unity, the unity that, beyond union in one flesh, leads to forming one heart and soul.
>
> —*The Christian Family in the Modern World (Familiaris Consortio)*, no. 13

Striving to grow in such a relationship of total self-giving is a lifelong vocation. Married couples face many obstacles as they strive for such a relationship. Sometimes the married life of Christians does not reflect God's love for humanity and Christ's love for his Church as fully as it might. St. Paul, as we learned in chapter 4, addressed this reality in the earliest days of the Church. In this chapter we will explore both the blessings of a true marriage and some of the problems encountered in marriage and family life. Knowledge and understanding of these blessings and challenges better enables us to recognize them, respond to God's grace, and face them effectively.

TALK IT OVER

⊙ How well does contemporary society support married couples in living a lifelong covenant of love?

THE HEART OF THE MARRIAGE COVENANT

The promises a man and a woman make to each other before God and the Church in the Sacrament of Marriage lie at the heart of a true and valid marriage covenant. These promises reflect God's covenant with his people and the saving and sanctifying love of God at work in the world. A true marriage covenant is:

⊙ **Lifelong:** It is indissoluble and lasts until the death of one of the spouses. God has proven time and again that his covenant with humankind is everlasting.

⊙ **Freely entered out of love:** Freedom is an essential dimension of all true relationships. True love must be an act of freedom; it cannot be compelled. This is true even of our relationship with God. For a marriage to be valid, both parties must enter into the marriage covenant freely and without coercion of any kind.

⊙ **Faithful:** It is an exclusive partnership. Marriage is a covenant that by its very nature brings about a bodily, intellectual and spiritual communion of life and love between a man and a woman. It is the total giving of the married woman and man to each other so that they become as one. (Check out Genesis 2:24.)

⊙ **Life-giving:** Marriage and the conjugal act are intended in the divine plan to be life-giving in two ways: life-giving for the good of the spouses and life-giving in the procreation of a new human person. A true and valid marriage is always open to children.

We will explore the meaning of the marriage vows in more detail in chapter 6 when we study the celebration of the Sacrament of Marriage.

JOURNAL EXERCISE

⊙ How do you see God's saving love being manifested through marriage? Give examples. Base your reasons on the essential elements for a true and valid marriage.

⊙ What are some of the blessings of married life that flow from the marriage vows? What are some of the challenges to being faithful to these promises?

⊙ Write your responses in your journal. Refer and add to your lists throughout your study of marriage.

True love must be an act of freedom; it cannot be compelled

Signs of Christ's saving love in marriage

TOTAL SELF-GIVING LOVE

A beautiful aspect of Catholic teaching is that for a marriage to be a true sacrament and an unbreakable union it must be consummated. In other words, the married man and woman do not seal their marriage at the altar but in their total giving of themselves in the sexual intimacy of conjugal love-making after their wedding ceremony. This teaching of the Catholic Church reflects her very positive understanding of the gift of human sexuality as a blessing for spouses and the human family.

OPENING REFLECTION

⊙ How does popular culture portray sexual intimacy? Does it support what you have learned to be the values of Scripture and the Catholic Church?

⊙ Does your expression of your sexuality reflect and promote your own self-respect and dignity? Your respect for the dignity of others?

⊙ What might you do to grow in the respectful expression of your sexuality?

GOD BLESSES THE WORLD THROUGH MARRIAGE

God shared his creative work with the first man and woman, saying, "Be fruitful and multiply" (Genesis 1:28). While this command is traditionally understood to apply to procreation, the partnership uniting a man and a woman in marriage is, in God's design, intended to be *fruitful* both in terms of procreation and the enrichment of the union and life of the spouses. In this and the next section of the chapter we explore some of the fruits of this committed, liberating and life-producing union of love. Among these fruits are:

⊙ participation in God's ongoing work of the creation of humanity;

⊙ greater awareness and growth in interpersonal relationships and holiness of life;

⊙ building and deepening of responsible relationships within the family, society and the Church;

⊙ promotion of respect for the dignity of both men and women.

JOURNAL EXERCISE

⊙ Sketch the outline of a multi-branched tree on a sheet of paper.

⊙ Write words and phrases hanging down from the branches that describe different ways a marriage can be fruitful.

SOURCE OF TRUE FREEDOM AND JOY

A true and committed marriage is a source of true **freedom** and **joy** for the married couple, their children and all the people whose lives they touch. (Take a moment and recall the marriage of Karen and Gary.) Spouses discover that their faithful and self-sacrificing love for God, for each other and for others is liberating, and that it bears out the wisdom "it is in giving that we receive."

A word about freedom. Freedom is never a license to do as we please. Achieving true freedom is always dependent on faithfully keeping one's freely given word and fulfilling one's responsibilities. Few of life's experiences can compare with the love expressed when two people commit to a lifetime of caring for each other in marriage. Total lifelong self-giving makes each partner secure in their love for each other and free from anxiety about whether the love is real.

The Church prays the *Benedictus* canticle in Morning Prayer of the Liturgy of the Hours, the official daily prayer of the Church. We praise God, who promised "to set us free from the hands of our enemies, / free to worship him without fear, / holy and righteous in his sight / all the days of our life" (see Luke 1:74–75, *New American Bible*). Through these words the Church professes her faith in the fidelity of God to his covenant with the Israelites (as Zachary, the husband of Elizabeth, did at the birth of their son, John the Baptist). By devoting themselves to God and reflecting the love of God in their lives as Zachary and Elizabeth did, the couple can experience married life as a source of true freedom and joy.

THINK, PAIR AND SHARE
- Work on your own at first and divide a piece of paper into two columns.
- In the left column list responsibilities, rituals or habits that might be part of a healthy marriage.
- In the right column describe the freedoms that might arise from each.
- Compare and discuss lists with a partner.

A BOOST TO INTERPERSONAL RELATIONSHIPS

Keeping our relationship with God at the center of our married, family and personal life, as Zachary and Elizabeth did, does not push others out of our life. On the contrary, it enlarges our ability to love family, friends, neighbors and the stranger as Jesus did. Loving God frees and enables us to love other people more than we previously thought possible. When we respond to God's grace to live the two Great Commandments, all other aspects of our life fall into place.

Encountering and receiving Christ in the Sacrament of Marriage and in the other sacraments, especially the Eucharist, deepens the married couple's union with God as well as with

THE BIRTH OF ST. JOHN THE BAPTIST | CHURCH OF ST. JOHN THE BAPTIST, ALLGÄU, GERMANY

each other. Empowered by the graces of the Holy Spirit, the couple's married love becomes both a source and an expression of God's love at work in their lives. Strengthened by the **theological virtues**, couples who celebrate and live the Sacrament of Marriage discover an endless reserve of faith, hope and love to share not only with each other but also with their children, relatives and others.

The couple's response to the graces of this sacrament can transform their relationship with each other and with all whose lives they touch. By acting faithfully and lovingly toward each other, toward family members and neighbors—even toward those who frustrate them—they can be beacons of faith, hope and love to themselves and others. The graces of this sacrament enable them to reflect the Trinitarian life and love revealed in Jesus Christ.

WHAT ABOUT YOU PERSONALLY?

⊙ Take a moment and read 1 Corinthians 13:1–8a.
⊙ Think about one personal relationship in your life that has improved the quality of other relationships in your life.
⊙ How might that relationship prepare you for marriage if that be your vocation?

RESPECT FOR THE DIGNITY OF ALL PEOPLE

God created humanity *male* and *female*. Each gender, in its own unique way and together, reflects the image and likeness of God. Working together as equal partners in the divine plan of creation and salvation, married couples witness to the mystery of God and to their dignity as human beings, whom God created in the divine image and likeness. The faithful love of Christian married couples, "in good times and bad times," bears witness to the respect married couples have for each other's sacred dignity. In reflecting on Genesis and other passages in Scripture the Catholic Church teaches that all people, male and female, have the equal and same dignity of images of God. We see this teaching reflected in this passage from the *Catechism of the Catholic Church*:

God transcends the human distinction between the sexes. He is neither man nor woman: he is God. He also transcends human fatherhood and motherhood, although he is their origin and standard.

—CCC, no. 239

There are constant opportunities in the ordinary events of daily life for married couples to show respect for this sacred dignity. On their wedding day the bridegroom and bride both make this promise: "I promise to be true to you in good times and in bad, in sickness and in health. I will love you and honor you all the days of my life" (*The Rites I*, "Rite of Marriage During Mass," no. 25). As a couple live out this promise and express their love for each other each and every day, they build respect for themselves, for their family and for all whom they interact with day in and day out.

Couples may experience challenges around everyday issues, such as misunderstandings or economic and career pressures, that can work against their living in mutual respect and love for each other. The graces of the Sacrament of Marriage empower a baptized man and woman to strive to meet those challenges. These graces help to offset what prevents us from achieving the holiness of life to which God calls all the baptized. (Check out 1 Corinthians 13:1–8a; 1 Thessalonians 4:1–8.)

TALK IT OVER
⊙ What traits of character or acts of service performed by wives and husbands, mothers and fathers, brothers and sisters show respect for others' dignity as children of God and partners in the work of God?
⊙ What concrete things can family members do to help one another to grow in holiness?

THE WEDDING AT CANA | JAN SWART VAN GRONINGEN

A WELLSPRING OF BLESSINGS FOR CHURCH AND SOCIETY

The effects of married love do not remain within the home but flow out into the Church and society. As much as our culture romanticizes marriage (mostly the wedding day and all its trappings), it does not even begin to capture the wealth of the blessings that Christian marriage can bring to the family, the Church and society. Indeed, the blessings of the married life of Christians are endless.

Jesus is the Savior of the world. At its heart salvation means God healing the brokenness in our relationship with him, with others and with creation by making us sharers, once again, in the very life and love of God. When two people live out the commitments they make to each other in the Sacrament of Marriage, their marriage relationship is an instrument of God's saving and sanctifying love at work not only in their lives but also in the lives of those with whom they interact outside their home.

In the next section of this chapter we will continue our exploration of the signs of Christ's saving work made present among us through sacramental married life.

TALK IT OVER
⊙ How has your discussion of the blessings of marriage increased your appreciation for the vocation of Christians to the married life?
⊙ Which of the blessings that you have explored is most overlooked in our culture? Why?
⊙ How might you change the way you talk about marriage to better reflect the blessings that God brings about through it?

JOURNAL EXERCISE
⊙ At home make a list of the good things about marriage that you see celebrated in music, TV, movies and magazines.
⊙ Add some other good things about marriage that you now recognize as a result of your study of this subject and explain your reasons for adding these.
⊙ Share and discuss this with your family.

Signs of Christ's saving love in marriage (continued)

Thanks, Mom and Dad!

I can't repay the lessons
That you taught when I was small.
Or give you gift for gift
The daily treasures I recall. . . .
I can't return encouragement
And loving words of praise
In quite the way you did for me
Through all my childhood days.
But there is one gift that I can give,
It's all the love you've earned.
For love is what you always taught . . .
And love is what I learned.

—Anonymous

OPENING REFLECTION

⊙ What do you think of this writer's expression of gratitude for parents?
⊙ For what are you most grateful to your parents?
⊙ How can you show them gratitude *today*?

THE GIFT OF PARENTHOOD

Parents are instruments of bodily and spiritual life for their children. They have the vocation and receive the graces to be the first teachers of their children in the faith and to raise them in the ways of faith, hope and love. The *Catechism* reaffirms this truth:

The fruitfulness of conjugal love extends to the fruits of the moral, spiritual, and supernatural life that parents hand on to their children by education. Parents are the principal and first educators of their children.

—CCC, no. 1653

After giving their child the gift of physical, or bodily, life, Christian parents present their child to the Church for Baptism. They ask for the gift of the faith for their child. They express their desire that their child receive the gift of sanctifying grace and share in the spiritual life of the Church. They promise to nurture their child in that faith and to teach them to live the Commandments as Christ taught by loving God and neighbor.

THINK, PAIR AND SHARE

⊙ Identify ways parents play a role in their children's spiritual life.
⊙ Identify ways children can play a role in the spiritual life of their parents.

FORMING DISCIPLES OF JESUS CHRIST

The family is, in the words of the Catholic Church, "a school for human enrichment." Typically we think of education as something that happens in classrooms and schools. But the Church rightly teaches that "parents are the principal and first educators of their children" (CCC, no. 1653). Parents' principal responsibility as Christian "educators" is to guide and support their children, in both words *and* deeds, to grow to be faithful disciples of Jesus Christ. Of the many gifts for life that children receive from their parents, few are more important than their formation in faith, which will prepare them to be responsible members of the Church and society.

Sometimes parents' education of their children is direct, but more often it is occasional and impromptu; it is provided by the silent and powerful witness of the parents' lives. This witness can occur through such activities as attending Mass and praying together at meals and at bedtime, and treating family members, relatives, neighbors and strangers with respect and compassion, care and love. Growing as a disciple of Christ is a total way of life; and parents are the first people to bring their children into that way of life. After the gift of bodily life, there is no greater gift that parents can give their children than to nurture in them the gift of faith and guide them to discern the vocation to which God calls them.

OVER TO YOU

- ⊙ What important life and faith lessons have you learned from your family?
- ⊙ What can you contribute to the growth in faith that happens in your family?

AGAPE: THE FOUNDATION AND DYNAMIC OF LIFE

The world of infants revolves entirely around having their needs met. Infants experience "love"

A Community of Faith, Hope and Charity

[The Christian family] is a community of faith, hope, and charity; it assumes singular importance in the Church, as is evident in the New Testament (see Ephesians 5:21—6:4; Colossians 3:18–21; 1 Peter 3:1–7).

—CCC, no. 2204

STAINED GLASS FROM ST. PATRICK'S CHURCH, ANN ARBOR, MI

through their parents and other family members meeting those needs. The human journey is a growth toward maturity in love, toward *agape*, a life of self-sacrificing love for God and others. God, through the instrumentality of our parents and other family members, leads us out of our initial self-centeredness to be more self-giving people.

The Christian family is a place of *agape*. Christian married life begins and ends with *agape*. Christian spouses promise to support and maintain a healthy and loving relationship among themselves and with their family. Anyone who has grown up in a family knows that family life involves plenty of letting-go and sacrifice as well as love and joy.

Every society needs selfless citizens if it is to flourish. The Christian family is a "school of selflessness." It prepares us to give of ourselves freely in our family, in society and in the Church. Christian families serve an invaluable role in building up and fostering the life of the Church and society.

Remembering the blessings of the Sacrament of Marriage and being aware of the work of Christian families helps us recognize the signs of the presence of God at work in the world saving and sanctifying humanity. This work will finally come to fruition when Christ comes again in glory and it will be celebrated in the heavenly wedding banquet, or "marriage supper" (Revelation 19:9).

TALK IT OVER

- ⊙ Recall the definition of the Kingdom, or Reign, of God.
- ⊙ What new insights have you gained into the role of Christian marriage and the Christian family in bringing about the Reign of God?

WHAT ABOUT YOU PERSONALLY?

- ⊙ What sacrifices have your parents made for you? You for your parents?
- ⊙ How has receiving and making those sacrifices made a difference in your life?

The First School of the Christian Life

It is in the Christian family . . . one learns endurance and the joy of work, fraternal love, generous—even repeated— forgiveness, and above all divine worship in prayer and the offering of one's life.

—CCC, no. 1657

Challenges to Christian marriage and family life

WHEN THE ROMANCE WEARS OFF

Marriages are the *stuff* of fiction and poetry, of music and opera, of stage and screen. The portrayal of romance, marriage and family life is daily food for consumption. How true to life or to the human desire for true love are these stories? Why do so many people, young and old, have an insatiable appetite for marriage and romance stories?

OPENING REFLECTION

- ◉ Do you think media portrayals reflect marriage and family life as it is lived by most people you know? Why or why not?
- ◉ What are some of the difficulties and challenges to marriage and family life portrayed in the media? How common are those difficulties and challenges?
- ◉ How do you think faith in Christ and the Church helps Christian married couples deal with obstacles to living their marriage?

ELIZABETH AND DARCY IN AUSTEN'S *PRIDE AND PREJUDICE* | C.E. BROCK

REAL MARITAL LOVE IS MUCH MORE THAN ROMANCE

Marital love requires trust and sacrifice on the part of both spouses for each other. Such trust and sacrifice are the source of deepening the marital relationship; they are the source of 2 becoming 1. This is a reality and a mystery of marital life that is not so easy for people to grasp, namely $1 + 1 = 1$. While bad math, this formula conveys the truth that in God's plan for humanity *one* man and *one* woman are to come together to form *one* community. In that community of covenantal love, husband and wife fulfill the divine command to multiply, to give birth to new life, to realize the human desire to live in community, and to bring God's plan of creation to fulfillment. (Take a moment and reread Genesis 1:28, 2:18–24.)

There is another reality. We struggle with trust and self-giving, as the biblical story of the fall of Adam and Eve teaches. We tend, as a consequence of Original Sin, to look after what we perceive to be in our best self-interest. Adam and Eve's self-centered and self-serving decision not only distanced them from God but also damaged their own relationship. The human story became marred by concupiscence.

This weakness of our fallen nature is at the heart of why newlyweds can find it hard to settle into their new roles of becoming one as husband and wife. One spouse or the other, or both spouses, may desire to hold on to their independence rather than give themselves over to the interdependence and mutual support and sacrifice demanded by the marriage covenant. The reality is that a marriage is anything but easy;

making a marriage work requires and demands effort. Marriages of people who honestly face these problems reflect God's joyful and healing love. These challenges arise both from within the marital relationship and from the outside world in which a marriage is lived.

TALK IT OVER
⊙ What advice have you heard people in the media give married couples about facing the problems that can arise within a marriage? About sustaining a healthy marriage?
⊙ What wisdom does the Catholic faith have to offer?

OVER TO YOU
⊙ From your coming to know God, why would you place your trust in him?
⊙ What personal qualities in others would enable you to trust them?
⊙ What experiences have you had where you trusted someone? Did it make a difference? Explain.

CONTEMPORARY CHALLENGES
No one can think that the weakening of the family as that natural society founded on marriage will prove beneficial to society as a whole. The contrary is true: it poses a threat to the mature growth of individuals, the cultivation of community values and the moral progress of cities and countries. There is a failure to realize that only the exclusive and indissoluble union between a man and a woman has a plenary role to play in society as a stable commitment that bears fruit in new life. We need to acknowledge the great variety of family situations that can offer a certain stability, but de facto or same-sex unions, for example, may not simply be equated with marriage. No union that is temporary or closed to the transmission of life can ensure the future of society.

—Pope Francis, *The Joy of Love* (*Amoris Laetitia*), no. 52

CHALLENGES TO COMMITTED LOVE
There are many common practices in contemporary culture that undermine and weaken a person's ability to live a lifelong marital commitment of sacrificial love. Two very common practices are free unions, such as cohabitation, and the use of artificial contraception. (*We will look at cohabitation in this chapter and explore artificial contraception in chapter 6.*)

Cohabitation and other free unions eat away at the possibility of a couple truly entering the marriage commitment to a lifelong union. The term "free unions" refers to several types of relationship, including cohabitation and hooking up, between an unmarried and romantically involved man and woman living together. Some unmarried couples cohabit, that is, they choose to live together and seek sexual intimacy outside of marriage. They sometimes call this arrangement a *trial marriage*. Such a living

Promiscuous behavior can make it difficult for a married couple to trust each other and develop a sense of deep intimacy

Free unions

The term "free unions" refers to several types of intimate relationships between a man and a woman. These include trial marriages, cohabitation and concubinage. All these relationships have one thing in common: the partners have chosen to live together without being married and they remain "free" from entering a full marriage commitment. The partners do not commit themselves to all or some of the indispensable elements that make a marriage a marriage.

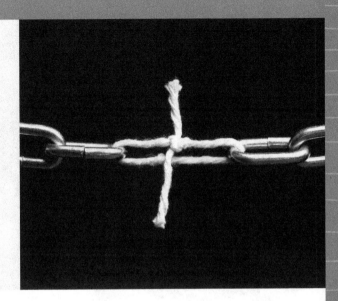

arrangement is contrary to both the natural and revealed moral law.

The practice of cohabitation and other free unions creates an impoverished mentality about sexuality. Using one's own body or the body of another person simply for personal gratification violates the sacredness of one's own body and of the other person's body as well as denying the personal dignity of both individuals. These attitudes and behavior are hard to overcome. They make it all the more difficult to express one's sexuality appropriately when one finally marries. Likewise, prior promiscuous behavior can make it difficult for a married couple to trust each other and develop a sense of deep intimacy. This contributes to the ease with which married couples who have cohabited find themselves seeking a divorce.

We will explore the Church's teaching on divorce and remarriage in detail in chapter 7.

SAME-SEX MARRIAGES

Some men and women living in same-sex, or homosexual and lesbian, relationships now seek to be legally "married." They seek to have their relationship recognized in civil law as equal to the marriage of a man and a woman, with the same rights and benefits that flow from a civil marriage. In the United States, same-sex marriage is now recognized by the federal government and is legal in all states. These civil laws, which are contrary to the teachings of Scripture and the Catholic Church, have divided the public deeply and given rise to much public debate. In answer to the question "Why can't marriage be redefined?" our bishops teach:

The word "marriage" isn't simply a label that can be attached to different types of relationships. Instead, "marriage" reflects a deep reality—the reality of the unique, fruitful, lifelong union that is only possible between a man and a woman. Just as oxygen and hydrogen are essential to water, sexual difference is essential to marriage. The attempt to "redefine" marriage to include two persons of the same sex denies the reality of what marriage is. It is as impossible as trying to "redefine" water to include oxygen and nitrogen.
—USCCB website, *Frequently Asked Questions about the Defense of Marriage*, "The Meaning of Marriage & Sexual Difference"

This teaching on same-sex marriage does not contradict the teaching of the Catholic Church on the love and respect that all homosexual and lesbian persons deserve. Christians must always condemn and avoid prejudicial attitudes and behavior toward homosexuals and lesbians that violate their dignity as children of God.

The *Catechism* teaches that the church community is to welcome homosexual persons and support them as they, too, strive for holiness of life

The teachings of the Catholic Church on marriage are to be understood within a holistic sexuality. God creates men and women as partners to complement each other physically, emotionally and spiritually. This equal and complementary partnership is fulfilled in the marriage of a man and a woman. For these reasons, the Catholic Church teaches that "homosexual acts are intrinsically disordered" (CCC, no. 2357). While it is not a sin to be attracted to persons of the same gender, homosexual acts are gravely sinful. The *Catechism* teaches:

Homosexuality refers to relations between men or between women who experience an exclusive or predominant sexual attraction toward persons of the same sex. It has taken a great variety of forms through the centuries and in different cultures. Its psychological genesis remains largely unexplained. Basing itself on Sacred Scripture, which presents homosexual acts as acts of grave depravity (see Genesis 19:1-29; Romans 12:4-27; 1 Corinthians 6:10; 1 Timothy 1:10), Tradition has always declared that "homosexual acts are intrinsically disordered" (Congregation of the Faith, *Persona Humana*, 8). They are contrary to the natural law. They close the sexual act to the gift of life. They do not proceed from a genuine affective and sexual complementarity. Under no circumstances can they be approved.

—CCC, no. 2357

Engaging in homosexual acts, therefore, leads to the person being prohibited from receiving Holy Communion in the Church without first receiving the Sacrament of Reconciliation.

The *Catechism* also teaches that the church community is to welcome homosexual persons and support them as they, too, strive for holiness of life. The *Catechism* teaches:

The number of men and women who have deep-seated homosexual tendencies is not negligible. This inclination, which is objectively disordered, constitutes for most of them a trial. They must be accepted with respect, compassion, and sensitivity. Every sign of unjust discrimination in their regard should be avoided. These persons are called to fulfill God's will in their lives and, if they are Christians, to unite to the sacrifice of the Lord's Cross the difficulties they may encounter from their condition.

—CCC, no. 2358

LET'S PROBE DEEPER: A CLASS DISCUSSION

- ⊙ What wisdom do you see in the Church's teachings on cohabitation, homosexual unions and same-sex marriages?
- ⊙ Does the practice of cohabitation foster the good of family life and society? Why or why not?
- ⊙ Does the practice of legalizing same-sex civil marriages foster the good of family life and society? Why or why not?
- ⊙ Share responses as a class.

FULLNESS OF LIFE AND TRUE JOY

Faithful married love is a wonderful path for growth into holiness and fullness of life. We have explored several of many challenges to marriage and family life, from both within and without the home, that can be obstacles to finding that holiness and fullness of life. By following the teaching of Jesus and his Church, Christian married couples can address these challenges and discover the joy that comes from committed, selfless love.

In his letter to families in 2014, on the feast of the Presentation of the Lord in the Temple, Pope Francis wrote "to help families face their present challenges with the light and strength that comes from the Gospel." The Pope wrote, in part:

It is a beautiful image: two young parents and two elderly people, brought together by Jesus. He is the one who brings together and unites generations! He is the inexhaustible font of that love which overcomes every occasion of self-absorption, solitude, and sadness. In your journey as a family, you share so many beautiful moments: meals, rest, housework, leisure, prayer, trips and pilgrimages, and times of mutual support. . . . Nevertheless, if there is no love then there is no joy, and authentic love comes to us from Jesus. He offers us his word, which illuminates our path; he gives us the Bread of life which sustains us on our journey.

OVER TO YOU

- ⊙ How has this discussion given you a more realistic understanding of the joys and challenges of married life?
- ⊙ What habits could you develop now that will help you to work through the challenges to marriage and family life in the future?

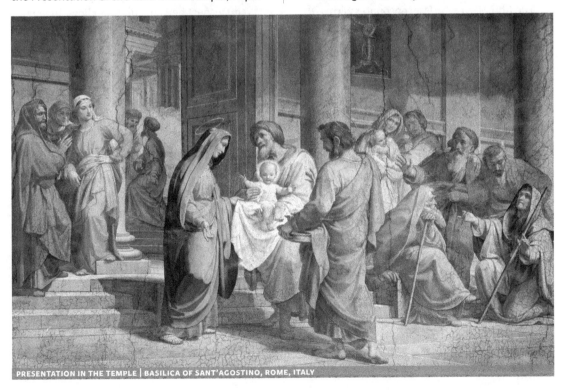

PRESENTATION IN THE TEMPLE | BASILICA OF SANT'AGOSTINO, ROME, ITALY

JUDGE AND ACT

REVIEW AND SHARE WHAT YOU HAVE LEARNED

Look back over this chapter and reflect on what you have learned about God's creation of man and woman and the role of marriage in God's plan for humanity. Share the teachings of the Catholic Church on these statements:

- ◉ The attraction between a man and a woman is most intimately fulfilled in the lifelong marriage covenant.
- ◉ Christ always offers his grace to Christian spouses and families to grow in holiness of life.
- ◉ Christian spouses commit to love, honor and respect each other as children of God.
- ◉ Christian marriage and family life are a source for growing in true freedom, fullness of life and joy.
- ◉ Cohabitation and sexual intimacy prior to and outside of marriage weaken a couple's ability to enter and live out the commitments of a true marriage.
- ◉ Homosexual unions and same-sex marriages are contrary to revealed and natural moral law.
- ◉ The Christian home is an encounter with Christ and a source of grace for building a healthy Church and society.

OVER TO YOU

- ◉ What wisdom did you discover about the relationship of men and women in God's plan for creation from your study of this chapter?
- ◉ How can you integrate that wisdom now into your attitudes and behavior?

JUSTICE AND RESPECT FOR ALL

Some traditional cultural attitudes and behaviors regarding marriage tend to promote dominance of the husband over his wife. Indeed, some have quoted the Book of Genesis and St. Paul to legitimize such dominance in marriage. Recent and more accurate translations and interpretations of biblical texts make it clear that husband and wife are to honor and respect each other as equal partners. Christians are called to practice justice within the home as well as within the world outside the home.

TALK IT OVER

- ◉ What can young people do to promote justice and respect between girls and boys, women and men? Give examples from life in school, in the family and in broader society.

LEARN BY EXAMPLE

Saint Gianna Beretta Molla (1922–62), wife, mother and physician

Gianna, after earning degrees in medicine and surgery in 1949, opened a medical clinic that soon specialized in working with mothers, infants, the elderly and people living in poverty. While engaged in this work, Gianna experienced an inner desire for marriage and family life; and in 1955 she and Pietro Molla married.

In September 1961, while pregnant with their fourth child, Gianna experienced severe and abnormal pains. An examination determined that she had developed a tumor on her uterus, which was surgically removed. However, the danger to her life and the life of her unborn child was not over. When the time came to deliver her baby, Gianna instructed the doctor, "If you must decide between me and the child, do not hesitate: choose the child. I insist on it." Labor brought complications and on the morning of April 28, 1962 Gianna died after giving birth to her child, whom her husband named Gianna Emanuela.

St. John Paul II named Gianna a blessed of the Church on April 24, 1994, during the international Year of the Family, and on May 16, 2004 he named her a saint of the Church. Gianna's husband and her children Laura and Gianna Emanuela were present; it was the first time a husband took part in the canonization of his wife. As they listened, they heard the Pope describe Gianna's love, saying, in part:

Following the example of Christ, who "having loved his own . . . loved them to the end" (John 13:1), this holy mother of a family remained heroically faithful to the commitment she made on the day of her marriage. The extreme sacrifice she sealed with her life testifies that only those who have the courage to give of themselves totally to God and to others are able to fulfill themselves.

TALK IT OVER

- ⊙ How is the sacrificial love of Gianna and Pietro a model for living as a Christian family?
- ⊙ What makes such a sacrifice possible?

SHARE FAITH WITH FAMILY AND FRIENDS

- ⊙ What can you do this week to support married and family life within your family? Your parish? Your community?
- ⊙ What advice would you give a young person who is contemplating marriage based on the insights you have gained from this chapter?

REFLECT AND DECIDE

- ⊙ What worries or excites you about marriage and family life?
- ⊙ What married couples can you support in living their sacrament? How?

JOURNAL EXERCISE

- ⊙ After considering the insights into marriage and family life in this chapter, do you think you might be up to the challenge of committing to and living a Christian marriage? Why or why not?
- ⊙ What could you be doing right now to better prepare yourself for the possibility of a future marriage and family life?
- ⊙ Compose a prayer to the Holy Family asking for strength and guidance to discern whether God is calling you to married life. Return to this prayer and pray it regularly.

All pray the Sign of the Cross together.

Opening Prayer

LEADER

Loving God,
we thank you for the many blessings
that you offer us through our families.
Send your Spirit upon us as we gather here today
so that we may give of ourselves lovingly and
selflessly to the people in our lives,
especially to the families to which we belong—
our home family, our parish and our community.
We ask this in the name of your Son, Jesus Christ.

ALL

Amen.

Proclamation of the Word of God

READER

A reading from the First Letter of St. John.
Proclaim 1 John 4:16–18.
The word of the Lord.

ALL

Thanks be to God.

LEADER

Reflect on what you heard for your life from this
reading. (*Pause*)
I invite all who wish to share their reflections
with the class to do so now.

Students share reflections.

LEADER

Let us take a moment to express in the silence of
our hearts gratitude to the Lord for the gifts we
have received from our parents, guardians and
family members, in the hope that one day we
will show the same kind of generosity in return.
(*Pause*)

Students spend a few moments in silent reflection.

Concluding Prayer

LEADER

Let us join together and ask our Lord to bless our
families.

ALL

Lord Jesus,
you belonged to a family, the Holy Family in
Nazareth.
In that family you experienced the selfless love of
Mary and Joseph and "increased in wisdom and in
years and in divine and human favor" (Luke 2:52).
We know that you dwell within our families.
Fill our families with the love of your saving and
sanctifying grace,
and make all of us one in heart and mind,
a joy-filled communion of life and love.
Amen.

Share a sign of peace.
Pray the Sign of the Cross together.

Let us express gratitude
to the Lord for the gifts
we have received from
our parents, guardians
and family members

CHAPTER 6

Celebrating the Sacrament of Marriage

CHRISTIAN MARRIAGE IS A PUBLIC ACT THAT REQUIRES A LITURGICAL CELEBRATION

THE RITE OF MARRIAGE CAN BE CELEBRATED EITHER DURING MASS OR OUTSIDE OF MASS

IN THE LATIN CHURCH THE BRIDE AND GROOM ARE THE MINISTERS OF THE SACRAMENT

PREPARING FOR MARRIAGE | REMOTE PREPARATION | PROXIMATE PREPARATION

THE CATHOLIC CHURCH CELEBRATES THE Sacrament of Marriage during the celebration of Mass or outside of Mass. The liturgical celebration points to the reality that marriage is more than a personal or private matter; it is a public act. Preparation for the reception of this sacrament begins in the home and parish community during one's childhood and youth, and it continues throughout one's formal education and faith formation, and culminates in the engaged couple's immediate preparation for their marriage.

ELEMENTS OF THE MARRIAGE RITE

INTRODUCTION

QUESTIONS

CONSENT AND EXCHANGE OF PROMISES

BLESSING AND EXCHANGE OF RINGS

NUPTIAL BLESSING

SOLEMN BLESSING

Faith Focus: These teachings of the Catholic Church are the primary focus of the doctrinal content presented in this chapter:

⊙ A sacramental marriage is a public act that requires a liturgical celebration.
⊙ In the Latin Church the spouses are the ministers of the sacrament.
⊙ Consent freely given, lifelong, exclusive and faithful commitment, and openness to children are essential for a valid sacramental marriage.
⊙ The Catholic Church encourages Catholics to marry another Catholic.
⊙ Those who wish to marry have the responsibility to prepare for marriage.

Discipleship Formation: As a result of studying this chapter and discovering the meaning of the faith of the Catholic Church for your life, you should be better able to:

⊙ explain the liturgical celebration of marriage;
⊙ understand the importance of the promises made at the celebration of marriage;
⊙ recognize how your present life can prepare you for married and family life;
⊙ value the significance of a Catholic marrying another Catholic.

Scripture References: These Scripture references are quoted or referred to in this chapter:
OLD TESTAMENT: **Genesis** 2:18–24; **Tobit** 7:9–10 and 11–15; **Song of Songs** 2:8–10, 14, 16a; 8:6–7a
NEW TESTAMENT: **Matthew** 5:1–16, 7:21 and 24–29, 19:3–6, 22:35–40; **Mark** 10:6–9; **John** 2:1–11, 15:9–16, 17:20–26; **Romans** 8:31b–35 and 37–39, 12:1–2 and 9–18, 15:1b–3a, 5–7 and 13; **1 Corinthians** 6:12–20, 12:31—13:8a; **Ephesians** 5:2a and 21–33; **Colossians** 3:12–17; **Hebrews** 13:1–4a and 5–6b; **1 Peter** 3:1–9; **1 John** 3:18–24, 4:7–12; **Revelation** 19:1 and 5–9a

Faith Glossary: Familiarize yourself with or recall the meaning of these key terms. Definitions are found in the Glossary: **artificial contraception, chastity, disparity of cult, dispensation, mixed marriage, Natural Family Planning (NFP), purity of heart**

Faith Words: disparity of cult; mixed marriage
Learn by Heart: Words from St. John XXIII
Learn by Example: Blessed Pope Paul VI

Why is the marriage ceremony so important?

THE BIG DAY—THE BEGINNING OF A JOURNEY

After months of planning and preparations, the big day is finally here. Kim and the bridesmaids wait in the church vestibule; Felipe and the groomsmen stand at the front of the church. All are feeling a bit anxious as they wait for Mass to begin. Friends and family have gathered in the church and are shifting in their seats, looking forward with excitement to their first glimpse of Kim. So much has led up to this one defining moment that will set Kim and Felipe on a journey they will follow together for the rest of their lives. At last the music swells, each takes a deep breath and the procession down the aisle begins.

OPENING REFLECTION

◉ Have you ever waited for some event that you had spent a long time preparing for? Describe your feelings.

◉ Imagine what it was like for Kim and Felipe as they waited for the Nuptial Mass to begin. Your thoughts? Your feelings?

A COMMUNITY AFFAIR

Marriage is far more than a personal act. The Sacrament of Marriage is designed, in God's plan, not only for the good of the couples celebrating the sacrament, but primarily for the good of the church community and as a source of God's creative, saving, sanctifying and transforming love for society. For this reason, Christian marriage is a public act that requires a public liturgical celebration, a public act of worship by the church community.

Marriage and family life are the foundation of society. The Sixth and Ninth Commandments teach that everyone, individuals and society, and not only the man and woman who enter the marriage covenant, must respect and support the sanctity of the marriage vows that spouses freely and fully commit to live. This is another reason why marriage is by its nature a public act.

For Catholics, the setting of the celebration of their marriage gives witness to this public nature of marriage. Not just any time or place will do. The nature of the Sacrament of Marriage requires that it be celebrated during a celebration of the liturgy. In the Latin Rite the marriage of two Catholics normally takes place during the celebration of Mass. This gives witness to the connection of this sacrament with the Paschal Mystery of God's saving and sanctifying work in the Death, Resurrection and Ascension of Jesus Christ, which is made present in the Eucharist. Though celebrating this sacrament during Mass is the norm, it is sometimes permissible to celebrate the Sacrament of Matrimony outside of Mass. This often happens in marriages where either the bride or bridegroom is not a Catholic.

CELEBRATION OF THE RITE OF MARRIAGE

The *Catechism of the Catholic Church* teaches: "Christian spouses are fortified and, as it were, *consecrated* for the duties and dignity of their state by a special sacrament" (CCC, no. 1535). "Consecrated" means "to set aside and dedicate to God for a holy purpose." Remembering that the couple are "consecrated" helps us appreciate the significance of the mystery of what is happening at the celebration of this sacrament. This, in turn, makes very clear the need and responsibility to prepare well for this day.

The Rite of Marriage can be celebrated either during Mass or outside of Mass. In both settings the celebration of the sacrament takes place after the homily, during the Liturgy of the Word. The celebration begins with the bishop, priest or deacon welcoming the couple and their guests.

ELEMENTS OF THE MARRIAGE RITE

After the proclamation of Scripture (which the bride and bridegroom often select in consultation with the priest, deacon or marriage preparation team) and the homily, the celebration of the sacrament begins. What many people might not realize is that in the Latin Church the bride and groom are the ministers of the sacrament. The bishop, priest or deacon serves as the witness to the marriage for the Church. This is not the case in the Eastern Churches, where the bishop or priest confers the sacrament. We will now take a brief look at the Rite of Celebrating Marriage during Mass.

Introduction: The priest (or bishop or deacon), using these or similar words, introduces the celebration of the rite by addressing the bride and bridegroom:

My dear friends, you have come together in this church so that the Lord may seal and strengthen your love in the presence of the Church's minister and this community. Christ abundantly blesses this love. He has already consecrated you in baptism and now he enriches and strengthens you by a special sacrament so that you may assume the duties of marriage in mutual and lasting fidelity. And so, in the presence of the Church, I ask you to state your intentions.
—*The Rites I*, "Rite for Celebrating Marriage During Mass," no. 23

The questions: The priest or deacon questions the bride and bridegroom about their intention to commit to the three elements necessary for a valid sacramental marriage. As you learned in chapter 5, the freedom of the man and woman uniting themselves in marriage is one of those essential elements. The couple about to marry must be free to marry, be of sufficient age, be neither already married nor closely related by blood to each other. The bride and bridegroom must also intend to enter an exclusive, faithful and lifelong marriage. Each must come to the sacrament with the intention of participating

Culture note

In Hispanic countries such as Mexico, the Philippines and Spain, it is common practice to place a "wedding cord" around the bride and the groom after they have made their vows and as they receive the nuptial blessing. The wedding cord, which looks like a large, figure-eight-shaped rosary, symbolizes the spouses' everlasting union and God's protection upon their marriage.

in God's life-giving creative love. They must be open to bringing about new life with the intention of helping their future children grow in faith and love as disciples of Jesus.

The consent and exchange of promises: After freely and truthfully stating their intentions, the bride and bridegroom, one at a time, give their consent by exchanging marriage promises, or vows, before God and the Church. By the *giving of their word*, they marry publicly, saying, one at a time:

I, N., take you, N., to be my wife [husband]. I promise to be true to you in good times and in bad, in sickness and in health. I will love you and honor you all the days of my life.
—*The Rites I*, "Rite for Celebrating Marriage During Mass," no. 25

The bride and bridegroom's profession of their promises reveals that they are the ministers of

this sacrament. The priest or deacon witnesses and accepts the consent of the couple on behalf of the Church and reaffirms that the marriage just entered is an inseparable union. He declares:

You have declared your consent before the Church. May the Lord in his goodness strengthen your consent and fill you both with his blessings.
What God has joined, men must not divide.
—*The Rites I*, "Rite for Celebrating Marriage During Mass," no. 26

THINK, PAIR AND SHARE
- What do the questions and the consent and exchange of promises reveal about the essence of the marriage covenant?
- What do you see as the significance of the fact that the couple administers this sacrament to each other?

The blessing and exchange of rings: Matrimony, like all the sacraments, uses words, actions and material objects to signify the mystery that is taking place. In addition to giving their consent verbally, the newly married couple may exchange wedding rings, if they so choose, as a sign of their love and fidelity.

After the priest or deacon blesses the ring (or rings), the bridegroom places a ring on the bride's finger, using these or similar approved words: "N., take this ring as a sign of my love and fidelity. In the name of the Father, and of the Son, and of the Holy Spirit." The bride then does the same.

The Prayer of the Faithful (and the Creed if called for) concludes the Rite of Marriage, and the Liturgy of the Eucharist begins.

Nuptial Blessing: The Liturgy of the Eucharist is now celebrated. Immediately after the Lord's Prayer, the priest offers the Nuptial Blessing for the couple. (In a marriage celebrated outside of Mass, the Nuptial Blessing takes place at the conclusion of the Prayer of the Faithful.) In the Nuptial Blessing the priest asks God to seal and bless the covenant of life and love that the newly-wed couple have entered. Among the prayers approved by the Church, the priest prays, in part:

O God, who consecrated the bond of
      Marriage
by so great a mystery
that in the wedding covenant you
      foreshadow
the Sacrament of Christ and his Church;
      . . .

Look now with favor on these your
      servants,
joined together in Marriage,
who ask to be strengthened by your
      blessing.
Send down on them the grace of the
      Holy Spirit
and pour your love into their hearts,
that they may remain faithful in the
      Marriage covenant. . . .

And now, Lord, we implore you:
may these your servants
hold fast to the faith and keep your
      commandments;
made one in flesh,
may they be blameless in all they do;
and with the strength that comes from the
      Gospel,
may they bear true witness to Christ before all;
      . . . .

And grant that
reaching at last together the fullness of years
for which they hope,
may they come to the life of the blessed
in the Kingdom of Heaven.
      —Nuptial Blessing, *The Roman Missal*, Ritual
      Masses for the Celebration of Marriage A

Solemn Blessing: Mass continues in its normal
fashion with the exchange of a sign of peace
and Holy Communion. Before the priest blesses
and dismisses the people, he blesses the newly
married couple. In part, he may pray:

May God the eternal Father
keep you of one heart in love for one another,
that the peace of Christ may dwell in you
and abide always in your home.

May you be blessed in your children,
have solace in your friends
and enjoy true peace with everyone.

May you be witnesses in the world to God's
      charity,
so that the afflicted and needy who have known
      your kindness
may one day receive you thankfully
into the eternal dwelling of God.
      —Solemn Blessing at the End of Mass,
      The Roman Missal, Ritual Masses for the
      Celebration of Marriage A

TALK IT OVER

⊙ How has your appreciation for the Sacrament
  of Matrimony grown in light of the discussion
  about the Rite of Marriage?

⊙ How will this lesson change your experience
  of weddings in the future? As you think about
  your own possible wedding?

JOURNAL EXERCISE

⊙ Read and reflect on these Scripture passages.
  They are among the readings approved by the
  Church for use during the celebration of the
  Sacrament of Marriage.
  – Tobit 7:9–10, 11–15; Song of Songs 2:8–10,
    14, 16a; 8:6–7a
  – Colossians 3:12–17; 1 John 3:18–24

⊙ Describe the insight these passages give you
  into the vocation of marriage.

Marriages uniting people of different faiths

LOOKING FOR DIRECTION

Jamie's parents practice different Christian faith traditions. His father is Methodist; his mother, who is Catholic, brought him up in the Catholic faith. Jamie, a junior in a Catholic high school, has attended Catholic schools since pre-school. His Catholic faith means a lot to him. Having been raised by a Catholic mother and a Methodist father, he often wonders if he, too, might marry a non-Catholic. He realizes from his theology courses that the Catholic Church encourages Catholics to marry another Catholic. He also knows from his experience that many homes, like his own, are of mixed faith traditions.

DON'T MARRY A CATHOLIC

Rev. Daniel A. Lord, s.j.

CATHOLIC PAMPHLET ABOUT MIXED-FAITH MARRIAGE FROM THE 1950S

OPENING REFLECTION

⊙ Do you live, or know someone who lives, in a household of mixed faith traditions?
⊙ What challenges does that present?
⊙ What unique challenges might it present for Catholics?

MARRIAGE INVOLVING DIFFERENT FAITH TRADITIONS

The people of the United States of America profess a wide variety of faith traditions. It is not uncommon for a Catholic to marry a non-Catholic. A marriage between a Catholic and a non-Catholic baptized person is a **mixed marriage**. A marriage between a Catholic and a non-Christian or a non-believer is a marriage with **disparity of cult**, or an interfaith marriage. In recognition of this reality the Catholic Church grants permission for Catholics to enter into a mixed marriage and a marriage with disparity of cult. The *Catechism* teaches:

> Difference of confession between the spouses does not constitute an insurmountable obstacle for marriage, when they succeed in placing in common what they have received from their respective communities, and learn from each other the way in which each lives in fidelity to Christ.
>
> —CCC, no. 1634

Knowing the particular challenges of a marriage in which the spouses practice different faith traditions, the Catholic Church encourages Catholics to marry another Catholic.

DEALING WITH DIFFERENCES

Many matters vital to marriage and family life are centered in one's religion—the way one sees the world, one's moral codes and convictions

Mixed marriage

A marriage between a Catholic and a non-Catholic baptized person. The law of the Catholic Church requires specific permission from the local ordinary (bishop) for the celebration of a sacramental mixed marriage. The process involved highlights the unique challenges the Catholic partner will face.

Disparity of cult

A marriage with disparity of cult is a marriage between a Catholic and a non-Christian, or an interfaith marriage. The law of the Catholic Church requires specific permission for a Catholic to marry a non-Christian. The process involved highlights the unique challenges the Catholic partner will face.

about family life and raising children, one's views on how authority and roles are shared within a marriage, to name just a few. Such differences can add stress and introduce specific areas of conflict into a marriage. Such conflict can make marriage and raising a family more challenging than when spouses share a common faith tradition.

Though the challenges are not insurmountable, couples from different religious traditions should not overlook the potential difficulties they might encounter in their marriage. In a mixed marriage both spouses need to bring together the common elements from their respective Christian communities and live together as disciples of Jesus in fidelity and service to each other, to their families and to the Church. In this way their marriage will enrich their own life as a Christian couple, the life of the family of God, the Church, and the life of society.

The marriage of a Catholic to a non-baptized person can have elements that become an even greater source of tension or conflict for living the marriage vocation. These tensions can sometimes lead to religious indifference. These are serious matters that require the careful attention of spouses and their pastors.

Canon law, the law of the Catholic Church, requires specific permissions for both mixed marriages and marriages with disparity of cult. The process involved highlights the unique challenges the Catholic partner will face. Throughout it all, the Catholic spouse accepts "the responsibility of training [children] in the practice of the faith" (*Rite of Baptism for Several Children*, "Reception of the Children," no. 39)

THINK, PAIR AND SHARE

- Work with a partner. Take turns playing each role in this activity.
- Imagine that you, a Catholic, are considering marrying your partner, who is a member of a different Christian denomination. Engage in a conversation about issues that might arise in your marriage.
- Speaking as a future Catholic spouse, discuss how you would work to address each of the issues.
- Share your discussion with the class.

PERMISSION TO MARRY

According to canon law, a mixed marriage must receive the express permission of ecclesiastical

When a couple agree to fulfill these conditions, the Catholic Church can bless their marriage. As in the case of any married couple, the real work is only just beginning once a Catholic and a non-Catholic person are married. The real challenges—as well as many joys—will be in the day-to-day living of their marriage.

ONGOING COMMUNITY SUPPORT

Thanks to efforts in ecumenical dialogue, Christian communities in many regions now offer a shared pastoral practice to prepare couples for and support them in mixed marriages. These programs help engaged couples to fulfill their obligations both to each other and to their faith communities. Catholic couples can take advantage of this resource by speaking to their local priest or parish marriage preparation team. In marriages of Catholics with non-baptized persons, the challenges can be even greater. With the help of God's grace, such a marriage may be the occasion for a non-Catholic spouse to ask to become a member of the Catholic Church.

TALK IT OVER

- What wisdom do you see in the Church's three conditions for a Catholic to marry a non-Catholic?
- Do you agree that the Church serves couples well by insisting that they discuss these matters before marriage? Why or why not?
- How might the way the Catholic Church addresses mixed marriages and disparity of cult support couples to grow closer to God and each other?

WHAT ABOUT YOU PERSONALLY?

- How might you as a Christian think differently from non-Christians about the actual wedding ceremony?
- How might you personally cultivate respectful relationships with people of different faith traditions?

authority, usually the bishop of the diocese, for the marriage to be lawful. This permission is usually requested through the priest who is preparing the couple for sacramental marriage in the Church. The Catholic Church requires a **dispensation** for a Catholic to marry a non-baptized person. A dispensation is the granting of freedom from the requirement(s) of a church law by the appropriate Church authority. This dispensation is also usually granted through the local ordinary, or bishop of the diocese.

Considering the potential difficulties for a Catholic marrying a non-Catholic Christian or a non-baptized person, the Catholic Church requires couples seeking to marry to satisfy certain conditions. For a Catholic to marry a non-Catholic, the Church sets out three basic requirements:

- First, both spouses know and do not exclude what the Catholic Church teaches to be the essential nature and purposes of marriage.
- Second, the Catholic spouse promises to continue practicing his or her faith.
- Third, the Catholic spouse agrees to do everything in her or his power to raise their children in the Catholic faith.

Preparing for marriage from infancy through school years

GOOD PREPARATION IS KEY

Imagine it is the opening night of your annual school drama production. You are taking the lead role. You had been very sick and missed almost a month of school and rehearsals, but the director insisted you keep your role. The rest of the cast are feeling uneasy about your lack of preparation. The truth is that you used your time at home to learn your lines and study the script. You are confident that you will make it work.

OPENING REFLECTION

- ⊙ How well do you prepare for taking part in events in which others rely on you?
- ⊙ How does your preparing for an event impact the outcome?
- ⊙ Make a list of the things you consider necessary for a couple to do in order to prepare themselves well for marriage. Discuss the importance of each.

MORE THAN A SPECIAL DAY

Engaged couples often stretch their resources to the limit and prepare lavishly for their wedding day. But marriage is about much more than a special day and demands far greater preparation; the wedding day is but one day of a lifetime together. Couples are commonly under the illusion that, having been raised within a family, they know all about the ups and downs of marriage. That is far from the truth.

The Church has a responsibility to prepare couples for marriage. In this and the next section of the chapter we take a look at the wisdom the Church offers us for preparing for the adventure and challenges of a Christian marriage. In this section you will explore both the remote preparation and the proximate preparation, and in the next section you will examine the immediate preparation for married life.

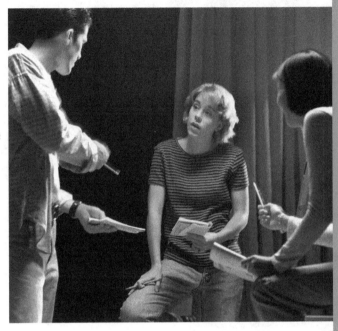

TALK IT OVER

- ⊙ When do you think preparation for marriage begins?
- ⊙ What are the most important elements of a couple's preparation for marriage?

REMOTE PREPARATION

Our life experiences are a source of preparation for our future. Through our experience of living as a member of a Christian family we develop a sense of who we are as a person and who we are as a member of a community. This development takes place over a period of time.

First, the early formative years are the time when we begin to develop our vision of our self, to develop a solid self-concept. Within the life of our family we come to know and develop our unique personality and discover some of our gifts and talents. We also learn about our strengths and weaknesses.

Becoming a responsible adult requires education and practice

just prior to the celebration of marriage. For every couple marriage preparation begins at birth. What they received from their family should prepare them to know themselves and to make a full and definitive commitment. Those best prepared for marriage are probably those who learned what Christian marriage is from their own parents who chose each other unconditionally and daily renew this decision.
—*The Joy of Love* (*Amoris Lætitia*), no. 208

WHAT ABOUT YOU PERSONALLY?

- ◉ What key values and wisdom about relationships have you learned from your parents and mentors?
- ◉ How does this wisdom help you, right now, to form and sustain healthy relationships?

PROXIMATE PREPARATION

Becoming a responsible adult requires education and practice. Preparing *proximately* for marriage and parenthood requires acquiring the resources, habits and competencies necessary for sustaining a well-ordered and disciplined adult life. Though we pick up a lot in our childhood homes, we cannot count on mere observation to guide us later in life. Formal education is necessary.

Building on a good foundation from our early years of life, we take on more explicit preparation for marriage (and for other vocations) through a more formal education both at home and in school and by participating in the faith life of our Church. In this course of study you have already explored many of the areas that need to be part of the proximate preparation for marriage. These include having a sound understanding that:

- ◉ human beings are images of God, and human sexuality is part of our very being, through which we relate to others;

Second, the experiences of childhood involve significant learning for developing healthy relationships. Much is made of sibling rivalry, manipulation of parents, resistance to doing household chores, and so on. In these and other areas we first learn (or do not learn) to restrain our self-centered impulses and respond to the good of others; we learn how to communicate clearly and negotiate differences when necessary. During these early stages of our life we are learning the foundational moral and spiritual values and virtues that will mark the way we relate well (or not so well) with others.

Pope Francis in his 2016 apostolic exhortation on love in the family addressed the essential role of family life in the development of one's growth in love. The pope wrote, in part:

Learning to love someone does not happen automatically nor can it be taught in a workshop

- God created man and woman as partners with a natural complementarity;
- God decreed that sexual intimacy be reserved for marriage;
- marriage involves a total self-giving of spouses; requires a sense of discipline, generosity and an understanding of true love;
- marriage reflects Christ's relationship to the Church.

LET'S PROBE DEEPER: A CLASS DISCUSSION

- Reflect on what you have already learned in this course of study or in other courses of study about the teachings of Scripture and the Catholic Church on marriage.
- From what you have learned, draw up a list of what you would see as a necessary part of one's proximate preparation for a Christian marriage.
- Share recollections as a class.

HUMAN SEXUALITY AND CONJUGAL LOVE

God creates men and women with a natural complementarity. In and through the man-woman God-given partnership, a man and woman become as "one" in marriage. This unique divinely ordered partnership expresses the fullness of human love—a love God creates to reflect or image the life-giving love of God. The *Catechism* teaches: "Since God created him man and woman, their mutual love becomes an image of an absolute and unfailing love with which God loves man" (CCC, no. 1604).

In their marital mutual self-giving, a married man and woman come to the fullness of life and become co-creators with God of new life. Preparing for a healthy and holy marriage that is in harmony with the divine plan necessarily includes coming to an authentic and accurate understanding and appreciation of the relationship between conjugal love and human sexuality. In the words of Pope Francis, "Sexuality is inseparably at the service of this conjugal friendship for it is meant to aid the fulfillment of the other" (*The Joy of Love*, no. 156).

CONTEMPORARY CHALLENGES TO CONJUGAL LOVE

Contemporary culture routinely promotes the separation of human sexuality and sexual intimacy from the fullness and integrity of conjugal love. Sexual intimacy is portrayed erroneously as an end in itself. The requirement

The Holiness of Marriage and the Family

Marriage is not a purely human institution. "The intimate partnership of life and the love which constitutes the married state has been established by the creator and endowed by him with its own proper laws. . . . It is an institution confirmed by divine law. . . . For God himself is the author of marriage and has endowed it with various values and purposes: all of these have a very important bearing on the continuation of the human race, on the personal development and eternal destiny of every member of the family, on the dignity, stability, peace, and prosperity of the family and of the whole human race" (Vatican II, *Pastoral Constitution on the Church in the Modern World* [*Gaudium et Spes*], no. 48).

for openness to conceiving a new life in every act of sexual intercourse is also portrayed erroneously as an obstacle to achieving personal growth and intimacy. Developing and practicing marital chastity, along with temperance, self-control and the other human virtues, strengthens married spouses to deal successfully with these challenges and temptations. In the words of our bishops:

Married people are called to love with conjugal chastity. That is, their love is to be total, faithful, exclusive, and open to life. Conjugal love merges "the human and the divine," leading the "partners to a free and mutual self-giving" (*Pastoral Constitution on the Church in the Modern World*, no. 49). The practice of marital chastity ensures that both husband and wife will strive to live as a gift of self, one to the other, generously. In other words, marital chastity protects a great good: the communion of persons and the procreative purposes of marriage.

— *Marriage: Love and Life in the Divine Plan*, A Pastoral Letter of the United States Conference of Catholic Bishops, 49

Pope Francis has reaffirmed this constant teaching of the Church:

The child who is born "does not come from outside as something added on to the mutual love of the spouses, but springs from the very heart of that mutual giving, as its fruit and fulfillment" (CCC, no. 2366). He or she does not appear at the end of a process, but is present from the beginning of love as an essential feature, one that cannot be denied without disfiguring that love itself. From the outset, love refuses every impulse to close in on itself; it is open to a fruitfulness that draws it beyond itself. Hence no genital act of husband and wife can refuse this meaning (see Blessed Paul VI, Encyclical Letter *Humanae Vitae*, July 25, 1968, nos. 11 and 12), even when for various reasons it may not always in fact beget a new life.

— *The Joy of Love*, no. 80

Children are "the supreme gift of marriage" (*Pastoral Constitution on the Church in the Modern World*, no. 50). Being open to receiving this gift of a new life is a privilege and sacred responsibility. This openness, contrary to what some assert, neither hinders a married couple's growth in intimacy nor commands a married couple to "generate" new life in an irresponsible way. "It is the nature of love to overflow, to be life-giving. . . . Thus, it is no surprise that marriage is ordained not only to growing in love but to transmitting life" (*Marriage: Love and Life in the Divine Plan*, 14).

Responsible Parenthood

"Living according to God's design for love and life does not mean that married couples cannot plan their families. The principle of responsible parenthood describes the way spouses can work with God's gift of fertility."
— *Marriage: Love and Life in the Divine Plan*, 20

RESPONSIBLE PARENTHOOD: NURTURING THE GIFT OF A NEW LIFE

"Making decisions about when and how many children to have in marriage is a sacred responsibility that God has entrusted to husband and wife. This is the foundation of what the Church calls 'Responsible Parenthood'—the call to discern God's will for your marriage while respecting His design for life and love" ("Natural Family Planning," United States Conference of Catholic Bishops). Family life requires a secure and loving environment for nurturing and educating children, spiritually and physically. The Church teaches:

A particular aspect of this responsibility concerns the regulation of procreation. For just reasons, spouses may wish to space the births of their children. It is their duty to make certain that their desire is not motivated by selfishness but is in conformity with the generosity appropriate to responsible parenthood. Moreover, they should conform their behavior to the objective criteria of morality:

> When it is a question of harmonizing married love with the responsible transmission of life, the morality of the behavior does not depend on sincere intention and evaluation of motives alone; but it must be determined by objective criteria, criteria drawn from the nature of the person and his acts, criteria that respect the total meaning of mutual self-giving and human procreation in the context of true love; this is possible only if the virtue of married chastity is practiced with sincerity of heart. (*Pastoral Constitution on the Church in the Modern World*, no. 51)
> —*Catechism of the Catholic Church*, no. 2368

Natural Family Planning (NFP): The Catholic Church teaches that the refined scientific methods of Natural Family Planning are in harmony with both the natural law and the unitive and procreative ends of marriage. Couples who use Natural Family Planning to space the birth of their children freely choose to abstain from conjugal relations during the portion of the woman's menstrual cycle when conception is most likely and to do nothing to alter the fullness and integrity of the conjugal act. "NFP reflects the dignity of the human person within the context of marriage and family life, promotes openness to life, and recognizes the value of the child. By respecting the love-giving and life-giving natures of marriage, NFP can enrich the bond between husband and wife" ("Natural Family Planning," United States Conference of Catholic Bishops). This is essentially different from contraception.

Contraception: Some would argue that they are "open" to children—but just not at this time. To resolve this dilemma they choose contraceptive methods to *block* the possibility of conceiving a new life. They judge that taking such precautions to *prevent* a pregnancy is justified because they are in principle open to new birth, but being open to new life all the time endangers the depth of intimacy uniting the spouses. They choose to separate the inseparable. In the words of the Church, they choose to separate the unitive from the procreative dimension of sexual intercourse.

The Catholic Church rejects this reasoning, which attempts to justify the use of contraceptives.

Deliberately intervening, by the use of contraceptive practices, to close off an act of intercourse to the possibility of procreation is a way of separating the unitive meaning of marriage from the procreative meaning. This is objectively wrong in and of itself and is essentially opposed to God's plan for marriage and proper human development. It makes the act of intercourse signify, or speak, something less than the unreserved self-gift intended in the marriage promises.
—*Marriage: Love and Life in the Divine Plan*, 18

Methods of contraception include chemical methods (the pill), mechanical methods (condoms) and surgical methods (direct sterilization). All contraceptive methods inhibit the completeness and fullness of conjugal love. They subvert the "complete and mutual" self-giving of the spouses one to another.

TALK IT OVER
◉ What issues are spouses to consider in planning the size of their family?
◉ What is the guiding moral principle for spouses in planning the size of their family?

THE BLESSING OF CREATING NEW LIFE

All marriages have the vocation to be life-giving. St. John Paul II in his 1981 apostolic exhortation, *The Christian Family in the Modern World*, taught that the fundamental task of marriage and family is to be at the service of life. By God's desire and design the sexual intimacy of conjugal love is reserved for marriage and is to be life-giving in two ways. It is ordered simultaneously to both the spiritual and bodily well-being of the spouses *and* to giving birth to new life. In procreating children, a married couple's love functions in deep and intimate partnership with God's creative love. To call this event a miracle is no exaggeration. Procreation and parenthood are precious gifts. The lack of willingness to have children by either of the spouses is contrary to the very essence of a marriage.

Spouses who are unable to give birth naturally often give witness to their openness to children through adoption or foster parenting, or by their special care for nieces and nephews and other people's children. Adoptive and foster parents are true parents. Their welcoming a child into their family as one of their own is an act of unselfish and committed love. Catholic Charities USA and other Catholic agencies serving the pastoral ministry of the Church play a significant role in uniting children with loving families.

REFLECT, DISCUSS AND SHARE
◉ Work in groups of three. Discuss:
  – Why is a child to be valued as a gift from God both by a family and by society?
  – How does respect for the gifts of fertility and children promote the well-being and joy of the family?
  – What impact does the birth rate have on a society?
◉ Share reflections as a class.

Immediate preparation for marriage

OPENING REFLECTION

- Have you felt pressured when a key event in your life was just around the corner? What were the key sources of that pressure? Did you overlook anything in preparing for that event?
- What would be some of the most important things for an engaged couple to focus and work on in the months immediately leading up to their wedding day? How would that help the couple deal better with the pressures they might be feeling?

A NOT UNCOMMON EXPERIENCE

Kim and Felipe slump back against the couch and sigh in exasperation. They look at the lists scattered on the table and floor in front of them and think of all that has yet to be done: flower catalogs to be sorted through, photographers to choose from, seating charts that need to be arranged, and the guest list that still needs to be finalized. And then, of course, there will be the invitations to send out. Kim looks at Felipe and asks, "How are we going to get it all done? With all the planning, we've had hardly any time for each other."

THINK, PAIR AND SHARE

- Reflect: Is there anything missing from Kim and Felipe's preparation plans and schedule?
- Share your reflections with a partner.

Pre-Cana Marriage Preparation

The Church has a responsibility to prepare engaged couples for marriage. Many dioceses and parishes offer Pre-Cana programs (named after the wedding feast Jesus attended at Cana) during which engaged couples meet with a parish priest, deacon and other married couples over a period of six to nine months. Pre-Cana helps engaged couples to deepen their understanding of the Catholic Church's teaching on marriage and the Sacrament of Marriage. Together, couples who share each other's hopes, dreams, fears and desires regarding marriage identify and discuss areas of agreement and areas of potential conflict, and how to put in place practices that foster mutual respect and good communication. They learn certain practical skills on forming and building a home, for example, budgeting and preparing for and raising children. In some cases, parishes and dioceses will offer daylong or weekend retreats to supplement other parish programs.

Couples need to be very clear that they are committing to a lifetime of growth in holiness and service to others together

IMMEDIATE MARRIAGE PREPARATION

The final months of preparing for one's marriage can, understandably, be very stressful. As we have been exploring, preparation for a sacramental marriage is a long-term, continuous process that includes many elements. All these elements receive focused attention during the *immediate marriage preparation* period. "Because Christian marriage is a sacrament, the Catholic Church wants couples to be well-prepared. Dioceses and parishes offer marriage preparation to help couples develop a better understanding of the sacrament; to evaluate and deepen their readiness to live married life; and to gain insights into themselves as individuals and as a couple" ("Marriage Preparation," USCCB website).

To support an engaged couple to meet that responsibility, the Catholic Church encourages and requires engaged couples to invest the time and energy to take part in an in-depth and immediate preparation for celebrating the sacrament. This preparation is multi-dimensional and includes both spiritual and practical concerns. In short, the immediate preparation for marriage focuses on the couple's understanding of and commitment to living the promises they will make on their wedding day.

Spiritual concerns: Whatever its format, an effective immediate preparation for marriage helps engaged couples to grow in their understanding of and commitment to living the three promises they will make in the Sacrament of Matrimony.

⊙ First, couples need to be very clear that they are committing to a lifetime of growth in holiness and service to others together. The prevalence of divorce in our culture may tempt Christian couples to believe that they can always leave their marriage if they feel it isn't "working out." Such an attitude sets couples up for failure from the beginning.

- Second, couples need to understand that they are committing themselves to this one person only. Any intimate romantic relationship outside the marriage is strictly forbidden by their marriage vows.
- Third, it is important for couples to be open to God's gift of children, whether by their own procreation or by adoption.

Practical concerns: In addition to these spiritual concerns, the Catholic Church strives to prepare engaged couples for the practicalities of marriage and family life. Attention to practical concerns is no small matter because it is in the details of the day to day that spouses live out the promises they first make to each other on their wedding day.

Growing in the understanding of one's self, of one's future spouse, and of one's relationship is essential. Knowing how to communicate effectively is one very practical skill that all spouses should develop. Effective communication involves listening patiently to the other person, expressing one's own views clearly, controlling one's emotions, and taking the other person's views seriously. Other important practicalities include managing family finances, relating to each other's families, and, should the couple be of child-bearing age, how to plan the size of their family using Natural Family Planning.

REFLECT AND DISCUSS
- Work in small groups.
- Brainstorm a detailed list of spiritual and practical habits, skills and resources that should be included in an immediate preparation for marriage.
- How would attending to these issues help a bride and bridegroom to profess and commit themselves to living their marriage promises?

WHAT ABOUT YOU PERSONALLY?
- Why is it vital that couples openly and honestly discuss their marriage and future hopes and dreams?
- What for you would be most important in preparing for marriage?

> **Knowing how to communicate effectively is one very practical skill that all spouses should develop**

LAST BUT NOT LEAST: PREPARING FOR THE CELEBRATION

We have emphasized the importance of preparing for a lifetime of marriage, but the couple must also take great care in preparing the wedding ceremony itself. The Church provides couples with both the support and the freedom to make their celebration of the sacrament a personal, meaningful event. For example, when the parish priest or marriage preparation team meets with the couple, they usually review together the prayers and readings that the couple can choose to include in the ceremony. The couple should put time into choosing what is most meaningful for them. As the big day approaches, couples are encouraged to receive the Sacrament of Reconciliation so they can be sure to enter into marriage in the state of sanctifying grace.

OVER TO YOU

- What do you feel you need to investigate further in order to better prepare yourself for marriage (if this be the vocation to which God calls you)?
- You can find more detailed information on Catholic teaching on marriage and marriage preparation programs on the website of the United States Conference of Catholic Bishops (*www.usccb.org*).

JOURNAL EXERCISE

- Think of what the vocation to the married life has come to mean to you.
- Identify some Scripture readings, prayers and hymns that you would include in your marriage celebration, and explain the reasons for your choices.

The Church provides couples with both the support and the freedom to make their celebration of the sacrament a personal, meaningful event

JUDGE AND ACT

REVIEW AND SHARE WHAT YOU HAVE LEARNED

Look back over this chapter and reflect on what you have learned about the preparation for and celebration of the Sacrament of Marriage. Share the teachings of the Catholic Church on these statements:

- ◉ The Catholic Church encourages Catholics to marry another Catholic.
- ◉ A sacramental marriage is a public act that requires a liturgical celebration.
- ◉ In the Latin Church the spouses are the ministers of the sacrament.
- ◉ Consent freely given by the spouses, lifelong, exclusive and faithful commitment, and openness to children are essential elements for a valid sacramental marriage.
- ◉ Those who wish to marry have a serious responsibility to prepare for their marriage.
- ◉ A mixed marriage and a marriage involving disparity of cult present unique challenges for spouses and their children.
- ◉ Spouses may limit the size of their family for just reasons.

OVER TO YOU

- ◉ What insights for living your Baptism right now have you received from studying this chapter?
- ◉ How will these insights help you prepare to respond to God's call to marriage, if this be your vocation?

LEARN BY EXAMPLE

Blessed Paul VI (1897–1978), Pope, "Humble and prophetic witness of love of Christ for his Church"

The Vatican website begins its profile of Giovanni Battista Montini by saying that his father was a lawyer, editor and "courageous promoter of social action." Giovanni, in his own way, learned well at home from his father's example. He was elected as pope on June 21, 1963, and took the name Paul VI after the great missionary and Apostle to the Gentiles. After becoming pope Paul VI's immediate task was to shepherd the Church through the Second Vatican Council, which St. John XXIII convened in 1962.

Paul VI would, as St. Paul did, travel extensively to proclaim the Gospel. Building on the social teachings of the Church, Paul VI promulgated the encyclical *Populorum Progessio* (*On the Development of Peoples*) in 1967 and the apostolic letter *Octogesima Adveniens* (*On the Eightieth Anniversary*) in 1971 to commemorate *Rerum Novarum* (*On Capital and Labor*), Pope Leo XIII's 1891 groundbreaking encyclical on social issues. These letters were followed by his apostolic exhortation *Evangelii Nuntiandi* (*Evangelization in the Modern World*) on December 8, 1975, which Pope Francis has described as the "greatest pastoral document that has ever been written."

The teaching of Blessed Paul VI that is perhaps most remembered is his 1968 encyclical *Humanae Vitae* (*On Human Life*). In this letter the Pope both extolled the beauty and joy of married life and also warned that marriage and family would suffer as the use of artificial contraception became widespread. The Pope wrote:

In humble obedience then to her voice, let Christian husbands and wives be mindful of their vocation to the Christian life, a vocation which, deriving from their Baptism, has been confirmed anew and made more explicit by the Sacrament of Matrimony. For by this sacrament they are strengthened and, one might almost say, consecrated to the faithful fulfillment of their duties. Thus will they realize to the full their calling and bear witness as becomes them, to Christ before the world. For the Lord has entrusted to them the task of making visible to men and women the holiness and joy of the law which united inseparably their love for one another and the cooperation they give to God's love, God who is the Author of human life.

—*Humanae Vitae*, no. 25

On October 19, 2014 at the Mass closing the 2014 Extraordinary General Assembly of the Synod of Bishops, Pope Francis declared Pope Paul VI to be a blessed of the Church. In his homily, he thanked Blessed Paul VI, saying, "Thank you, our dear and beloved Pope Paul VI! Thank you for your humble and prophetic witness of love for Christ and his Church!"

TALK IT OVER

- How does Blessed Paul VI's teaching on marriage describe the connection between God's love and conjugal love?
- How does this teaching deepen and clarify our understanding of married life as a vocation?
- How can young people bear witness "to Christ before the world" as a preparation for married life?

SHARE FAITH WITH FAMILY AND FRIENDS

- Do your relationships give authentic witness to the love of Christ? How might you give a clearer witness of that love?

JOURNAL EXERCISE

- Reflect on your relationships with other young people.
- Describe how respect for the human body guides you in living those relationships.
- How can your present relationships prepare you for the married life or for whatever vocation to which God calls you.

LEARN BY HEART

"Human life is sacred— all men must recognize that fact."

ST. JOHN XXIII

PRAYER REFLECTION

All pray the Sign of the Cross together.

LEADER
Loving and faithful God,
thank you for the learning and wisdom we have
received over these past days.
Bless us as we gather now in prayer
with the grace of your Holy Spirit.
May our knowledge about the Sacrament of
Marriage transform our lives into lives of love.
We ask this in the name of your Son, Christ Jesus.
ALL
Amen.

LEADER
Please form into groups of three or four. Look
over this list of readings from the New Testament
approved by the Church for the celebration of
the Sacrament of Marriage. Select and read one
or several of these passages. Reflect on what
the Word of God is saying to you about marriage
and family life, and decide how you can begin to
make that wisdom part of your life right now.

Matthew 5:1–12a
Matthew 5:13–16
Matthew 7:21, 24–29
Matthew 19:3–6
Matthew 22:35–40
Mark 10:6–9
John 2:1–11
John 15:9–12
John 15:12–16
John 17:20–26
Romans 8:31b–35, 37–39
Romans 12:1–2, 9–18
Romans 15:1b–3a, 5–7, 13
1 Corinthians 6:13c–15a, 17–20
1 Corinthians 12:31—13:8a
Ephesians 5:2a, 21–33
Philippians 4:4–9
Colossians 3:12–17
Hebrews 13: 1–4a, 5–6b
1 Peter 3:1–9

1 John 3:18–24
1 John 4:7–12
Revelation 19:1, 5–9a

*Invite a member from each group to share their
reading and reflection with the class.*

LEADER
We now turn to God in prayer.
Lord God, Creator and giver of all life,
we lift up our prayers in the name of your Son,
Jesus Christ.

READER
For the Church, that the whole faith community
may be built up by the marriages of the faithful,
we pray to the Lord.
ALL
Lord, hear our prayer.

READER
For married couples, that we may support them
to live their vows, we pray to the Lord.
ALL
Lord, hear our prayer.

READER
For our own parents, grandparents and married
friends, that God may renew in them the graces
of the Sacrament of Marriage so they may love
one another as Christ loves his Church, we pray
to the Lord.
ALL
Lord, hear our prayer.

READER
For all of us gathered here who are discerning
a possible vocation to marriage, that we may
devote ourselves to loving the people around us
and so prepare for a lifetime partnership of love,
we pray to the Lord.
ALL
Lord, hear our prayer.

READER

Let us now add our personal intentions in the quiet of our heart. (*Pause*)

ALL

Lord, hear our prayer.

LEADER

Loving God, maker of the whole world,
you created man and woman in your own image
and willed that their union in marriage be
crowned with your blessing.
We humbly beseech you as your servants,
who are discerning our vocations,
that you may shower your abundant blessings
upon us,
and may the power of your Holy Spirit set our
hearts aflame from on high,
so that, living out together the gift of the Spirit,
we may enrich the whole Church.
We ask this through Christ our Lord.

ALL

Amen.

Pray the Sign of the Cross together.

You created man and woman in your own image and willed that their union in marriage be crowned with your blessing

CHAPTER 7

Christian Marriage in Today's World

CHRISTIAN MARRIAGE IS . . .

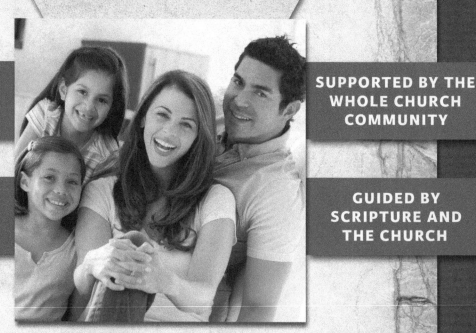

A UNIQUE AND LIFELONG VOCATION

SUPPORTED BY THE WHOLE CHURCH COMMUNITY

A SPIRITUAL JOURNEY

GUIDED BY SCRIPTURE AND THE CHURCH

GIFTED WITH UNIQUE GRACES FROM CHRIST

FOR CATHOLIC SPOUSES, LIVING THE PROMISES that they knowingly and freely make to each other before God and the Church is the path to salvation. The practices and laws of society today challenge marriage and family life. However, the graces of the Sacrament of Matrimony and the teachings of Scripture and the Catholic Church support Catholic spouses and families to confront those challenges.

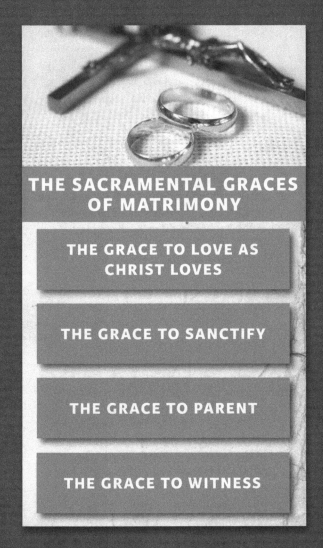

THE SACRAMENTAL GRACES OF MATRIMONY

THE GRACE TO LOVE AS CHRIST LOVES

THE GRACE TO SANCTIFY

THE GRACE TO PARENT

THE GRACE TO WITNESS

Faith Focus: These teachings of the Catholic Church are the primary focus of the doctrinal content presented in this chapter:
- A true marriage lasts as long as both parties are alive.
- Civil divorce does not end a valid sacramental marriage.
- Catholics who seek and receive a civil divorce and remarry without a declaration of nullity are still required to honor their sacramental marriage.
- The Catholic Church has the authority to issue a declaration of nullity, declaring that a valid and true sacramental marriage never took place.
- Catholics whose marriage has been declared to be invalid, that is, a true sacramental marriage never took place, are free to marry.

Discipleship Formation: As a result of studying this chapter and discovering the meaning of the faith of the Catholic Church for your life, you should be better able to:
- deepen your understanding of today's challenges to marriage and family life;
- support your parents in their efforts to live their marriage;
- recognize the negative impact of media images about marriage and sexual intimacy on your attitudes and behavior;
- develop those habits that will strengthen you to live the lifelong faithful commitment to Christian marriage, if that be your vocation.

Scripture References: These Scripture references are quoted or referred to in this chapter:
NEW TESTAMENT: **Matthew** 5:14–16, 19:1–9; **Mark** 10:1–12; **Acts of the Apostles** 11:14, 16:31, 18:8; **Romans** 15:2–6

Faith Glossary: Familiarize yourself with or recall the meaning of these key terms. Definitions are found in the Glossary: **annulment, declaration of nullity, divorce, fruits of the Holy Spirit, gifts of the Holy Spirit, scandal, separation**

Faith Words: annulment; divorce
Learn by Heart: Statement from *Pastoral Constitution on the Church in the Modern World*, no. 48
Learn by Example: St. Philip Howard

What challenges does a Christian marriage face today?

WHAT NOW? WHAT NEXT?

Kim and Felipe are sitting in their apartment. The honeymoon is over and their mood has changed; they're feeling a little down. All of the planning and preparation for their wedding paid off; everyone had a wonderful time. The newly married couple now find themselves with new questions: What now? What next?

OPENING REFLECTION

⊙ "What now?" and "What next?" are natural questions for newlyweds to ask. Have you ever asked yourself these same questions? What were the circumstances? How did you answer these questions?

⊙ Why do you think newlyweds might ask these questions after the excitement of the wedding celebration has ended? How might Kim and Felipe have answered these questions?

WHEN THE WEDDING DAY IS OVER

After the pre-wedding stress and the emotional high of the wedding day, post-wedding letdown is a common experience for couples who have focused so much of their energy on the wedding day. The reality of married life can catch them off guard. Couples who have engaged in pre-marriage preparation will be alert to such experiences and will be better able to move into the reality of married life with confidence.

We devote this final chapter on the Sacrament of Marriage to discussing some of the challenges to marriage and family life prevalent in contemporary society. In particular, we focus on how the sacramental graces, or effects, that Christ offers help couples who celebrate the Sacrament of Marriage to face those challenges.

TALK IT OVER

⊙ What challenges might you expect newlyweds to encounter in their first years of marriage?

⊙ What concerns and desires distract people from the true purpose of married and family life?

⊙ What blessings might married couples overlook if they become overwhelmed by the challenges they meet?

THE GRACES OF MARRIAGE

Christian couples best prepare for both the challenges and joys of marriage by reflecting on marriage as a unique Christian vocation through which they live their Baptism. Christ offers Christian married couples special graces to meet the universal vocation of all the baptized, which is to holiness of life, in a unique way. One of the graces of the Sacrament of Marriage is the grace to love unselfishly—with the *agape* that Christ manifested in the events of his life and Paschal Mystery. In addition to this grace, Christ offers the couple the graces to:

⊙ strengthen their commitment to live their lifelong, permanent union faithfully;

⊙ appreciate and be nourished by the joys of their union;

- live their marriage commitments in good times and bad;
- support each other as they strive for holiness of life on the way to eternal life;
- nurture their children, if so blessed, in faith and love;
- contribute to the good not only of their family, but also of the Church and society.

(*We will look at these effects of the sacrament in more detail in the next section of this chapter.*)

When seen in this light, the day to day of marriage takes on a spiritual significance. Couples who lose sight of this vision of marriage as a vocation might fall into thinking that married life is just a series of chores and obligations that contribute to their material well-being. Christian spouses who embrace a vocational understanding of their marriage come to recognize even mundane tasks, such as paying the rent or mortgage, putting gas in the car, preparing and cleaning up after meals, changing diapers and so on, to be opportunities to serve others and to grow in holiness of life.

LET'S PROBE DEEPER: A CLASS ACTIVITY

- Brainstorm a list of everyday tasks, obligations and chores that you would include as part of the *routine* of married and family life.

- Then discuss: Seen from a Christian vocation perspective, how can each of these activities serve as an opportunity to grow in love and holiness?

A VOCATION TO THE EVERYDAY

We do not respond to God's call to live as disciples of Jesus in one instant, once and for all. We respond to our vocation over the course of our lifetime. Most of our responses are not dramatic or extraordinary; they happen as part of the fabric of everyday life, as we go about our daily activities and interact with other people.

When a bride and groom affirm their marriage vows before God and the Christian community, they have only just begun to live out that vocation. Their "I do's" must be continually reinforced and deepened over the course of their lifetime, as they support each other on good and bad days, share responsibility for raising their children, look after each other in sickness as well as in health, and forgive each other's shortcomings.

When Christian spouses pray "give us this day our daily bread" in the Lord's Prayer, they might *intentionally* pray for the graces (the spiritual food) they need to nourish and strengthen them to live their marriage vocation one day at a time.

Hope, the Leaven of a Marriage

Young love needs to keep dancing towards the future with immense hope. Hope is the leaven that, in those first years of engagement and marriage, makes it possible to look beyond arguments, conflicts and problems and to see things in a broader perspective. It harnesses our uncertainties and concerns so that growth can take place. Hope also bids us live fully in the present, giving our all to the life of the family, for the best way to prepare a solid future is to live well in the present.
—Pope Francis, *The Joy of Love* (*Amoris Lætitia*), no. 219

Married love cannot deepen unless it faces and overcomes hard times and adversity.

In an address to more than twelve thousand engaged couples on February 15, 2014, Pope Francis offered a vision and some wisdom for their upcoming marriages. Among his many tips for making a marriage work, the Pope said:

"Marriage is also a daily job. We could even say it's like craftsmanship. In a way it's like being a goldsmith, because a husband makes his wife more of a woman, and she in turn should make her husband a better man. Growing together in their humanity, as man and woman."

"Love is something that comes about. It's a reality that grows. As an example, we could even say that it's like building a home. You build a home together, not alone."

"You can't base a marriage on feelings that come and go. But rather on the rock of true love, the love that comes from God."

"When we pray the 'Our Father' we say: Give us this day our daily Bread. When it comes to marriage, we can say: Give us this day, our daily love."

OVER TO YOU

- Is having a Christian understanding of marriage as a vocation likely to help spouses transition into their new life together? Why or why not?
- How can you respond to your baptismal vocation to love throughout your day today? How might this prepare you for married life should that be your personal vocation?

JOURNAL EXERCISE

- Keep a log of the family activities and interactions that occur within your home on a typical day.
- Observe the responsibilities and opportunities for love that come with being a spouse and parent and child.
- When you are finished, look over the activities and interactions and reflect on how each offered an opportunity to grow in holiness and loving service to God and to one another.
- Consider including such a reflection each evening in your prayers at bedtime.

The sacramental graces of Matrimony

AN IRRESISTIBLE MOMENT

It is a pleasant evening in Sabadell, Spain. The Plaza de Sant Roc is bustling with people enjoying an evening stroll or wrapping up the day's business before heading home for dinner. Amidst the crowds, a tall man stands motionless with his double bass in hand. A little girl drops a coin in his hat, and he begins to play. A woman with a cello soon walks out and begins playing alongside him . . . and then a bassoon and two violins and then several more. Pretty soon a full symphony has gathered, filling the plaza with Beethoven's "Ode to Joy" and as many people as can fit in between the buildings. Caught up in the beauty of the music and the joy of the moment, people in the crowd dance about and add their voices to the song.

OPENING REFLECTION

- What do you think it would have been like to be present for this moment?
- Have you ever been swept up in the moment by something beautiful or exciting? What was it like?
- When might such moments arise in the life of a married couple? In the life of a family?
- How might the married and family life of Christians have a similar impact outside their family?

FOREVER TRANSFORMED IN UNSELFISH LOVE

The lives of a man and woman are forever changed by their marrying in the Sacrament of Matrimony. They may look the same as they did before marrying; but, through the gift of the Holy Spirit, God the Father has bonded them to each other and to Jesus Christ. Having committing themselves to each other exclusively and inseparably, their love imitates God's love and "is caught up into divine love" (*Catechism of the Catholic Church* [CCC], no. 1639). Like the flash mob symphony sweeping up the crowd in their music in Plaza de Sant Roc, God's love draws married couples into a new joy that possesses their hearts.

In responding to their vocation and committing to this lifelong, permanent union through a life of selfless love (*agape*), a married couple grow not only in union with each other but also in their communion with God the Holy Trinity. In the Sacrament of Matrimony a couple encounter Jesus and welcome him into their relationship as they strive to love God, each other and their neighbor as Jesus commanded them. It is a transformation wrought by the couple's best efforts to cooperate with Christ's offer of grace and with the help of the whole church community.

This transformation of a couple's love bears fruit in their marriage in many ways. We will now explore four of the blessings or graces of

Jesus gave us a model of love, which was fully revealed in his dying for us

their union can bring to themselves and to all those whom they meet.

Jesus gave us a model of love, which was fully revealed in his dying for us. Gifted with the grace to love unselfishly in the Sacrament of Marriage, couples discover the joy to be found in committing themselves totally to each other.

TALK IT OVER
- What do you imagine would be difficult about sharing more than your belongings, home, money and time with someone for the rest of your life? About sharing your very self?
- How would loving as Jesus modeled enable a couple to grow in holiness of life and in love for each other as well as for others?
- What would help a couple to love in this way?
- What might make it difficult for them to love in this way?

THE GRACE TO SANCTIFY
A vocation to the married state of life goes well beyond the spouses helping each other with caring for the home, adapting to busy schedules, and so on. As with all vocations, God calls people to marriage so that in striving to grow in their love for each other they also grow in their love for God. The intimate love at the heart of the marriage relationship uniting a man and woman is a primary source of their living a life of holiness as they strive to attain eternal life.

Married life is a spiritual journey. It involves married couples sharing their lives as fully as possible in all they do. In the words of Pope Francis, "Marriage . . . is a friendship marked

the Sacrament of Marriage: the grace to love as Christ loves, the grace to sanctify, the grace to parent, and the grace to witness.

REFLECT AND DISCUSS
- How do you think marriage can bring a couple into a closer relationship with Jesus?
- How might that deepen their relationship with each other?
- What other aspects of a couple's relationship might be influenced by their relationship with Jesus?

THE GRACE TO LOVE AS CHRIST LOVES
At Baptism we are joined to Christ. When a baptized man and woman unite themselves in a sacramental marriage, the Spirit of Christ gives them the graces they need to love unselfishly— to love as Christ loves. The Sacrament of Matrimony gives them the grace to love each other with tender love, to act with humility toward each other, to bear each other's burdens, and to forgive each other when necessary. Making the love of Christ their own, the couple are better able to strengthen the permanent nature of their union and to appreciate the joy

by passion, but a passion always directed to an ever more stable and intense union" (*The Joy of Love*, no. 125). This sharing includes deepening their relationship not only with each other but also with the Holy Trinity. One challenge and blessing of marriage is forming a shared spirituality, or way of responding to the graces of the Holy Spirit. This includes rooting their lives in living the theological virtues and the **gifts of the Holy Spirit** and enriching their marriage with the **fruits of the Holy Spirit**. Together, spouses encourage each other to receive spiritual nourishment from the Church and her sacraments, especially through the regular celebration of the Eucharist.

The prayer life of spouses is also vital to a marriage. While it is healthy for spouses to set aside time to pray alone and deepen their personal relationship with the Holy Trinity, it is no less essential and vital for spouses to pray together. The shared prayer of spouses is one of the most transformative aspects of a marriage. It is indispensable for solidifying a couple's partnership with each other and with God, who has made them sharers in his very own life.

LETS PROBE DEEPER: A GROUP ACTIVITY

⊙ Take a poll to identify how each person in the class most likes to pray.

⊙ Discuss what might be difficult but also rewarding about sharing in the prayer life of another person who prays differently than you do.

THE GRACE TO PARENT

If you were to survey parents about their experiences of raising their children, you would likely hear one particular response repeated more than a few times: "It is the most challenging and most rewarding thing I have ever done." Whether spouses are blessed with children by procreation or adoption or foster parenting, children are among the greatest blessings of married life. Children open parents' eyes to many of life's wonders and teach their parents to love more than they ever thought they could.

There are few things more stressful for Christian parents than feeling that they failed in this responsibility, and few more rewarding than seeing their children embrace the faith of the Church, keep God at the center of their lives and commit to living as disciples of Jesus. God gives parents the grace to hand on their Catholic faith, as well as the consolation of knowing that, even if they fail to see this faith flourish, God is constantly nurturing the seeds of faith the Spirit has planted in their children. Christian parents encounter Christ in the Sacrament of Matrimony.

There are few things more rewarding for Christian parents than seeing their children embrace the faith of the Church

This mystery of Christ's love for his Church assures Christian parents that God is always present in their married life. God always offers them the graces they need to raise their children and nurture them in faith and love.

THINK, PAIR AND SHARE

⊙ Recall what you learned about the vocation of Christian parenthood in chapter 5.
⊙ How does the teaching of the Catholic Church on parenting give Christian parents a vision for living their vocation?
⊙ How does it support Christian parents in living their vocation day in and day out?

WHAT ABOUT YOU PERSONALLY?

⊙ What do you think would be the most challenging and most rewarding parts of being a parent?
⊙ Where can you recognize God working through your parents? In your family?

THE GRACE TO WITNESS

The Church has always recognized the unique role of married couples in the sanctifying and saving work of the Church.

From the beginning, the core of the Church was often constituted by those who had become believers "together with all [their] household" (Acts of the Apostles 18:8). When they were converted, they desired that "their whole household" should be saved. (See Acts of the Apostles 16:31; 11:14.) These families who became believers were islands of the Christian life in an unbelieving world.

—CCC, no. 1655

You will recall that the Sacrament of Marriage is one of the two Sacraments at the Service of Communion. By the graces God offers in the Sacrament of Matrimony, married couples become "centers of living, radiant faith" (CCC, no. 1656) within the community of the Church and within society. The graces of the sacrament enable them to be lights in the world (check out Matthew 5:14–16) by bearing witness to the love of God in the way that only spouses can. Married couples thus serve to sanctify and foster the good of the Church and society. The joint witness of married couples encourages others to "give glory to [their] Father in heaven" (Matthew 5:16). Catholics who marry outside the Sacrament of Marriage in a civil marriage are living in an objective state of sin; they may be a source of scandal for others.

TALK IT OVER

⊙ In light of your study of this section of the chapter, how important is the Sacrament of Matrimony to a Catholic married couple's ability to share their faith and love with their children? With their neighbors?

OVER TO YOU

⊙ How would you respond if a non-Catholic friend were to ask you, "Why does it matter whether Catholics marry in the Sacrament of Marriage?"

Working through contemporary challenges

SAVING THE DAY

In one episode of a popular television sitcom, the dad accidently kills his daughter's hamster. When he breaks the bad news to everyone, his wife insists that the family give the beloved pet a proper burial—eulogies and all—to help their daughter through the difficult moment. This all seems ridiculous to the dad, but he eventually realizes that his relationships with his wife and daughter are on the line and so he joins in the family ceremony—which turns out to be a profoundly emotional and healing experience.

OPENING REFLECTION

- ⊙ All families sometimes experience conflicts. How has your family dealt with those conflicts?
- ⊙ Has anyone in your church family, for example, your parish youth minister, been instrumental in helping you deal with any family conflict you may have experienced? Why did you turn to the Church?

CHALLENGES TO MARRIAGE AND FAMILY LIFE

Pope Francis reminds us that married and family life "is a journey full of challenges, difficult at times, and also with its conflicts, but that is life" (February 14, 2014). Family members can get on one another's nerves, finances can become pressured, and there can be a growing need for both parents to work outside the home. The graces of a sacramental marriage do not magically erase the reality of life's difficulties; but, as we have seen, these graces offer married couples the support to face those challenges and live out their commitments.

In addition to dealing with the challenges that arise within the daily routine of married and family life in the home, Christian married couples also have to deal with many challenges from the broader society that threaten the traditional values of Christian marriage and family life. Christian marriages and families are constantly bombarded with images and messages from the media which promote ways of living that are contrary to the Christian way of life.

Many of these challenges arise from widely accepted, popular practices, and at times the laws of society are contrary to the law of God, Scripture and the teachings of the Church. The prevalence of these social practices makes them *seem normal*; and, as a consequence, they can tempt Christians to abandon or dilute their commitment to faithful Christian living.

These values and practices include the legal efforts to redefine the very nature and meaning of marriage; the growing practice of cohabitation, homosexual unions and same sex marriages, and other free unions; the lack of willingness to be open to children for other than just reasons; the loss of respect for the sacredness and dignity of all human beings; and the objectification of the human person as a source of pleasure and profit. It is vital for us, therefore, to be aware of how these social structures have become part of the very fabric of society and contribute to the devaluation of Christian marriage and family life.

As more spouses are both working outside the home, more effort is needed to promote open and honest dialog that addresses issues as they occur

Christian married couples need to respond to the grace of God and meet these challenges head on. They need to be confident that the Holy Spirit enables them to face these challenges courageously with the vision and power of the Gospel. They need to be confident that their efforts are kneading the leaven of the Gospel into the dough of contemporary culture. These efforts will contribute to the gradual diminishing of the prevalence of these practices and the bringing about of the Kingdom of God.

TALK IT OVER

- ◉ What messages and images from popular media undermine the values of Christian marriage?
- ◉ How do you think such messages and images influence couples who are preparing for or living the married life?
- ◉ What other social challenges could create tension or spark conflict within married or family life?

CHALLENGES FROM WITHIN

Not all the challenges to marriage and family life have their roots outside the home. Many arise from the interpersonal dynamics of married and family life. Let's take a brief look at several of these challenges.

Financial and career success: Financial concerns and the impact of time spent away from home

due to work commitments are often cited as the main reasons for family discord and divorce. Many people's sense of self-worth and security is wrapped up in their finances and career. As more spouses are both working outside the home, more effort is needed to promote open and honest dialog that addresses issues as they occur; this is the surest road to healing conflicts concerning money and careers. Silence only leads to the festering of resentment and an increase in discord, and it even leads to divorce.

Parent–children relationships: The changing nature of the parent–child relationship in contemporary society is putting strain on married and family life. The natural authority of parents has been increasingly challenged in recent years. Recall the well-known case of the daughter who accused her parents of violating her rights to a college education and sued her parents for college tuition. Some parents try to be pals with their children, fearing that if they don't give in to their children's demands they may lose their *friendship* with them. Other parents shield their children from the challenges of life by overprotecting them; they quickly defend or excuse their children's lack of achievement in academics or athletics as the teacher's or coach's fault. Parents sometimes neglect to provide the strong adult guidance that their children need.

Remarriage and blended families: The number of blended families is continuously on the rise in our times. A blended family is a remarried couple and their children from a previous marriage. In the United States of America about 65 percent of remarriages involve children from a prior marriage. Given that over 50 percent of first marriages and 75 percent of second marriages end in a divorce, the blended family is becoming more and more common. Some estimate that the blended family will become the most common form of family life in the United States. Among the many challenges a blended family faces is the building of trust among the members of the new family, adapting to the dynamics within the new family, and addressing such common issues as fighting among siblings and stepparent–child conflict. Achieving these goals is often a slow and difficult process.

Extended, or multi-generational, families: The extended family usually includes two or more adults from different generations living in the same household. An extended family may include the immediate family (parents and children), grandparents, aunts, uncles and cousins who live in the same household or nearby. After World War II the United States of America slowly became a nation of people on the move into the suburbs. People today are more mobile than at any previous time in history. This means grown children are more likely to move far away from the family and place where they grew up.

The loss of extended family relationships deprives families of many blessings. These include the deepening of family identity through the passing on of family history and traditions; support of family life during times of sickness and economic hardship; sharing of wisdom in dealing with conflicts and challenges, and so on. Social media communication via Skype or Facetime is not a real substitute for face-to-face interpersonal sharing and companionship.

LET'S PROBE DEEPER: EXTENDED FAMILY PROFILES

⊙ Create a class profile of how many students live in an extended family.

⊙ In small groups share your experiences of extended family life. Discuss:
 – How often do you see grandparents, aunts, uncles and cousins?
 – Do you communicate when you are apart, and, if so, how?
 – Do you wish you could see one another more often?
 – What is nice about having extended family nearby?

OVER TO YOU

⊙ Has your understanding of the challenges and difficulties of contemporary married and family life increased? Give examples.

⊙ How can this increased understanding help you contribute to building a harmonious and healthy family life in your home?

⊙ Act on your insights!

> The extended family usually includes two or more adults from different generations living in the same household

Divorce, annulment and remarriage

A SHORT-TERM CONTRACT?

The tabloids feed on gossip surrounding the off-again/on-again married relationships of celebrities. The ease with which celebrities divorce and remarry reflects both the culture and civil law of the United States. Simply put, civil law has made it easy to divorce and remarry. All states offer a legal no-fault civil divorce. In a no-fault divorce, a spouse does not have to claim that the other spouse did anything wrong. Some states only require that the spouse seeking the divorce simply claims that the couple can no longer get along.

OPENING REFLECTION

- Are you surprised by the attention given to the breakup of celebrity marriages? Why or why not?
- What possible effect might reading about so many celebrity breakups and remarriages have on you and other young people?

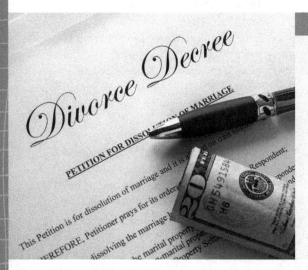

FAITH WORD

Divorce

The claim that the indissoluble marriage bond validly entered into between a man and a woman is broken. A civil dissolution of the marriage contract (divorce) does not free persons from a valid marriage before God; remarriage would not be morally licit.
—CCC, Glossary

GUIDANCE FOR MARITAL DIFFICULTIES

The reality is that marriage takes work. Married couples need to work at facing and dealing with conflicts that arise within their marriage; they need to communicate honestly and to seek lovingly to reconcile their differences. They need to work at the marriage "in good times and bad times." We have already discussed some of the challenges that married couples face today. Perhaps a married couple's financial situation gets dicey, or their careers conflict, or the original attraction to each other fades, or they discover they just do not have as much in common as they once thought.

Some couples find themselves in marital situations where *they feel* they simply cannot continue to live together. This is especially true where domestic and spousal violence, physical or verbal, is a reality. In such situations, living together is unsustainable and couples may separate.

Whatever the reason, many couples find themselves contemplating separating or seeking a civil divorce. The Catholic Church acknowledges these difficult situations and offers her wisdom on the issues of separation, divorce and remarriage.

The Good of Marriage

At a time when divorce and single-parent homes have become much more common, the benefits of marriage are becoming increasingly apparent. According to numerous studies, children raised by two married parents are physically and emotionally healthier, are more likely to attend college, are less likely to use drugs or abuse alcohol or commit delinquent behaviors, and have a decreased risk of divorcing when they get married. These findings in no way diminish the loving care and heroic sacrifices made by single parents, but the advantage is clear. A loving marriage provides the best foundation for a healthy family life.

TALK IT OVER

⦿ What is your understanding of the Catholic Church's teaching on civil divorce and separation?

⦿ What questions do you have about that teaching?

THE INDISSOLUBILITY OF MARRIAGE

Over 50 percent of spouses who enter marriage in the United States of America seek and obtain a civil divorce. The Catholic Church does not recognize that a civil divorce ends a marriage because no government has the authority to dissolve what divine law reveals to be indissoluble. Some Catholics see this teaching as unreasonable or harsh. In truth, it safeguards not only the couples' spiritual well-being but also the well-being of the family and of society as a whole.

In Matthew 19:1–9 Jesus clearly taught that marriage is for life and that divorce is contrary to divine law. He taught, you will recall, that the Law of Moses only permitted divorce because God's people had become "hard-hearted" (Matthew 19:8), and he declared, "Therefore, what God has joined together, let no one separate" (Matthew 19:6b). The love uniting spouses is to be a sign of God's faithful and never-ending love for us. God has promised to love us forever, in good times and bad times. God has proven that he does not break his promises; neither should we break our marital promises.

The Catholic Church has consistently held fast to this teaching of Jesus. Following the example of Jesus, the Church shows compassion for and supports the faithful who divorce. Difficult though it may be, spouses can still show love for God and each other by honoring Jesus' teaching and their marital promises when they no longer live together. This teaching and practice of the Church leaves open the possibility of reconciliation between spouses; it enables them to remain in full communion with the Church and to continue receiving the sacraments.

SEPARATION AND CIVIL DIVORCE

The Catholic Church has come to understand Jesus' teaching on divorce to mean that married couples, first and foremost, are to work to overcome the hardness of heart that can emerge and create a wall between spouses. (Check out Mark 10:1–12.) This teaching, however, does not command that spouses and their children continue to live in a dangerous or harmful marital situation.

The home may become a place where a spouse or children may suffer severe physical, mental and spiritual harm, where the safety of a spouse and children are at risk. In such situations, spouses may separate from living with each other and, if necessary, seek a civil divorce. On this point the Church teaches: "If civil divorce remains the only possible way of ensuring certain legal rights, the care of the children, or the protection of inheritance, it can be tolerated and does not constitute a moral offense" (CCC, no. 2383).

When couples united in the Sacrament of Marriage obtain a civil divorce, they change only their legal standing in the eyes of the state; the civil divorce does not undo the spiritual and sacramental covenant they have freely entered. If and when a civil divorce is obtained, the sacramental marriage still exists. The divorced spouses are still bound to fidelity to their marriage promises. They remain married in the eyes of God and the Church and therefore cannot remarry without obtaining a declaration of nullity, also known as an annulment, from the Church.

TALK IT OVER

⊙ How would you explain the difference between a civil marriage and a sacramental marriage?
⊙ What does the requirement to remain faithful to one's marriage vows even while separated or civilly divorced reveal about the Sacrament of Marriage?

⊙ How might such fidelity contribute to a person's growth in holiness?
⊙ What hope might such fidelity hold for the couple's reconciliation in the future? And how might it be beneficial to children of the couple?

DECLARATION OF NULLITY, OR ANNULMENT

In some cases it becomes evident after careful review of a marriage by a Church authority that one or more of the indispensable conditions for a true and valid marriage was not present at the time the spouses married. For example, the Church can declare that no true sacramental marriage occurred if one or both spouses (1) were too young or too immature to knowingly and freely consent to a lifetime commitment, or (2) were forced or coerced into a marriage, or (3) lacked the psychological capacity (for example, because of a mental disorder) to assume the essential obligations of marriage, or (4) were not open to raising children, or (5) the couple are blood relatives.

If any of these circumstances were present, the Church can issue a declaration of nullity and annul the marriage. When the Church issues a

HENRY VIII, WHO WAS REFUSED AN ANNULMENT BY POPE CLEMENT VII | HOLBEIN

FAITH WORD

Annulment (Declaration of Nullity of a Marriage)

The consent of the spouses entering into marriage must be a free act of the will, devoid of external or internal invalidating factors. If this freedom is absent, the marriage is invalid. For this reason, the Church, after an examination of the situation by a competent Church court, can declare the nullity of a marriage, i.e., that the sacramental marriage never existed. In this case, the contracting parties are free to marry, provided the natural obligations of the previous union are discharged.
—*United States Catholic Catechism for Adults (USCCA)* Glossary, 503–504

declaration of nullity, she declares that a true and valid marriage never existed, and the man and the woman are free to marry provided there are no other impediments to their marrying.

Divorce or separation can be a difficult and painful experience. Anger and a sense of betrayal are often experienced by spouses and children alike. Whatever the reason behind a marriage failing, we follow the example of Christ and are not to judge those whose marriages fail.

TALK IT OVER
- What is the difference between an annulment and a civil divorce?
- What wisdom do you see in the Catholic Church's efforts to encourage and support couples to reconcile and to work to heal their marriage?

WHAT ABOUT YOU PERSONALLY?
- What might you do personally to support a friend who shares with you that their parents are considering a divorce?

CATHOLICS WHO REMARRY WITHOUT A DECLARATION OF NULLITY
Due to the impact of popular cultural values in relation to divorce and remarriage, Catholics who divorce and remarry without a declaration of nullity may not anticipate or understand the consequences of their decision for both themselves and others. The Church calls them to honor the vows of the sacramental marriage as long as their spouse is alive. Divorced Catholics who remarry in a civil ceremony without a declaration of nullity are living in a state of objective sin. Their civil marriage is also a source of spiritual harm to them and a scandal for others.

Catholics who remarry without a declaration of nullity are not, as many believe, automatically excommunicated from the life of the Church. They remain members of the Church, but they cannot participate fully in the life of the Church. They may not receive the sacraments, including Holy Communion, except in danger of death, nor serve as a sponsor for Baptism or Confirmation.

Remarried Catholics have the responsibility to live out their Baptism. They are to give witness to their identity as children of God and brothers and sisters of Jesus Christ. They are to live the Gospel, attend Sunday Mass, and strive for holiness of life, "especially by educating their children in the faith" (CCC, no. 1665).

WALKING WITH THE WOUNDED
Pope Francis reminded us, as did his predecessors, of the Church's ministry with the members of the Church who divorce or separate. He taught, in part:

Although she constantly holds up the call to perfection, and asks for a fuller response to God, the Church must accompany with attention and care the weakest of her children, who show signs of a wounded and troubled love, by restoring in them hope and confidence, like the beacon of a lighthouse in a port or a torch carried among people to enlighten those who have lost their way or who are in the midst of a storm.
—*The Joy of Love*, no. 291

OVER TO YOU
- How does the teaching and discipline of the Catholic Church hold out hope and compassion for all Catholic couples, including those who separate or remarry without a declaration of nullity?

JUDGE AND ACT

REVIEW AND SHARE WHAT YOU HAVE LEARNED

Look back over this chapter and reflect on what you have learned about the Sacrament of Marriage. Share the teachings of the Catholic Church on these statements:

⊙ In God's plan, marriage is a lifelong faithful commitment between a man and a woman.

⊙ There are social practices and laws and popular contemporary values that are contrary to God's plan for marriage.

⊙ God always offers married couples the grace to address the many challenges of living their marriage partnership.

⊙ The love between spouses is an image of the unending aspect of God's love for us.

⊙ A civil divorce does not dissolve the indissoluble marriage validly entered into by a man and a woman.

⊙ The Church has the authority to declare a sacramental marriage to be null and void if she judges that the conditions required for a valid marriage have been lacking from the beginning of the marriage.

⊙ Catholics who remarry without a declaration of nullity may not participate fully in the life of the Church.

OVER TO YOU

⊙ What is the most valuable wisdom you have learned in this chapter about living out the vocation to marriage?

⊙ What efforts can you make right now so that you will be able to live a committed lifelong Christian marriage if you discern that God calls you to married life?

LEARN BY EXAMPLE

Saint Philip Howard (1557–95), English nobleman, husband and martyr

St. Philip Howard's life gives witness to marriage as a path to salvation and holiness. The story of this nobleman, husband and saint, who was canonized by Blessed Pope Paul VI in 1979, points to the difficulties and challenges that can arise from entering into a marriage for the wrong reasons and the personal transformation that can come about through God's grace.

Philip did not marry freely. His father prearranged his marriage, as was customary, giving Philip no say in the matter. It perhaps comes as little surprise, then, that Philip did not pay much attention to his wife, Anne, during the early part of their marriage.

During the course of their marriage Anne converted to Catholicism and became a generous benefactor of many priests in the area. Her generosity conflicted with Philip's excessive concern for worldly gain. This Twelfth Earl of Arundel spent much of his time away from Anne at Queen Elizabeth's court, fixated entirely on improving his status. Ironically, it was during his time at the queen's court that Philip began to turn away from his "worldly" desires.

In 1581 Philip witnessed a debate between Protestant theologians and the Jesuit priest St. Edmund Campion. While listening attentively to Campion's eloquent argument in defense of the Catholic faith, Philip began to have a change of heart. At last he recognized the beauty of his wife's faith and all that she had done for him. Philip became a devoted husband and, in 1584, he professed his faith in the Catholic Church.

It may have been Edmund Campion who planted the seed, but it was Anne who nurtured Philip's faith. He was arrested and detained in the Tower of London and martyred for his Catholic faith on October 19, 1595. He professed his devotion to Christ and to his wife Anne until the end.

TALK IT OVER

⊙ What role did Philip's wife's faith in Christ and devotion to Philip play in their married life?
⊙ What lessons can we learn from the marriage of Philip and Anne?

SHARE FAITH WITH FAMILY AND FRIENDS

⊙ How does our Christian faith support and guide us in striving for holiness in married and family life?
⊙ How does the Catholic Church support and guide us in striving for holiness in married and family life?

HOW WOULD YOU RESPOND?

You are at dinner with your family. Your older brother, a senior in college, has come home on a weekend visit and a classmate has joined him. The conversation begins to center around a celebrity couple, whose divorce the media has been covering for days. Your brother's classmate remarks, "Just as people fall in love, they also fall out of love. Isn't a failed marriage just a regular part of life?"

⊙ Using what you have learned in your study of marriage, what would you say to respond to your brother's classmate's remark?
⊙ Share responses as a class.

JOURNAL EXERCISE

⊙ What do you experience as the greatest difficulties of family life?
⊙ How do your experiences of interacting with your peers help you to foster unity in your family now? How are these experiences preparing you for married and family life in the future?

LEARN BY HEART

"Authentic married love is caught up into divine love."

VATICAN II, *PASTORAL CONSTITUTION ON THE CHURCH IN THE MODERN WORLD*, NO. 48

PRAYER REFLECTION

All pray the Sign of the Cross together.

LEADER

Loving God, send your Spirit upon us.
Strengthen us by your grace
so that we may boldly face the challenges
and gratefully welcome the joys
of responding to Jesus' invitation to love
in all our relationships now
and so prepare well for all future relationships,
in particular for marriage if that be the vocation
to which you will call us.

ALL

Amen.

READER

A reading from the Letter of St. Paul to the
Romans.
Proclaim Romans 15:2–6.
The word of the Lord.

ALL

Thanks be to God.

LEADER

Let us pause and reflect on how we can "glorify
God" in all our relationships. (*Pause*)

Loving God, in your Son you have given us a
perfect example of selfless love.
Give us the gifts of charity, patience and humility
so that we can bear the challenges of our present
relationships and love one another by sharing the
love with which you love us.

ALL

Amen.

LEADER

I invite you to form into groups of three and
discuss the gifts from God that you most desire
to help you in your present relationships.

Students form groups and share their thoughts.

LEADER

Let us now bring our prayers before God. Please
respond, "Loving God, bless us" to each petition.

THE SERMON ON THE MOUNT | JORISKERK, ANTWERP, BELGIUM

READER
For the gift of discernment, we pray:
ALL
Loving God, bless us.

READER
For the grace to love unselfishly, we pray:
ALL
Loving God, bless us.

READER
For the grace to remain faithful in all our
relationships, we pray:
ALL
Loving God, bless us.

READER
For the grace to grow in holiness as disciples of
Jesus, we pray:
ALL
Loving God, bless us.

READER
For the grace to be good models of Christian faith
to others, we pray:
ALL
Loving God, bless us.

READER
For the grace to build up the Church and the
common good of society, we pray:
ALL
Loving God, bless us.

LEADER
I invite all who wish to add their own petitions to
do so now.

Students add their own petitions.

LEADER
God, you are always faithful in your love for us.
You know our needs better than we know them
ourselves.
Stay always by our side and in our hearts,
and guide us in the way of holiness that leads to
true peace and fulfillment.
We pray this in the name of your Son, Jesus.
ALL
Amen.

Pray the Sign of the Cross together.

CHAPTER 8

Ordained to Serve the Communion of the Church

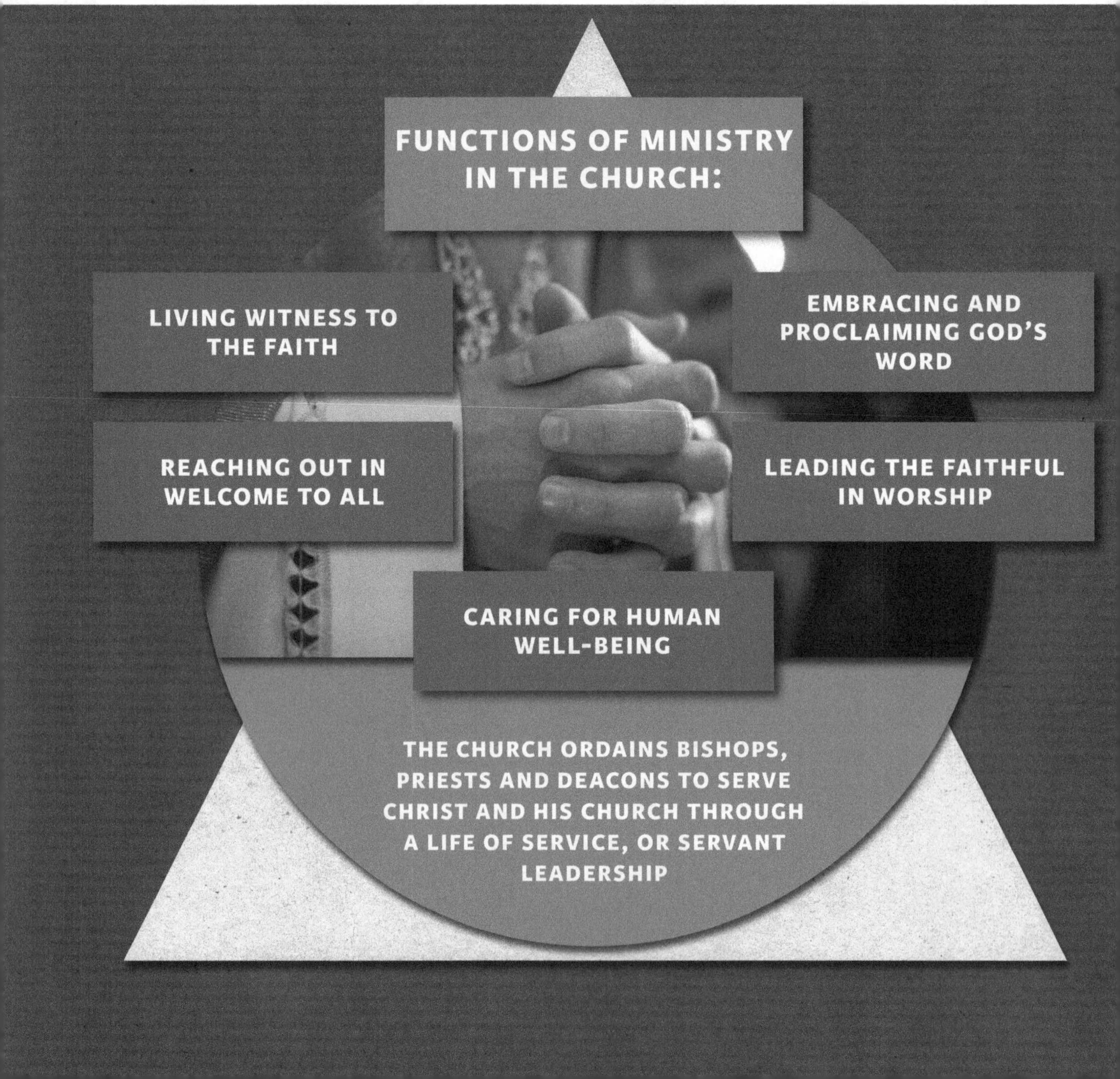

FUNCTIONS OF MINISTRY IN THE CHURCH:

LIVING WITNESS TO THE FAITH

EMBRACING AND PROCLAIMING GOD'S WORD

REACHING OUT IN WELCOME TO ALL

LEADING THE FAITHFUL IN WORSHIP

CARING FOR HUMAN WELL-BEING

THE CHURCH ORDAINS BISHOPS, PRIESTS AND DEACONS TO SERVE CHRIST AND HIS CHURCH THROUGH A LIFE OF SERVICE, OR SERVANT LEADERSHIP

A BAPTIZED MAN BECOMES A MEMBER OF THE ORDER OF bishops, the order of priests or the order of deacons through the Sacrament of Holy Orders. Each of these three degrees of Holy Orders shares, in its own way, in the hierarchy's threefold office of teaching, sanctifying and governing the faithful. Through the graces of this sacrament, ordained members of the faithful become living signs of Christ the Priest, Prophet and King. They are made instruments of Christ's continued saving and sanctifying presence and priestly action in, through and with his Church.

THE THREE DEGREES OF HOLY ORDERS:

ORDER OF BISHOPS

ORDER OF PRIESTS

ORDER OF DEACONS

THE MINISTRY OF DEACONS IS ONE OF COMPASSION AND JUSTICE

THE CHURCH ORDAINS DEACONS TO BE OF SERVICE TO BISHOPS AND PRIESTS

Faith Focus: These teachings of the Catholic Church are the primary focus of the doctrinal content presented in this chapter:

⊙ All the faithful are called to a life of selfless service to God and the Church.
⊙ Holy Orders is one of the two Sacraments at the Service of Communion in the Church.
⊙ Jesus Christ instituted the Sacrament of Holy Orders at the Last Supper.
⊙ Jesus chose the Apostles to be the first servant leaders of his Church on earth.
⊙ There are three degrees of Holy Orders: bishops, priests and deacons.
⊙ The essential elements of the sacramental celebration of each order are the laying on of hands and the consecratory prayer.
⊙ Those ordained are marked with a permanent seal, or indelible spiritual character.
⊙ There are two ways of living the diaconate: as a transitional deacon or as a permanent deacon.
⊙ The Church ordains deacons to be of service to bishops and priests.

Discipleship Formation: As a result of studying this chapter and discovering the meaning of the faith of the Catholic Church for your life, you should be better able to:

⊙ discover and put to use your own personal leadership characteristics;
⊙ deepen your commitment to a life of selfless service to God and others;
⊙ join with others to build up the Church, the *communio*, or community, of the disciples of Jesus Christ;
⊙ see the ministry of deacons as a model for your own participation in the life of the Church.

Scripture References: These Scripture references are quoted or referred to in this chapter:
OLD TESTAMENT: **Isaiah** 42:1–7, 49:1–6, 50:4–11, 52:13—53:12
NEW TESTAMENT: **Matthew** 23:1–12, 25:31–46, 28:16–20; **Mark** 1:16–20, 6:7–13, 9:35, 10:41–45, 15:40–41; **Luke** 6:12–16, 22:24–30; **John** 11:1–44, 13:1–16, **Acts of the Apostles** 1:12–14, 2:1–4 and 14–36, 6:1–7, 16:14–15; **Romans** 12:3–8; **Ephesians** 6:21; **Philippians** 1:1; **Colossians** 4:7; **1 Timothy** 3:8–10 and 12–13, 4:11–16

Faith Glossary: Familiarize yourself with or recall the meaning of these key terms. Definitions are found in the Glossary: **Apostle, bishop, catechesis, deacon, Eastern Catholic Churches, evangelization, Holy Orders, laying on of hands, Magisterium, priest, Sacraments at the Service of Communion, Sacred Chrism, Western Church (Latin Church)**

Faith Words: Holy Orders; deacons; laying on of hands
Learn by Heart: Mark 9:35
Learn by Example: St. Ephrem

What makes a good and effective leader?

LEADERSHIP IN ACTION

The U.S.A. women's soccer team won the 1999 World Cup. The championship game against China was a hard-fought thriller played in front of a packed stadium and before a huge television audience. Coach Tony DiCicco pointed out that what made the team a champion was the example of the team's leaders both *on and off* the field. The team *became* a team off the field. The team's superstars and other leaders were always the first to take on jobs for the good of the team. For example, unloading equipment from the team bus after a late-night arrival at the hotel was not a chore the superstars delegated to younger or less-famous teammates. These team leaders, no matter how tired, were always the first to get to work and lead by example by serving the good of the whole team.

OPENING REFLECTION

⊙ What qualities do you think make for an effective leader?

⊙ Skipping false humility, what qualities do *you* have for leadership?

⊙ What leader do you admire in the world today? Why?

⊙ What leadership qualities do you admire in church leaders? How are church leaders building up the Church by serving the faithful? Give examples from your own experience.

JESUS CHOOSES HIS CHURCH'S FIRST LEADERS

Jesus, at the very beginning of his public ministry, began to call disciples to accompany him, saying, "Follow me." (Check out Mark 1:16–20.) Eventually, he chose twelve disciples, "whom he also named apostles" (Luke 6:13), to be his closest companions and leaders among all his disciples. Luke wrote:

Now during those days [Jesus] went out to the mountain to pray; and he spent the night in prayer to God. And when day came, he called his disciples and chose twelve of them, whom he also named apostles: Simon, whom he named Peter, and his brother Andrew, and James, and John, and Philip, and Bartholomew, and Matthew, and Thomas, and James son of Alphaeus, and Simon, who was called the Zealot, and Judas son of James, and Judas Iscariot, who became a traitor.

—Luke 6:12–16

The word "apostle" comes from the Greek *apostellein*, which means "to send forth" (*Dictionary of the Bible*, 46). After the Resurrection, the risen and glorified Christ gave the **Apostles** a share in his authority and sent them forth to announce the Gospel and make disciples of all nations. Matthew wrote:

Now the eleven disciples went to Galilee, to the mountain to which Jesus had directed them. When they saw him, they worshiped him; but some doubted. And Jesus came and said to them, "All authority in heaven and on earth has been given to me. Go therefore and make disciples of all nations, baptizing them in the name of the Father and of the Son and of the Holy Spirit, and teaching them to obey everything that I have commanded you. And remember, I am with you always, to the end of the age."

—Matthew 28:16–20

This work, the work of **evangelization**, is the primary work of the Church.

READ, REFLECT AND SHARE

- ⊙ Work with a partner. Read and reflect on Luke 6:12–16.
- ⊙ Why might Jesus have prayed all night about his decision to choose the Twelve Apostles?
- ⊙ What do you imagine Jesus saw in the Twelve that led him to choose them to become leaders for his community of disciples?

JESUS INSTITUTES THE SACRAMENT OF HOLY ORDERS

At the Last Supper Jesus instituted the Sacrament of the Eucharist and the Sacrament of **Holy Orders**. These two sacraments are signs of his abiding presence and priestly action in the Church. Holy Orders, as you have already learned, is one of the two **Sacraments at the Service of Communion**. The word "orders," which the Church uses to name this sacrament, comes from the Latin verb *ordinare*, literally "to put in order." The Romans used the verb *ordinare* to designate the acts of governing and organizing of the Roman Empire.

As the Church grew, the Apostles and their successors ordained priests as their co-workers. They also ordained deacons to assist the Apostles, their successors and priests in serving the material needs of the community (Acts of the Apostles 6:1–7). Since apostolic times the Church has ordained, or conferred, the Sacrament of Holy Orders on baptized men to govern and organize the whole community of Jesus' disciples as **bishops**, **priests** and **deacons** to serve Christ and his Church through a life of service, or servant leadership.

FAITH WORD

Holy Orders

The Sacrament in which a bishop ordains a [baptized] man to be conformed to Jesus Christ by grace, to service and leadership in the Church. A man can be ordained a deacon, priest, or bishop. Through this Sacrament, the mission entrusted by Christ to his Apostles continues to be exercised in the Church. The Sacrament confers a permanent mark or character on the one who receives it.

—*United States Catholic Catechism for Adults* (USCCA), Glossary, 514–15

> Through the ordained ministry, especially that of bishops and priests, the presence of Christ as head of the Church is made visible in the midst of the community of believers.
>
> *CATECHISM OF THE CATHOLIC CHURCH [CCC], NO. 1549*

SERVANT LEADERSHIP—NO EASY CALLING

The vocation to serve the Church in the state of life of Holy Orders is no easy calling. Being a *servant* requires those who are ordained to live a life of self-sacrificing love, or *agape*, of God and others. The model for living such a life, of course, is Jesus Christ, the Suffering Servant Messiah. Jesus taught his Apostles that as he served they also were to serve.

On one occasion, when the Apostles were arguing among themselves as to who would be the "first" among them, Jesus responded by declaring that servant leadership was at the heart of their calling as Apostles.

When the ten heard this, they began to be angry with James and John. So Jesus called them and said to them, "You know that among the Gentiles those whom they recognize as their rulers lord it over them, and their great ones are tyrants over them. But it is not so among you; but whoever wishes to become great among you must be your servant, and whoever wishes to be first among you must be slave of all. For the Son of Man came not to be served but to serve, and to give his life a ransom for many."

—Mark 10:41–45

Jesus called James, John and others to a form of leadership within his Church that required serving others. The disciples were not to "lord it over" others or act as "tyrants." The servant leadership that Jesus demanded of his disciples was contrary to the prevalent understanding of leadership among the Gentiles in Jesus' time, as it sometimes is in our own times. The servant leadership that Jesus demanded of his Apostles should not have been unexpected; for it is rooted deep in the tradition of Ancient Israel.

LET'S PROBE DEEPER: A SCRIPTURE ACTIVITY

- ⊙ The prophet Isaiah described the Messiah whom God promised to send to save his people as a suffering servant.
- ⊙ Check out the suffering servant songs in Isaiah 42:1–7, 49:1–6, 50:4–11 and 52:13—53:12.
- ⊙ What commitment do these songs ask of bishops, priests and deacons and all in leadership roles in the Church?
- ⊙ Share your reflections as a class.

JOURNAL EXERCISE

- ⊙ Reflect on the qualities of leadership that you identified in the "Opening Reflection."
- ⊙ Compare and contrast those qualities with the qualities of leadership in Matthew 23:1–12, Mark 6:7–13, Luke 22:24–30, John 13:1–16, Romans 12:3–8 and 1 Timothy 4:11–16.
- ⊙ Describe why servant leaders build up and foster the good of the Church.
- ⊙ Spend some time thinking about how you will incorporate what you have learned from this section into your own life now. Write a summary of your intentions.

A Church in need of servant leaders

MARIAN HOUSE SOUP KITCHEN

As a young priest, Fr. Steve started sharing his food with a homeless man who sometimes visited his rectory. After a little while the man began to bring a few friends with him. As word spread, Fr. Steve quickly found that he had more dinner guests than he could cook for by himself. So he invited some parishioners to donate food and help prepare and serve meals. Soon these parish meals moved out of the rectory and eventually led to the founding of the Marian House soup kitchen and the Bijou hospitality house in Colorado Springs.

OPENING REFLECTION

- ⊙ Why did Fr. Steve's serving others require additional "servants"?
- ⊙ How does what Fr. Steve did give witness to the servant leadership that Jesus preached?
- ⊙ Who in your parish community gives witness to the servant leadership modeled by Fr. Steve?
- ⊙ What opportunities might you have to participate in the Church's mission and ministries of serving others? How might you respond?

HEAL THE WOUNDS! WARM THE HEARTS!

"The thing the church needs most today is the ability to heal wounds and to warm the hearts of the faithful; it needs nearness, proximity. I see the church as a field hospital after battle. It is useless to ask a seriously injured person if he has high cholesterol and about the level of his blood sugars! You have to heal his wounds. Then we can talk about everything else. Heal the wounds, heal the wounds. . . . And you have to start from the ground up."

—Pope Francis, in an interview for *America* magazine, September 19, 2013

CHURCH AS SACRAMENT OF GOD'S REIGN

The Church has the divine calling to heal the spiritual and bodily wounds of people. Vatican Council II reminded us: "The church, in Christ, is a sacrament—a sign and instrument, that is, of communion with God and of the unity of the entire human race" (*Dogmatic Constitution on the Church [Lumen Gentium]*, no. 1). All the faithful are anointed with **Sacred Chrism** at their Baptism. This anointing signifies their vocation to take part in the saving, healing and sanctifying work of Christ the Priest, Prophet and King, according to their state of life in the Church.

What is the nature of this work of the Church? Pope Francis' image of the Church as a "field hospital" gives us some insight into this teaching. The Church is a sacrament bringing about the Reign of God by healing people's wounds. She is "the community of the faithful on earth under the leadership of the Pope, the common Head, and of the bishops in communion with him.

They are the Church" (St. John Paul II, Apostolic Exhortation, *Lay Members of Christ's Faithful People*, no. 9, quoting Pope Pius XII; quoted in *Catechism of the Catholic Church* [CCC], no. 899). She is an effective agent of God's saving and healing work in the world.

Joined to Christ, the Head of the Church, all the faithful are to work to bring about justice, compassion and fullness of life for all. All the faithful, both men and women, are called to a life of service to the Church and to society.

WOMEN AND MEN SERVED THE EARLY CHURCH

Men and women have always played a major role in carrying on the servant ministry of Jesus Christ. The New Testament is very clear that both men and women were among the first disciples of Jesus. Jesus welcomed women, such as Mary Magdalene and the sisters Martha and Mary, into his inner core of disciples. All three synoptic Gospels record that women disciples traveled with Jesus, as the Twelve did, throughout his public life and ministry. Along with the beloved disciple, these women were faithful to Jesus from the beginning to the very end, accompanying and remaining with him during his Passion and Crucifixion.

After the Resurrection and Ascension, women disciples of Jesus along with men continued to have a significant role in the life of the churches that the Apostles had established. The Acts of the Apostles notes that there were "certain women including Mary the mother of Jesus" among about one hundred and twenty disciples who waited for the coming of the Holy Spirit in an upper room in Jerusalem. (Check out Acts of the Apostles 1:12–14.) Then, on that Pentecost, *all present* "were filled with the Holy Spirit." (Check out Acts of the Apostles 2:1–4.) From that great launching of the Church to take up the work that Christ handed on to the Apostles, both men and women have been empowered by the Holy Spirit to carry forth Jesus' ministry to the world. (Check out Acts of the Apostles 16:14–15.)

In the final chapter of his letter to the Church in Rome, St. Paul gave particular evidence of the role of women in the Church there. He wrote, in part:

I commend to you Phoebe our sister, who is [also] a minister of the church at Cenchreae, that you may receive her in the Lord in a manner worthy of the holy ones, and help her in whatever she may need from you, for she has been a benefactor to many and to me as well.

PENTECOST (TRIPTYCH) | ST. JOHN'S CHURCH, MECHELEN, BELGIUM

Greet Prisca and Aquila, my co-workers in Christ Jesus, who risked their necks for my life, to whom not only I am grateful but also all the churches of the Gentiles; greet also the church at their house. Greet my beloved Epaenetus, who was the first fruits in Asia for Christ. Greet Mary, who has worked hard for you. Greet Andronicus and Junia, my relatives and my fellow prisoners; they are prominent among the apostles and they were in Christ before me.

—Romans 16:1–7 (*New American Bible [NAB]*)

Holding up the example of these women whose service contributed to building up the early Church, Pope Francis wrote: "We need to create still broader opportunities for a more incisive female presence in the Church" and "recognize more fully what this entails with regard to the possible role of women in decision-making in different areas of the Church's life" (*The Joy of the Gospel [Evangelii Gaudium]*, nos. 103 and 104).

WHAT ABOUT YOU PERSONALLY?

- ⊙ Read Mark 15:40–41. What does this Scripture passage teach about the role of women in the public ministry of Jesus?
- ⊙ Name some of the women who have played a significant role in your journey of faith.
- ⊙ Has these women's faith in Christ and service to the Church inspired you to live your baptismal anointing? Explain.

FUNCTIONS OF MINISTRY IN THE CHURCH

Many ministries of the faithful serve the communion of the Church and foster unity among all peoples. All these ministries of service share five common characteristics or functions: "Witness," "Welcome," "Word," "Worship," and "Well-being."

Witness: Giving witness requires Christians, personally and as a community of Jesus' disciples, to give living example to their faith, hope and love. We are to walk the walk and not just talk the talk. The New Testament word for witness is *marturia*, which is translated "martyr." Though you will not likely be called upon to die physically for your faith, all disciples of Christ are to die to themselves and live a life of self-sacrificing love

JESUS AND THE SAMARITAN WOMAN | ST- SULPICE- DE- FAVIÈRES, PARIS, FRANCE

for God and other people. There is no greater service that we can render.

- ⊙ What are some effective ways that young people today can fulfill their ministry of Christian witness?

Welcome: The risen Christ instructed his disciples to "go therefore and make disciples of all nations, baptizing them in the name of the Father and of the Son and of the Holy Spirit" (Matthew 28:19). The lives of all the baptized are to reflect this "catholic" nature of service. The word "catholic," as you may recall, comes from two Greek terms, *katha holos*, which can be translated as *universal in welcoming all*. The Church reaches out in service to all people and invites all to become members of the Body of Christ.

- ⊙ How can you be truly "catholic" in your own practice of the faith of the Church?

Word: The primary mission of the Church is to proclaim Jesus Christ, the Incarnate Word of God. Guided by the Holy Spirit and the **Magisterium** of the Church, all the faithful, according to their state of life in the Church, are to proclaim, in both word and deed, Christ and his teachings. The Church is to teach through word and example the Divine Revelation that comes to us through Scripture and Christian Tradition. As Pope Francis

How do you practice works of mercy, justice and reconciliation in your life now?

exhorts all Christians, we are to share "the joy of the Gospel" with others.

⊙ How can you embrace God's word revealed in Scripture and Tradition? How can you share it with joy?

Worship: The Eucharist and other sacraments are vital to the Christian life. The Church carries out her ministry of serving the Church through her celebration of the liturgy, especially the celebration of the Seven Sacraments. The Second Vatican Council declared that "all the faithful should be led to take that full, conscious, and active part in liturgical celebrations which is demanded by the very nature of the liturgy" (*Constitution on the Sacred Liturgy [Sacrosanctum Concilium]*, no. 14). In other words, we must engage in the liturgy as active participants; this is particularly true when we join together in celebrating Mass.

⊙ On a scale of 1 (lowest) to 10 (highest), how do you score your own participation in Sunday Mass? How might you make it more active and "fully conscious"?

Well-being: From the beginning, imitating the example of Jesus, the Church has recognized

serving others to include all forms of human need—spiritual, psychological and material. In addition to doing the corporal and spiritual works of mercy on a personal level, caring for human well-being demands of Christians the works of mercy, justice and reconciliation.

⊙ How do you practice works of mercy, justice and reconciliation in your life now? How can you grow in these works of service?

A GROWING CHURCH IN NEED OF SERVANT LEADERS

The Apostles, the first bishops of the Church, served as the first pastors and leaders of the Church. But as the Church and her needs grew, so did the expanse of the ministry of the Apostles, and there was a need for the Apostles to have others to join with them in their ministry. The New Testament letters and the Acts of the Apostles describe this growing need and the Apostles' response to it.

The Pentecost story in Acts of the Apostles 2:14–36 attests that St. Peter was the leader and first among the Apostles. The Acts of the Apostles tells us (as do some of the letters of St. Paul) that the Church gathered, usually in the home of one of her members, to listen to the *teachings of the Apostles* and celebrate the Eucharist. The members would also collect funds to distribute to the needy among them. Empowered by the Holy Spirit, the Apostles and their companions, along with other disciples, undertook the work the risen Christ had commissioned them to do.

These writings also recount the Apostles' need for co-workers. The New Testament attests to the Apostles sharing their ministry with bishops (*episcopoi*), with priests (*presbyteroi*) and with deacons (*diakonoi*). This gave rise within the Church to the Order of Bishops, the Order of Priests and the Order of Deacons. As she grew in her understanding of her mission and authority, the Church reserved the Sacrament of Holy Orders for baptized men. This discipline was made not because there was any question regarding the ability of women to carry out the functions of ministry—life in the early Church had made women's abilities very clear.

In his Apostolic Letter *The Dignity of Women* (*Mulieris Dignitatem*), St. John Paul II wrote:

In the history of the Church, even from earliest times, there were side-by-side with men a number of women, for whom the response of the Bride to the Bridegroom's redemptive love acquired full expressive force. First we see those women who had personally encountered Christ and followed him. . . . (no. 27§3)

The same thing is repeated down the centuries, from one generation to the next, as *the history of the Church* demonstrates. . . . (no. 27§4)

The witness and the achievements of Christian women have had a significant impact on the life of the Church as well as of society. Even in the face of serious social discrimination, holy women have acted "freely," strengthened by their union with Christ. Such union and freedom rooted in God explain, for example, the great work of Saint Catherine of Siena in the life of the Church, and the work of Saint Teresa of Jesus in the monastic life. (no. 27§6)

In our own days too the Church is constantly enriched by the witness of the many women who fulfill their vocation to holiness. Holy women are an incarnation of the feminine ideal; they are also a model for all Christians, a model of the "sequela Christi," an example of how the Bride must respond with love to the love of the Bridegroom. (no. 27§7)

Rather, it was a matter of being faithful to what the Church came to understand to be the model that Christ had established.

The Lord Jesus chose men (*viri*) to form the college of the twelve apostles, and the apostles did the same when they chose collaborators to succeed them in their ministry. The college of bishops, with whom the priests are united in the priesthood, makes the college of the twelve an ever-present and ever-active reality until Christ's return. The Church recognizes herself to be bound by this choice made by the Lord himself. For this reason the ordination of women is not possible.

—CCC, no. 1577

THINK, PAIR AND SHARE
⊙ What problems did the growing Church face?
⊙ How does the Church today welcome all the faithful into servant-leadership roles?

OVER TO YOU
⊙ How do the functions of ministry listed above enrich your own understanding of the Church as Servant? Of your role within the Church?
⊙ How might you help the whole Body of Christ, the Church, to be an effective servant to all?

In the next two sections of this chapter we will take a closer look at the vocation of ordained deacons. In chapter 9 we will explore the teaching of the Catholic Church on the vocation and ministry of bishops and priests.

ST. PETER AND THE VIRGIN MARY | NOTRE DAME DU SABLON, BRUSSELS, BELGIUM

Deacons as ministers of God's compassion and justice

WE'RE ALL IN THIS TOGETHER

Deacon Jim had served his parish community faithfully for many years. Now he was facing a life-threatening illness and a hazardous operation. At the end of his homily, he shared his anxiety and asked for his parishioners' prayers. At the conclusion of the Prayer of the Faithful the priest celebrant called Jim to come to the front of the altar. He invited all the worshipers to stand and extend their hands toward Deacon Jim, as he led a prayer for him. The people followed with lengthy applause to express their appreciation for and solidarity with Deacon Jim. He responded, "I have tried to be your good deacon; now you have all been like a community of deacons to me."

MASS IN THE CATHEDRAL OF NOTRE DAME, STRASBOURG, FRANCE

OPENING REFLECTION

⊙ Do you know any deacons? Is there a deacon who serves your parish or school community? What ministries do you see him doing?

⊙ How does his serving you and others inspire you to live out your own calling to Christian service?

THE ORIGIN OF THE ORDER OF DEACONS

Take a moment and read Acts of the Apostles 6:1–7. This passage from Acts affirms the ministry of deacons in the early days of the Church. The text attests that the Church was growing in numbers and, in the Church in Jerusalem, the needs of Hellenists (Greeks) who had become disciples were not being adequately met. The Apostles listened and agreed that they needed assistance in caring for the material needs of the people.

FAITH WORD

Deacons

Men ordained by the bishop to serve. They receive the Sacrament of Holy Orders but not the ministerial priesthood. Through ordination, the deacon is conformed to Christ who said he came to serve, not to be served. Deacons in the Latin Church may baptize, read the Gospel, preach the homily, assist the bishop or priest in the celebration of the Eucharist, assist at and bless marriages, and preside at funerals. They dedicate themselves to charitable endeavors, which was their ministerial role in New Testament times.

—USCCA, Glossary, 509

Laying on of hands

The laying on, or imposition, of hands signifies the bestowing of the gift of the Holy Spirit. This ritual finds its roots in both the Old Testament and the New Testament and has been part of the Tradition of the Church from the time of the Apostles. The laying on of hands, or extending of hands over, is used by the Catholic Church both in the celebration of the sacraments and in the celebration of her sacramentals, for example, in the blessing of people and objects.

JESUS HEALS THE BLIND MAN | DUCCIO DI BUONINSEGNA

The Hellenists met and identified "seven men of good standing, full of the Spirit and of wisdom. . . . Stephen, a man full of faith and the Holy Spirit, together with Philip, Prochorus, Nicanor, Timon, Parmenas, and Nicolaus, a proselyte of Antioch. They had these men stand before the apostles, who prayed and laid their hands on them" (Acts of the Apostles 6:3, 5–6).

The seven men, who were appointed by the Apostles to serve the Church in Jerusalem, came to be known as deacons. The word "deacon," from the Greek word *diakonos*, means "primarily one who serves at table" (*Dictionary of the Bible*, 182). The whole Church in Jerusalem knew that it, *as a community*, had the responsibility to care for the widows, among the most vulnerable members of their community, who "were being neglected in the daily distribution of food" (Acts of the Apostles 6:1). Deacons enabled the Apostles to devote more time "to prayer and to serving the word" (Acts of the Apostles 6:4).

Note well that these first deacons were not simply doing their own good works. They were tasked with helping the Apostles, "who prayed and laid their hands on them" (Acts of the Apostles 6:6). You will recall that the laying on of hands was a ritual gesture invoking the Holy Spirit to come upon a person to strengthen them to serve God and his people. Adhering

to the earliest traditions of the Church, the Church today teaches that only baptized men are ordained to the diaconate, or Order of Deacons. There is no historical evidence of women serving as deacons in the diaconate as we now know and understand it.

QUALITIES OF A DEACON

What did it take to be a deacon? Acts 6:1–6 gives a brief description of the qualities that the Apostles and early Church were looking for in a deacon. Timothy, a disciple and companion of St. Paul, described other qualities. In the First Letter to Timothy, which is one of the seven pastoral letters in the New Testament, we read:

Deacons likewise must be serious, not double-tongued, not indulging in much wine, not greedy for money; they must hold fast to the mystery of the faith with a clear conscience. And let them first be tested; then, if they prove themselves blameless, let them serve as deacons.

—1 Timothy 3:8–10

The letter adds that deacons should "be married only once, and let them manage their children and their households well"; they were to be growing with "great boldness in the faith that is in Christ Jesus." (Check out 1 Timothy 3:12–13.) In addition to these passages from Acts and First Timothy, other passages in the New Testament give further evidence for the existence of the ministry of deacons in the early Church. (Check out Philippians 1:1, Ephesians 6:21 and Colossians 4:7.)

Other early Church writings not included in the Scriptures speak of the qualities of deacons. For example, St. Ignatius of Antioch (c. AD 35–c. 107), martyr and third bishop of Antioch, wrote: "The deacons, too, who are ministers of the mysteries of Jesus Christ, should please all in every way, for they are not servers of food and drink, but ministers of the Church of God" (*To the Trallians*, 2, 3). St. Polycarp (c. AD 69–160), Bishop of Smyrna in modern Turkey, exhorted deacons to be "disciplined in all things, merciful, diligent, walking according to the truth of the Lord, who became the servant of all" (On the Letter to the Philippians, 5, 2). The ministry of deacons

ST. STEPHEN IS CONSECRATED DEACON | CARPACCIO

eventually became a vital support to the ministry of bishops and priests.

The deacon became the eyes and ears of the bishop, "his right hand man." The bishop's principal assistant became known as the "archdeacon," and was often charged with heavy responsibilities, especially in the financial administration of the local church, above all in distribution of funds and goods to the poor. . . .

During the first Christian millennium deacons undertook, as the bishops' assistants, the functions that are today those of the vicar general, the judicial vicar, the vicar capitular, the cathedral chapter and the oeconome, or finance officer. In current canon law these are almost exclusively priests' functions [Duane L.C.M. Galles, "Deacons Yesterday and Today," 1995].

—From the website of the Archdiocese of Newark, New Jersey

LET'S PROBE DEEPER: A SCRIPTURE ACTIVITY

⊙ Read and reflect on Acts 6:8—8:1, the story of St. Stephen the Deacon. Note the boldness with which he preached the Gospel. Stephen was a victim of religious violence.
⊙ What do you learn from this passage about the qualities required of a deacon?
⊙ How do these qualities reflect the role of the deacon as a servant leader? Explain.

THINK, PAIR AND SHARE

⊙ Do the requirements for being a deacon in the early Church mirror the qualities of the Apostles? Are these same requirements necessary for the ministry of deacons, as well as bishops and priests, in the Church today?

TWO WAYS OF LIVING THE DIACONATE

There are two ways of living the diaconate, namely, as a transitional deacon or as a permanent deacon. Transitional deacons are those who are ordained to the diaconate before they are ordained a priest. Transitional deacons generally serve in that role for six months to a year. Preparation for their ordination and ministry as a deacon is part of their training for priesthood. Permanent deacons are baptized men, and they may include men who were married prior to their ordination to the diaconate. Permanent deacons may not remarry should their spouse die. Preparation for the permanent diaconate takes place over several years. This preparation is part-time and includes human, intellectual, spiritual and pastoral formation.

By the middle of the fifth century, the ministry of permanent deacon, or deacons who were not seeking ordination to the priesthood, began to decline in the Western Church, or Latin Church. The term "transitional deacon" is used to designate those men who are ordained deacons as a step in the process of being ordained to the ministerial priesthood. In 1967 Blessed Paul VI in his apostolic letter *Sacrum Diaconatus Ordinem* (*The Sacred Order of the Diaconate*) decreed that the permanent diaconate be "restored as a particular and permanent rank of the hierarchy" in the Latin Church.

The Church ordains deacons, giving them the commission to carry on her work of justice and compassion toward all. The Sacrament of Holy Orders "configures them to Christ, who made himself the 'deacon' or servant of all" (CCC, no. 1570). Deacons are to see to it that the Church is truly a "field hospital" providing care to those who are wounded spiritually, physically, emotionally and psychologically. They perform this ministry by anchoring their work in the works of justice and compassion to bring the joy of the Gospel to all whom they serve.

THINK, PAIR AND SHARE

◉ What do you consider to be the necessary gifts for the vocation of a deacon?

◉ What gifts do you have for Christian service?

◉ Share with a partner how you try to use those gifts in the service of the Church.

MINISTERS OF JUSTICE

The first deacons were chosen to help the Apostles resolve a true pastoral issue in the early Church concerning how to care for the poor and vulnerable. The earliest Church in Jerusalem was made up of both Jewish and Hellenist disciples of Jesus. There were linguistic and cultural divisions. The Greek-speaking widows, as we have already seen, were being neglected

THE JUDGMENT OF NATIONS | VORONET MONASTERY, ROMANIA

in the daily distribution of food (Acts of the Apostle 6:1). In appointing deacons to rectify this inequity, the Apostles stipulated that all of the needy, regardless of background, were to be treated fairly. There was no group that was "more deserving" of resources and service than others.

Today, even in the United States, career and other opportunities and providing for one's basic needs are still very much connected with a person's identity. Race, language and geography are closely correlated with disparities in education, job opportunities, health and income. All Christians are called to be concerned with these inequities and injustices. We are to work to undo the personal attitudes and systemic structures that can perpetuate and reinforce structures of injustice. In a special way, the service of deacons stands as a symbol against systemic discrimination that treats anyone as less than fully human.

OVER TO YOU

◉ Read carefully Matthew 25:31–46, the parable of the judgment of nations.

◉ In your own personal life, how can you increase your efforts to feed the hungry, give drink to the thirsty, welcome the stranger, clothe the naked, care for the ill and visit those in prison?

◉ How about in your life with your family? Can you do any of these things *for* your family? Can you do any of them *with* your family? Imagine how!

MINISTERS OF COMPASSION

Few events challenge us to make meaning out of sorrow more than the death of a loved one. Jesus, who would conquer death by his Resurrection, was himself brought to tears as he shared in the sorrow of his beloved friends Martha and Mary when their brother Lazarus died. Read the story in John 11:1–44. Notice that Jesus himself "began to weep" at the tomb of Lazarus (John 11:35). Reflecting this compassion of Jesus, deacons have a special ministry to people in times of mourning. They can preside at funerals and they often lead wake services. These works reflect God's compassion for those mourning their beloved. In this ministry deacons can offer hope and meaning in a time of great sorrow.

TALK IT OVER

⊙ What strikes you in what you have learned so far about the ministry of deacons?

⊙ How might you join with deacons and/or other members of your school and parish to take part in the Church's works of justice and compassion?

WHAT ABOUT YOU PERSONALLY?

⊙ Recall a time when you did something generous and compassionate for someone in need.

⊙ What difference did it make for the person? For you?

⊙ What did you learn from that experience?

THE RAISING OF LAZARUS | SAINT NICOLÒ, TREVISO, ITALY

Ordination and duties of deacons

BRINGING CHRIST TO OTHERS

With the enthusiastic support of his wife and their children, Mike was ordained a deacon in 1994. Mike had spent several years discerning and preparing for his ministry as a deacon. While Deacon Mike serves the people of his parish, his work also extends out beyond the parish into the wider community, where he pays particular attention to the spiritual needs of people with intellectual disabilities. Like all deacons, Deacon Mike makes Christ and his Church present through his service in the local community.

OPENING CONVERSATION

- ⊙ Where do you see members of your parish serving others as Deacon Mike does?
- ⊙ What is the best lesson you can learn from Deacon Mike for living your own faith in Christ?

The Ministry Of Deacons

Deacons in the Latin Church may baptize, read the Gospel, preach the homily, assist the bishop or priest in the celebration of the Eucharist, assist at and bless marriages, and preside at funerals. They dedicate themselves to charitable endeavors, which was their ministerial role in New Testament times.

—USCCA, Glossary, "Deacons," 509

THE DUTIES OF DEACONS: WORSHIP, WORD AND WORKS

Deacons are usually assigned by their bishop to serve a parish. Their ministry, however, often extends further into the community. Deacons, as agents of their bishop, make God's healing and saving presence visible throughout the diocese in schools, hospitals, prisons and many other venues that serve the bodily or spiritual needs of people. The diaconate symbolizes the truth that the sacramental and the social ministries of the Church are inseparable and inextricably intertwined. Public worship, personal prayer and acts of service nourish and inform one another. This unity is made visible in the diaconal ministry.

In the Catholic Church deacons "assist the bishop and priests in the celebration of the divine mysteries" (CCC, no. 1570). While deacons cannot serve as celebrants of Mass, they often assist the priest at the celebration of the Eucharist. At Mass and under other circumstances, deacons proclaim the Gospel and may preach the homily. They may also sometimes preside over a prayer service or a communion service where the faithful receive the Body and Blood of Christ, the Eucharist, under the appearances of bread and wine that have been previously consecrated at Mass. In the Latin Church deacons may serve, along with bishops and priests, as ordinary ministers of Baptism. This is not the case in the Eastern Catholic Churches.

In the Latin Church the deacon may also preside over the celebration of the rite of a sacramental marriage. He receives the consent of the spouses, who are the ministers of this sacrament, and acts as a witness to and blesses the marriage on behalf of the whole Church. This is not the case in a sacramental marriage in the Eastern Churches, in which the bishop or priest confers (rather than solemnizing and witnessing) the sacrament—and not the woman and man marrying.

Whatever services deacons render, their primary function is one of loving service to the People of God. As the Second Vatican Council taught clearly, the defining vocation of a deacon is to be "dedicated to works of charity" (*Dogmatic Constitution on the Church*, no. 29).

RITE OF ORDINATION OF A DEACON

The essential elements in the rite of ordination of deacons are the laying on of the bishop's hands in silence and his praying aloud the Prayer of Ordination, or Prayer of Consecration. Both these elements are required for the valid celebration of this sacrament. These elements of the rite of ordination of a deacon are celebrated during Mass during the Liturgy of the Word after the proclamation of the Scriptures and the homily. We will now take a brief look at several of these ritual elements. Each will give us insights into the mystery of faith that is being celebrated.

Homily: "The bishop, while all are seated, gives the homily. Taking his theme from the readings proclaimed in the Liturgy of the Word, he addresses the people and the elect on the office of deacon. In his homily he should take into consideration whether the one to be ordained is married or unmarried." Using these or similar words, the ordaining bishop first addresses the people, saying, in part:

Dearly beloved brothers and sisters: because this our son, your relative and friend, is now to be advanced to the Order of deacons, consider carefully the ministerial rank to which he is about to be raised.

Strengthened by the gift of the Holy Spirit, he will help the Bishops and his priests in the ministry of the word, of the altar, and of charity, showing himself to be a servant to all. . . . With the help of God, he is to go about all these duties in such a way that you will recognize him as a disciple of him who came not to be served, but to serve.

—*The Roman Pontifical*, Rite of Ordination of a Deacon, no. 227

The deacon will draw new strength from the gift of the Holy Spirit

The bishop lays his hands on the elect's head, in silence. Then the bishop extends his hands over the elect and prays the Prayer of Ordination aloud

THE LAYING ON OF HANDS | ORDINATION OF DEACONS, IOWA

The bishop then addresses the elect, saying, in part:

You, dearly beloved son, are now to be raised to the Order of the diaconate. The Lord has set an example that just as he himself has done, you also should do.

As a deacon, that is, as a minister of Jesus Christ, who came among his disciples as one who served, do the will of God from the heart: serve the people in love and joy as you would the Lord. Since no one can serve two masters, look upon all defilement and avarice as serving false gods.

—*The Roman Pontifical*, Rite of Ordination of a Deacon, no. 227

The bishop then proceeds to question the elect, asking him to state publicly his resolve to accept the duties and responsibilities of a deacon. The elect makes his promise to serve his bishop. The bishop then leads the people in prayer for the elect, who kneels before the bishop.

Laying on of Hands and Prayer of Ordination (Consecration): The essential rituals of the sacrament, the matter and form, are now celebrated. The elect goes up to and kneels before the bishop. The bishop lays his hands on the elect's head, in silence. Then the bishop extends his hands over the elect and prays the Prayer of Ordination aloud. The bishop prays, in part:

Lord, we implore you:
send forth upon him the Holy Spirit,
that he may be strengthened
by the gift of your sevenfold grace
to carry out faithfully the work of his ministry.

May every Gospel virtue abound in him:
unfeigned love,
concern for the sick and poor,
unassuming authority,
the purity of innocence
and the observance of spiritual discipline.

May your commandments shine forth in his
   conduct,
so that by the example of his way of life
he may inspire the imitation of your holy
   people.
Offering the witness of a clear conscience,
may he remain strong and steadfast in Christ,
who came not to be served but to serve,
so that by imitating your Son on earth
he may be found worthy to reign in heaven with
   him,
who lives and reigns with you in the unity of the
   Holy Spirit,
God for ever and ever.

—*The Roman Pontifical*, Rite of Ordination of a Deacon, no. 235

> # Let them be merciful and zealous, and let them walk according to the truth of the Lord, who became the servant of all.
>
> **EPISTLE TO THE PHILIPPIANS, 5.2**

ST. POLYCARP | CHURCH OF ST. POLYCARP, IZMIR, TURKEY

Investiture with deacon's stole and dalmatic:
The investiture with stole and dalmatic and the presentation of the Book of the Gospels follows the Prayer of Ordination. These items symbolize the liturgical office of a deacon and the deacon's ministry to proclaim and live the Gospel at all times.

THINK, PAIR AND SHARE
- ◉ Does knowing the rite and prayers of the rite of the ordination of a deacon deepen your understanding of the ministry of deacons?
- ◉ Does it give you insight into your own baptismal vocation to serve as Jesus served?

EFFECTS OF THE SACRAMENT
Holy Orders, like all the sacraments, confers unique graces. All who receive the Sacrament of Holy Orders are marked with a permanent seal or indelible spiritual character. This means that ordination as a bishop, priest or deacon cannot be repeated, nor is ordination only a temporary state of life in the Church. "The grace of the Holy Spirit proper to this sacrament is configuration to Christ as Priest, Teacher, and Pastor, of whom the ordained is made a minister" (CCC, no. 1585).

Strengthened by sacramental grace, [deacons] are dedicated to the people of God, in communion with the bishop and his presbyterate, to the service of the liturgy, of the word and of charity. . . . Dedicated to the works of charity and functions of administration, deacons should recall the admonition of St. Polycarp: "Let them be merciful and zealous, and let them walk according to the truth of the Lord, who became the servant of all (*Epistle to the Philippians*, 5.2)."
> —Vatican II, *Dogmatic Constitution on the Church*, no. 29

Ordination to the diaconate gives the deacon a special relationship with Jesus and with the community that he serves. "Deacons share in Christ's mission and grace in a special way. The sacrament of Holy Orders marks them with an *imprint* ('character') that cannot be removed and which configures them to Christ, who made himself the 'deacon' or servant of all" (CCC, no. 1570).

WHAT ABOUT YOU PERSONALLY?
- ◉ Reflect: The ordaining bishop addresses the candidate for ordination to the diaconate, saying, in part: "Never turn away from the hope which the Gospel offers; now you must not only listen to God's word but preach it; . . . Express in action what you proclaim by word of mouth."
- ◉ How does this exhortation apply to you? To all the baptized?
- ◉ How do you proclaim the Gospel by your actions?

JUDGE AND ACT

REVIEW AND SHARE WHAT YOU HAVE LEARNED

Look back over this chapter and reflect on what you have learned about the Sacrament of Holy Orders and, in particular, the ministry of deacons within the Church. Share the teachings of the Catholic Church on these statements:

- ⊙ Baptism is a call and empowerment to a life of selfless service to God and the Church.
- ⊙ Holy Orders is one of the two Sacraments at the Service of Communion in the Church.
- ⊙ Jesus Christ instituted the Sacrament of Holy Orders at the Last Supper.
- ⊙ Jesus chose the Apostles to be the first servant leaders of his Church on earth.
- ⊙ There are three degrees of Holy Orders: bishops, priests and deacons.
- ⊙ The essential elements of the sacramental celebration of each order are the laying on of hands and the consecratory prayer.
- ⊙ Those ordained are marked with a permanent seal, or indelible spiritual character.
- ⊙ There are two ways of living the diaconate, namely, as a transitional deacon or as a permanent deacon.
- ⊙ The Church ordains deacons to be of service to bishops and priests.

OVER TO YOU

- ⊙ What is the most valuable wisdom from this chapter that you want to incorporate into your own life of faith?
- ⊙ What can you do in your life now to prepare for how you will live your own vocation to serve the Church?

PROCLAIMING THE GOSPEL ALWAYS AND WITH JOY

Learning about and understanding the faith of the Church is a lifelong process. Christians who seek to deepen their relationship with Christ and with his Church continue to ask about and study their faith. Deacons often accompany the faithful on this journey by taking part in their parish's ministry of catechesis. For example, they take part in a variety of adult faith formation programs, including marriage preparation and RCIA (Rite of Christian Initiation of Adults) programs.

Whatever their ministry, deacons bring the joy of the Gospel to all those whom they serve. They reflect the sentiments of Pope Francis, who advises that the Church must teach so that "the joy of the Gospel fills the hearts and lives of all who encounter Jesus" (*The Joy of the Gospel*, no. 1). St. Ephrem was a deacon of the Church who proclaimed the joy of the Gospel through music and song.

LEARN BY EXAMPLE

Saint Ephrem (c. 306–373), deacon, Doctor of the Church, poet and hymn-writer

St. Ephrem served the Church in Edessa, a city not far from Antioch in Syria. Born about AD 306, Ephrem was baptized at the age of eighteen. He was later ordained a deacon but declined his bishop's invitation to become a priest. Ephrem lived during a time of great theological debate within the Church. The debate, which was discussed at the early Church councils of Nicaea (325) and Constantinople I (381), centered on the relationship of the divine nature and human nature in Christ.

In response to heretics, Ephrem proclaimed the Gospel by writing hymns. He would take the popular songs of the heretical groups and, using their melodies, compose beautiful hymns that embodied orthodox doctrine. In writing about the mysteries of humanity's redemption, Ephrem revealed a realistic and humanly sympathetic spirit and a great devotion to the humanity of Jesus. Ephrem also wrote many of his sermons in verse. His poetic account of the Last Judgment, some claim, inspired Dante.

One of St. Ephrem's major contributions to the life of the Church is the use of singing and song to profess one's faith. Here is one example from a hymn in which Ephrem addressed the controversy over the humanity of Christ at the Council of Nicaea:

> From God Christ's deity came forth,
>   his manhood from humanity;
> his priesthood from Melchizedek,
>   his royalty from David's tree:
> praised be his Oneness.
> He joined with guests at wedding feast,
>   yet in the wilderness did fast;
> he taught within the temple's gates;
>   his people saw him die at last:
> praised be his teaching.

Our Church celebrates the memory and life of St. Ephrem the deacon each year on July 26.

TALK IT OVER

- What might the life and ministry of St. Ephrem teach those of us who belong to the Church today?
- Where do you see deacons using their gifts to serve the Church? What contributions are those deacons making to the life of the Church?
- What are your favorite hymns? How do they inspire you to live the faith of the Church in Jesus?

SHARE FAITH WITH FAMILY AND FRIENDS

- Do we seek more to serve or be served by one another? What are some ways we serve? What are some ways we seek to be served?
- How does that give witness to our faith in Jesus?
- How does "serving" or "seeking to be served" impact our relationships with one another? With other people?

REFLECT AND DECIDE

- Reflect: The ministry of deacons also serves the Church by reminding all the faithful of their baptismal call to serve God and one's neighbor with one's whole heart, mind and strength.
- What gifts do you have that you can use to serve the Church, your school and local community, people you know and those whom you do not know? How generously do you use those gifts?
- Choose some work of justice or compassion that you can do now. Decide on how you will do it and then make a commitment to see it through.

LEARN BY HEART

"Whoever wants to be first must be last of all and servant of all."

MARK 9:35

PRAYER REFLECTION

All pray the Sign of the Cross together.

LEADER
Loving God, who creates us as gifted human beings,
whose Son provided us with a model of servant leadership,
whose Holy Spirit makes our gifts effective,
we thank you for your ever-loving concern for us.
We ask that you give us the grace to respond to your promptings with courage and faith.
ALL
Amen.

READER
A reading from the First Letter of Paul to Timothy.
Proclaim 1 Timothy 4:11–16.
The word of the Lord.
ALL
Thanks be to God.

LEADER
Reflect for a moment on what you hear from this reading for your own life. You might focus on the desires it elicits from your heart. When ready, share your reflections with the group if you wish.

Allow a couple of minutes for conversation.

LEADER
Loving God, who gives us servant leaders,
help us to use our gifts to contribute to the building up of your Church.
You know us more intimately than we know ourselves.
We ask you to make known to us our vocation to minister to others as servants.
We now ask you for the graces of your Holy Spirit to join with your Son to serve your people.

READER
Please respond "Help us serve" to each petition.

For the gift of seeing our own gifts, we pray . . .
ALL
Help us serve.

READER
For the vision to see the needs in our communities, we pray . . .
ALL
Help us serve.

READER
For the heart of a servant leader, we pray . . .
ALL
Help us serve.

READER
For the courage to serve and lead regardless of our age, we pray . . .
ALL
Help us serve.

READER
That we may seek and find ways to support others who lead us, we pray . . .
ALL
Help us serve.

READER
I now invite all who wish to do so to add their own petitions.
Students may speak their petitions aloud or in the silence of their hearts.
ALL
Help us serve.

LEADER
Loving God, who wants the best for us and the best from us,
you never cease to gift us yourself through and for one another.
Grant us the vision to recognize your presence with and among us,
and the courage to respond with joy.
This we ask through Jesus Christ, who lives and reigns with you and the Holy Spirit.
ALL
Amen.

Pray the Sign of the Cross together.

CHAPTER 9

The Ministry of Bishops and Priests

PASTORS OF THE FLOCK OF JESUS CHRIST

SERVE, SANCTIFY, TEACH AND GOVERN THE PEOPLE OF GOD

SHARE IN THE ONE PRIESTHOOD AND MINISTRY OF CHRIST

BISHOPS AND PRIESTS

BISHOPS RECEIVE THE FULLNESS OF THE Sacrament of Holy Orders. They are the direct successors of the Apostles, the first bishops and priests of the Church. Bishops and their co-workers, priests, are pastors, or shepherds, of the flock of Jesus Christ. They have the threefold office of sanctifying, teaching and governing the Church. Bishops and priests serve as icons of Jesus Christ, "the Priest, the Good Shepherd, the Teacher and Servant of all" (*The Roman Missal*, "Thursday of Holy Week: The Chrism Mass," no. 9)

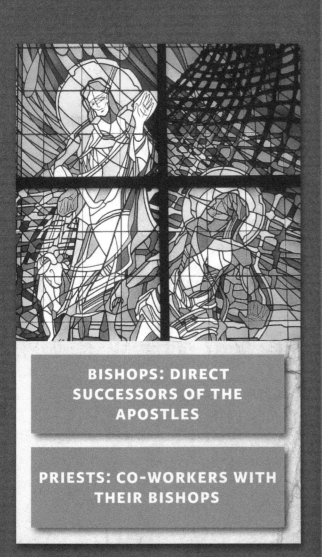

BISHOPS: DIRECT SUCCESSORS OF THE APOSTLES

PRIESTS: CO-WORKERS WITH THEIR BISHOPS

Faith Focus: These teachings of the Catholic Church are the primary focus of the doctrinal content presented in this chapter:

- ◉ Christ instituted the Sacrament of Holy Orders at the Last Supper.
- ◉ The Apostles appointed and ordained bishops to be their direct successors.
- ◉ Priests are called to be the bishops' co-workers.
- ◉ Bishops and priests act in the person of Christ and serve as icons of Christ.
- ◉ The ministry of both bishops and priests includes the threefold office of sanctifying, teaching and governing.
- ◉ The essential elements of the ordination of a bishop or priest are the laying on of hands and the Prayer of Ordination, or Prayer of Consecration.

Discipleship Formation: As a result of studying this chapter and discovering the meaning of the faith of the Catholic Church for your life, you should be better able to:

- ◉ understand and value the ministry of bishops and priests;
- ◉ support your bishops and priests;
- ◉ proclaim the Word of God courageously;
- ◉ participate more fully and actively in the sacramental life of the Church.

Scripture References: These Scripture references are quoted or referred to in this chapter:
NEW TESTAMENT: Matthew 22:1–14, 25:1–3; **Mark** 2:19, 10:42–45; **Luke** 10:2, 22:19; **John** 3:29, 10:1–18 and 14–15, 13:1–17, 21:15–19; **Acts of the Apostles** 6:7, 11:1–18, 12:24; **1 Corinthians** 6:15–17; **2 Corinthians** 11:3; **1 Timothy** 3:1–7; **2 Timothy** 3:10–12 and 14; **Hebrews** 4:14, 5:10, 6:20, 13:15; **1 Peter** 1:23; **Revelation** 1:6, 5:9–10

Faith Glossary: Familiarize yourself with or recall the meaning of these key terms. Definitions are found in the Glossary: **apostolate, Apostolic Succession, archbishop, archdiocese, bishop, cardinal, college of bishops, collegiality, diocese, Donatism, Eastern Catholic Churches, episcopacy, evangelization, local ordinary, obedience, pope, presbyter, presbyterate, priest, priesthood (ordained/ministerial), priesthood of the faithful, seminary**

Faith Words: bishop; college of bishops; priest
Learn by Heart: Mark 10:43, 45
Learn by Example: Terence Cardinal Cooke

What does the Church celebrate on Holy Thursday?

JESUS ENTERS JERUSALEM ON PALM SUNDAY | 19TH-CENTURY ENGRAVING

During Holy Week the Church remembers and celebrates the final entry of Jesus into Jerusalem, the Last Supper and the events of Jesus' Paschal Mystery—his Passion, Death and Resurrection. The Paschal, or Easter, Triduum, the last three days of Holy Week, is the center and high point of the Church's liturgical year. The Triduum begins with the celebration of the evening Mass of the Lord's Supper on Holy Thursday, continues with the celebration of the Passion of Christ on Good Friday, has as its culmination the celebration of the Easter Vigil, and concludes with Evening Prayer on Easter Sunday.

OPENING REFLECTION

- Which of the liturgical celebrations of the Easter Triduum do you take part in?
- Which of them appeals most to you? Why?
- What do you recall about the Holy Thursday celebration?

A CLOSER LOOK AT HOLY THURSDAY

Jesus Christ is the one Eternal High Priest. He is the one, true and only Mediator between God and humanity. (Check out Hebrews 5:10 and 6:20.) He is the perfect "sacrifice of praise to God" (Hebrews 13:15; see also Hebrews 4:14). The sacrifices of the Old Covenant only prefigure the salvation and redemption of humankind brought about by the Sacrifice of Jesus on the Cross.

On Holy Thursday at the evening Mass of the Lord's Supper the Church remembers and celebrates the sacrifice and priesthood of Jesus Christ. We remember and celebrate that Jesus gave his Church the Sacrament of the Eucharist and the Sacrament of Holy Orders. At the Last Supper Jesus commissioned the Apostles to celebrate the Eucharist in remembrance of him. (Check out Luke 22:19.) "By doing so, the Lord institutes his apostles as priests of the New Covenant" (*Catechism of the Catholic Church* [CCC], no. 611).

On Holy Thursday morning (or on another day earlier in Holy Week) the bishop and the **priests** of his diocese gather for the celebration of "The Chrism Mass." At this Mass the bishop blesses the holy oils used by the Church, namely, the Oil of Catechumens, the Oil of the Sick, and the Sacred Chrism. At this Chrism Mass the priests also renew their priestly promises. The bishop, speaking to the priests, begins with these or similar words:

Beloved sons,
on the anniversary of that day
when Christ conferred his priesthood
on his Apostles and on us,
are you resolved to renew,
in the presence of your Bishop and God's holy people,
the promises you once made?

Jesus commissioned Peter to shepherd his flock, saying, "Feed my lambs"; "Tend my sheep"; "Feed my sheep."

FEED MY SHEEP | SAINT PETER CHURCH, COLUMBUS, OH

After the priests have renewed their promises, the bishop asks all present to pray for him:

And pray also for me,
that I may be faithful to the apostolic office
entrusted to me in my lowliness
and that in your midst I may be made day by day
a living and more perfect image of Christ,
the Priest, the Good Shepherd,
the Teacher and Servant of all.

The bishop then asks all faithful who are present to pray for their priests and for him, saying:

May the Lord keep us all in his charity
and lead all of us,
shepherds and flock,
to eternal life.

All present respond, "Amen."
—*The Roman Missal*, "Thursday of Holy Week: The Chrism Mass," no. 9

OVER TO YOU
⊙ Who is your bishop? Who are the priests who serve you?
⊙ Take a moment and pray for them, using these or similar words, "May the Lord pour out his gifts abundantly [on our bishop and priests], / and keep them faithful as ministers of Christ, the High Priest, / so that they may lead [us] to him, / who is the source of salvation" (*The Roman Missal*, "Thursday of Holy Week: The Chrism Mass," no. 9).

BISHOPS SHEPHERD THE FLOCK OF CHRIST

Bishops are ordained to shepherd (to tend and feed) the flock of Christ. The English word "shepherd" is the translation of the Latin word *pastor*. Take a moment and recall the encounter of the risen Christ with St. Peter and six other Apostles on the shore of the Sea of Tiberias.

John the Evangelist tells us that after Simon Peter and the others had eaten a breakfast of fish and bread with the risen Jesus, the risen Jesus asked Simon Peter three times, "Do you love me?" Three times the Apostle professed his love for Jesus and each time the risen Jesus commissioned him to shepherd his flock, saying, "Feed my lambs"; "Tend my sheep"; "Feed my sheep." (Check out the whole encounter in John 21:15–19.)

The Apostles would come, over time, to understand the full meaning and depth of this commission. Led by St. Peter, they were to

Keep watch over the whole flock, in which the Holy Spirit appoints you to govern the Church of God

THE GOOD SHEPHERD | 17TH-CENTURY GOAN IVORY

With the charity of a father and a brother, love all whom God places in your care, especially priests and deacons, your co-workers in the ministry of Christ, but also the poor and weak, immigrants and strangers. Exhort the faithful to work with you in your apostolic labor; do not refuse to listen willingly to them. . . . And so, keep watch over the whole flock, in which the Holy Spirit appoints you to govern the Church of God: in the name of the Father, whose image you represent in the Church; and in the name of his Son, Jesus Christ, whose office of Teacher, Priest, and Shepherd you will discharge; and in the name of the Holy Spirit, who gives life to the Church of Christ and by his power strengthens us in our weakness.

— The Roman Pontifical, Rite of Ordination of a Bishop, "Homily," no. 39

care for the flock of Jesus the Good Shepherd. Their Lord had described his own ministry of shepherding:

"I am the good shepherd. The good shepherd lays down his life for the sheep. . . . I know my own and my own know me, just as the Father knows me and I know the Father. And I lay down my life for the sheep. . . . For this reason the Father loves me, because I lay down my life in order to take it up again. No one takes it from me, but I lay it down of my own accord.

—John 10:11, 14, 17, 18a

In the homily of the Mass during which the ordination of a bishop is celebrated, the principal ordaining, or consecrating, bishop describes, in these or similar words, some of the ways that the bishop-elect is to shepherd the flock entrusted to his care:

LET'S PROBE DEEPER: A RESEARCH ACTIVITY

⊙ Learn more about your diocesan bishop. Find out:
- when he was ordained a priest and a bishop;
- when he was appointed the bishop of your diocese;
- what the symbols and wording on his coat of arms reveal about his ministry.

⊙ How might you support your bishop in his serving the people of your diocese?

⊙ Share your research with the class during the next section of the chapter. Work together to create a profile of your bishop.

OVER TO YOU

⊙ Pause for a moment and pray for your bishop.

Bishops, successors of the Apostles

HABEMUS PAPAM

On March 13, 2013, the papal conclave elected Cardinal Jorge Bergoglio, the Archbishop of Buenos Aires, Argentina, a Jesuit, to be the 266th pope. The new pope amazed everyone by taking the name Francis (after St. Francis of Assisi), asking the people to bless him before he blessed them, and returning to his hotel to pay his own bill. These initial actions of the newly elected pope gave the world an insight into the manner in which he would fulfill his ministry as Shepherd of the Universal Church.

OPENING REFLECTION

⊙ What have you come to know about Pope Francis?

⊙ What qualities of Pope Francis' ministry most appeal to you? Why is that?

⊙ How can Catholic young people imitate those qualities?

ORIGIN OF THE ORDER OF BISHOPS

From her earliest days the Church has acknowledged her bishops to be the direct successors of the Apostles, and the successor of St. Peter, the pope, to be the first among the bishops. This unbroken line connecting the Apostles to the bishops of the Church is called **Apostolic Succession**. Apostolic Succession is the "passing on of the office of bishop from the Apostles to bishops, and from them to other bishops down each generation, by means of ordination" (*United States Catholic Catechism for Adults* [USCCA], Glossary, "Apostolic Succession," 504).

The Acts of the Apostles, the New Testament letters of 1 and 2 Timothy, and other non-biblical writings of the early Church attest to this ancient Tradition. Those non-biblical sources include the writings of St. Ignatius (AD c. 35–98), the third Bishop of Antioch; the Greek theologian

A CARDINAL'S BIRETTA

Did you know?

Cardinals, usually archbishops or bishops, are named by the pope in recognition of their service to the Church. A bishop (and sometimes a priest) does not become a cardinal through receiving the Sacrament of Holy Orders. The pope appoints cardinals to serve as his senior counselors and assist him in governing the Church. Cardinals become members of the Sacred College of Cardinals who have the honor and responsibility to elect the pope.

St. Clement of Alexandria (AD c. 150–215); the Roman theologian Hippolytus (AD 170–235); and the Council of Elvira (AD c. 300).

After the death of St. Peter, his successor became the Bishop of Rome. The leadership and authority of the Bishop of Rome has held pre-eminence among all the bishops of the Church, just as the leadership and authority of Simon Peter did among the Apostles.

In the eleventh century the title of **pope**, from the Greek word *pappas*, meaning "father," was used exclusively for the successor of St. Peter.

The pope is the "visible and juridical head of the Catholic Church" (USCCA, Glossary, "Pope," 523). He is the supreme and final authority in the universal Church on earth. The leadership office and ministry of the pope is called the Petrine office, or "office of Peter."

THE OFFICE AND DUTIES OF A BISHOP

The **bishop** of a **diocese** or the **archbishop** of an **archdiocese** is called the **local ordinary**. He is the visible head and pastor of the particular Church that the pope has appointed and entrusted to him to shepherd. The term "particular Church" refers to the Church in local communities, or in dioceses or archdioceses in the Latin Church and in eparchies in the Eastern Churches. Sometimes the pope appoints a bishop to assist the local ordinary; this bishop is called an auxiliary bishop. While each local ordinary is responsible for the particular Church the pope entrusts to him, the collegial character of the office of bishops unites all bishops in service to the mission of the whole Church. The pastoral, or shepherd's, office of a bishop includes "sanctifying, teaching, and governing roles within the Church" (USCCA, Glossary, "Apostolic Succession," 504).

ST. AMBROSE WAS BISHOP OF MILAN IN THE 4TH CENTURY

Bishops are *sanctifiers*. They are ministers of the sacraments, the most powerful source of God's grace for our lives. In this sense, a bishop may be seen as the "High Priest" of a diocese. He is " 'the steward of the grace of the supreme priesthood' (Vatican II, *Dogmatic Constitution on the Church [Lumen Gentium]*, no. 26), especially in the Eucharist which he offers personally or whose offering he assures through the priests, his co-workers" (CCC, no. 893).

Bishops are *teachers*. They have a special duty to evangelize—to spread the Gospel through their teaching and preaching. They are the leading teachers and catechists in their diocese who are entrusted to be good stewards of the faith handed down from the Apostles. They guide the faithful to cooperate with the Holy Spirit in living the new life of faith in Christ that they first receive in Baptism.

Bishops *govern*. They have the authority of pastoral leadership in their diocese. " 'The bishops, as vicars and legates of Christ, govern the particular Churches assigned to them by their counsels, exhortations, and example, but over and above that also by the authority and sacred power' (Vatican II, *Dogmatic Constitution on the Church*, no. 27) which indeed they ought to exercise so as to edify, in the spirit of service which is that of their Master" (CCC, no. 894).

The miter, the pastoral staff, or crozier, and ring a bishop receives at his ordination are the insignia, or signs of his pastoral office. The miter is a reminder of his priestly duties and that "the splendor of holiness shine[s] forth in [him]." The crozier symbolizes that the bishop is to "keep watch over the whole flock / in which the Holy

FAITH WORD

Bishop

The highest of the three degrees of Holy Orders; a bishop is normally ordained to teach, to sanctify, and to govern a diocese or local church; a bishop is a successor of the Apostles.

—USCCA, Glossary, 505

College of Bishops

All bishops, with the Pope as their head, form a single college, which succeeds in every generation the college of the Twelve Apostles, with Peter at their head. Christ instituted this college as the foundation of the Church. The college of bishops, together with—but never without—the pope, has the supreme and full authority over the universal Church.

—USCCA, 507

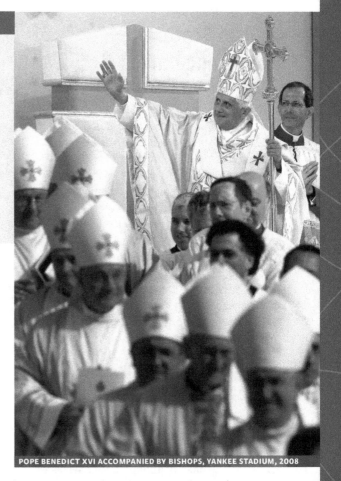

POPE BENEDICT XVI ACCOMPANIED BY BISHOPS, YANKEE STADIUM, 2008

Spirit has placed [him] as Bishop / to govern the Church of God." The ring symbolizes and is a reminder of the newly ordained bishop's fidelity to "the bride of God, the holy Church" (*The Roman Pontifical*, Rite of Ordination of a Bishop, no. 51). A bishop also wears the ring because he is understood as "married," not only to the whole Church, but specifically to his particular diocese.

READ, REFLECT AND SHARE

⊙ Work in small groups. Read Matthew 22:1–14, 25:1–3; Mark 2:19; John 3:29; 1 Corinthians 6:15–17 and 2 Corinthians 11:3.
⊙ What image for the Church is found in these passages? What does this image tell you about a bishop and the people of his diocese?

OVER TO YOU

⊙ What image would you use to describe the relationship of a bishop to his diocese? Why?

THE COLLEGE OF BISHOPS

The New Testament teaches clearly that St. Peter and the other Apostles worked collaboratively to exercise the authority that Jesus had given them. For example, recall the gathering of the Apostles and other Church elders in Jerusalem as recorded in Acts of the Apostles 11:1–18. The bishops of the Church today serve the Church in the same way. They serve collegially, that is, in unity as the **college of bishops**.

The pope is the Supreme Pontiff of the Universal Church. The word "pontiff" comes from the Latin word *pontifex*, which means

"bridge-builder." The pope is the instrument and the visible sign of unity of the whole Church in her faith, sacraments and Christian living. The **collegiality** uniting the pope and all the bishops serves as a visible reminder that all the particular Churches around the world are united together as the one Body of Christ. Through the exercise of collegiality the pope and the bishops in communion with him give living witness to the unity of the one Church of Christ throughout the world.

This charism of collegiality also unites bishops with other bishops in the fulfillment of their ministry. The bishops of a country work collegially to fulfill their threefold office of service in the Church in a particular country. They accomplish this work through national episcopal conferences. The Catholic Bishops of the Church in the United States of America work collegially as members of the United States Conference of Catholic Bishops (USCCB).

United States Conference of Catholic Bishops (USCCB)

The mission of the United States Conference of Catholic Bishops (see Code of Canon Law, c. 447) is to support the ministry of bishops with an emphasis on evangelization, by which the bishops exercise in a communal and collegial manner certain pastoral functions entrusted to them by the Lord Jesus of sanctifying, teaching, and governing (see Vatican II, *Dogmatic Constitution on the Church*, no. 21).

This mission calls the Conference to:

- ⊙ Act collaboratively and consistently on vital issues confronting the Church and society (see Vatican II, *Decree on the Pastoral Office of Bishops*, no. 38.1)
- ⊙ Foster communion with the Church in other nations, within the Church universal, under the leadership of its supreme pastor, the Roman Pontiff
- ⊙ Offer appropriate assistance to each bishop in fulfilling his particular ministry in the local Church (see St. John Paul II, Apostolic Letter on Episcopal Conferences, 1998.)

—Website of United States Conference of Catholic Bishops (*www.usccb.org*)

THE SELECTION OF A PRIEST TO THE ORDER OF BISHOPS

The selection of a priest for ordination to the **episcopacy**, or order of bishops, is very deliberate. After a very careful and thorough selection process the pope directly appoints a bishop from among the priests recommended to him. These priests will have had years of experience serving the People of God. In summary:

The process for selecting candidates for the episcopacy normally begins at the diocesan level and works its way through a series of consultations until it reaches Rome. It is a process bound by strict confidentiality and involves a number of important players—the most influential being the apostolic nuncio, the Congregation for Bishops, and the pope. It can be a time consuming process, often taking eight months or more to complete.

—*www.usccb.org*

Central to the selection process is discerning that a priest has consistently demonstrated qualities that are desirable in a bishop. These qualities are enumerated briefly during the ordination of a bishop in the questions the consecrating bishop publicly asks the bishop-elect about his readiness for ordination. These qualities include lifelong commitment, faithfulness and constancy in proclaiming the Gospel, fidelity to the deposit of faith, building up the Body of Christ in communion with the pope, kindness and compassion, seeking out those who stray, praying for the People of God, and conducting oneself "so as to afford no grounds for reproach."

READ, REFLECT AND SHARE
- ⊙ Read 1 Timothy 3:1–7. How does this passage describe a bishop?
- ⊙ Compare the qualities referred to in this passage with the qualities named in the ordination rite of a bishop today.
- ⊙ Discuss: How are those qualities at the heart of a bishop's ministry?

LET'S PROBE DEEPER: A RESEARCH ACTIVITY
- ⊙ Visit the website of the United States Conference of Catholic Bishops.

- Research "How Bishops Are Appointed."
- Explore and become familiar with these terms: *apostolic nuncio, auxiliary bishop, coadjutor bishop, Congregation for Bishops, diocesan bishop,* and *province.*

CONSECRATION, OR ORDINATION, OF BISHOPS

Only a bishop can ordain a bishop. The ordination of a bishop is most often referred to as his "consecration." This highlights that "the fullness of the sacrament of Holy Orders" is conferred by episcopal consecration (CCC, no. 1557). The ordination of a bishop always takes place within Mass and is celebrated after the Liturgy of the Word. Typically, more than one bishop (usually three or more) participate at the ordination, or consecration, of a new bishop. However, one bishop is designated as the principal ordaining bishop, or the principal consecrating bishop, and he presides over the ordination.

Questioning of bishop-elect: After the homily the principal ordaining bishop examines, or questions, the bishop-elect as to his readiness for ordination. He then leads everyone present in praying the Litany of the Supplication invoking the saints to pray for the bishop-elect. The essential rite of the sacrament then takes place during the laying on of hands and Prayer of Ordination, or Prayer of Consecration.

Laying on of Hands and Prayer of Ordination: The principal ordaining bishop lays his hands silently on the bishop-elect, and all the other bishops do the same. In this way the priesthood of Jesus Christ, which he first shared with the Apostles, is handed on in an unbroken line to the new bishop. Next, the principal ordaining bishop receives the Book of the Gospels from one of the assisting deacons and places it open upon the head of the bishop-elect. Then, two deacons hold the open book over the head of the bishop-elect as the principal ordaining bishop with hands outstretched prays the Prayer of Ordination. All the other bishops join with the principal ordaining bishop in praying in a low voice the following part of the Prayer of Ordination:

Now upon this chosen one
pour out the power that is from you,
the governing Spirit,
whom you gave to your beloved Son, Jesus Christ,
the Spirit he bestowed on those holy Apostles

DEACONS HOLDING THE BOOK OF GOSPELS DURING THE ORDINATION OF THE AUXILIARY BISHOP OF BRASÍLIA, 2013

who established the Church in every place
as your sanctuary
for the unceasing praise and glory of your name.
> —*Rite of Ordination of a Bishop,* "Prayer of
> Ordination," no. 47

Anointing with Chrism: Next, the principal ordaining bishop anoints the head of the newly ordained bishop with Chrism, praying:

May God, who has made you a sharer in the
High Priesthood of Christ,
pour upon you the oil of mystical anointing
and make you fruitful with an abundance of
spiritual blessings.
> —*Rite of Ordination of a Bishop,* "Anointing
> of the Head and Handing on of the Book of
> Gospels and the Insignia," no. 49

He then hands the newly ordained bishop the Book of the Gospels, saying, "Receive the Gospel and preach the word of God / with all patience and sound teaching." As the ceremony continues, the new bishop is presented with the insignia of his office, namely, a ring, miter and crozier.

THINK, PAIR AND SHARE

- ⊙ What images come to mind when you think of your local bishop? How do these images help you share with others the nature of the office and ministry of a bishop in the Church?
- ⊙ Bishops have a responsibility to lead and serve all the people of their diocese. How would you describe the responsibilities of the people toward their bishop?

OVER TO YOU

- ⊙ How has this lesson given you a better understanding of the office and ministry of bishops in the Catholic Church?
- ⊙ What do you consider most important about bishops in the life of the Church?
- ⊙ Decide now what you can and will do to support the bishop of your diocese. (At a minimum, you can pray for him.)

PRESENTATION OF THE MITER

As the ceremony continues, the new bishop is presented with the insignia of his office, namely, a ring, miter and crozier

Priests, co-workers with bishops

A JOURNEY TOWARD PRIESTLY ORDINATION

Jim grew up in a Catholic home in Philadelphia. In his youth he was active in his parish as an altar server and as a member of the parish youth group. After high school he attended a prestigious university staffed by Jesuits to study for a career in finance. After graduating, Jim settled into what he thought was his dream job—working in corporate finance at a Fortune 500 Company. He chose to remain single as he built his professional career. As time went on, the attraction of his dream job soon began to wear off. Remembering the priests who taught and counseled him at the university, Jim began to ponder whether he might become a priest in the Society of Jesus, or the Jesuits. After much prayer, discernment, and conversation with some of his former Jesuit professors, Jim began the very long and formal journey toward ordination as a Jesuit priest.

OPENING REFLECTION

- ⊙ Think about the priests whom you know personally.
- ⊙ How are they serving the Church?
- ⊙ What talents do they have that help them serve the Church?
- ⊙ How can you use your talents to serve the Church?

CO-WORKERS WITH BISHOPS

The Apostles and other bishops, as we have already discovered, responded to their need for co-workers, or co-laborers. They ordained men as priests, whom the writings of the early Church identify as *presbyteroi*, or presbyters. The term presbyter can be translated as "elder" or "priest." Only a bishop can ordain a priest.

FAITH WORD

Priest

A baptized man ordained through the Sacrament of Holy Orders. "Priests are united with the bishops in priestly dignity and at the same time depend on them in the exercise of their pastoral functions; they are called to be the bishops' prudent co-workers" (CCC, no. 1595). With the bishop, priests form a presbyteral (priestly) community and assume with him the pastoral mission for a particular parish. They serve God's People in the work of sanctification by their preaching, teaching, and offering the Sacraments, especially the Eucharist and the forgiving of sins.

—USCCA, Glossary, 524

A prayer for vocations to the priesthood

O Father, raise up among Christians
abundant and holy vocations to the
   priesthood,
who keep the faith alive
and guard the blessed memory of your
   Son Jesus
through the preaching of his Word
and the administration of the
   sacraments,
with which you continually renew your
   faithful.
      —*Catholic Household Blessings & Prayers*
             (Revised Edition), 385

All the priests in a diocese form one priestly body. With their bishop they serve the Church as a unified body of priests, or **presbyterate**. The Church at the Second Vatican Council reiterated this ancient Tradition of the Church.

All priests share with their bishops the one identical priesthood and ministry of Christ. Consequently the very unity of their consecration and mission requires their [priests'] hierarchical union with the order of bishops. . . . Bishops, therefore, because of the gift of the Holy Spirit that has been given to priests at their ordination, will regard them as indispensable helpers and advisers in the ministry of and in the task of teaching, sanctifying and shepherding the people of God. This has been forcefully emphasized from the earliest ages of the church by liturgical texts.
   —Vatican II, *Decree on the Ministry and Life of Priests (Presbyterorum Ordinis)*, no. 7

NURTURING PRIESTLY VOCATIONS

The Lord has "made us [his Church] a kingdom, priests serving his God and Father" (Revelation 1:6; see also Revelation 5:9–10). The whole Church is a priestly people. Through Baptism all the faithful are made sharers in the **priesthood of the faithful**. The baptized receive the vocation and the graces to share in the one priesthood of Jesus Christ according to their state of life in the Church.

Christ calls some of the faithful to lead the communion of the Church in a way that is essentially different from the priesthood of the faithful. Christ calls baptized men to the ordained ministry, or the **ministerial priesthood**. Ordination into the ministerial priesthood, as we have already seen, is reserved to men alone. St. John Paul II reaffirmed this apostolic tradition. He wrote: "The Church has no authority whatsoever to confer priestly ordination on women" (Apostolic Letter, *On Priestly Ordination [Ordinatio Sacerdotalis]*, no. 4). This teaching, the Pope affirmed, cannot be interpreted to "mean that women are of lesser dignity" than men (*On Priestly Ordination*, no. 3).

While Jesus was journeying with the Apostles through Samaria, he appointed seventy disciples and sent them in pairs ahead of him to every town and place that he intended to visit. He then said to the Apostles, "The harvest is plentiful, but the laborers are few; therefore ask the Lord of the harvest to send out laborers" (Luke 10:2). The Church sees in these words of the Lord the need for priests and the responsibility of all the faithful to pray for and encourage vocations to the ministerial priesthood.

All the faithful can pray that many will respond to the Lord's invitation to serve his Church as priests. Parents and other family members can encourage their sons, grandsons and nephews to consider whether the Lord is calling them to the priesthood. Parish priests and other members of the parish and Catholic school communities through the example of their life and prayer can support youth and men of the parish to discern whether the Lord is calling them to serve God's people as ordained priests.

PREPARING FOR ORDINATION

Once a man acknowledges through prayer and discernment that the Lord is calling him to the ordained priesthood, he begins a period of formal, lengthy study and formation for the priestly ministry in a seminary. St. John Paul II, in chapter 5 of his 1992 apostolic exhortation, *On the Formation of Priests in the Circumstances of the Present Day (Pastores Dabo Vobis)*, identified four essential characteristics that are to be part of the formal formation and training of priests. These are: "Human formation, the Basis of All Priestly Formation"; "Spiritual Formation: In Communion with God and in Search of Christ"; "Intellectual Formation: Understanding the Faith"; and "Pastoral Formation: Communion with the Charity of Jesus Christ the Good Shepherd."

While at seminary the candidate studies philosophy and theology and engages in intense and supervised formation in all four areas. Along the way, the seminary faculty and others discern and assess the candidate's formation and readiness for ordination. Throughout this time of formal preparation, candidates must come to understand clearly and embrace freely the lifelong promises they will make at their ordination.

OVER TO YOU

◉ Take a moment and pray that young men whom the Lord calls to the priestly life will respond to that call.

RITE OF ORDINATION OF PRIESTS

The essential elements of the rite of ordination of priests are the same as those for the ordination of bishops and deacons, namely, the laying on of hands and the Prayer of Ordination, or Prayer of Consecration.

The promises of the elect: After the homily, the elect rise and stand before the ordaining bishop, who questions the elects' resolve to:

◉ cooperate with the grace of the Holy Spirit to "discharge without fail the office of priesthood in the presbyteral rank, as worthy co-workers with the Order of Bishops in caring for the Lord's flock";

◉ "exercise the ministry of the word worthily and wisely, preaching the Gospel, and teaching the Catholic faith";

◉ "celebrate the mysteries of Christ faithfully and reverently, in accord with the Church's tradition, especially in the sacrifice of the Eucharist and in the sacrament of Reconciliation, for the glory of God and the sanctification of the Christian people";

While at seminary the candidate studies philosophy and theology and engages in intense and supervised formation

ST. JOHN'S SEMINARY, BRIGHTON, MA

- ⊙ "implore with us God's mercy upon the people entrusted to your care by observing the command to pray without ceasing"; and
- ⊙ "be united more closely every day to Christ the High Priest, who offered himself for us to the Father as a pure sacrifice, and to consecrate yourselves to God for the salvation of all."
  —*The Roman Pontifical*, Rite of Ordination of Priests, "Promise of the Elect," no. 124

The elect then place their joined hands between those of the bishop and promise respect and obedience to their Ordinary and, if the elect is a member of a religious order, to their legitimate superior. As in the rite of the ordination of a bishop, the Litany of Supplication follows.

Laying on of Hands and Prayer of Ordination: Each of the elect go up to the ordaining bishop and kneel before him. The bishop lays his hands on the head of each of the elect without saying anything. The priests present then come and do the same. Then with the priests standing alongside, the bishop with hands outstretched sings or prays aloud the Prayer of Ordination.

Anointing of Hands and Handing On of Bread and Wine: After the Prayer of Ordination, the newly ordained priests are vested with stole and chasuble, the insignia of the priestly office. Then the bishop anoints the palms of the hands of each of the newly ordained priests with Chrism as he prays:

The Lord Jesus Christ,
whom the Father anointed with the Holy Spirit and power,
guard and preserve you,
that you may sanctify the Christian people
and offer sacrifice to God.
—*The Roman Pontifical*, Rite of Ordination of Priests, no. 133

The Liturgy of the Eucharist is then celebrated. After he receives the gifts of bread and wine from the deacon, the bishop hands them to each of the newly ordained priests as he says: "Receive the offering of the holy people to be rendered to God. / Understand what you do, imitate what you celebrate, / and conform your life to the mystery of the Lord's cross." After the bishop and the priests present exchange a sign of peace with the newly ordained, the bishop and the new priests concelebrate the Liturgy of the Eucharist.

TALK IT OVER
- ⊙ What does the celebration of the ordination of a priest reveal about the vocation to the priesthood?

THE EFFECTS OF THE SACRAMENT

In the Sacrament of Holy Orders bishops and priests are marked with an indelible, or permanent, seal or character that cannot be repeated. This character configures them "to Christ as Priest, Teacher and Pastor" (CCC, no. 1585) "by a special grace of the Holy Spirit, so that [they] may serve as Christ's instrument for his Church" (CCC, no. 1581).

Christ, who is the Head of the Church, is the source of all priesthood. He is visible and present in the whole community of believers in a unique way through his bishops and priests. A traditional way of expressing this reality is to say that the bishop or priest acts *in persona Christi Capitis*, or "in the person of Christ, the Head (of his Body, the Church)." Through the Sacrament of Holy Orders, the ordained is "truly made like to the high priest and possesses the authority to act in the power and place of the person of Christ himself" (CCC, no. 1548). "The presence of Christ as head of the Church is made visible in the midst of the community of believers" (CCC, no. 1549). St. Thomas of Aquinas summed up this ancient teaching of the Church: "Christ is the source of all priesthood: the priest of the old law was a figure of Christ, and the priest of the new law acts in the person of Christ" (St. Thomas Aquinas, *Summa Theologiae* III, 22, 4c, quoted in CCC, no. 1548).

"This presence of Christ in the minister is not to be understood as if the latter were preserved from all human weaknesses, the spirit of domination, error, even sin" (CCC, no. 1550). What it does mean is that despite the inevitable human weakness of the bishop or priest as a person, the Spirit of Christ always offers his grace in the sacraments to all the faithful who properly receive a sacrament.

The Church has always taught that no human person is really holy enough to administer the sacraments. In its rejection and condemnation of the heresy Donatism, the Church in the fourth century affirmed, as she continues to do today, that the power of the sacrament comes through the power of God, not through the personal holiness of the minister who administers the sacrament in the name and Person of Jesus Christ.

In persona Christi Capitis

In the ecclesial service of the ordained minister, it is Christ himself who is present to his Church as Head of his Body, Shepherd of his flock, high priest of the redemptive sacrifice, Teacher of Truth. This is what the Church means by saying that the priest, by virtue of the sacrament of Holy Orders, acts *in persona Christi Capitis*.

—CCC, no. 1548

THINK, PAIR AND SHARE

⊙ Jot down some of your thoughts on these questions:
  – Should the faithful expect a priest to be "perfect"?
  – How can the faithful support their priests?
⊙ Share your reflections with a partner.

OVER TO YOU

⊙ How has your discussion of the ministerial priesthood increased your understanding and appreciation of the ministry of your parish priest(s)?
⊙ Take a moment and pray for the priests who minister to and with you.

In the next section of this chapter we will explore the priestly life in more detail.

The priestly life

WASHING OF THE FEET

Read John 13:1–17 slowly. As you do so, picture the scene and imagine that you are there. Let Jesus wash your feet. When St. Peter objected to Jesus washing his feet, Jesus explained the deeper meaning and reason for his action—performing humble tasks of service to others manifests both God's love and one's own love for those whom we serve.

OPENING REFLECTION

◉ Turn your attention once again to your memories of evening Mass on Holy Thursday. What do you remember about the ritual of washing of the feet?

◉ Have you ever "washed the feet" of another person? Why would you do so?

◉ How do you see people "washing the feet" of others? Give specific examples.

HOLINESS OF LIFE

Jesus gave his Apostles the model and criterion for their ministry. Their ministry was to be a life of service, of "washing the feet" of people out of love for them. Through the Sacrament of Holy Orders, one of the two Sacraments at the Service of Communion, the ordained—bishops, priests and deacons—commit themselves to serve the People of God as Jesus himself did and continues to do through them. Their path to their own salvation and holiness is serving God and the People of God. Through service rendered out of love for God and for others, priests can grow in holiness of life. As co-workers with their bishop they deepen their communion with God and the People of God by sanctifying, teaching and governing the faithful.

JESUS WASHING THE DISCIPLES' FEET | GERMAN, LATE 15TH CENTURY

Living images, or icons, of Christ

"Beloved, through ordination, you have received the same Spirit of Christ, who makes you like him, so that you can act in his name and so that his very mind and heart might live in you. This intimate communion with the Spirit of Christ—while guaranteeing the efficacy of the sacramental actions which you perform in persona Christi—seeks to be expressed in fervent prayer, in integrity of life, in the pastoral charity of a ministry tirelessly spending itself for the salvation of the brethren. In a word, it calls for your personal sanctification" (St. John Paul II, "*On the Formation of Priests in the Circumstances of the Present Day*," no. 33 §5).

St. Charles Randolph Uncles and the Josephites

Father Charles Randolph Uncles (1859–1933) was the first black seminarian ordained a Roman Catholic priest in the United States. In 1895, four years after his ordination, Father Uncles and four other priests founded the Society of St. Joseph of the Sacred Heart, which is known as the Josephites. The mission of the Josephites, as stated on their website, is: "The Josephites, a religious community of Catholic priests and brothers, is committed to serving the African American Community through the proclamation of the Gospel and our personal witness. Our commitment is expressed through sacramental, educational and pastoral ministry, service to those in need, and working for social justice."

ST. JOSEPH'S JOSEPHITE SEMINARY, WASHINGTON, DC

THINK, PAIR AND SHARE

- Recall our discussion of the Christian vocation to holiness of life in chapter 1.
- What do you understand to be "holiness of life"?
- How might service to others be essential to growing in holiness of life?

DIOCESAN PRIESTS AND RELIGIOUS INSTITUTE PRIESTS

The Church is served by diocesan priests and religious order priests. Priests ordained to serve the people of a particular church or diocese are known as diocesan priests. Prior to their ordination as a priest, when they have been ordained a transitional deacon, they are incardinated into, or officially connected to, a diocese and its bishop. (You will recall that ordination to the transitional diaconate is the step just prior to ordination as a priest.) Priests who are members of a religious community, for example the Franciscans, Dominicans, Jesuits or Josephites, may also be appointed to work with the bishop of a diocese, or local ordinary, to serve the people of a diocese.

Most often a priest will serve in a parish as its pastor or as a parochial vicar, or associate pastor. In the Catholic Church only a priest can serve as a pastor of a parish. You will recall that the word "pastor" comes from the Latin word *pastor*, which means "shepherd." Pope Francis at the celebration of the Chrism Mass in 2013 reminded priests of what it means to be a pastor, or shepherd of the flock of Jesus Christ, the Good Shepherd. The Pope said, "This is what I am asking you, 'be shepherds with the smell of sheep.'" These words of the Pope open up the meaning of these words of Jesus, "I am the good shepherd. I know my own and my own know me, just as the Father knows me and I know the Father" (John 10:14–15).

WHAT ABOUT YOU PERSONALLY?

- What are the many ways priests serve you?
- Take the opportunity to thank them.

MINISTERS OF THE WORD AND SACRAMENTS

Priests are co-workers with their bishop in fulfilling the threefold ministry of sanctifying, teaching and governing the Church. Priests have a variety of pastoral duties. In the parish they attend to the day-to-day duties of running a parish. They work closely with lay leaders in overseeing finances and the general upkeep of the parish facilities. They interface with other community leaders. They also work with their bishop in various governing offices, such as vicar

FR. FRANCIS P. DUFFY, CATHOLIC CHAPLIN AND HERO OF WORLD WAR I

regard they counsel people to seek the will of God in meeting the small and large challenges of living an authentic Christian life and service. Priests are often educators in schools and universities and in parish religious formation programs. They serve as counselors, chaplains and spiritual directors. They attend to the military and to those in prison and may help run social services for people with material needs. In this regard, priests especially serve the poor and other vulnerable people entrusted to their care. They visit with the sick and dying at home or in hospitals and other healthcare facilities, often bringing them the Eucharist. They console people who are grieving over the suffering or the death of relatives or friends. In all these and other ways they are heralds of the Gospel of mercy.

The sacraments: Priests exercise their ministry most profoundly in the celebration of the sacraments, especially the Eucharist, which is the source and summit of the Christian life. "For in the most blessed Eucharist is contained the entire spiritual wealth of the Church" (*Decree on the Ministry and Life of Priests*, no. 5). The *Catechism*, quoting the *Dogmatic Constitution on the Church* (*Lumen Gentium*) and citing the *Decree on the Ministry and Life of Priests* (*Presbyterorum Ordinis*) promulgated by the Second Vatican Council, teaches further:

"It is in the Eucharistic cult or in the *Eucharistic assembly* of the faithful (*synaxis*) that they exercise in a supreme degree their sacred office; there, acting in the person of Christ and proclaiming his mystery, they unite the votive offerings of the faithful to the sacrifice of Christ their head, and in the sacrifice of the Mass they make present again and apply, until the coming of the Lord, the unique sacrifice of the New Testament, that namely of Christ offering himself once for all a spotless victim to the Father" (*Lumen Gentium*, no. 28). From this unique sacrifice their whole priestly ministry draws its strength (see *Presbyterorum Ordinis*, no. 5).

— CCC, no. 1566

general, to assist him in the administration of the diocese. In these and other ways they fulfill the Church's primary work of **evangelization** within and outside the parish. But the priestly ministry has a special focus on preaching the Word of God, especially at the liturgy, and on celebrating the sacraments, with a privileged place for celebrating the Eucharist.

The Word of God: The Church at Vatican II taught: "The people of God is formed into one in the first place by the word of the living God (see 1 Peter 1:23; Acts of the Apostles 6:7, 12:24), which is quite rightly expected from the mouths of priests. . . . For by the saving word of God faith is aroused in the heart of unbelievers and is nourished in the heart of believers" (*Decree on the Ministry and Life of Priests*, no. 4).

Priests exercise this ministry of the Word of God in particular by their preaching and example, or word, of their lives. Priests also exercise this ministry in their instruction of the people to live the Gospel authentically. In this

Priests in the Latin Church are the ordinary ministers of Baptism, Confirmation, Eucharist, Penance and Anointing of the Sick. In certain circumstances priests in the Latin Church may confer the Sacrament of Confirmation. (In the Eastern Churches bishops and priests are the ordinary ministers of Chrismation, or Confirmation.) Priests administer God's forgiveness, healing and reconciliation in the Sacrament of Penance and Reconciliation, or Confession. They bring spiritual graces and healing through the Sacrament of the Anointing of the Sick to the faithful who are seriously or terminally ill.

Priests in the Latin Church are the Church's witness to the Sacrament of Marriage. They receive the consent of the spouses, who are the ministers of this sacrament, in the name of the Church and they give the blessing of the Church. (As you learned in chapter 8, in the Eastern Churches the priest confers the Sacrament of Marriage.)

THINK, PAIR AND SHARE

- ⊙ Take a moment to jot down all the different ways you see priests serving your parish and the broader community.
- ⊙ Then with a partner discuss:
  - How can you support the work of the priest(s) in your parish?
  - How can you encourage your priest(s) to live holy lives among a community that is "a holy priesthood"?
- ⊙ Share your discussions with the class.

EMBRACING THE PRIESTLY PROMISES

Think about it: life, family, society, indeed nothing could function well without promises made and kept faithfully. We all make various promises in the course of our lives. We promise to do a favor for a friend; we promise to be loyal to someone; we promise to play our part. Some of the promises we make are simple and easy to fulfill; others require more focused attention and a long-term commitment. For example, married people promise to spend the rest of their lives together and to love each other even when it is difficult. But, no matter what kind of promises we make, they all involve a commitment to another person who trusts us to keep our word. As you have learned in the previous

section of this chapter, diocesan priests make two promises during their ordination. They commit to living a life of celibacy and promise obedience to their bishop. Religious priests also embrace vows as a requirement to enter their religious order or institute. Most commonly, religious priests vow to live the evangelical counsels of poverty, chastity and obedience.

A life of celibacy: "In the Latin Church, celibacy is obligatory for bishops and priests. In some Eastern Churches, celibacy is a prerequisite for the ordination only of bishops; priests may not marry after they have been ordained" (CCC, Glossary).

In reflecting on the spiritual gift of celibacy, St. John Paul II taught:

Priestly celibacy should not be considered just as a legal norm or as a totally external condition for admission to ordination, but rather as a value that is profoundly connected with ordination, whereby a man takes on the likeness of Jesus Christ, the good shepherd and spouse of the Church, and therefore as a choice of a greater and undivided love for Christ and his Church, as a full and joyful availability in his heart for the pastoral ministry.

—*On the Formation of Priests in the Circumstances of the Present Day*, no. 50 §2

EASTERN ORTHODOX CLERGY IN THE 19TH CENTURY

But you may ask, "Aren't some priests married?" While the Roman Catholic (Latin) Church requires the promise of celibacy from its bishops, priests and transitional deacons, Eastern Churches permit a married man to be ordained a priest. Like all married people, they are to practice chastity, but do not make the promise of celibacy.

A second group of married priests are those married ministers who come into the Catholic Church from a Protestant denomination. These priests, usually Episcopalian, Anglican or Lutheran, were married and ordained as priests in those ecclesial communions before deciding to become members of the Roman Catholic Church. The Catholic Church allows these priests to serve the Church as married priests. Should their spouses die, they may not remarry and must commit to a life of celibacy.

THINK, PAIR AND SHARE
- How would a priest's life of celibacy contribute to the building up of the Body of Christ and advance the Reign of God in the world?

WHAT ABOUT YOU PERSONALLY?
- What do you think are the biggest challenges

to living the promise of celibacy? What might be some of its rewards?
- Would you be willing to promise to live a life of celibacy to serve the Church? Why or why not?

Obedience to the bishop: You have already learned that priests are ordained to be co-workers with their bishop. St. John Paul II opened up the meaning of priestly obedience. He taught that authentic priestly obedience is apostolic, communal, ascetical and pastoral. Let us take a moment to read and reflect on what the Pope taught:

First of all, obedience is "apostolic" in the sense that it recognizes, loves and serves the Church in her hierarchical structure. . . .

Priestly obedience has also a "community" dimension: It is not the obedience of an individual who alone relates to authority, but rather an obedience which is deeply a part of the unity of the presbyterate, which as such is called to cooperate harmoniously with the bishop and, through him, with Peter's successor.

This aspect of the priest's obedience demands a marked spirit of asceticism, both in the sense of a tendency not to become too bound up in one's own preferences or points of view and in the sense of giving brother priests the opportunity to make good use of their talents, and abilities, setting aside all forms of jealousy, envy and rivalry. . . .

Finally, priestly obedience has a particular "pastoral" character. It is lived in an atmosphere of constant readiness to allow oneself to be taken up, as it were "consumed," by the needs and demands of the flock. . . .
—*On the Formation of Priests in the Circumstances of the Present Day*, no. 28

THINK, PAIR AND SHARE
- How would a priest's life of obedience build up the Body of Christ and advance the Reign of God in the world?

Religious order priests vow to accept and practice voluntary poverty; each member of the religious order owns nothing as strictly his own

OVER TO YOU

- Think about the role of true obedience within your family and within your school community?
- What are the biggest challenges to your living the virtue of obedience?
- What are some of its rewards?

THE EVANGELICAL COUNSELS

Religious priests consecrate themselves to serve their community and its apostolate and to seek holiness of life by living the radicalism of the gospel life. Upon entering a community, religious priests most commonly vow or promise to live the evangelical counsels of poverty, chastity and obedience. We will explore this state of life in more detail in chapter 10, "The Consecrated Life." Here, we reflect briefly on those vows or promises that religious order priests commit to live.

Poverty: Religious order priests vow to accept and practice voluntary poverty. Voluntary poverty is freely chosen as an expression of the person's and the community's total reliance on God. In practice, each member of the religious order owns nothing as strictly his own. Diocesan priests, as are all Christians, are called to practice the evangelical counsel of poverty according to their state of life. They are to be poor as Christ, in whose priesthood they share, was poor. Diocesan priests, however, do not vow to live a life of poverty as religious order priests do.

Chastity: Religious order priests vow to live a life of chastity. This vow of chastity is broader than the obligation of all the faithful to live the virtue of chastity according to their state of life. The vow of chastity a religious order priest makes also includes a commitment to lifelong celibacy.

Obedience: Religious order priests vow obedience to their religious superior. In this way they promise to work, as directed by the superior, with the other members of the community collaboratively to attain the mission of the institute or order. If appointed by their superior and a bishop to serve the people of a diocese as a co-worker of the bishop, religious order priests, as members of the presbyterate, fulfill all their pastoral duties in obedience to the bishop. They work in communion with the bishop and all the priests of the diocese.

THINK, PAIR AND SHARE

- Given everything that you have learned about the vocation to the ministerial priesthood, discuss with a partner:
  - What is the importance of the priesthood for the Church?
  - What are some of the challenges of serving the Church as a priest?
  - What are the rewards of serving the Church as a priest?
- Share your reflections with the class.

JOURNAL EXERCISE

- How does your living a life of voluntary obedience, chastity and poverty contribute to the mission of the Church? To your attaining holiness of life?

JUDGE AND ACT

REVIEW AND SHARE WHAT YOU HAVE LEARNED

Look back over this chapter and reflect on what you have learned about the vocation, ministry and life of bishops and priests. Share the teachings of the Catholic Church on these statements:

- ⊙ Christ instituted the Sacrament of Holy Orders at the Last Supper.
- ⊙ Holy Orders is a sacrament reserved to men.
- ⊙ The ordained are marked with a permanent seal or character that configures them to Christ.
- ⊙ As the Church grew, the Apostles appointed and ordained both their successors and priests to be their co-workers.
- ⊙ The bishops are the direct successors of the Apostles.
- ⊙ Bishops are directly appointed by the pope.
- ⊙ Bishops and priests act in the person of Christ and serve as icons of Christ.

SAINT BRIGID OF KILDARE CHURCH, DUBLIN, OH

- ⊙ The ministry of bishops and priests includes the threefold office of sanctifying, teaching and governing.
- ⊙ The essential elements of the ordination of a bishop or priest are the laying on of hands and the Prayer of Ordination, or Prayer of Consecration.
- ⊙ Priests are co-workers with their bishop.

OVER TO YOU

- ⊙ What wisdom did you discover for living your life as a disciple of Jesus Christ from your study of this chapter?
- ⊙ What did you learn about the relationship uniting bishops and priests?
- ⊙ What did you learn about the relationship uniting bishops and priests with the people entrusted to their care?

HEALING THE WOUNDS OF THE WORLD

Pope Francis is the Shepherd of the Universal Church. He described the work of the Church, saying, in part: "I see clearly that the thing the church needs most today is the ability to heal wounds and to warm the hearts of the faithful; it needs nearness, proximity. I see the church as a field hospital after battle. It is useless to ask a seriously injured person if he has high cholesterol and about the level of his blood sugars! You have to heal his wounds. Then we can talk about everything else. Heal the wounds, heal the wounds" ("A Big Heart Open to God," *America* magazine, September 30, 2013).

TALK IT OVER

- ⊙ How does what you have learned in this chapter help you understand Pope Francis' description of the work of the Church?
  - – Did the Pope's description of the Church as a "field hospital after battle" surprise you?
  - – Does it inspire you to work with your bishop and the priests of your parish?
- ⊙ Share your reflections as a class.

Terence Cardinal Cooke (1921–83), Archbishop of New York and Servant of God

Terence Cooke was born and raised in New York City. Francis Cardinal Spellman, Archbishop of New York, ordained him as a priest on December 1, 1945. In his priestly ministry Father Cooke served in a variety of pastoral ministries. These included as a parish priest, chaplain at St. Agatha's Home for Children, CYO (Catholic Youth Organization) director, an administrator at St. Joseph's Seminary, a secretary for Cardinal Spellman, and vicar general of the archdiocese. Throughout his ministry as priest and archbishop Cooke deeply committed himself to consultation in his decision-making and to reaching out in dialogue to people of all faiths.

Blessed Paul VI named Cooke an auxiliary bishop of New York in 1962; and when Cardinal Spellman died in 1965, Paul VI named Cooke the Archbishop of New York. On the day of Cooke's installation as the Archbishop, Martin Luther King, Jr. was assassinated in Memphis, Tennessee. This tragic murder set off rioting in New York City and across the country. One of the new Archbishop's first acts was to visit Harlem, a section of New York City whose residents were predominantly Black, to work with the community to heal their wounds and strive for peace. Cooke later attended King's funeral as a sign of solidarity and to share in the nation's mourning.

Archbishop Cooke also committed his ministry to serve the needs of those most vulnerable among his flock. He founded a number of agencies and services to address the particular needs of imprisoned, disabled and disadvantaged people. Under his leadership the Archdiocese of New York cared for 60 percent of the abandoned and neglected children in New York City, and established nine nursing homes and other health care facilities.

Cardinal Cooke suffered with leukemia and he took a particular interest in providing care for terminally ill cancer patients. As early as 1975 his own cancer had become terminal. During these last years of his life the Archbishop continued to live joyfully and fully in the service of others. He recognized that life was a gift from God, no matter what the circumstances. He wrote: "Life is no less beautiful when it is accompanied by illness, weakness, hunger or poverty, physical or mental diseases, loneliness or old age."

Cardinal Cooke died on October 16, 1983. Men and women from all walks of life and faith traditions, grateful for his selfless service, mourned his death and paid him tribute. The front page of *El Diario*, New York's Spanish language newspaper, said it for all: "*Adios Amigo.*" In 1992 the Church officially declared Cardinal Cooke a "Servant of God"— the first step toward being officially declared a saint of the Church.

TALK IT OVER

⊙ Cardinal Cooke was particularly dedicated to healing the wounded and vulnerable members of the Church. How do you see priests taking part in this work?

SHARE FAITH WITH FAMILY AND FRIENDS

⊙ Talk about ways to incorporate a ministry of healing into your life together.

⊙ Come up with one concrete way that you can put this service into practice.

REFLECT AND DECIDE

⊙ Reflect: Pope Francis said: "I see clearly that the thing the church needs most today is the ability to heal wounds and to warm the hearts of the faithful."

⊙ Recall and name ways that Jesus reached out to people to heal their wounds and warm their hearts.

⊙ What inspiration can you draw from the example of Cardinal Terence Cooke and Pope Francis to take part in this work? How will you act on that inspiration?

LEARN BY HEART

"Whoever wishes to become great among you must be your servant. . . . For the Son of Man came not to be served but to serve, and to give his life a ransom for many."

MARK 10:43, 45

PRAYER REFLECTION

Pray the Sign of the Cross together.

LEADER
Let us join in prayer that our Church serves her Lord and his flock with compassion and mercy. (*Pause*)
God of love and mercy,
you created and care for each of us with an infinite compassion and mercy.
Make us attentive and responsive to the promptings of the Spirit of Christ,
who calls your Church to be the servant of your compassion and mercy in the world.
We ask this in the name of Jesus Christ, the Good Shepherd.
ALL
Amen.

READER
A reading from the holy Gospel according to Mark.
ALL
Glory to you, O Lord.

READER
Proclaim Mark 10:42–45.
The Gospel of the Lord.
ALL
Praise to you, Lord Jesus Christ.

LEADER
Reflect for a moment on what you hear the Lord calling you to be and do right now to render service as a member of the Church. Be attentive to how the Spirit prompts your desires. (*Pause*) If you wish, share your reflections with the group.

Allow a brief time for sharing.

LEADER
Spirit of Christ, light the fire of your love and mercy within us.
May your Church respond to your grace to be instruments of your healing compassion and mercy through our service to all in need.
In this spirit we lift up our minds and hearts in prayer.

READER
May those whom you invite to serve your Church as bishops and priests hear and respond to your call.
ALL
Lord, grant us your sevenfold gift to do your work in the world.

READER
May all the faithful support and work with the bishops and priests whom you send to shepherd them.
ALL
Lord, grant us your sevenfold gift to do your work in the world.

READER
May we and all the faithful recognize and respond to your promptings to serve as Jesus did.
ALL
Lord, grant us your sevenfold gift to do your work in the world.

READER
Let us now pray in our hearts for our bishops and priests who serve us. (*Pause*)
ALL
Lord, grant us your sevenfold gift to do your work in the world.

LEADER
Lord Jesus Christ, Eternal High Priest,
raise up compassionate and merciful shepherds to proclaim your love in the world,
and to provide the living Bread of Life to all the faithful.
ALL
Amen.

Pray the Sign of the Cross together.

CHAPTER 10

The Consecrated Life

MEMBERS OF THE CONSECRATED LIFE . . .

RESPOND TO CHRIST'S CALL TO PERFECTION

PUT ON THE MIND OF CHRIST

LIVE THE EVANGELICAL COUNSELS

GIVE TOTAL SURRENDER TO THE WILL OF GOD

DETACH THEMSELVES FROM EARTHLY GOODS

STRIVE TO LIVE IN THE WORLD FREE FROM ITS DISTRACTIONS

LIVE CHASTE AND CELIBATE LIVES

ALL CHRISTIANS ARE CALLED TO LIVE THEIR LIFE FOR THE SAKE OF THE KINGDOM OF GOD

JESUS CENTERED HIS LIFE AND MINISTRY ON building the Reign of God. Christ calls some Christians to "consecrate" their lives to joining him in this mission. They respond to this call and live the consecrated life. They profess to live the evangelical counsels of poverty, chastity and obedience. Their choice to live the consecrated life frees them from the many distractions that impede a life lived in intimacy with God.

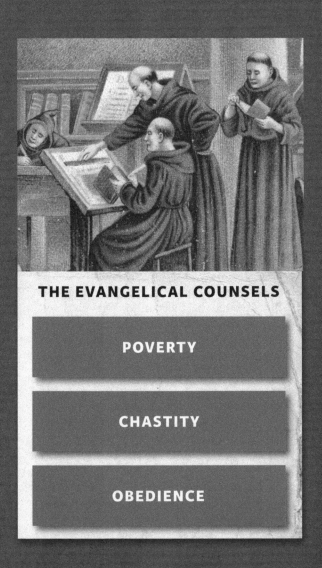

THE EVANGELICAL COUNSELS

POVERTY

CHASTITY

OBEDIENCE

Faith Focus: These teachings of the Catholic Church are the primary focus of the doctrinal content presented in this chapter:

⊙ All the faithful are called to live for the Kingdom of God.

⊙ The practice of the three evangelical counsels of poverty, chastity and obedience leads to the perfection of the Christian life.

⊙ The consecrated life is one of the three states of life in the Church.

⊙ "In the consecrated life, Christ's faithful, moved by the Holy Spirit, propose to follow Christ more nearly, to give themselves to God who is loved above all and, pursuing the perfection of charity in the service of the Kingdom, to signify and proclaim in the Church the glory of the world to come" (*Catechism of the Catholic Church*, no. 916).

⊙ The consecrated life gives witness to the Paschal Mystery of Jesus Christ and to Christ in the world.

⊙ The Blessed Virgin Mary is the model of consecration and discipleship.

Discipleship Formation: As a result of studying this chapter and discovering the meaning of the faith of the Catholic Church for your life, you should be better able to:

⊙ understand the evangelical counsels of poverty, chastity and obedience;

⊙ recognize the various forms of the consecrated life;

⊙ cultivate the attitude and practice of gospel detachment;

⊙ adopt the spirit of the consecrated life;

⊙ discern whether Christ is calling you to the consecrated life;

⊙ model your life as a disciple of Jesus on the life of the Blessed Virgin Mary.

Scripture References: These Scripture references are quoted or referred to in this chapter:
NEW TESTAMENT: **Matthew** 4:1–11, 5:48, 6:24b, 19:16–22 and 27; **Luke** 1:26–38, 7:11–17, 10:38–42, 12:13–29 and 31, 18:24–25; **Philippians** 2:5; **Colossians** 3:1–4; **1 Timothy** 5:3, 5, 9–10 and 16; **Revelation** 14:4

Faith Glossary: Familiarize yourself with or recall the meaning of these key terms. Definitions are found in the Glossary: **asceticism, celibacy, chastity, cloister, consecrated life, contemplation, detachment, eremitical life, eschatology, evangelical counsels, hermit, inculturation, Kingdom of God, monasticism, obedience, Paschal Mystery, poverty (voluntary), secular institutes, societies of apostolic life, states of life, temptation, works of mercy**

Faith Words: consecrated life; evangelical counsels
Learn by Heart: Matthew 19:21
Learn by Example: Blessed Virgin Mary

What does it take to be truly free and alive for Christ?

FROM RAGS TO RICHES

The phrase "from rags to riches" is often used to describe the worldly success of people who have raised themselves up from poverty to wealth! It summarizes the successful pursuit of the American dream—the pursuit of wealth, professional success and social status. Some Christians adapt this saying and use it to preach a "gospel of prosperity." Material riches, they falsely teach, are a sign that a person is "blessed" by God.

OPENING REFLECTION

◉ Can you give examples of people who have made the journey from rags to riches? Where did that journey lead them?

◉ How could the phrase "from rags to riches" describe the life of a Christian?

CINDERELLA: A TIMELESS RAGS-TO-RICHES STORY | GUSTAVE DORÉ

FULLY ALIVE AND FREE—SURRENDERING ONE'S LIFE TO GOD

The gospel mandate "Go, sell your possessions, and give the money to the poor, and you will have treasure in heaven" gives quite another meaning to the phrase "from rags to riches." By giving up everything that the world identifies as riches and a source of security, out of love for God and others, we become truly rich. By committing oneself freely and unselfishly to live the Great Commandment, we attain a wealth far greater than this world can ever provide. Take a moment and reflect on these words of Jesus to a wealthy young man:

"Teacher, what good deed must I do to have eternal life?" And [Jesus] said to him, "Why do you ask me about what is good? There is only one who is good. If you wish to enter into life, keep the commandments." He said to him, "Which ones?" And Jesus said, "You shall not murder; You shall not commit adultery; You shall not steal; You shall not bear false witness; Honor your father and mother; also, You shall love your neighbor as yourself." The young man said to him, "I have kept all these; what do I still lack?" Jesus said to him, "If you wish to be perfect, go, sell your possessions, and give the money to the poor, and you will have treasure in heaven; then come, follow me." When the young man heard this word, he went away grieving, for he had many possessions.

—Matthew 19:16–22

True wealth is found in living one's life rooted in *agape*, the unselfish and self-sacrificing love for God and others. This was how Jesus lived. Freedom from the enslaving power of wealth, whatever form it takes, frees us to gain the fullness of human life. Surrendering to the will

of the Father and consecrating ourselves to him, as Christ did, by living for the **Kingdom of God** is the pursuit of true wealth. Christ's whole way of life, which culminated in the **Paschal Mystery** of his Passion, Death and Resurrection, revealed this way of life. It is only by dying to oneself that one is freed to live for the Kingdom of God. It is this gospel way of life that Jesus invites all his disciples to embrace.

THINK, PAIR AND SHARE

- The young man could not detach himself from his possessions; he rejected Jesus' counsel and went away grieving. Why do you think he responded that way?
- Share your reflections with a partner.

WHAT ABOUT YOU PERSONALLY?

- Do you find it difficult to detach yourself from your possessions? From pursuing the latest style of clothes or the latest tech gadget?
- What does real freedom mean in your life? In what ways can you share this freedom with others?

DETACHMENT

The Gospel calls us to practice the virtue of **detachment**. We are to "strive for [God's] kingdom" (Luke 12:31). We are to respond to the wisdom of the gospel precept of detachment with poverty of heart and simplicity of life. This will enable us to give priority to our relationship with Jesus Christ and to live for the sake of the Kingdom of God that he announced and inaugurated.

The call of the world is the **temptation** to a life of attachment to worldly goods—to their pursuit and possession. The Devil tried to lure Jesus to give in to this very temptation. (Check out Matthew 4:1–11.) In the parable of the rich fool (Luke 12:13–23), Jesus warned about the deceiving, alluring and enslaving power of this temptation. He summarized his teaching:

"Therefore I tell you, do not worry about your life, what you will eat, or about your body, what you will wear. For life is more than food, and the body more than clothing. Consider the ravens: they neither sow nor reap, they have neither storehouse nor barn, and yet God feeds them. Of how much more value are you than the birds!"
—Luke 12:22–23

Consumerism tempts us to live a life of acquiring and finding security in "stuff"; materialism tempts us to seek our well-being in this world. When our identities become tied to our possessions, we lose our true freedom to live fully human lives.

Joined to Christ in Baptism, we receive the grace of the Spirit of Christ to live as Christ did. We receive the wisdom and knowledge to transform our attitudes and behavior into those of Christ. We receive the courage to resist the seduction of the world's prevailing attitudes toward earthly goods, which are contrary to both the natural and the revealed law of God.

Jesus revealed that he truly understood the inner conflict that exists within every heart. Recall his words: "How hard it is for those who have wealth to enter the kingdom of God! Indeed, it is easier for a camel to go through the eye of a needle than for someone who is rich to enter the kingdom of God" (Luke 18:24–25). Jesus' whole life revealed our need to detach ourselves from slavery to material goods and, most importantly, to abandon ourselves to the caring presence of God who "frees us from anxiety about tomorrow" (*Catechism of the Catholic Church* [CCC], no. 2547). Competition for and a preoccupation with worldly success can undermine our efforts to give authentic witness to Christ in the world.

THINK, PAIR AND SHARE
- What can distract a person from building life-giving and loving relationships with God and others?
- Share examples of how a life of "detachment" can help a person to focus on living for the sake of the Kingdom of God.

OVER TO YOU
- What can you do to cultivate the attitude and practice of gospel detachment?
- What difference might that make for your living as a disciple of Jesus?

THE EVANGELICAL COUNSELS
All Christians are to strive to live their life for the sake of the Kingdom of God. The **evangelical counsels** are at the center of that effort. They are "in general, the teachings of the New Law proposed by Jesus to his disciples which lead to the perfection of Christian life" (CCC, Glossary, "Evangelical Counsels"). "Christ proposes the evangelical counsels, in their great variety, to every disciple" (CCC, no. 915).

FAITH WORD

Evangelical counsels

Those vows taken by men or women who enter religious life; there are three vows: poverty, chastity, and obedience.
—*United States Catholic Catechism for Adults* (USCCA), Glossary, 511

CHRIST AND THE RICH YOUNG MAN | A.N. MIRONOV

The Greek root word for "evangelical" is *euangelion*, which means "good news." A counsel differs from a precept or commandment that one has the obligation or responsibility to follow. A counsel is wise advice taken on or followed voluntarily. (Recall once again the conversation between Jesus and the rich young man who claimed he obeyed all the precepts of the Commandments; but he then rejected Jesus' counsel to go and sell his many possessions.) Christians voluntarily respond to Christ and embrace the evangelical counsels. When they do so, they go the extra mile in living the Gospel.

Some members of the Church make a public promise and vow to surrender their life to living the evangelical counsels, making them the blueprint for their life. They vow to live a life rooted in **poverty**, **chastity** and **obedience**. By living the evangelical counsel of poverty, the faithful who have the vocation to the consecrated life witness that nothing created will distract them from keeping God at the center of their life. They live the counsel of chastity by a life of **celibacy** for the sake of the Kingdom of God. They vow obedience to God and to their religious superior. By obeying their religious superior regarding life in their community and its apostolic work they come to know the will of God for their lives.

These three vows are not about escaping from the world; they are about voluntarily living a way of life in the world that frees one to focus fully on God and join with Christ to bring about the Kingdom of God which he inaugurated. The evangelical counsels free a person to live a life totally committed to the Good News, or Gospel, of Jesus in a radical, complete and uncompromising way. Traditionally, the Church describes the decision to live in this way as "entering the religious life."

TALK IT OVER
- What do you think is required of people who vow to live a life of poverty, chastity and obedience?
- What might be the challenges for living such a life? The blessings?

Forms of the consecrated life

LEARNING FROM JESUS' FRIEND MARY

As a class, read Luke 10:38–42, the gospel story of Martha and Mary. During Jesus' visit with Martha and Mary, Mary was attentive to Jesus and listened to what he was saying. Martha, on the other hand, was "distracted by her many tasks." Perhaps, in her efforts to be a good host, Martha was filled with anxiety and stress. She became upset that Jesus was not troubled by the fact that she was doing all the work while Mary seemed to be just sitting around and doing nothing. Jesus responded to Martha, "you are worried and distracted by many things; there is need of only one thing. Mary has chosen the better part."

JESUS WITH MARY AND MARTHA | 19TH-CENTURY ENGRAVING

OPENING REFLECTION

◉ What sources of stress and pressure do you experience in your daily life? What aspects of your daily life cause you to be frustrated and anxious?

◉ Do these pressures impact the way you live your faith? How?

◉ What place or places provide stillness and quiet for you? Does being in these places help you to be more attentive to God? Can you talk to God in such moments? How?

TALK IT OVER

◉ Why might Martha have been trying to fill her encounter with Jesus with so many activities?

◉ Why was Mary content with sitting at the feet of Jesus, seemingly avoiding all the work that one might have thought necessary to make Jesus' visit a good one?

◉ Put yourself in Martha's place. How might you have responded, and why?

THE CONSECRATED LIFE

The "religious life" is a form of the **consecrated life**, which you have already learned is one of the three **states of life** in the Church. While all the baptized are called to live the evangelical counsels, Christ calls some members of the Church, both lay and ordained, to live those counsels in a public way. The consecrated life is the "public profession of the evangelical counsels of poverty, chastity, and obedience [that] is a constitutive element of the state of consecrated life in the Church" (CCC, Glossary, "Evangelical Counsels"). The word "consecrate" comes from the Latin verb *consecrare*, which means "to dedicate or set apart for a holy purpose." What is that holy purpose? In the Sermon on the Mount Jesus described it this

Put on the Mind of Christ

Consecrated life is a call to incarnate the Good News, to *follow Christ*, the crucified and risen one, to take on "Jesus' way of living and acting as the Incarnate Word in relation to the Father and in relation to the brothers and sisters" (St. John Paul II, Apostolic Exhortation, *The Consecrated Life* [Vita Consecrata], no. 22). In practical terms, it is a call to take up his way of life, to adopt his interior attitude, to allow oneself to be invaded by his Spirit, to absorb his surprising logic and his scale of values, to share in his risks and his hopes. "Be guided by the humble yet joyful certainty of those who have been *found, touched and transformed by the Truth* who is Christ, ever to be proclaimed" (Pope Francis, *Homily at the Holy Mass with Bishops, Priests, Religious and Seminarians on the XXVIII World Youth Day*, Rio de Janeiro, 27 July 2013).

—*Rejoice! A Letter to Consecrated Men and Women: A Message from the Teachings of Pope Francis*, no. 5 §3

CRISTO REDENTOR, RIO DE JANEIRO, BRAZIL

way: "Be perfect, therefore, as your heavenly Father is perfect" (Matthew 5:48).

Members of the consecrated life have a unique identity among the faithful. Members of religious communities may be ordained or members of the laity. They "consecrate" their lives to serve God and the Church as members of a religious community approved by the Church. Their vocation calls them to a new way of being. They give of themselves in total surrender to the will of God and the service of the Church for the sake of the Kingdom of God.

Members of the consecrated life follow the counsel of St. Paul, who wrote to the Church in Philippi, "Let the same mind be in you that was in Christ Jesus" (Philippians 2:5); and to the Church in Colossae:

So if you have been raised with Christ, seek the things that are above, where Christ is, seated at the right hand of God. Set your minds on things that are above, not on things that are on earth, for you have died, and your life is hidden with Christ in God. When Christ who is your life is revealed, then you also will be revealed with him in glory.

—Colossians 3:1–4

To respond to the call to the consecrated life is not to reject the world as evil or to deny its beauty and goodness. It is a call to *detachment*. Members of the consecrated life *detach* themselves from "earthly goods" and strive to live in the world free from its distractions. The life of a person called to the consecrated life is a deepening of a *life hidden with Christ in God* (see Colossians 3:2), a life that furthers God's reign of love, justice and peace. Members of the consecrated life live chaste and celibate lives as Christ did. "[Of] those called to the consecrated life, [Christ] asks a total commitment, one which involves leaving everything behind (see Matthew 19:27) in order to live at his side and to follow him wherever he goes (see Revelation 14:4) (St. John Paul II, Apostolic Exhortation, *On the Consecrated Life and Its Mission in the Church and in the World*, no. 18).

TALK IT OVER

⊙ Do you know or have you learned about someone who lives the consecrated life? How does that person give witness to the goodness and purpose of human life?

⊙ How does that person give you insight into the Christian's life in Christ?

A SIGN OF THE MYSTERY OF REDEMPTION

"In the Church, which is like the sacrament . . . of God's own life, the consecrated life is seen as a special sign of the mystery of redemption" (CCC, no. 932). The faithful who have a vocation to the consecrated life put on the mind of Christ and conform their life to the Paschal Mystery of his Passion, Death and Resurrection. They live in hope and assurance of life in the kingdom to come. This dimension of the consecrated life is referred to as its eschatological dimension. The adjective "eschatological" comes from the Greek noun *eschaton*, which means "last." "Whether their witness is public, as in the religious state, or less public, or even secret, Christ's coming remains for all those consecrated both the origin and rising sun of their life" (CCC, no. 933).

Many members of the consecrated life choose to live in a religious community approved by the Church, such as the Franciscans or Benedictines or Carmelites. Others, without professing the three evangelical counsels, may live the vocation to the **eremitical life**, the life of a **hermit**; others as members of societies of the apostolic life, such as the Society of St. Vincent de Paul, the Daughters of Charity, or the Missionaries of Charity. Some may choose not to live as a member of a religious community, but opt instead to live as a consecrated virgin or widow, or as a member of a secular institute. We shall explore these and other forms of the consecrated life in the next three sections of this chapter. Whatever form living the consecrated life takes, it manifests "to everyone the interior aspect of the mystery of the Church, that is, personal intimacy with Christ" (CCC, no. 921) through "a stricter separation from the world, the silence of solitude and assiduous prayer and penance" (*Code of Canon Law*, canon 603 §1).

JOURNAL EXERCISE

⊙ What are the ways you can bring the spirit of the consecrated life into your vocation as a student, and to your future vocation, whatever it might be?

⊙ How would such a commitment give witness to the Kingdom of God and advance the Reign of God?

THE EREMITICAL LIFE: THE VOCATION OF THE HERMIT

The Roman Emperor Constantine, after he converted to Christianity, passed laws of tolerance

FAITH WORD

Consecrated Life

A permanent state of life recognized by the Church, entered freely in response to the call of Christ to perfection, and characterized by the profession of the evangelical counsels of poverty, chastity, and obedience.

—CCC, Glossary

and then of favor for the Christian religion in AD 312 and AD 313. Soon after that the persecution of Christians ended and Christians could freely and openly practice their faith. Some Christians became troubled when they saw the relationship between the Christian faith and the world of imperial power and privilege grow closer and closer. These Christians feared that some of the essential teachings of Jesus, such as "You cannot serve God and wealth" (Matthew 6:24b), were being watered down and even cast aside. In other words, the newfound freedom of Christians was becoming a serious distraction from living the Gospel.

Some Christians, desiring to focus on living in a more radically Christian way and to be free from these distractions, moved out to the edges of cities or into the desert so as to be away from the centers of power. These Christians were known as eremitic monks or hermits. The word "monk" comes from the Greek adjective *monos*, meaning "single, alone, or solitary." The word "eremitic" means "relating to a monk." St. Paul the Hermit (c. 230–242) and St. Anthony of Egypt (c. 251–356) were among these hermits.

Hermits lived simple lives of self-denial and prayer in silence and solitude. They rejected power-grabbing, social climbing, the pursuit of wealth and other distractions that turned their focus from the Kingdom of God. They sought an ever-deepening communion with God through living a life of **asceticism**—a life of prayer and penance for the coming of God's reign.

The hermit's life of gospel simplicity provides a powerful witness to Christians. While they did not always profess the three evangelical counsels, hermits "devoted their life to the praise of God and salvation of the world through a stricter separation from the world, the silence of solitude and assiduous prayer and penance" (*Code of Canon Law*, canon 603 §1; quoted in CCC, no. 920).

This ancient eremitical tradition is alive and well in the Church. Today, hermits such as the Hermits of Bethlehem in Paterson, New Jersey, and the Hermits of the Blessed Virgin Mary of Our Lady of Mount Carmel in Cristoval, Texas live under the direction of the local ordinary, or bishop, of their diocese, who approves their Rule of Life. It is also customary today

PETER THE HERMIT | GÉDÉON DE FORCEVILLE

for hermits to make a public profession of the evangelical counsels, which the local ordinary receives in the name of the Church, and to live together in community in a hermitage. "A hermit is recognized by [church] law as one dedicated to God in consecrated life if he or she publicly professes in the hands of the diocesan bishop the three evangelical counsels, confirmed by vow or promise or other sacred bond, and observes a proper program of living under his direction" (canon 603 §2). The *Catechism* teaches:

They manifest to everyone the interior aspect of the mystery of the Church, that is, personal intimacy with Christ. Hidden from the eyes of men, the life of the hermit is a silent preaching of the Lord, to whom he has surrendered his life simply because he is everything to him. Here is a particular call to find in the desert, in the thick of spiritual battle, the glory of the Crucified One.

—CCC, no. 921

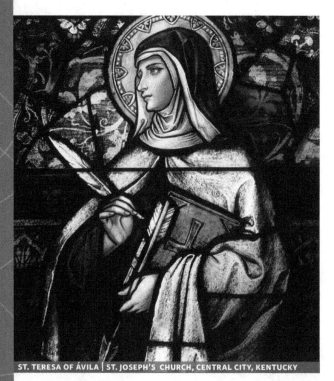

ST. TERESA OF ÁVILA | ST. JOSEPH'S CHURCH, CENTRAL CITY, KENTUCKY

Contemplative prayer . . . means taking time frequently to be alone with him who we know loves us.

ST. TERESA OF ÁVILA

the Curé of Ars, described contemplative prayer in a similar way. He wrote: "I look at him and he looks at me."

In Christian tradition, various forms, or Institutes, of the contemplative life have emerged. Among these are the Poor Clares and the Order of Discalced Carmelites. "By their lives and mission, the members of these Institutes imitate Christ in his prayer on the mountain, bear witness to God's lordship over history and anticipate the glory which is to come. . . . In this way they offer the ecclesial community a singular testimony of the Church's love for her Lord, and they contribute, with hidden apostolic fruitfulness, to the growth of the People of God" (St. John Paul II, *The Consecrated Life*, no. 8). St. Clare of Assisi (1194–1253) and St. Thérèse of Lisieux (1873–97) consecrated themselves to the contemplative life. The fact that the Church has named St. Clare the patron saint of television and St. Thérèse the patron saint of missionaries gives testimony to the essential connection between the contemplative in the **cloister** and the apostolic life in the outside world.

All disciples of the Lord should embrace a contemplative disposition. To do this they should sit at the feet of our Lord before and after entering into decisions and activity. The contemplative life reminds us that we are called to listen to God's Spirit before springing into action.

THINK, PAIR AND SHARE

- ⊙ How comfortable are you with silence? Do you seek solitude and silence? Why or why not?
- ⊙ What do you do when you find yourself in a place of silence?

THE CONTEMPLATIVE WAY OF LIFE

Silence and solitude in the presence of our Lord are essential to the life of every disciple of Christ, just as they are to the life of a hermit. Recall Jesus' response to Martha in the gospel story in Luke 10:38–42. Jesus was not counseling a life of inactivity; he was teaching that we should take time frequently to sit in his presence, "to be alone with him" in prayer. Contemplative prayer is vital to the Christian life. **Contemplation** creates stillness and quiet and a prayerful openness to the Spirit of God. It opens our mind and heart to listen to the depths of our own inner spirit, where the Holy Spirit abides.

St. Teresa of Jesus (of Ávila) named such prayer contemplative prayer. She wrote: "Contemplative prayer [mental prayer] in my opinion is nothing else than a close sharing between friends; it means taking time frequently to be alone with him who we know loves us" (*The Book of Her Life*, 8, 5; quoted in CCC, no. 2709). St. John Vianney,

OVER TO YOU

- ⊙ Do you sit in the presence of the Lord just to be alone with him?
- ⊙ How can you "unplug" at different times during the day or week?
- ⊙ What wisdom does monastic life have for our living as a Christian family in the world?

The monastic and the apostolic religious life

GOING ON RETREAT

Catholic high school programs and parish youth ministry programs often include going on, or making, a retreat as an annual event. A retreat is a time away from one's normal routine; it is a time for more intense personal and communal prayer and for reflection and discussion. Retreats are part of the preparation process for the celebration of Confirmation and Marriage.

OPENING REFLECTION

- Think back to a time when you took part in a retreat. What was the occasion?
- Recall the various parts of the retreat. What was the role of prayer and reflection and of discussion and other activities?
- What was the high point of that retreat for you?
- How did going on retreat help you grow in your faith? Help you live your faith in a more focused manner?

MONASTIC LIFE

After several years of living as a hermit in solitude and prayer, as the early hermits of the Church had lived, St. Benedict of Nursia (c. 480–c. 547) founded a monastic community for men in Italy, which came to be known as the Benedictines. He is acknowledged to be the founder of monasticism, or the monastic way of life, in the Church in the West. Monks organize themselves into communities for mutual support in living the Gospel.

The first Benedictines followed a defined way, or rule, of life, written by St. Benedict, which Benedictines continue to follow today. The Benedictine *Rule of Life* is rooted in the practice of asceticism, prayer, study and work. Benedictines promise *stability* (or to remain for life in a particular monastery), *conversion of life*,

ST. BENEDICT | F.L. SCHMITNER

and *obedience* to the community's superior, or the abbot. These promises are similar to the evangelical counsels promised by members of other religious orders. Benedict's motto, "Prayer and Work," is a reminder that both prayer and work are essential for a whole and holy life.

St. Scholastica (c. 480–c. 547), Benedict's twin sister, formed a similar community for women. These religious women came to be called nuns. A monk or nun who lives in a community is called "coenobitic," as compared to the "eremitic" monk who lives alone.

THINK, PAIR AND SHARE

- Compare the eremitical life with the monastic life. In what ways are they similar? In what ways do they differ?
- Do you see your life as a disciple of Christ reflected in one or both of these forms of religious life?

MONASTERIES AS CENTERS OF CHRISTIAN LIFE

Monasteries were not only places where monks lived, prayed and worked. In addition to being an environment that nurtured a monk's growth in holiness of life, monasteries preserved the cultural and spiritual heritage of the people. For example, monks hand-copied the texts of Sacred Scripture and the writings of the great teachers of the Church. They also developed monastery schools to educate children of the nobility as future leaders of the Church and society.

Monks and nuns not only sought their own holiness of life and salvation, but, as the Gospel calls all the faithful to do, they practiced the gospel works of mercy through their life of prayer *and* good words. Monks practiced the biblical mandate of hospitality for the stranger and monasteries became places where travelers could rest, seek spiritual counsel and find the solitude and quiet needed to reflect on their own lives of faith. St. Benedict emphasized the ministry of hospitality in his *Rule of Life*; he wrote: "All guests who present themselves are to be welcomed as Christ, for he himself will say: *I was a stranger and you welcomed me*" (chap. 52). The life of monks and nuns provides all Christians with a model of how to be with God in prayer and to live for the sake of the Reign of God.

Many Christians today discover the monastery to be a place where they can experience God's presence more readily and be free from distractions and worries that turn them away from God. By going on retreats in monasteries or adopting some monastic practices in our own lives we can become more like Christ and live as his disciples. Regularly, all of us need to "unplug" for a period of time and reconnect with God.

Some Christians today are forming "monastic-like" communities. A growing phenomenon in Christianity is one form of a "new monasticism" that is renewing the Church and the lives of the faithful. Members of these communities live and pray together, study and share their possessions, and celebrate their faith in Christ together. They work in a variety of settings outside their monastic community and return for daily support in living the Gospel. Those of us who are not called to live in a monastery or in a monastic-like community can still find ways to bring the values of the monastery and monastic life into the world and our personal lives.

MONKS AT WORK IN A SCRIPTORIUM | CHROMOLITHOGRAPH C. 1900

- Research communities of monastic life in the Catholic Church today in the United States of America.
- Work in small groups and create a profile of a monastic community. Include details of:
  - The founding of the community
  - The origins of their spiritual tradition
  - The specifics of their way of life
- Share your profiles with the class, perhaps during your discussions for the "Judge and Act" section of this chapter.

MOVING OUTSIDE THE MONASTERY WALLS

In the early centuries of the Church a life of solitude and prayer lived away from the world was the choice for many seeking to live a life consecrated to God. Gradually, another form of the consecrated, vowed life emerged, whose hallmark was apostolic activity outside the walls of the community. Those who adopt this lifestyle are often referred to as contemplatives in action. Saints Francis of Assisi and Ignatius of Loyola are examples of founders of religious communities whose lives united contemplation and activity into a holistic way of living the Gospel. Both of these saints gave up wealth and privilege to embrace a life of poverty for the sake of the Kingdom of God.

St. Francis of Assisi (c. 1181–1226), also known as the Poverello ("The Little Poor Man") of Assisi, lived in a time when the excessive pursuit of material possessions and power had weakened the life and mission of the Church. Francis was the son of a wealthy cloth merchant. After failing in his pursuit of worldly fame as a soldier, Francis became disillusioned and turned to solitude and prayer. While in deep prayer before a crucifix in the chapel of San Damiano, which was in need of great repair, Francis responded to the Lord's call, "Rebuild my Church."

At first Francis interpreted this command literally, but he soon came to understand its deeper meaning. He detached himself totally from all possessions and from his social status. He traveled about preaching Christ and the Gospel, begging for food and whatever bodily

ST. FRANCIS OF ASSISI | MISSION CHURCH, RANCHOS DE TAOS, NEW MEXICO

needs were necessary along the way. Others began to join with him, and eventually, with the approval of the Church, the Order of Friars Minor, commonly called "The Franciscans," was established.

The Franciscan way of life is rooted in professing and living the evangelical counsels of poverty, chastity and obedience, and in a community life that is centered in prayer. This communal and personal prayer is the driving force of the Franciscans' apostolic work of preaching, teaching and serving the Church outside the walls of their community.

St. Ignatius of Loyola (1491–1556) responded to the needs of the Church in the sixteenth century, as St. Francis had done in the thirteenth century. Ignatius led a life of poverty, contemplation and action. He founded the Jesuits, or the Society of Jesus, whose initial mission was to renew the education of priests and set straight the false teachings proposed by the Protestant Reformation. This mission soon gave birth to a missionary spirit that led St. Francis Xavier, SJ (1506–1552) and St. Isaac Jogues, SJ (1607–1646) and others to bring the Gospel to Asia and North America.

Religious orders and congregations of men and of women continue to bring the contemplative life into the noisiness of the world. For them, prayer precedes and directs action, which in turn leads to prayer, again in an ongoing cycle. The *Catechism of the Catholic Church*, in its discussion of "religious life," notes:

History witnesses to the outstanding service rendered by religious families in the propagation of the faith and in the formation of new Churches: from the ancient monastic institutions to the medieval orders, all the way to the more recent congregations.

—St. John Paul II, *Redemptoris Missio* (Mission of the Redeemer), no. 69; quoted in CCC, no. 927

SOCIETIES OF APOSTOLIC LIFE

The members of a society of apostolic life live a common life in a community. They promise to live a life of gospel simplicity without religious vows according a constitution, or rule of life, approved by the Church. Some of these communities observe the evangelical counsels as directed in their rule of life. Members of a society of apostolic life support one another as they strive for the perfection of charity.

Societies of apostolic life collaborate with the diocesan bishop in his pastoral duty as they pursue the specific mission or apostolate of the society. They serve in parishes, schools and universities and in hospitals and hospices. They serve as missioners at home and in countries other than their native lands. Examples of societies of apostolic life include:

Daughters of Charity of St. Vincent De Paul: St. Vincent de Paul (1581–1660), the founder of the Vincentians, and St. Louise de Marillac (1591–1660) co-founded this apostolic society in the seventeenth century. The Daughters of Charity gave women religious the freedom to leave their cloisters and go into the streets. They met the poor in their homes and founded hospitals, schools and orphanages. This type of witness continues today.

Opus Dei: St. Josemaría Escrivá (1902–75), who is called the "Saint of the Ordinary Life," founded Opus Dei in 1928 in Spain. The name Opus Dei means "Work of God." The mission of Opus Dei is "to spread the Christian message that every person is called to holiness and that every honest work can be sanctified." Members of Opus Dei

St. Vincent de Paul and St. Louise de Marillac co-founded the apostolic society the Daughters of Charity in the seventeenth century

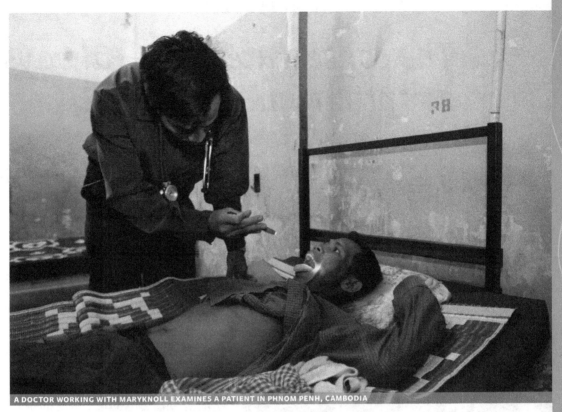

A DOCTOR WORKING WITH MARYKNOLL EXAMINES A PATIENT IN PHNOM PENH, CAMBODIA

include priests and lay people, men and women, both married and single. Opus Dei serves the mission of the Church in sixty-six countries.

Society of Our Mother of Peace: Father Placid Guste, SMP founded the Society of Our Mother of Peace in Oklahoma City, Oklahoma in 1966. It comprised three separate communities, namely: (1) Sons of Our Mother of Peace for Religious Priests and Brothers; (2) Daughters of Our Mother of Peace for Religious Sisters; and (3) Lay Members Community for lay married, or single lay men or lay women.

The Society of Our Mother of Peace states its mission to be "to establish a setting in which the *contemplative life*, with a strong focus on solitude and solitary prayer, will be available *in the context of austere simplicity, with two apostolates*, namely, one of helping persons deepen in prayer and self-discipline, and the apostolate of making the Catholic Faith available primarily to non-Catholics, especially to African-Americans, by door-to-door visitation."

Two other prominent examples in the United States are the Glenmary Home Missioners and Maryknoll priests, brothers and sisters. Glenmary Home Missioners serve the poor in rural America, especially the Appalachian region. Maryknoll does similar work in an international context. All the societies of apostolic life are marked by their commitment to compassion for the poor and to the works of justice.

ANALYZE, COMPARE AND SHARE

⊙ What need do you see in the world today for compassion for the poor and for the works of justice?
⊙ Are you aware of the ways members of religious orders, religious congregations and societies of apostolic life are responding to these needs?
⊙ Share reflections as a class.

JOURNAL EXERCISE

⊙ What gospel issues do you want to respond to? How can you and other Catholic youth get involved?
⊙ Revisit these questions often.
⊙ Rewrite and compare your responses.

The consecrated life—always adapting and developing

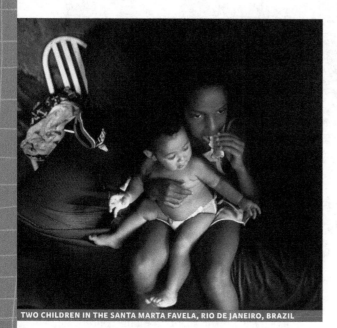

TWO CHILDREN IN THE SANTA MARTA FAVELA, RIO DE JANEIRO, BRAZIL

WITNESSING TO THE LOVE OF GOD

Sr. Dorothy Stang, SND (1931–2005) is a profound example of what it means to live one's life for the sake of the Kingdom of God. From childhood Dorothy expressed her desire to serve the poor as Jesus did. At the age of seventeen she became a member of the Congregation of the Sisters of Notre Dame de Namur—a community of religious sisters whose apostolic work gives witness to God's preferential option for the poor. In 1966, after teaching in Chicago and Phoenix, Sr. Dorothy traveled with five other sisters to serve the people of Brazil as missioners.

Sr. Dorothy lived a life of radical poverty alongside the poor of Brazil. Her only possessions were a few items of clothing and furnishings and a Bible. In the 1970s she became an outspoken advocate for the poor landless farmers and for the environment in the Amazon. Her work for justice so angered and threatened landowners and corporations that her name was added to

their "hit list" in the late 1990s. In 2005 she was murdered by "hired guns" for her commitment to Christ and the Gospel's work of justice.

OPENING REFLECTION

- ⊙ Does a person have to be a member of a religious community to live the Gospel as radically as Sr. Dorothy? Why or why not?
- ⊙ How do you think Sr. Dorothy's commitment to live the consecrated life, especially the evangelical counsel of poverty, strengthened her for the work of a missioner?
- ⊙ What can you learn from Dorothy about giving witness to the love of God where you live right now? What can you do to give such witness?

CONSECRATED VIRGINS

From apostolic times virgins have committed themselves to follow Christ more closely. They are "betrothed mystically to Christ, the Son of God, and are dedicated to the service of the Church" (CCC, no. 923). Virgins were very much part of the everyday life of the early Church. They freely surrendered their life for the sake of the Kingdom of God. The Church continues to honor these women and presents them as models for living the faith today. For example, at Mass in Eucharistic Prayer I the priest prays that we may live in "fellowship with" the virgin-martyrs "Agatha, Lucy, Agnes, Cecilia . . . and all your Saints."

Virgins who consecrate their life to Christ continue to have a unique vocation in the Church today. After the Second Vatican Council the Church officially restored the Order of Virgins as a way of life in the Church.

It is a source of joy and hope to witness in our time a new flowering of *the ancient Order of Virgins*, known in Christian communities ever since apostolic times. Consecrated by the diocesan Bishop, these women acquire a particular link with the Church, which they are committed to serve while remaining in the world. Either alone or in association with others, they constitute *a special eschatological image of the Heavenly Bride and of the life to come*, when the Church will at last fully live her love for Christ the Bridegroom.

—St. John Paul II, *The Consecrated Life* (*Vita Consecrata*), no. 7

A Catholic woman who has never been married and has lived a chaste life commits to this way of life in the Rite of Consecration to a Life of Virginity. After praying the Prayer of Consecration the bishop-celebrant presents a ring to the newly consecrated woman, saying: "Receive the ring that marks you as a bride of Christ. / Keep unstained your fidelity to your Bridegroom, / that you may one day be admitted to the wedding feast of everlasting joy" (*Rite of Consecration*, no. 26).

LET'S PROBE DEEPER: A RESEARCH ACTIVITY
- During the liturgical year the Catholic Church celebrates more than twenty feast days of saints who were virgins, some of whom were also martyrs.
- Work in small groups. Find out the names of some of these saints. Choose several of them and create a profile of how their lives model living the Gospel for Catholic youth today.
- Share your profiles with the class.

CONSECRATED WIDOWS
Sacred Scripture often speaks of God's love for widows. Widows also held a place of honor and service in the early Church. Some widows in the early Church did not remarry; they committed themselves to a life centered in Christ and focused on the Kingdom of God. The Apostle Paul commanded churches to assist widows. He wrote, in part: "Honor widows who are really widows. . . . The real widow, left alone, has set her hope on God and continues in supplications and prayers night and day; . . . If any believing woman has relatives who are really widows, let her assist them; let the church not be burdened, so that it can assist those who are real widows" (1 Timothy 5:3, 5, 16). Paul went on to extol the unmarried widow who "has been married only once; . . . well attested for her good works, as one who has brought up children, shown hospitality, washed the saints' feet, helped the afflicted, and devoted herself to doing good in every way" (1 Timothy 5:9–10).

Pope Francis in reflecting on Luke 7:11–17 emphasized Jesus' compassion for the widow who was grieving over her only son who had just died. He then went on to describe how the widow is "an icon of the Church, because the Church is in a sense a widow." The Pope said, in part:

The Bridegroom is gone and she walks in history, hoping to find him, to meet with him—and she will be his true bride. In the meantime she—the Church—is alone! The Lord is nowhere to be seen. She has a certain dimension of widowhood . . . and that makes me think of the widowhood of the Church.

ST. LUCY, VIRGIN AND MARTYR | SEVILLE, 18TH CENTURY

This courageous Church, which defends her children, like the widow who went to the corrupt judge to [press her rights] and eventually won. Our Mother Church is courageous! She has the courage of a woman who knows that her children are her own, and must defend them and bring them to the meeting with her Spouse.
—Pope Francis, Sermon, September 16, 2013

Today some widows and widowers freely choose not to remarry and they dedicate themselves to Christ by living a simple gospel life marked by prayer and penance. Most of these widows and widowers live out their commitment alone in the ordinary routine of daily life; others seek and find support by living together in a community approved by the Church.

TALK IT OVER

⊙ Do you know a widow or widower serving the Church? Are they honored and respected in the community?
⊙ What experiences and graces might widows and widowers bring to serving the Church and her work in the world?
⊙ Share your reflections in small groups.

SECULAR INSTITUTES

While societies of apostolic life connect one's apostolic work to the apostolate and mission of the society in a direct way, secular institutes allow people to labor at an individual profession, not necessarily connected to the institute. This way of living a consecrated life began in 1947 "for people who wish to combine the contemplative and the apostolic life while living in the world. Secular institutes provide members with a community of like-minded people who put God first in their lives and everything else second" (United States Conference of Secular Institutes). People who belong to secular institutes work within the world, but they commit their lives first to God. While members of secular institutes do not always live in community, the institution and its meetings provide a structure of support for those seeking to live the vowed life within the world.

Members of secular institutes, rather than dedicating themselves to a single mission or charism, live the Gospel in a wide variety of settings, professions and ministries. They work as teachers, doctors, lawyers, social workers, artists, and in many other fields. In an increasingly diverse, mobile and specialized world, the work of these "consecrated seculars" is a unique witness to the Gospel and the mission of Christian discipleship. Perhaps it is especially suited to the modern world of the twenty-first century. Secular institutes provide a witness to gospel values in professional settings. They provide focus and grounding to people seeking to live as contemplatives in action in the context of an always changing world.

THINK, PAIR AND SHARE

⊙ How might vows of chastity, poverty and obedience change the way a person engages in their profession?
⊙ In what ways might a contemplative attitude to one's profession make a person more "free" in the Christian sense?

SEEK FIRST THE KINGDOM: THE GOSPEL LIFE

Regardless of the path in life we choose, God calls the faithful "by name" in every time and place to live out their baptismal promises.

Throughout this chapter you have learned that from the earliest days of the Church to the present God has called the faithful to the consecrated life and to other forms of religious life to proclaim the Second Coming of Christ to the people of their own time. As we have seen, new expressions of the religious life have arisen in our own time to proclaim and give witness to the truth that life on earth is a pilgrimage to "the glory of the heavenly kingdom."

For the People of God has here no lasting city, . . . [and this state] reveals more clearly to all believers the heavenly goods which are already present in this age, witnessing to the new and eternal life which we have acquired through the redemptive work of Christ and precluding our future resurrection and the glory of the heavenly kingdom.

—Vatican II, *Dogmatic Constitution on the Church* (*Lumen Gentium*), 44; quoted in CCC, no. 933

Some of you may feel called by Christ to live out your Baptism in some form of consecrated life. For you, the key is to discern the religious community or institute whose spiritual charism and work are most attractive and provide the best fit for your unique characteristics and personality. For example, Benedictines and Carmelites dedicate themselves to the contemplative life. The Sisters of Mercy emphasize works of mercy, while the Sisters of Saint Joseph focus on grade and high school education.

The call to such a vocation must be well tested, ever listening for the movements and invitations of the Holy Spirit. Be sure to talk it through with a wise spiritual mentor who can help you to listen to what God is inviting you to consider. It can also help to spend a few days living in the midst of a community, experiencing their ministry and good works.

JOURNAL EXERCISE

⊙ Sit for a moment at the feet of the Lord. Imagine Jesus saying to you *personally*, "I have called you by name, you are mine."
⊙ What does this say to your heart? How do these words impact your living as a disciple of Jesus now?
⊙ What elements of the consecrated life might you integrate into your life to respond to the call of Jesus now and in the future? Is a commitment to the consecrated life a possibility in your vision for your life?
⊙ Write your reflections in your journal.

Imagine Jesus saying to you personally, "I have called you by name, you are mine."

CHRIST THE REDEEMER OF MARATEA, BASILICATA, ITALY

REVIEW AND SHARE WHAT YOU HAVE LEARNED

Look back over this chapter and reflect on what you have learned about the call to the consecrated life as a way of living one's Baptism. Share the teachings of the Catholic Church on these statements:

- ◉ The consecrated life enables the faithful to dedicate their lives to the service of the Kingdom of God.
- ◉ The evangelical counsels are at the heart of consecrating one's life to God.
- ◉ All the faithful are called to live the evangelical counsels, no matter what their vocation or state of life in the Church may be.
- ◉ There are a variety of ways of living the consecrated life.
- ◉ The consecrated life gives witness to Christ in the world.
- ◉ "Religious life in its various forms is called to signify the very charity of God in the language of our time" (CCC, no. 926).
- ◉ The Blessed Virgin is the model of consecration and discipleship.

OVER TO YOU

- ◉ What wisdom for discerning your vocation as a disciple of Jesus Christ have you learned from studying this chapter?

A LIFE OFTEN NOT UNDERSTOOD

Many people, including some Catholics, cannot conceive why a man or woman could respond to God's invitation to live a life of celibacy or lifelong chastity. They truly believe that men and women who choose such a vocation and do not marry live lonely, unhappy lives. It is true that some who promise lifelong celibacy and chastity may *experience* loneliness, but this is not to say that they live lonely lives. Married people also experience loneliness, as do all people.

There are numerous testimonies to prove that most men who become priests, monks or brothers and most women who become nuns, sisters or consecrated virgins generally live happy and fulfilling lives. Sexual intimacy with another is not essential for personal fulfillment and happiness.

The heart of celibacy is a *truly loving relationship* with the Lord, expressed in a self-gift to others in his name. Committed celibacy for the sake of Jesus Christ and his kingdom brings consolation that cannot be appreciated by someone who has not lived it. Living a life of committed celibacy or chastity gives one a sense of the gifts of the eternal life to come. God gives us the grace we need to live out our commitments.

NUN AT PRAYER IN THE CHURCH OF THE HOLY SEPULCHRE, JERUSALEM

The Virgin Mary, model of consecration and discipleship

The Blessed Virgin Mary is the model of living a life of Christian discipleship consecrated to God. Mary lived her life most fully through her commitment to her Son and his mission. Mary's life, like that of her Son, was totally dedicated to God for the sake of the Kingdom of God. We first see this dedication and faith in the response of a "perplexed" Virgin Mary to the angel's words to her, "Here am I, the servant of the Lord; let it be with me according to your word" (Luke 1:38). Recall for a moment the gospel account of the Annunciation. (Read Luke 1:26–38.)

Notice that Luke tells us that Mary was "much perplexed by [the angel's] words and pondered what sort of greeting this might be" (Luke 1:29) and she asked the angel, "How can this be, since I am a virgin?" (Luke 1:34). Mary's response, "Here am I, the servant of the Lord; let it be with me according to your word" (Luke 1:38) reveals the depth of her faith. She consecrated her very being to God and to the divine work of salvation.

Soon after the birth of Jesus, Mary and Joseph brought Jesus to Jerusalem and presented him to God according to "the law of the Lord." Upon entering the Temple, they were greeted by a "righteous and devout man" named Simeon. "Simeon took him in his arms and praised God"; and after blessing Joseph and Mary, Simeon said to Mary, "This child is destined for the falling and the rising of many in Israel, and to be a sign that will be opposed so that the inner thoughts of many will be revealed—and a sword will pierce your own soul too" (Luke 2:34–35). The reality behind these words of Simeon was experienced most fully by Our Lady of Sorrows at the foot of the Cross.

The motherhood of Mary exemplifies for Christians what it means to consecrate one's heart and soul, one's whole being, to the will of the Triune God. Mary, in turn, came to know the joy of her consecration in the Resurrection of her Son. "From the Church [the Christian] learns the *example of holiness* and recognizes its model and source in the all-holy Virgin Mary" (CCC, no. 2030).

As men and women seeking to conform our lives to Christ, all of us can be inspired and supported by the motherhood of Mary and her faithfulness to her vocation in life. She is indeed the Mother of the Church, our "advocate, helper, benefactress, and mediatrix" (Vatican II, *Dogmatic Constitution on the Church*, no. 62). She was assumed into heaven, body and soul, and we continue to receive the gifts of salvation through her intercession. We can always ask her to pray for us as we make our vocational choices. Meanwhile, the vocation of every Christian is to say a big "YES" to God, as Mary did. Whether our vocation is to the married, vowed, or single life, and regardless of what work or career we choose at any given time, our first vocation is to live as disciples of Jesus by consecrating our life to God as Mary did. Whether we say "Yes" to God and commit to the married life, the ordained life or the consecrated life, or we discern to conform our life to Christ as a lay single person, all the faithful share the common vocation to seek holiness of life. Mary's example and prayers will help us follow the way of her Son Jesus, ever seeking to transform our own lives and the world toward God's reign by living lives rooted in the virtues of faith, hope and love.

THINK, PAIR AND SHARE
⊙ Share examples of ways Mary is your model for living as a disciple of her Son.

SHARE FAITH WITH FAMILY AND FRIENDS
⊙ What value do you see in rooting your discipleship in prayer?
⊙ What can you learn for living your faith from Christians who embrace the evangelical virtues of poverty, chastity and obedience?

REFLECT AND DECIDE
⊙ How might God be inviting you to give witness to Christ through poverty, chastity and obedience?
⊙ What commitments are you called to make toward living a life in true Christian freedom for love and justice—for the sake of the Kingdom of God?

LEARN BY HEART

"If you wish to be perfect, go, sell your possessions, and give the money to the poor, and you will have treasure in heaven; then come, follow me."

MATTHEW 19:21

PRAYER REFLECTION

Note: Each student will need a Bible, a large sheet of art paper and a colored marker.

LEADER

God of loving kindness,
you know each of us better than we know ourselves.
You call each of us by name to witness and continue to do the work begun by your Son, Jesus.
Give us the grace to discern our gifts and how best to put them to work for the sake of your reign.

ALL

Amen.

LEADER

All the baptized, every one of us, need to listen to God and discern our particular vocation in life. Let us listen to Jesus' invitation to the rich young man.

ALL

Quietly read and reflect on Matthew 19:16–22, the parable of the rich young man.

LEADER

Why do you think the rich young man went away sad?
Put yourself in that story. What might your response have been?

ALL

Quietly reflect on and respond to the two questions.

LEADER

All of us need to take time to discern our particular vocation in life and make new decisions as life unfolds. In such times of discernment it is imperative to be in prayerful conversation with God. Seeking answers to these three questions will go a long way to your recognizing the vocation to which God is calling you.

⊙ What am I good at? (Look at your gifts.)
⊙ What would I enjoy doing? (Living one's God-given vocation is a source of true joy.)
⊙ Does it need to be done? (Responding to others who are in need is central to living as Christ did.)

JESUS AND THE RICH YOUNG MAN | HEINRICH HOFFMANN

When we answer these questions honestly and in conversation with God, then we can be confident that God will bless our decision. For God meets us where we are in life, and invites us to use our talents and passions for the life of the world. *Work* becomes *vocation* when we enter into it with a desire to live for the sake of the Kingdom of God.

ALL

Quietly reflect on and respond to the three questions.

LEADER

We are all called to live our life in the freedom of the children of God by responding to the gospel call to poverty, chastity and obedience.
We are to love for the sake of the Kingdom of God and bring the Good News to the poor and oppressed.
We are to remove the things in our life that prevent us from fulfilling this mission.
Reread Matthew 19:16–22, the parable of the rich young man. (*Pause*)

- ⊙ What is the wisdom you take from this story? (*Pause*)
- ⊙ Take some quiet time to reflect on the ways you sense God calling you to live your Baptism.

- – What vocations or what ways of life attract you?
- – Is the consecrated life one of those vocations?
- – What stands in the way of your responding?
- – What can you do now to prepare the way?

ALL

Quietly reflect on and respond to the questions.

LEADER

When you are ready, use a marker to trace an outline of your own foot on the art paper. Write your responses to the questions in it.

LEADER

God of the journey,
send your Spirit to lead and guide us.
May the waters of Baptism refresh us,
the bread of the Eucharist strengthen us,
and the community of the faithful support us,
Above all, may the words and life of Christ guide us,
and may your love always remind us of the sacred gift that is each of us.

ALL

Amen.

God of the journey, send your Spirit to lead and guide us

CHAPTER 11

The Lay Faithful

THE LAITY IN THE CHURCH . . .

ARE CALLED TO HOLINESS OF LIFE

SERVE THE MISSION AND UNITY OF THE CHURCH

SHARE IN THE THREEFOLD MINISTRY OF CHRIST THE PRIEST, PROPHET AND KING

ALL THE FAITHFUL—THE ORDAINED (BISHOPS, PRIESTS AND deacons), the laity and those who commit to the consecrated life—are called to holiness of life and to serve God and the Church and the broader community of the world. The laity, who constitute the largest number of the faithful, have been aptly described as the leaven of the love of God in society. Some members of the laity marry and others choose to remain single permanently. Some of the lay faithful, married and unmarried, work more closely than others with the hierarchy in serving the Church. These members of the laity are called lay ecclesial ministers.

LAY ECCLESIAL MINISTERS AND LAY VOLUNTEERS SUPPORT THE CHURCH IN ACCOMPLISHING HER MISSION

Faith Focus: These teachings of the Catholic Church are the primary focus of the doctrinal content presented in this chapter:

⊙ The Church is "the sacrament of Christ's action at work in her through the mission of the Holy Spirit" (*Catechism of the Catholic Church*, no. 1118).

⊙ The laity serve the People of God in a diversity of leadership roles.

⊙ Scripture and the teaching of the Church are the foundation for lay people undertaking ministries within the Church.

⊙ Lay ecclesial ministers assist the hierarchy in serving the Church in a variety of full-time and part-time responsibilities.

⊙ The title "lay ecclesial minister" names and describes a specific role the laity have in working for the good of the whole Church.

Discipleship Formation: As a result of studying this chapter and discovering the meaning of the faith of the Catholic Church for your life, you should be better able to:

⊙ appreciate the diversity of lay ministries within the Church;

⊙ volunteer your time and talents to serve your parish community;

⊙ consider serving the Church as a lay ecclesial minister;

⊙ discern the vocation to which God is calling you.

Scripture References: These Scripture references are quoted or referred to in this chapter:
OLD TESTAMENT: 1 Samuel 3:2–10; **Jeremiah** 8:8
NEW TESTAMENT: Matthew 7:29, 9:3 and 35–38, 12:38, 21:15, 28:16–20; **Mark** 1:21–22, 2:16, 3:22, 11:27; **Luke** 6:7, 10:2, 11:53; **John** 1:38 and 49, 3:2, 6:25 and 51; **Acts of the Apostles** 7:54–58, 11:19–21, 18:26; **Romans** 16:1–16; **1 Corinthians** 9:16; 12:1–31; **Ephesians** 4:12; **Philippians** 4:3; **Hebrews** 4:14—5:5–10, 8:1–7, **1 Peter** 2:9–10a, 3:15

Faith Glossary: Familiarize yourself with or recall the meaning of these key terms. Definitions are found in the Glossary: **charism, priesthood of the faithful, lay ecclesial ministers, lay ecclesial ministry, lay ecclesial movements, pastoral associate, pastoral life director, rabbi, Sanhedrin, scribe**

Faith Words: the laity, or lay faithful; lay ecclesial ministry; lay ecclesial ministers
Learn by Heart: Matthew 9:37–38
Learn by Example: National Association for Lay Ministry (NALM)

What does the Bible say about the laity?

OPENING REFLECTION

- Prayerfully read and reflect on 1 Peter 2:9–10a.
- In what ways do these words of St. Peter the Apostle capture your current understanding of the Church? Of your identity as a member of the Church?
- How might these words deepen the way you participate in the life and mission of the Church?

LAY LEADERS SERVING THE CHOSEN PEOPLE OF GOD

In the tradition and practice of Ancient Israel, priests were vital to the life of the Chosen People of God. Priests, however, were not the only members of the Jewish people who had significant leadership roles. The Old Testament and the four accounts of the Gospel attest to a diversity of religious leaders, in addition to priests, within Judaism. During Jesus' time these leaders included **rabbis**, **scribes**, elders and the **Sanhedrin**.

Rabbis: Rabbis were recognized as teachers and interpreters of the Law and of Jewish tradition. They instructed the people to know and live their faith. Rabbis had no authority to perform the sacrifices and other sacred rituals of the Jews. This authority belonged to priests alone.

Jesus' disciples, leading Pharisees and others acknowledged and respected Jesus as a rabbi. (Take a moment and check out John 1:38 and 49; 3:2; and 6:25.) The people revered Jesus over other rabbis because of the authority with which he taught. The Evangelist Mark tells us that the people acknowledged this "authority" of Jesus from the very beginning of his ministry. Mark wrote that after Jesus chose his first disciples:

AARON THE HIGH PRIEST | JOSEPH SCHONMAN

You are God's people

You are a chosen race, a royal priesthood, a holy nation, God's own people, in order that you may proclaim the mighty acts of him who called you out of darkness into his marvelous light.

Once you were not a people,
but now you are God's people; . . .

—1 Peter 2:9–10a

They went to Capernaum; and when the sabbath came, he entered the synagogue and taught. They were astounded at his teaching, for he taught them as one having authority, and not as the scribes.

—Mark 1:21–22

THE SANHEDRIN (DETAIL) | ENGRAVING AFTER ALEXANDRE BIDA

Priests: Jewish priests were descendants of Aaron and members of the tribe of Levi. A priest could be a rabbi, but a rabbi need not be a priest. Jesus is the fulfillment of the priesthood of Ancient Israel. He is the Lamb of God who sacrificed himself to atone for the sins of humanity. He is the Great High Priest, the Savior and Redeemer of the world. (Check out Hebrews 4:14—5:5–10 and 8:1–7.)

Scribes: Scribes were acknowledged leaders of the Chosen People well before the time of Jesus. The writings of the seventh-century-BC prophet Jeremiah attest to the centrality of the role of a scribe. We read:

"How can you say, 'We are wise,
    and the law of the LORD is with us,'
when, in fact, the false pen of the scribes
    has made it into a lie?"

—Jeremiah 8:8

Scribes played a significant leadership role within the Jewish community of which Jesus was a member. "The Jewish scribe in NT times is the scholar and the intellectual of Judaism, who receives the title rabbi. His scholarship was the knowledge of the law, which he regarded as the sum of wisdom and the only true learning. His position in the Jewish community was a respected position of leadership; it is somewhat surprising but revealing that Mt 7:29 says that Jesus taught with authority, not like the scribes" (John L. McKenzie, SJ, *Dictionary of the Bible*, 780). Matthew 7:29 is but one account of the numerous times that the scribes found themselves at odds with Jesus and his teachings on the Law. (Take a moment to check out Matthew 9:3, 12:38, 21:15; Mark 2:16, 3:22, 11:27; Luke 6:7, 11:53.)

Sanhedrin: The Sanhedrin was the highest governing and judicial body of the Jewish religious community in Jesus' time. The Great Sanhedrin in Jerusalem was a governing body of seventy-one priests, scribes and elders. It convened daily except on the Sabbath to pass judgment on violations of Jewish law. For example, it was members of the Sanhedrin who falsely accused Jesus of blasphemy and handed him over to Pilate to be put to death. It was also members of the Sanhedrin, Luke tells us in Acts of the Apostles 7:54–58, who examined St. Stephen and condemned him to be stoned to death.

LAY LEADERS OF THE NEW PEOPLE OF GOD

The Gospels attest that Jesus called upon and invited others, in addition to the Twelve, to assist him in fulfilling the mission his Father sent him to do. For example, Luke 10:1 tells us "the Lord appointed seventy others and sent them on ahead of him in pairs to every town and place where he himself intended to go. He said to them, 'The harvest is plentiful, but the laborers are few.'" The accounts of the Gospel also tell us that women, such as the sisters Martha and Mary, accompanied and supported Jesus and the

CHRIST WITH MARY AND MARTHA | LITHOGRAPH BY C. HAHN

Apostles. These women disciples were with Jesus and supported him from the very beginning of his ministry in Galilee.

After Jesus' Death, Resurrection and Ascension, the Apostles appointed a diversity of people to assist them in leading and serving the early Church community. In addition to the central roles of *episkopoi* (overseers or bishops), *presbuteroi* (elders or priests), and *deaconoi* (servants or deacons), there were many other recognized leaders who were not ordained. St. Paul identifies some of these leaders in the early Church in Corinth in 1 Corinthians 12:1–11, 27–31. The Letter to the Ephesians sums up the purpose of the diversity of these ministries. The Spirit gifts the Church with a variety of gifts, or **charisms**, "for building up the body of Christ" (Ephesians 4:12).

St. John Paul II reaffirmed this vision and practice of the apostolic Church. As the Catholic Church entered the new millennium the Pope wrote:

The unity of the Church is not uniformity, but an organic blending of legitimate diversities. It is the reality of many members joined in a single body, the one Body of Christ (see 1 Corinthians 12:12). Therefore the Church of the Third Millennium will need to encourage all the baptized and confirmed to be aware of their active responsibility in the Church's life. Together with the ordained ministry, other ministries, whether formally instituted or simply recognized, can flourish for the good of the whole community, sustaining it in all its many needs: from catechesis to liturgy, from education of the young to the widest array of charitable works.

—Apostolic Letter, *At the Close of the Great Jubilee Year 2000 (Novo Millennio Ineunte)*, no. 46

LET'S PROBE DEEPER: A SCRIPTURE ACTIVITY

⊙ The New Testament speaks about ministries undertaken by the non-ordained members of the early Church.

⊙ Read 1 Corinthians 12:1–11, 27–31.

⊙ Reflect:
  − What do these passages say about the wide diversity of roles within the early Church?
  − What different forms of ministry, in addition to those of priests and deacons and religious sisters and brothers, do you see in your parish?
  − How do these roles contribute to the work of the Church?

⊙ Share your reflections as a class.

JOURNAL EXERCISE

⊙ From your experience and your reflections on this lesson, what are your thoughts about how the laity may serve the mission of the Church?

⊙ What gifts might you have to contribute to your parish or school community? Might you see yourself using those gifts as an adult lay person?

⊙ Write your thoughts in your journal.

A ROYAL PRIESTHOOD, A HOLY NATION

In Baptism a person is joined to Christ, reborn as an adopted son or daughter of God the Father, and becomes a temple of the Holy Spirit. The Sacrament of Confirmation perfects the graces of Baptism; the baptized being confirmed are "sealed" with the gift of the Holy Spirit. Lay people "exhibit the graces of Baptism and Confirmation in all dimensions of their personal, family, social, and ecclesial lives, and so fulfill the call to holiness addressed to all the baptized" (*Catechism of the Catholic Church* [CCC], no. 941).

During the rite of Baptism the newly baptized are anointed with Sacred Chrism. This baptismal anointing signifies that through Baptism they have been made participants in the threefold ministry of Christ—Priest, Prophet and King: "Jesus Christ is the one whom the Father anointed with the Holy Spirit and established as priest, prophet and king. The whole People of God participates in these three offices of Christ and bears the responsibilities for mission and service that flow from them" (CCC, no. 783; referencing St. John Paul II, *Redemptor Hominis [Redeemer of Man]*, nos. 18-21).

THE COMMON PRIESTHOOD OF THE FAITHFUL

Through Baptism we are made sharers in the priesthood of Christ. The Church names this sharing by the baptized in the one priesthood of Jesus Christ the common **priesthood of the faithful**. The *Catechism* summarizes the common priestly vocation of all the faithful:

> On entering the People of God through faith and Baptism, one receives a share in this people's unique, *priestly* vocation: "Christ the Lord, high priest taken from among men, has made this new people 'a kingdom of priests to God, his Father.' The baptized, by regeneration and the anointing of the Holy Spirit, are *consecrated* to be a spiritual house and a holy priesthood" (Vatican II, *Dogmatic Constitution on the Church*, no. 10.)
>
> —CCC, no. 784

Through Baptism we are made sharers in the priesthood of Christ

CHRIST THE REDEEMER, RIO DE JANEIRO, BRAZIL

The Church from her earliest days believed and taught that the ordained ministries are essential for the structure and the life of the Church

ST. IGNATIUS OF ANTIOCH | SAINT IGNAZ CHURCH, MAINZ, GERMANY

The common priesthood of the faithful *differs* in *essence* from the ordained, or ministerial, priesthood. The ordained priesthood, as you have already learned, is conferred by the Sacrament of Holy Orders. The Church from her earliest days, as attested to in the writings of St. Ignatius of Antioch (d. c. AD 110), has believed and taught that the ordained ministries are essential for the structure and the life of the Church. In other words, we cannot speak of the Church without her ordained ministers.

Lay people are to give witness to their baptismal participation in the priesthood of Jesus Christ in all aspects of their lives. This participation includes not only their life within the Church but also their personal and family life, and in their workplace and the communities in which they live. In this way the laity strive both to fulfill the call to holiness to which God calls all the faithful and to bring the leaven of the Gospel into every nook and cranny of the world.

REFLECT, COMPARE AND SHARE

- ◉ Recall what you have already learned in chapter 9 about the ordained, or ministerial, priesthood, namely:

- Priests act *in persona Christi capitis*. This means: "The office of priests shares in the authority by which Christ himself builds up and sanctifies and rules his Body" (CCC, no. 1563).
- Priests "are consecrated in order to preach the Gospel and shepherd the faithful as well as to celebrate divine worship" (CCC, no. 1564). They fulfill this service by teaching, divine worship and pastoral governance.
- In addition, while lay people may preside at some sacramentals, "the more a blessing concerns ecclesial and sacramental life, the more is its administration reserved to the ordained ministry (bishops, priests or deacons)" (CCC, no. 1669).

◉ In what ways do you see lay people in your parish collaborating with your parish priests in serving the parish?

◉ What do you see your priest doing that a lay person cannot do?

◉ Share reflections as a class.

Leading by the Spirit of Christ

SERVING *ALL PEOPLE* IN THE NAME OF CHRIST

The Catholic bishops of the United States founded Catholic Relief Services (CRS) in 1943 to serve World War II survivors in Europe. Catholic Relief Services today "eases suffering and provides assistance to people in need in more than 100 countries around the world without regard to race, religion or nationality."

Sean Callahan, a lay person, after serving with CRS for more than twenty-eight years, became the organization's Catholic lay President and CEO in 2017. Callahan serves the Church full time; he works in collaboration with bishops, religious, other members of the laity, as well as non-Catholics. He coordinates the efforts of CRS to serve more than 120 million people in more than 100 countries on five continents. CRS describes its mission, in part:

> Our mission is to assist impoverished and disadvantaged people overseas, working in the spirit of Catholic social teaching to promote the sacredness of human life and the dignity of the human person. Although our mission is rooted in the Catholic faith, our operations serve people based solely on need, regardless of their race, religion or ethnicity. Within the United States, CRS engages Catholics to live their faith in solidarity with the poor and suffering people of the world. CRS is motivated by the example of Jesus Christ to ease suffering, provide development assistance, and foster charity and justice.

OPENING REFLECTION

⊙ Have you ever heard of CRS? Share what you know.

⊙ How does the ministry of the organization's President and CEO image the work of Jesus Christ?

PRIMARY SCHOOL STUDENTS IN NORTHERN SIERRA LEONE FED BY CRS

⊙ What other lay people do you know who serve the Church full time in a formal way? Describe their ministries.

⊙ How might you serve suffering people both in your community and around the world?

THE CHURCH, THE SACRAMENT OF CHRIST'S ACTION

The Church, as you have already learned, is first and foremost a *people*, the new People of God. She is both a visible and an invisible hierarchical society. Christ is the source of the Church's ministry. She is "the sacrament of Christ's action at work in her through the mission of the Holy Spirit" (CCC, no. 1118). She is the instrument of the life-giving communion uniting the Blessed Trinity, the People of God and all humanity.

The Church has always fulfilled her mission of being the sacrament of Christ's action in the world. One way that the Church has faithfully done this is by addressing the circumstances and needs of the Church. We have already seen that the Apostles ordained bishops as their successors; priests as their co-workers; and deacons to assist them in attending to the needs of the Church.

PENTECOST

All the members of the Church have a role in continuing "Christ's action at work in her through the mission of the Holy Spirit"

St. Paul, writing some fifteen to twenty years after Pentecost, using the image of the human body, taught that all the baptized are to take part in that mission. As members of the Body of Christ, all the members of the Church have a Spirit-led role in continuing "Christ's action at work in her through the mission of the Holy Spirit." (Check out 1 Corinthians 12:12–26.)

As history unfolded, the Church began to organize her diversity of ministries into the work of those who were ordained and members of religious orders. The ordained and the consecrated began, over time, to take on the various forms of ministry that were present in the apostolic Church.

In turn, the laity began to expect that the ministries of the Church were the responsibility of those who were ordained or who were members of religious orders. This arrangement of ecclesial ministries worked well for many centuries, as there were sufficient priests and religious sisters and brothers to meet the pastoral needs of the Church.

The Church at the Second Vatican Council (1962–65) took an in-depth look at the circumstances in which the Church found herself. Then, as is the case today, there was an increasing shortage of priests and a dwindling number of vowed religious men and women. Reading these *signs of the times* and reflecting on her Apostolic Tradition, the Church imagined *renewed* ways of engaging the laity, the largest number of her members, in the Church's ministries.

While reaffirming both the divinely given hierarchical structure of the visible Church and the invaluable role of religious orders, the Council gave impetus to the restoration of the vocation of the laity. As a result, the ministerial profile of the Church began to reflect the profile of the early Church. The Council taught:

The Church can never be without the lay apostolate; it is something that derives from the lay person's very vocation as a Christian. Scripture clearly shows how spontaneous and fruitful was this activity in the church's early days (see Acts of the Apostles 11:19–21; 18:26; Romans 16:1–16; Philippians 4:3).

No less fervent a zeal on the part of lay people is called for today; present circumstances, in fact, demand from them a more extensive and more vigorous apostolate.

—*Decree on the Apostolate of Lay People (Apostolicam Actuositatem),* no. 1 §§1 and 2

PAIR, CREATE AND SHARE

- Work with a partner.
- Create an image that portrays the Church as "the sacrament of Christ's action at work in her through the mission of the Holy Spirit" (CCC, no. 1118).
- Create your image using words (story, song lyrics, verse) or a graphic. Come up with an image that speaks to your peers.

OVER TO YOU

- What might be the advantages of a greater number of lay people serving the Church and her mission?

LED BY THE SPIRIT OF CHRIST

The laity have always responded to the needs of the Church. Led by the Spirit of Christ, lay people have contributed significantly to the life and mission of the Church by responding— sometimes in ways that were new or unfamiliar— to the circumstances of their own time. During this course of study you have learned about several such lay people, namely, Maisie Ward and Frank Sheed, St. Gianna Beretta Molla and St. Philip Howard. We will now pause and recall several other members of the Church's laity who served the mission of the Church.

St. Catherine of Alexandria (287–305): Catherine, a virgin and martyr, evangelizer and defender of the Church, lived during a time when Christians were still being persecuted. She was born into a wealthy pagan family, was well educated and became a Christian in her teenage years. At the age of eighteen Catherine confronted the Roman Emperor Maxentius and demanded that he order his soldiers to stop persecuting Christians. Maxentius imprisoned her and eventually had her beheaded after she convinced many others to become Christians; the wife of Maxentius and 200 of his soldiers were among those converts. The life of this saint and martyr of the Church serves as a model for Christian apologists and preachers, philosophers and theologians.

St. Catherine of Siena (1347–80): The Spirit of Christ blessed Catherine of Siena, a single lay woman, with the gifts of wisdom, counsel and courage. She became a Dominican tertiary at the age of sixteen, and later became an advisor to popes and bishops as well as to Italian princes. Catherine's counsel contributed to the life of the Church in several ways; from the renewal of the faith life of the Church in Siena and surrounding areas, to the settling of divisive disputes within the Church, to convincing the pope, who had been living in Avignon, France, to return to Rome. Catherine was also a prolific writer on the spiritual life. Catherine of Siena is revered as the patron saint of Italy and Europe.

St. Thomas More (1478–1535): Thomas More, husband and father of four children, was a well-educated scholar who studied the classics, theology, philosophy and law. His professional career as a civil and public servant included being a barrister (lawyer), judge, member of Parliament, diplomat and statesman who served as Lord Chancellor (key counselor) to King Henry VIII.

ST. THOMAS MORE | ENGRAVING AFTER HOLBEIN

When Henry established the Church of England and made himself its head so that he could claim the authority to divorce his wife, Catherine of Aragon, and marry Anne Boleyn, More staunchly defended the pope's supremacy and authority as head of the Church. He adamantly refused to side with the king against the pope and upheld the Church's teachings on marriage and divorce. In 1534 Henry VIII imprisoned More in the Tower of London and eventually ordered him to be beheaded on July 6, 1535. The life of this saint and martyr of the Church serves as a model for Christian lawyers, political leaders and civil and public servants.

St. Charles Lwanga (1860–86): Charles, a convert to the Catholic Church, an evangelist, catechist and martyr, assisted the White Fathers (The Society of Missionaries in Africa) in their work of evangelization in Uganda in Central Eastern Africa. The pedophile King Mwanga ordered Charles, aged twenty-six, to be burned at the stake in retaliation for his defending imprisoned Anglican youth and young men, between the ages of thirteen and twenty-five, from being sexually abused by Mwanga. Blessed Paul VI named Charles Lwanga and the twenty-one other young people whom he was instructing in the Catholic faith, saints of the Church. Charles Lwanga is the patron of youth and Catholic Action in Uganda and most of tropical Africa.

Dorothy Day, Servant of God (1897–1980): Dorothy Day has been described as a "radical lay Catholic." Dorothy, a convert to the Catholic Church, was a journalist, prophetic voice and tireless servant in promoting and living the Catholic Church's social principle of preferential option for the poor and vulnerable. The vision and efforts of Dorothy Day live on in the Catholic Worker movement that she and Peter Maurin founded in 1933 during the Great Depression, in the more than one hundred hospitality houses in the United States, and in the movement's newspaper, *The Catholic Worker*. In 1997 on the 100th anniversary of Dorothy's death, John Cardinal O'Connor, the Archbishop of New York, began the process of the Church naming her a saint. And in 2012 the Catholic bishops of the United States unanimously supported and recommended her canonization. The Catholic Church honors Dorothy Day with the title Servant of God, a title given to the faithful whose life and teachings the Church is investigating as part of the canonization process.

HOMELESS FAMILY WALKING FROM ARIZONA TO CALIFORNIA DURING THE GREAT DEPRESSION

The Catholic Worker movement was founded by Dorothy Day and Peter Maurin during the Great Depression

Now you are the body of Christ and individually members of it.

1 CORINTHIANS 12:27

ST. PAUL | ENGRAVING BY J. MYNDE

WHAT ABOUT YOU PERSONALLY?

- Recall St. Paul's list of ministries in 1 Corinthians 12:27–31.
- Reflect:
  - How do Dorothy Day and the others named above reflect the diversity of ministries that served the early Church?
  - Are there any other lay people whom you have learned about who committed themselves to these ecclesial ministries?
- How do these people serve as models for your living your faith?
- Write your thoughts in your journal.

LAY ECCLESIAL MOVEMENTS

The Church at the Second Vatican Council (1962–65) sought to interpret the "signs of the times" and reflect on how the Church could dialogue more effectively with the modern world. The Council encouraged lay Catholics to imagine new ways of living out Christian discipleship together. The term "lay ecclesial movement" is often given to one of these attempts. **Lay ecclesial movements** have a strong spiritual component and emphasize shared experiences of prayer and, sometimes, intentional communal living.

"New Monasticism" is an example of a lay ecclesial movement. This movement was inspired by the monastic tradition within the Church. It is committed to ecumenism, evangelization, hospitality, and services of compassion and justice. With its origins in the 1980s, "New Monasticism" is part of a long tradition of innovative Christian communities in the United States. Those communities include, among others, the Catholic Worker Movement founded by Dorothy Day. Other examples of lay ecclesial movements are the Community of Sant'Egidio, Communion and Liberation, Focolare and the Legion of Mary.

- *Community of Sant'Egidio* focuses on promoting peace and reaching out to the poor and elderly and other people in need.
- *Communion and Liberation* aims to form its members into more fervent co-workers in the Church's mission in all realms of society by educating them both in Jesus' teachings and in human arts and knowledge.
- *Focolare* aims to unite people. It brings together people of all Christian traditions and from many of the world's religions, alongside people with no formal faith, to share the aim of building a united world according to the prayer of Jesus for his disciples, so that they may be witnesses to those who are not disciples of Christ, as the *Catechism* teaches:

THE LEGION OF MARY HOSTING AN EVENT IN MANILA, PHILIPPINES

The Legion of Mary aims to foster the holiness, the spiritual and social welfare, of people in union with Mary and the Church

"That they may all be one. As you, Father, are in me and I am in you, may they also be one in us . . . so that the world may know that you have sent me' " (John 17:21; quoted in CCC, no. 820).

⊙ *Legion of Mary* aims to foster the holiness, the spiritual and social welfare, of people in union with Mary and the Church.

It is important to emphasize that lay ecclesial movements and other lay organizations are not meant to replace the parish or church community as the center of a person's faith life. Instead, these movements offer a supplement that allows people to enrich and deepen their relationship with a parish or congregation and provide a support network of "friends in faith."

There is a tremendous diversity of ways in which people live out their baptismal vocation as Christians. These lay ecclesial movements encourage all the faithful to use their imagination in discerning how they can best live their discipleship. They also highlight the importance of surrounding ourselves with like-minded people who can support our faith commitments and kindle our imagination to address the spiritual and bodily needs of people as Jesus did.

REFLECT AND DECIDE

⊙ What communities, organizations or groups support you as you strive to follow the challenging and demanding way of Jesus?

⊙ What practices might you adopt in your daily life along with friends or others that would help you live the gospel life now?

⊙ What suggestions might help the Church reach out to those who are marginalized in society today?

Lay pastoral leadership

Did you know?

In 2005, the year our bishops issued *Co-Workers in the Vineyard of the Lord*:

⊙ 30,632 lay ecclesial ministers were working at least twenty hours per week in paid positions in parishes;

⊙ an additional 2,163 volunteers were working at least twenty hours per week in parishes;

⊙ the percentage of lay women was 64 percent, and lay men was 20 percent;

⊙ more than 2,000 lay persons ministered in the name of the Church in hospitals and health care settings, on college and university campuses, and in prisons, seaports, and airports; and

⊙ 5,466 lay women and lay men served as principals of elementary and secondary schools.

> —*Co-Workers in the Vineyard of the Lord*, "Reality of Lay Ecclesial Ministry," §§1, 2

OPENING REFLECTION

⊙ How do you see members of the laity serving your parish? Your school?

⊙ In what ways have lay workers in the vineyard of the Lord helped you grow in knowing and living the Catholic faith?

EMERGENCE OF LAY ECCLESIAL MINISTRIES

The lay faithful, married and single, participate in the life and mission of the Church in diverse ways. Lay people have roles in the celebration of the liturgy, for example, as readers at Mass, choir members and extraordinary ministers of Holy Communion; they take part in the teaching mission of the Church as parish catechists and youth ministers, as elementary school principals and teachers, and as high school administrators and theology teachers. Lay men and lay women serve as visitors to the sick and are actively engaged as agents of peace and justice. The lay faithful may also assist in the governance of the Church at diocesan and parish levels.

In 1999 our bishops in the United States addressed the issue of the growing need for the assistance and collaboration of laity to assume leadership roles in the Church. In their document *Lay Ecclesial Ministry: The State of the Questions* the Subcommittee on the Laity of the United States Conference of Catholic Bishops (USCCB)

Lay ecclesial ministry

The term reflects certain key realities. The ministry is *lay* because it is service done by lay persons. The sacramental basis is the Sacraments of Initiation, not the Sacrament of Ordination. The ministry is *ecclesial* because it has a place within the community of the Church, whose communion and mission it serves, and because it is submitted to the discernment, authorization, and supervision of the hierarchy. Finally, it is *ministry* because it is a participation in the threefold ministry of Christ, who is priest, prophet, and king.

—*Co-Workers in the Vineyard of the Lord*, "The Call to Lay Ecclesial Ministry," § 5

Lay ecclesial ministers

The men and women of every race and culture who serve in parishes, schools, diocesan agencies and Church institutions. Lay ecclesial ministers are lay people who give their lives in a full- or part-time capacity to carrying out the ministries of the Church.

acknowledged this emerging need in the United States. They wrote, in part:

a distinctly new and different group of lay ministers has emerged in the Church in the United States. This group consists of lay women and men performing roles that entail varying degrees of pastoral leadership and administration in parishes, church agencies, and organizations, and at diocesan and national levels. They are doing so in a public, stable, recognized, and authorized manner. Furthermore, when these lay ministers speak of their responsibilities, they emphasize ministering in ways that are distinguished from, yet complementary to, the roles of ordained ministers.

—*Lay Ecclesial Ministry: The State of the Questions*, no. 9

CO-WORKERS IN THE VINEYARD OF THE LORD
In their recognition of this emerging trend and the need for greater participation of the laity in *public, stable* and *authorized* pastoral leadership roles complementary to the roles of ordained ministers, the USCCB in 2005 issued the pastoral statement *Co-workers in the Vineyard of the Lord*. These lay workers are officially called **lay ecclesial ministers**. In the "Introduction" to their pastoral statement, the bishops state:

Co-Workers in the Vineyard of the Lord is a resource for diocesan bishops and for all others who are responsible for guiding the development of lay ecclesial ministry in the United States. For several decades and in growing numbers, lay men and women have been undertaking a wide variety of roles in Church ministries. Many of these roles presume a significant degree of preparation,

Lay ecclesial ministers serve in hospitals, prisons and in many other non-parish pastoral settings

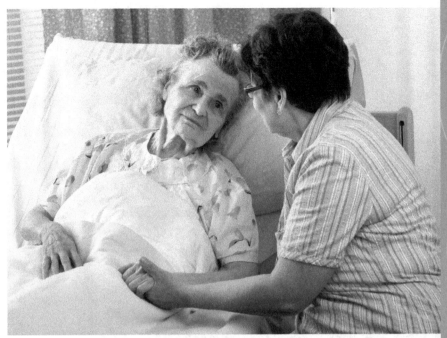

formation, and professional competence. They require authorization of the hierarchy in order for the person to serve publicly in the local church. They entrust to laity responsibilities for leadership in particular areas of ministry and thereby draw certain lay persons into a close mutual collaboration with the pastoral ministry of bishops, priests, and deacons. . . .

Co-Workers in the Vineyard of the Lord expresses our strong desire for the fruitful collaboration of ordained and lay ministers who, in distinct but complementary ways, continue in the Church the saving mission of Christ for the world, his vineyard.

The title "lay ecclesial minister" names and describes a specific role that the laity have in working for the good of the whole Church. On the parish level the bishops may appoint lay ecclesial ministers to serve as administrators in parishes as pastoral associates and pastoral life directors.

- **Pastoral associates:** Pastoral associates are appointed by the bishop *to assist a priest who serves as the pastor*. Pastoral associates assist the pastor in those ministries that are not reserved to the ordained.
- **Pastoral life directors:** Pastoral life directors are appointed by the bishop *to serve a parish*

that does not have a priest to serve as its pastor. Pastoral life directors, likewise, cannot perform all the ministries of the ordained. They can perform all pastoral duties, except those ministries reserved to the ordained.

Lay ecclesial ministers serve as the vicar general of a diocese. They also serve the Church as school principals and directors of parish religious education programs; as youth ministry directors and RCIA directors; and in a variety of other parish positions. Lay ecclesial ministers also serve in hospitals and prisons, on college and university campuses and in many other non-parish pastoral settings. The contribution of the laity in these ministries is so essential that "the apostolate of the pastors cannot be fully effective without it" (CCC, no. 900).

BRAINSTORM, REFLECT AND SHARE

- Brainstorm with a partner a list of ways you see lay people working full- or part-time in a church ministry in your parish, school and diocese.
- In what ways is the work of the Church more effective because of their presence and work?
- Why might the apostolate of the ordained not be fully effective without the contributions of lay ecclesial ministers?
- Share reflections as a class.

Jesus calls the lay faithful to be the leaven of the Gospel in the marketplace of life—in their homes and society

THE SACRAMENTAL FOUNDATION OF LAY ECCLESIAL MINISTRY

In the "Attend and Reflect" section of this chapter you explored that at Baptism you were made a sharer in the threefold ministry of Christ the Priest, Prophet and King, and that at Confirmation you were strengthened by the Spirit of Christ to take part in that ministry. These two Sacraments of Christian Initiation are the foundation of lay ecclesial ministry.

By "regeneration and the anointing of the holy Spirit, [the baptized] are consecrated as a spiritual house and a holy priesthood. . . . They should everywhere on earth bear witness to Christ and give an answer to everyone who asks a reason for their hope of eternal life (see 1 Peter 3:15)" (*Vatican II, Dogmatic Constitution on the Church* [*Lumen Gentium*], no. 10). Christ calls all the laity, lay ecclesial ministers and non-lay ecclesial ministers, to be active in ministering with one another "for the life of the world" (John 6:51).

WHAT ABOUT YOU PERSONALLY?

- ⊙ Might serving God and the Church as a lay ecclesial minister be on your radar?
- ⊙ What lay ecclesial ministry attracts you the most?

SERVICE TO THE CHURCH

Jesus Christ calls the lay faithful to be the leaven of the Gospel in the *marketplace* of life—in their homes and society. The Church at the Second Vatican Council reiterated this teaching: "The laity are called to participate actively in the entire life of the church; . . . they are to be witnesses to Christ in all circumstances and at the very heart of the human community" (Vatican II, *Pastoral Constitution on the Church in the Modern World* (*Gaudium et Spes*), no. 43). The *Catechism of the Catholic Church* reaffirms that mission of the lay faithful. It describes the mission of the laity as "permeating social, political, and economic realities with the demands of Christian doctrine and life" (CCC, no. 899). "Lay believers are in the front line of Church life; for them the Church is the animating principle of human society" (Pope Pius XII, Discourse, February 20, 1946).

While most of the laity fulfill this vocation in the "secular" world, some lay people are becoming increasingly involved in official leadership responsibilities beyond volunteering their time and talents. St. John Paul II, writing to the Church in America in 1999, encouraged such lay participation. The Pope wrote:

As pastors of the People of God in America, priests . . . should be careful to discern the charisms and strengths of the faithful who might be leaders in the community, listening to them and through dialogue encouraging their participation and co-responsibility. This will lead to a better distribution of tasks, enabling priests "to dedicate themselves to what is most closely tied to the encounter with and the proclamation of Jesus Christ, and thus to represent better within the community the presence of Jesus who draws his people together" (Synodal Proposition 49).

—Post-Synodal Apostolic Exhortation, *The Church in America (Ecclesia in America)*, no. 39 §3

St. Paul, in reflecting on his ministry as an Apostle, wrote: "for an obligation is laid on me, and woe to me if I do not preach the gospel!" (1 Corinthians 9:16). Paul's words have a particular meaning today when bishops are seeking to meet the contemporary challenges to their preaching the Gospel. Among these obstacles, as we have seen, is the decreasing number of priests and a growing Catholic population.

COLLABORATORS AND CO-WORKERS WITH THE HIERARCHY

Lay ecclesial ministry "entails an explicit relationship of mutual accountability to and collaboration with the Church hierarchy" (*Co-Workers in the Vineyard of the Lord*, "The Lay Faithful and Lay Ecclesial Ministers," §2). Lay ecclesial ministers do not have the same authority and vocation to serve the Church as ordained ministers have. Lay ecclesial ministers find their relationships with the local Church by virtue of the Sacraments of Christian Initiation *and* by virtue of the recognition and authorization they receive from the bishop.

Bishops, working with their co-workers, priests, have the Christ-given authority to celebrate the sacraments, to teach the faithful, and to govern the local, or particular, Church to which the pope has appointed them to serve. The emergence of lay ecclesial ministers in no way diminishes the ministries of the ordained. It simply broadens the Church's responsibility to include all the baptized in carrying out the mission Jesus Christ entrusted to his Church.

". . . an obligation is laid on me, and woe to me if I do not preach the gospel!"

1 CORINTHIANS 9:16

ST. PAUL PREACHING | VERIA, GREECE

LAY ECCLESIAL MINISTERS AND LAY VOLUNTEERS

Lay volunteers *and* lay ecclesial ministers are serving the Church in the United States of America at all levels. Their service supports the Church in accomplishing her mission effectively. It is important to distinguish the role of lay ecclesial ministers and that of lay people who volunteer their time and talents.

Lay volunteers serve parishes in a diversity of ways. For example, they serve as ushers, readers, choir members and extraordinary ministers of Holy Communion at Mass; they assist in faith formation programs as catechists in parish religious education, in RCIA programs, and in baptismal and marriage preparation programs; they serve as outreach volunteers and peace and justice workers; they assist in the pastoral management of parishes as members of the parish council, finance and building committees, or as heads of pastoral life committees. Lay volunteers are not lay ecclesial ministers; they are sometimes supervised and trained by lay ecclesial ministers.

TALK IT OVER

- Identify the many opportunities for the laity to serve your parish. Then create a lay ministry profile of your parish. Use the headings "Lay Volunteers" and "Lay Ecclesial Ministers" to organize your profile.
- From what you have learned in this chapter, which of those lay people would you describe as lay ecclesial ministers? Which would you describe as lay volunteers? Give specific reasons.
- Share and discuss as a class the importance of the laity to the life and mission of the local parish.

WHAT ABOUT YOU PERSONALLY?

- You can serve your parish as a lay volunteer. You do not need to be designated a lay ecclesial minister.
- Discern the best gifts you have to contribute to the Church's work in your local parish.
- What decision will you make in order to use those gifts?

Path to lay ecclesial ministry

Go into the Vineyard of the Lord

Working in the Church is a path of Christian discipleship to be encouraged by the hierarchy (see *Dogmatic Constitution on the Church*, nos. 30, 33, 37). The possibility that lay persons undertake Church ministries can be grounded in Scripture and the teachings of the Church, from St. Paul to the Second Vatican Council and in more recent documents.

—*Co-Workers in the Vineyard of the Lord*, "The Call to the Lay Faithful," §3

OPENING REFLECTION

⦿ Take a moment and reflect on the first disciples of Jesus, other than the Apostles, for example, Nicodemus, and Martha and Mary.

⦿ How did they accompany and support Jesus in his ministry? How might their support have contributed to the mission of Jesus? To the Apostles' fulfilling the mission Jesus gave them?

DISCERNING A CALL TO LAY ECCLESIAL MINISTRY

Many Catholic lay people see their Baptism as calling them into direct work in the Church as either a full-time or part-time lay ecclesial minister. Perhaps you see a role for you as a lay ecclesial minister. To help you discern whether you have such a calling, let us examine a few of the frequently asked questions about lay ecclesial ministry. The responses are based on *Co-Workers in the Vineyard of the Lord* and the USCCB's "Lay Ecclesial Ministry FAQs."

How do lay people hear a call to lay ecclesial ministry? "The pathway to lay ecclesial ministry for any individual is as unique as that individual" (*Co-Workers in the Vineyard of the Lord*, p. 27). Lay volunteers may desire a more formal and stable ministry within the Church. This desire may originate in the home, in other faith life experiences, or from the personal invitation of others, especially the invitation of a priest, deacon or lay ecclesial minister.

How do lay people discern and respond to a call to lay ministry? Exploring a call to lay ecclesial ministry involves both the discernment of that call and the evaluation and determination of a lay person's suitability for this ministry. The discernment process is a gradual process that involves many people. Prayer and dialogue with family and friends, mentor or spiritual director, priests and other pastoral leaders are essential to discerning whether one is truly called to such a ministry.

What are some of the essential dispositions of a lay ecclesial minister? "Lay persons with a call to lay ecclesial ministry possess certain dispositions. . . . These include:

⊙ Being in full communion with the Catholic Church, able to minister joyfully and faithfully within the hierarchical communion that is the Church

⊙ The desire to serve the Church and its mission, which proceeds from the love of God and God's people

⊙ A commitment to regular personal prayer, frequent participation in the Mass beyond the Sunday obligation and in the other sacraments, especially the Sacrament of Penance

⊙ Zeal to live a Christian life, and willingness to live and teach as the magisterium teaches

⊙ Emotional maturity, including the ability to sustain friendships and professional relationships and the management and appropriate expression of both anger and affection

⊙ The intellectual gifts needed for the specific ministry

⊙ A commitment to good communication and conflict resolution skills."
—*Co-Workers in the Vineyard of the Lord*, p. 30

What are the elements of the formation process for lay ecclesial ministry? The formation of lay ecclesial ministers is similar to that of ordained ministers. Their remote preparation begins in the home and in their participation in parish life. Their formal training includes education in the four areas of human, spiritual, intellectual and pastoral formation. The time and programs for this formal formation are set by each diocese and vary from individual to individual.

The lay ecclesial minister's formation does not end with their initial formal training. "Ongoing formation continues the process of learning and growing throughout the time one serves in ministry" (*Co-Workers in the Vineyard of the Lord*, p. 50). This ongoing formation may occur through participation in conferences, academic and professional skill development courses and workshops, peer support groups, and mentoring.

TALK IT OVER

⊙ How have you come to understand the call to lay ecclesial ministry? Discuss:
  – its significance for the mission of the Church;
  – its many opportunities;
  – its difference from lay volunteer ministry.

- How might high school Catholic youth begin to discern whether they might serve the Church as lay ecclesial ministers?

ENVISIONING YOUR FUTURE

Your personal vocation to live your Baptism is far more than a job or career. God calls you to a fulfillment and happiness that no job or career in and of itself can ever provide. No amount of wealth and possessions and power the world has to offer can ever fully satisfy you. If enduring happiness is to be found in this life, you will find it in living the two Great Commandments in selfless service to God and others. The baptized may live this way of life as members of the laity, of the hierarchy or of the consecrated life.

The goal of this course of study is to provide you with a vision and a framework to discern your personal vocation. Prayerful reflection and the spiritual discipline of discernment will enable you to come to know and live out that vocation.

Take a moment and return to chapter 2 of this text. Revisit and reread the "Attend and Reflect" section of that chapter. Then begin the journal exercise.

JOURNAL EXERCISE

- Begin a "Vocations" journal. In your journal:
  - write the vocation you feel God might be calling you to live;
  - describe the reasons why you feel that you are called to that vocation;
  - detail the talents you have to fulfill that vocation.
- Share your reflections with a mentor—a parent or other family member, a priest, deacon, religious brother or sister, youth minister or single or married lay person.
- Pray regularly to know your personal vocation and for the courage to respond to that call.
- Revisit and update your reflections often.

JUDGE AND ACT

REVIEW AND SHARE WHAT YOU HAVE LEARNED

Look back over this chapter and reflect on what you have learned about how the lay faithful serve the Church. Share the teachings of the Church on these statements:

⊙ The laity have the vocation to seek holiness of life by being the leaven of the Gospel in society.

⊙ The laity serve the People of God in a diversity of leadership roles.

⊙ Scripture and the teaching of the Church are the foundation for lay people undertaking ministries within the Church.

OVER TO YOU

⊙ What wisdom for discerning your vocation as a disciple of Jesus Christ have you learned from studying this chapter?

LEARN BY EXAMPLE

The National Association for Lay Ministry (NALM)

 National Association for Lay Ministry

The National Association for Lay Ministry (NALM) was founded in 1981. According to its website, NALM is the "professional organization that supports, educates and advocates for lay ministers and promotes the development of lay ministry in the Catholic Church."

NALM was instrumental in assisting the bishops in their writing of *Co-Workers in the Vineyard of the Lord* and continues to support its implementation in a variety of ways.

Among NALM's key accomplishments are the "Emerging Models for Pastoral Leadership" initiative and its advocacy on behalf of lay ecclesial ministers.

The Emerging Models initiative is designed to explore and support the wide variety of ways that lay ecclesial ministers are functioning effectively as pastoral leaders in the Catholic institutions in the United States of America. NALM's advocacy work centers around helping parishes and other Church institutions understand what it means to be a lay person who works for the Church. It supports the efforts of lay ecclesial ministers to receive just wages, sufficient health and retirement benefits, and appropriate educational, spiritual and personal formation and support in their ministry.

TALK IT OVER

⊙ What are some ways that Catholic youth can join together to explore and participate in the ministries of their parish or school?

SHARE FAITH WITH FAMILY AND FRIENDS

⊙ Read together the account of Jesus' commissioning of the Apostles in Matthew 28:16–20. Discuss:
 – What does it mean for the laity to be disciples of Jesus in the marketplaces of their lives?
 – How can we support one another in preaching and living the Gospel?

- As a result of this course of study, do you have a clearer vision of the personal vocation that God might be calling you to embrace?
- What vision do you have for your future? Do you have a plan in mind to prepare for that vocation?
- How does serving the mission of the Church fit into those plans?

Note: *A container of holy water will be needed for the concluding "Prayer Reflection."*

LEARN BY HEART

"The harvest is plentiful, but the laborers are few; therefore ask the Lord of the harvest to send out laborers into his harvest."

MATTHEW 9:37–38

All pray the Sign of the Cross together.

Call to prayer

LEADER
Let us quiet our minds and hearts and listen to
our Lord, who is always with us. (*Pause*)
Loving God,
you have gathered us together as your people
to listen and respond to your Word.
Send your Holy Spirit upon all of us
as we seek out ways you desire us to serve your
Church and one another.
ALL
Amen.

Proclamation of the Word of God

READER ONE
A reading from the holy Gospel according to
Matthew.
ALL
Glory to you, O Lord.
READER
Proclaim Matthew 9:35–38.
The Gospel of the Lord.
ALL
Praise to you, Lord Jesus Christ.

READER TWO
A reading from the First Book of Samuel.
Proclaim 1 Samuel 3:2–10.
The word of the Lord.
ALL
Thanks be to God.

Response to the Word of God

LEADER
Let us take a moment to listen to how God might
be calling each one of us to live out our baptismal
vocation. Reflect on:
⊙ How might we hear God's voice more clearly?
  (*Pause*)
⊙ Are we truly listening to God's call? (*Pause*)

God of love, you call each of us by name;
you invite us to cooperate with the Spirit of
Christ
by using the talents and gifts with which you
have blessed us
to give witness to your abundance of love at
work in the world.
May we truly listen to your voice and respond to
your call.
We ask this in the name of Jesus Christ our Lord.
ALL
Amen.

LEADER
I invite you to come forward and bless yourself
with holy water to recall your Baptism.

*All come forward, bless themselves and return to
their places.*

We now join our voices in prayer.

ALL
Loving Mother, Our Lady of Guadalupe,
you asked Juan Diego to help build a Church that
    would serve a new people in a new land.
You left your image upon his cloak as a visible
    sign of your love for us,
so that we may come to believe in your Son, Jesus
    the Christ.

Our Lady of Guadalupe and St. Juan Diego,
help us respond to God's call to build your Son's
    Church today.
Help us recognize our personal vocation to serve
    God as married or single persons or priests,
    brothers, or sisters as our way to help extend
    the Reign of God here on earth.
Help us to pay attention to the
    promptings of the Holy Spirit.
May all of us have the courage of Juan
    Diego to say "Yes" to our personal call!
May we encourage one another to follow Jesus,
    no matter where that path takes us. Amen.

All pray the Sign of the Cross together.

**Our Lady of Guadalupe
and St. Juan Diego,
help us respond to God's
call to build your Son's
Church today**

CHAPTER 12

Catholic Lay Singles

CHRISTIAN SINGLE LIFE . . .

AN UNSELFISH GIFT OF SELF TO GOD AND OTHERS

A SOURCE FOR JOY AND FULLNESS OF LIFE

A WAY OF LIVING ONE'S BAPTISM

GIFTED WITH GRACES FROM THE HOLY SPIRIT

A SOURCE OF UNIQUE BLESSINGS AND CHALLENGES

AN IMAGE AND REFLECTION OF TRINITARIAN LOVE

JESUS IS THE MODEL FOR THE CHRISTIAN SINGLE LIFE

THE SINGLE LIFE IS ONE EXPRESSION OF THE vocation of the laity. The Christian single life can be either a temporary or permanent choice by a lay person to live out their faith and give witness to Christ. The committed single life is a permanent chaste and celibate way of living the Gospel that a baptized woman or man freely chooses and promises to live.

SOME BLESSINGS OF THE SINGLE LIFE

TIME FOR FAMILY AND FRIENDS

SERVICE TO THE COMMUNITY

INTIMACY WITH GOD

Faith Focus: These teachings of the Catholic Church are the primary focus of the doctrinal content presented in this chapter:

- ⊙ The life of Jesus is the model for all Christians who choose to live the single life.
- ⊙ Jesus calls the faithful who choose to live the single life to make an unselfish gift of themselves to God and others.
- ⊙ The single life can be either a temporary or permanent committed way of living the Gospel.
- ⊙ The single life has its own blessings and challenges.
- ⊙ The single life is a source of joy and fullness of life.
- ⊙ The Holy Spirit offers the single person the graces to face the unique challenges of living the Gospel as a single person.

Discipleship Formation: As a result of studying this chapter and discovering the meaning of the faith of the Catholic Church for your life, you should be better able to:

- ⊙ understand and value the life of single people in the Church;
- ⊙ apply the blessings and challenges of living an authentic Christian life to your own life;
- ⊙ meet the challenges you now face in living as a Christian single person;
- ⊙ consider whether God might be calling you to the committed single life.

Scripture References: These Scripture references are quoted or referred to in this chapter:
NEW TESTAMENT: Matthew 9:11–12, 10:37–40 and 42, 12:48b–50, 19:11–12; **Mark** 1:14–15; **Luke** 4:14–21; 18:29–30; **John** 13:34–35, 19:25b–27; **1 Corinthians** 7:32–35, 13:4–8a, 13; **Philippians** 2:1–13; **1 John** 4:7–16

Faith Glossary: Familiarize yourself with or recall the meaning of these key terms. Definitions are found in the Glossary: **abstinence, Apostolic Tradition, celibacy, chastity, committed single life, joy, passions, single life, temperance, temptation, virginity, works of mercy**

Faith Words: committed single life; single life
Learn by Heart: Luke 18:29–30
Learn by Example: Blessed Pier Giorgio Frassati

How can the single life be a truly Christian way of life?

THE CHANGING FACE OF MARRIAGE

The latest available statistics reveal that less than half of all Americans choose to marry, a record low for the country. The age at which people marry is also increasing. Young adults now tend to view marriage not as the cornerstone of their life but as its capstone. They see successful employment as the foundation on which to build their personal life, including, perhaps, marriage and a family life. In fact, most young adults believe that they must be completely financially independent to be ready for marriage. Culturally, the effect of this changing face of marriage is that there are a growing number of Catholics living the single life for an extended period before marrying or entering the priesthood or religious life.

OPENING CONVERSATION

⊙ What are your thoughts about this profile of marriage in our country?

⊙ Do you have an older sibling or cousin who fits this profile? How would you describe their life?

OVER TO YOU

⊙ What about yourself? What are your thoughts about the right time to marry or respond to the call to the priesthood or to religious life?

THE CHRISTIAN SINGLE LIFE

As a single person, you may be giving some thought to the way of life, or vocation, to which God might be calling you. As we learned in chapter 2, that decision is best made when we engage in prayer, self-reflection and conversation with other people, for example, with family, a priest or spiritual director, and other adults whose wisdom and Christ-like lifestyle we respect. Discerning whether to remain single, or marry, or become a deacon or priest, or enter religious life takes time.

How long a lay person chooses to remain single is a personal decision—the length of time varies from person to person. Most often, a lay person chooses the **single life** as a temporary stage on their life journey. Some lay people, however, choose to make a personal consecration or commitment that takes on a permanent, celibate gift of self to God. When a Catholic single lay person chooses and commits to living this form of **celibacy**, they choose to live the **committed single life**.

THINK, PAIR AND SHARE

⊙ Oftentimes Catholics assume that someone who is interested in religion or in truly living the Gospel will become a priest or nun. Why do you think some make this assumption?

- How do you think the life of Jesus challenges such an assumption?

WHAT ABOUT YOU PERSONALLY?

- What, if anything, have you heard people say about Christians living the single life?
- What has been your own experience as a single person of living the divine command to love? What challenges have you faced?

JESUS: A MODEL FOR LIVING AS A CHRISTIAN SINGLE PERSON

Jesus began his public ministry by announcing the Kingdom of God; and he committed and devoted his life to bringing about that kingdom. (Recall and check out Mark 1:14–15 and Luke 4:14–21.) Jesus' entire life, Death, Resurrection and teachings made it clear that bringing about the Kingdom of God was his primary mission. He came to reconcile humanity with God and with one another and to heal all that divides humanity from God and separates people from one another and from God's creation. This mission determined everything else in his life. It was the heart and center of his teachings and other deeds.

Jesus was about thirty years old when he announced and began his public ministry. The four Gospels and the **Apostolic Tradition** of the Church clearly teach that Jesus did not marry. For the only son in a family to choose not to marry would have been very uncommon and, in a sense, counter cultural to Jewish practice at that time. It would have been expected of him, a carpenter's son, to marry in order to assure the continuance of his family line.

Many people today still have a difficult time accepting that Jesus did not marry. For example, contemporary works of popular fiction, music and theater speculate about the "married life" of Jesus. For a man (or woman) to choose to live a celibate single life committed to others, and not to marry, is a way of life beyond the understanding of many.

LOVE OF ANOTHER SORT

All Christians look to Jesus as the model for living their Baptism. Jesus' whole life, his actions and his words, model living the divine command to love God and others. You will recall that at the Last Supper Jesus commanded his Apostles (and his disciples for all times): "I give you a new commandment, that you love one another. Just as I have loved you, you also should love one another. By this everyone will know that you are my disciples, if you have love for one another" (John 13:34–35).

Selfless love, or *agape*, for God and for all people was at the heart of Jesus' life. All his life choices were rooted in and flowed from his identity as the Incarnate Son of God, who is love. His life of selfless sacrificial love culminated in his freely emptying himself and giving up his life on the Cross.

FAITH WORDS

Single life

Christian single life is a temporary or permanent choice by a lay person to live out their faith and give witness to Christ while remaining unmarried.

Committed single life

A permanent chaste and celibate way of living the Gospel that a baptized woman or man freely chooses and promises to live.

THE ASCENSION | SANTA MARIA IN VALLICELLA, ROME, ITALY

No one ever loved more freely, completely and selflessly than Jesus. To both women and men, to children and adults, Jesus gave his time, his wisdom, his compassion, his healing and, in the end, his life. He poured himself out in service to all. The life of Jesus is the model of living for all his disciples, then and now—for the ordained and religious, for the laity, the married and the single. This same mind, the Apostle Paul tells us in his letter to the Philippians, is to direct the way all Christians are to live, no matter their vocation or state of life in the Church.

THINK, PAIR AND SHARE
⊙ Take a moment to read and reflect on Philippians 2:1–13 and 1 John 4:7–16.
⊙ What do these passages reveal about the way of life that all disciples of Christ are to live?

WHAT ABOUT YOU PERSONALLY?
⊙ How might the teachings in these passages apply to you, right now?

GOD-CENTERED LOVE
As Jesus was teaching, someone in the crowd let him know that his mother and other family members were standing outside and wanted to speak to him. Jesus' response reveals the scope of his mission. He said: " 'Who is my mother, and who are my brothers?' And pointing to his disciples, he said, 'Here are my mother and my brothers! For whoever does the will of my Father in heaven is my brother and sister and mother' " (Matthew 12:48b–50).

Jesus revealed his relationship with his Father and that God is the Father of all. Jesus' mission was to the entire family of God. All people are called to be one with him and his Father. A person's *relationship* or *bond* with the Trinity

"Whoever does the will of my Father in heaven is my brother and sister and mother."

MATTHEW 12:48B

Jesus placed his Mother's care in the hands of the beloved disciple

THE CRUCIFIXION (DETAIL OF MARY AND JOHN) | ROGIER VAN DER WEYDEN

runs deeper than even family and other blood relationships. Recall these words of Jesus to all who wish to be his disciples:

"Whoever loves father or mother more than me is not worthy of me; and whoever loves son or daughter more than me is not worthy of me; and whoever does not take up the cross and follow me is not worthy of me. Those who find their life will lose it, and those who lose their life for my sake will find it. Whoever welcomes you welcomes me, and whoever welcomes me welcomes the one who sent me. . . . and whoever gives even a cup of cold water to one of these little ones in the name of a disciple—truly I tell you, none of these will lose their reward."

—Matthew 10:37–40, 42

Jesus was not teaching that we are not to love our parents, siblings and other family members. He was teaching that our relationship with God, our obedience and fidelity to God and our love for God, is to be at the center of all our relationships—no matter which way of life God calls us to live and we choose to live.

We know that Jesus always had a special love and concern for Mary. For example, the Fourth Gospel tells us that at the end of his life the crucified Jesus, moments before his Death, placed his Mother's care in the hands of the beloved disciple, the disciple whom the Tradition of the Church identifies to be John the Apostle. (Take a moment and read John 19:25b–27.)

TALK IT OVER
- Can you imagine something being more important to you than your family? Why or why not?
- How does the life of Jesus model for you how to place your love of God at the heart of your love for your family?

JOURNAL EXERCISE
- What aspect of Jesus' life would be most helpful for you to imitate at this time in your life?
- How will doing so help you grow in true, loving relationships with others?

The shape of the Christian single life

THE ULTIMATE SACRIFICE

Jean Donovan chose to remain single and live the Gospel as a Catholic lay missioner. After earning a master's degree in business, she began a promising professional career with a prestigious international accounting firm. She became engaged, but then experienced doubts about her decision to marry and felt an inner calling to do mission work. Donovan described her inner conflict, "I sit there and talk to God and say, 'Why are you doing this to me? Why can't I just be your little suburban housewife?' "

After much prayer and discernment, Jean Donovan chose to become a lay missioner, and she served the poor and oppressed people of El Salvador. On December 2, 1980, Jean Donovan,

ST. CATHERINE OF ALEXANDRIA | CARAVAGGIO

Ursuline Sister Dorothy Kazel, and Maryknoll Sisters Maura Clarke and Ita Ford were beaten, raped and murdered by Salvadoran soldiers. They gave their lives out of love for God, the Church and the people whom they served.

OPENING CONVERSATION

⊙ How did living as a single person empower Jean Donovan to live the Gospel?

⊙ How do you see single people serving the Church and the people of your community? Describe how the single way of life contributes to their doing so.

OVER TO YOU

⊙ Do you give any thought to remaining a single layperson so you can serve the Church? What value might you see in coming to such a decision?

THE VALUE OF THE SINGLE LIFE

One of the joys of discerning and living our vocation is discovering our talents and accomplishing feats we may never have even envisioned. Because God's plans and desires for us go well beyond what we can imagine for ourselves, we sometimes fail to understand or appreciate how God is working in our lives and bringing to fruition the person whom he created us to be. While this discovery is a lifetime adventure, responding to and cooperating with the Holy Spirit is central to discerning and living our vocation.

The biblical story of salvation contains many examples of people who heard God's personal invitation to them and responded. These biblical figures include Jeremiah, Elijah and Daniel in the Old Testament and John the Baptist in the New Testament. The story of the Church is also filled with examples of single faithful lay people who discerned and lived their vocations, such as

> # The celibate person becomes spiritually fruitful, the father and mother of many, cooperating in the realization of the family according to God's plan.
>
> ### THE CHRISTIAN FAMILY IN THE MODERN WORLD, NO. 16

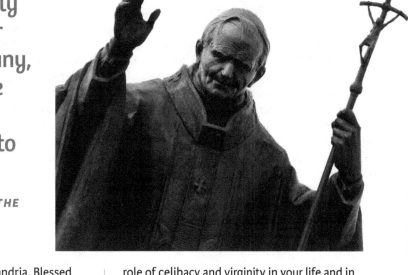

St. Agatha, St. Catherine of Alexandria, Blessed Pier Giorgio Frassati, Venerable Matt Talbot, the founder of the Legion of Mary, and Peter Maurin, the co-founder with Dorothy Day of the Catholic Worker movement. Today, God continues to bless and achieve great things through those who faithfully live out their Baptism through the single life, whether as a temporary or a permanent way of living the Gospel.

LET'S PROBE DEEPER: A SCRIPTURE ACTIVITY

- ⊙ What is the first thing that comes to mind when you hear the name John the Baptist? Share your thoughts with a partner.
- ⊙ Now read about the mission and work of John the Baptist in the Gospels.
- ⊙ Share what you find most inspirational about his life for your own spiritual growth and living of the Gospel.

CHASTITY AND CELIBACY OR VIRGINITY

Jesus neither married nor had children nor raised a family. He had close relationships with both men and women. (Recall his friendships with the Beloved Disciple, with Martha and Mary and Lazarus, and with Mary Magdalene.) Throughout his life Jesus modeled and gave witness to the meaning of living a life of **chastity** and **celibacy** or **virginity** for the sake of the Kingdom of God.

Before we continue our exploration of the single life, let us pause, read and reflect on the role of celibacy and virginity in your life and in the life of all single people. St. John Paul II in his 1981 apostolic exhortation *The Christian Family in the Modern World (Familiaris Consortio)* taught:

> Marriage and virginity or celibacy are two ways of expressing and living the one mystery of the covenant of God with His people. . . .
>
> In virginity or celibacy, the human being is awaiting, also in a bodily way, the eschatological marriage of Christ with the Church, giving himself or herself completely to the Church in the hope that Christ may give himself to the Church in the full truth of eternal life. The celibate person thus anticipates in his or her flesh the new world of the future resurrection. . . . Virginity or celibacy, by liberating the human heart in a unique way, "so as to make it burn with greater love for God and all humanity" (Second Vatican Council, *Decree on the Renewal of Religious Life*, no. 12), bears witness that the Kingdom of God and his justice is that pearl of great price which is preferred to every other value no matter how great, and hence must be sought as the only definitive value. . . .
>
> In spite of having renounced physical fecundity, the celibate person becomes spiritually fruitful, the father and mother of many, cooperating in the realization of the family according to God's plan.
> —*The Christian Family in the Modern World*, no. 16

All Christians, no matter what their vocation or state of life, are to live the virtue and evangelical, or gospel, counsel of chastity, as Jesus did. For unmarried people, this means that they are to practice **abstinence** from sexual intercourse and all forms of inappropriate sexual intimacy. This gospel counsel is often rejected by some Catholic and non-Catholic single people. They often falsely think that living a chaste life is dehumanizing, and that abstinence and premarital chastity work against their developing the strength of character that will contribute to a healthy and solid marriage.

WHAT ABOUT YOU PERSONALLY?

- ⦿ What challenges do you face in living as a single person?
- ⦿ What challenges might you face as you move on from high school?
- ⦿ Do you have a clear vision of how you will meet those challenges?

THE WITNESS OF THE SINGLE LIFE

In the chapters on marriage, you explored and discussed how married couples grow spiritually and bodily by giving witness to the life and love of the Trinity. In chapters 8, 9 and 10 you explored how deacons, priests, bishops and members of religious orders and institutes do the same. The life of a Christian single person is also to reflect the life and love of God the Father, God the Son and God the Holy Spirit. This is the universal vocation of all the faithful—to be an image and reflection of Trinitarian love.

Archbishop Robert Carlson of Saint Louis wrote these words of encouragement to those men and women who choose to remain single:

Single men and women who have given themselves wholeheartedly to Christ . . . bind themselves to the service of others, and they participate directly in the Church's mission and share themselves intimately with those who walk with them on the journey to Christ's kingdom. . . . They discern God's will for themselves through prayer, spiritual reading and retreats. They commit to their families—parents, siblings and extended family members. They partner with friends, co-workers, fellow parishioners, neighbors and all whom

What challenges do you face in living as a single person?

DETAIL FROM AN ILLUMINATED BOOK OF GOSPELS, ENGLAND, C. 1000 AD

Living a single life rooted in the Gospel contributes to the Church being a sacrament of God's reign in the world

they encounter in seeking to make our world a better place. The dedicated single life is a real vocation. It is a calling to be an authentic follower of Jesus Christ in the particular circumstances of daily life.

—Blog titled "A vocation to the dedicated single life leads to joy and fulfillment," November 1, 2010

No one lives in a vacuum. Each person responds to their life situation in a unique way. Single life may look very different depending on each person's situation. For some people, this way of life frees them, as it did for Jean Donovan, to make their greatest possible contribution to the Church and to the common good of society. Others remain single as they discern whether they may have the vocation to marry or to be ordained or to enter religious life. Other single people, it would appear, are open to marriage but simply never find the right person for such a partnership of life and love. And some find themselves living as a single person again after their spouse has died.

Some people live in situations or with conditions that make it impossible or undesirable for them to marry. In this case, some Christians choose the single life as the path to holiness of life. You will recall that, after Jesus' teaching on divorce, his disciples said to him, "If such is the case of a man with his wife, it is better not to marry." Jesus responded:

"Not everyone can accept this teaching, but only those to whom it is given. For there are eunuchs who have been so from birth, and there are eunuchs who have been made eunuchs by others, and there are eunuchs who have made themselves eunuchs for the sake of the kingdom of heaven. Let anyone accept this who can."

—Matthew 19:11–12

Living a single life rooted in the Gospel contributes to the Church being a sacrament of God's reign in the world. This life comes with its own unique blessings and challenges. We will take a more detailed look at these blessings and challenges in the next two sections of this chapter.

TALK IT OVER
⊙ What would it mean to live the single life faithfully while remaining open to marriage, to the ordained life or to the consecrated life?
⊙ What difficulties and joys might come with choosing to live the single life?

WHAT ABOUT YOU PERSONALLY?
⊙ How has your understanding of the single life changed in light of this discussion?
⊙ What piece of wisdom about the single life can you apply to your life right now?

Blessings of the single life

SERVING THE CHURCH THROUGH THE SINGLE LIFE

Sarah is fifty-five and single. She works four days a week in a job that she enjoys and finds that, because she doesn't have the responsibility of raising a family or caring for elderly family members or relatives, she can devote more of her free time to helping others less fortunate than herself. She helps out in a local charity shop on her day off and in the evenings she often visits elderly people in her neighborhood or participates in fund-raising or church activities. On Sundays she enjoys being a minister of the Eucharist and, occasionally, singing in the local church choir. Sarah enjoys her single life and finds great fulfillment from her work, her friendships and being an active and contributing member of her parish community.

OPENING CONVERSATION

⊙ Do you have a family member or know someone who lives the Gospel as Sara does? If so, share their story.

⊙ What joys and blessings come with such a dedicated commitment to Christ?

A SOURCE FOR JOY AND FULLNESS OF LIFE

Living the single life as a Christian is, for some, the pathway to fullness of life, through which they can seek true happiness and discover true joy. We now explore some of the many blessings of the single life.

Family and friends: When they commit to marriage and family life, spouses must often set parameters around the amount of time they can spend with friends, and, perhaps, even with parents and siblings. All the relationships that married couples enjoy tend to flow from and support their married and family life. Christians who are living a single life typically find that they have more time for both other family members and friends and for engaging in activities in their communities or in the wider society.

While some single people experience a longing for married and family life, many find great fulfillment and joy in their relationships with others. For example, single people often play a significant role in the lives of their parents and grandparents, of nieces, nephews and other family members, and of the children of friends, work colleagues and neighbors.

Service to the community: A blessing that Christian single people in particular discover and experience is the greater freedom to be available to invest time in serving their parish, the broader church community, as well as the local community. Christian single people, just like the married, ordained and religious, discover and experience great joy and fulfillment of life in bringing about the Kingdom of God through their practice of the corporal and spiritual works of mercy.

Oftentimes single people can attend more events and take on more responsibilities and leadership roles than their married friends and family members. They are generally freer to commit themselves more fully to volunteer ministries and works of charity and justice and mercy. They sometimes have more freedom to relocate when new opportunities to serve arise. St. Paul spoke about these blessings:

I want you to be free from anxieties. The unmarried man is anxious about the affairs of the Lord, how to please the Lord; but the married man is anxious about the affairs of the world, how to please his wife, and his interests are divided. And the unmarried woman and the virgin are anxious about the affairs of the Lord, so that they may be holy in body and spirit; but the married woman is anxious about the affairs of the world, how to please her husband. I say this for your own benefit, not to put any restraint upon you, but to promote good order and unhindered devotion to the Lord.

—1 Corinthians 7:32–35

Whether as parish or community volunteers, or as supportive daughters and sons, brothers and sisters, cousins, nieces and nephews, aunts and uncles, or as friends, coworkers or neighbors, the generous self-gift of single people renders invaluable service to the Church and the world.

Intimacy with God: Christians who choose the single life receive the grace to live in deep intimacy and communion with God. They receive many graces to live an authentic and true spiritual life rooted in the two Great Commandments. As Paul taught: "I say this for your own benefit, not to put any restraint upon you, but to promote good order and unhindered devotion to the Lord" (1 Corinthians 7:35).

Christians living the single way of life can discover the fundamental truth about human existence, namely, that we find completeness and fulfillment only in God. Above all other relationships, the human heart seeks communion and intimacy with God as the source of its deepest happiness. The life of a Christian single person, in its own unique way, can witness to this truth of human existence in tangible ways.

Of course, there is no shortage of distractions for any Christian living in today's fast-paced world. Single people, just like those with a vocation to the married life, ordained life or religious life, need to deal with the temptation to keep God and not their work or other activities at the center of their life.

OVER TO YOU

⊙ What aspects of the single life are most attractive to you?
⊙ What helps you to live this lifestyle in a healthy, holy way?

JOURNAL EXERCISE

⊙ Which of the above blessings of the single life had you not considered before?
⊙ How might those blessings enrich your happiness and joy right now?

ST. PAUL | BASILICA OF SAINTS PETER AND PAUL IN AGLIATE, LOMBARDY, ITALY

Challenges to living the single life

FLYING HIGH, FALLING SHORT

Nolan lives his life out of a suitcase. He is a well-educated and highly respected "corporate whiz." His acute problem-solving skills are in high demand in corporate America. To meet the demands on his time, Nolan has adopted a *jet setting* lifestyle, which has led to his hooking up in several no-strings-attached romances. One late night, while sitting waiting to board the red-eye flight to the East Coast, Nolan becomes overwhelmed by the emptiness of his life. He finds himself longing for a permanent and loving relationship that will give his life more meaning.

OPENING CONVERSATION

⊙ Why do you think Nolan eventually found himself unfulfilled by his lifestyle?

⊙ What are some unhealthy habits people can fall into while living the single life?

⊙ How might the Catholic faith help people live the single life in a healthier, more fulfilling way?

WHAT DO YOU LIVE FOR?

Nolan's life journey is far from uncommon. In fact, his style of living the single life is often portrayed as the preferred way to live "a good life." No family obligations, no one to tell you what to do, and all the fun and romance you want. But, as Nolan discovered, the single life has its fair share of responsibilities and challenges if a person is to find fullness of life.

Did you know?

According to the U.S. Census Bureau, there were 105 million people aged eighteen and older in the United States in 2013. Forty-four percent of these people were unmarried.

The United States Conference of Catholic Bishops (USCCB), in *Sons and Daughters of the Light: A Pastoral Plan for Ministry with Young Adults* (1996), summarized four particular challenges that both married and single young adults themselves have identified. These four challenges are:

⊙ Developing Personal Identity
⊙ Developing Relationships
⊙ Developing a Meaning of Work
⊙ Developing a Spiritual Life

In their closing comments on these concerns the bishops wrote:

These characteristics can be expressed as a desire of young adults to root their lives in something that gives them hope and conveys meaning. Their search for a personal identity, pursued in relationships and work, partially satisfies this hunger for meaning. However,

Have you ever feared that, should you remain single, you might be judged to be different or set apart from other people?

time and time again they told us of their thirst for a relationship with God. They ask, "What is the purpose of my life? What do I live for?"

Like any way of life, the single life is not to be lived rashly or without proper discernment. There are many **temptations** that challenge Christian single people as they strive to live as faithful disciples of Jesus Christ. Participating in the sacramental life of the Church, especially in the Eucharist and Penance, in prayer and living a life of virtue, is as vital for singles as it is for all Catholics in dealing with these challenges successfully. Let us examine some specific challenges single people encounter as they seek answers to the questions, "What is the purpose of my life? What do I live for?"

DEVELOPING PERSONAL IDENTITY

One common challenge to living the single life is the temptation to fear that family, friends and others will *judge you to be different*. Due to traditional cultural and family values and expectations, choosing to live the single life for an extended period is "unusual" and often misunderstood. Single people may feel, "Living as a single person sets me apart, makes me different."

Some Catholics may go through their youth thinking that making a lifelong permanent commitment to marriage or to the priesthood or the religious life is the norm for all Catholic adults. Such expectations sometimes move family members and others to pressure unmarried children and friends (intentionally or not) to find a mate and "tie the knot."

These expectations and pressures can make it difficult for some Catholic young adults to choose to remain single beyond the usual accepted period of time before choosing a permanent way of living their Baptism. Some Catholics may give in to these pressures and may choose immaturely to enter a marriage, or the priesthood or the religious life.

OVER TO YOU

⊙ Have you ever feared that, should you remain single, you might be judged to be different or set apart from other people? If so, what have you learned so far in this chapter that might help you to address or confront such fears?

RELATIONSHIPS: THE LONGING FOR INTIMACY

Our sexual identity is an integral part of our personal identity. Living the virtue of chastity is essential to developing our identity as sexual beings. Developing and practicing the virtue of chastity fosters our growth in the moral attitudes and behavior that enable us to honor and respect

Living a life of chastity and committed celibacy brings a consolation that cannot be appreciated by those who have not lived it

our own dignity and the dignity of other people as sexual persons. The chaste life nurtures the unity and wholeness of the human person, both body and soul.

Contrary to the widespread view, sexual intimacy with another is not essential for personal fulfillment and happiness. Chastity involves channeling the human drive for intimacy through moral and appropriate expressions of friendship with members of the opposite gender and with those of the same gender. For single people, as we have already discussed, this includes practicing the virtue of abstinence. Abstinence is refraining from sexual intercourse and other inappropriate expressions of intimacy until one marries.

Chastity calls for self-mastery, or self-control, so that we have the discipline to deal with the fires ignited by our passions. The cardinal virtue of temperance strengthens us to develop this self-control. Temperance enables us to moderate the desire for and attraction of pleasure and provides balance in our use of created goods. Among those created goods is the pleasure associated with the appropriate expression of

our sexuality. Like all the challenges of living as a disciple of Jesus, responsible living of one's gift of sexuality is possible by God's grace, which inspires and sustains our own best efforts.

We are social beings. Practicing the virtue of chastity is made easier when the surrounding culture supports and does not undermine this moral behavior. The average American hears far more about the satisfactions of sex than about the spiritual benefits of chastity and celibacy. Our culture glorifies sex as an end in itself and places little, if any, emphasis on sexual moderation. It is not only the media but also one's peers who encourage single people to engage in such contemporary sexual practices as cohabitation, which is contrary to the Gospel and to the natural and revealed law of God.

Living a life of chastity and committed celibacy for the sake of Jesus Christ and the Kingdom of God brings a consolation that cannot be appreciated by those who have not lived it. Living a life of committed celibacy or chastity gives one a sense of the gifts of the eternal life to come. God always offers us the grace to live such commitments.

OVER TO YOU

- Why is abstinence vital to non-married people achieving a healthy personal identity?
- What might be some creative and relational activities into which you as a single person could channel your sexuality?

MEANINGFUL WORK: IN THE SERVICE OF OUR VOCATION

Overwork and isolation moved the jet-setting Nolan to re-examine his career and lifestyle. Self-centered choices can easily lead single people to falsely think that their work, job and career is the ultimate source of fulfillment in life. Work can become their *whole life*, leaving no space either for God or for others. In contemporary terms, such choices contribute to their becoming "workaholics." In other words, they *become addicted* to their work and isolate themselves from authentic and live-giving relationships.

In chapter 1 we explored that no created object or created person or career can fulfill the deepest longing of our mind and heart to be loved and to love. No job or career is the same as our vocation. Our work is always in service to our vocation. There is a spiritual dimension to work that we must never overlook. Our bishops put it this way: "The ultimate search for a meaning and a spirituality of work in a Christian context is a response to God's call, which is our vocation" (*Sons and Daughters of the Light*, Section 3, "Developing a Meaning of Work: Work as Meaningful," §5).

OVER TO YOU

- Do you find yourself burying yourself in "work" in school or outside of school? If so, how does that affect your relationships with God, family and friends?
- How does that impact your developing your own identity?
- In light of what you have learned in this chapter, what advice would you give yourself now for striking a healthy balance between work and the rest of life—now and in the future?

ST. JOHN PAUL II IN 2003

"Everyone in the Church, precisely because they are members, receives and thereby shares in the common vocation to holiness."

ST. JOHN PAUL II, *THE LAY MEMBERS OF CHRIST'S FAITHFUL [CHRISTIFIDELES LAICI]*, NO. 16

STRIVING FOR HOLINESS AND WHOLENESS OF LIFE

We love and crave love because God, who is love, first loved us and he invites us to respond to his love. This craving is rooted in the very nature of the human person. It is, as we saw at the beginning of this course of study, the universal human vocation. We exist in order to love. Jesus made it amply clear that our response to the invitation to love God and one another as we love ourselves is the fundamental life choice we make.

Holiness of life is real success in life. God's abundant grace transforms our work and our relationships so that they contribute to our becoming the person God created us to be and to our achieving holiness and wholeness of life. This lifelong pilgrimage, however, is marked by many spiritual and moral challenges. These challenges include not allowing our job to take the place of God, or using other people as objects for our self-gratification. As Nolan discovered, people who keep God out of their life and make sexual and other pleasures their priority will eventually experience a longing for fuller life. They will discover, sooner or later, that their life is fragmented and incomplete, and that striving for wholeness of life necessarily includes striving for holiness of life—a life of intimate communion with God.

TALK IT OVER

⊙ What are some of the key challenges that all Christians face in growing in holiness and wholeness of life?

⊙ How might Christians who live the single life face those challenges?

WHAT ABOUT YOU PERSONALLY?

⊙ What new insights have you discovered into the Christian single life that give you a better understanding of why some people choose that way of life as a vocation?

Striving for wholeness of life necessarily includes striving for holiness of life

JUDGE AND ACT

REVIEW AND SHARE WHAT YOU HAVE LEARNED

Look back over this chapter and reflect on what you have learned about the single way of life and its role in living the Gospel faithfully and authentically. Share the teachings of the Catholic Church on these statements:

⊙ The life of Jesus is the model for all Christians, including those who choose to live the single life.

⊙ Jesus calls the faithful who choose to live the single life to make an unselfish gift of themselves to God and others.

⊙ The single life can be either a temporary or permanent committed way of living the Gospel.

⊙ The Christian single life is a source of joy and happiness.

⊙ The Holy Spirit offers the single person the graces to face the unique challenges of living the Gospel as a single person.

OVER TO YOU

⊙ What wisdom for your life right now did you learn from exploring the teachings of the Catholic Church in this chapter?

⊙ What did you learn that will help you discern the vocation to which God is calling you?

DISCERNING ONE'S VOCATION TO THE COMMITTED SINGLE LIFE

At this point you might be wondering, "Why would anyone want to choose the committed single life when they could be married or be a priest or a deacon or a religious? What's the payoff?" The truth is that not as many young people think about choosing the single life as a permanent lifelong commitment as they do about marriage, the priesthood and religious life.

More commonly, some people come to realize gradually that they have a desire and calling to the committed single life. What leads them to this realization? Some feel called to live a celibate life as an act of devotion to God. Others, while they may find some aspects of religious

community life attractive, also have a strong desire to work independently in the world. They see this as the best way to live their own personal discipleship.

In the end, discerning whether one is called to commit to living the single life as a permanent way of living the Gospel is the same as discerning any vocation. It is a matter of discerning how one can best respond to God's invitation to live the commandments as taught and modeled by Jesus. Hence, the most important question is, "What way of life will most empower me to live my Baptism as an authentic disciple of Jesus Christ?" In a moment you will learn of how Blessed Pier Giorgio Frassati answered such a question.

OVER TO YOU

⊙ What visions and dreams do you have for your life right now? For your future?

⊙ Who and what inspires you to follow those visions and pursue your dreams?

Blessed Pier Giorgio Frassati (1901–25), Catholic single lay man, "Man of the Eight Beatitudes"

Pier Giorgio Frassati was born in Turin, Italy on April 6, 1901 and died at the age of twenty-four on July 4, 1925. On May 20, 1990, St. John Paul II beatified Frassati, calling him the "Man of the Eight Beatitudes."

Early in his life Pier Giorgio developed a deep spirituality rooted in the Eucharist, devotion to the Blessed Mary and the practice of the Beatitudes. For example, at the age of seventeen he joined the St. Vincent de Paul Society and dedicated much of his spare time to serving the sick and the needy, caring for orphans, and assisting the demobilized servicemen returning from World War I. And later Pier Giorgio told friends that he chose a career as a mining engineer so he could "serve Christ better among the miners."

Pier Giorgio generously shared his possessions with the poor. The poor and the suffering were his masters, and he was literally their servant. For instance, he would give a poor person his bus fare and then run home to be on time for his meals. He often sacrificed vacations at the family summer home outside of Turin because, as he said, "If everybody leaves Turin, who will take care of the poor?"

Just before receiving his university degree, Pier Giorgio contracted poliomyelitis, which doctors later speculated he caught from the sick people whom he tended. His selfless commitment to people who were poor and suffering remained his primary concern right up to the time of his death. Having neglected his own health to care for his grandmother who was dying, Pier Giorgio died at the young age of twenty-four. On the eve of his death he scribbled a message to a friend, asking him to take medicine to a poor sick man whom Pier Giorgio had been visiting.

St. John Paul II, after visiting Pier Giorgio's tomb in 1989, said: "I wanted to pay homage to a young man who was able to witness to

> "When I was a young man, I, too, felt the beneficial influence of [Frassati's] example and, as a student, I was impressed by the force of his testimony."

ST. JOHN PAUL II

Christ with singular effectiveness in this century of ours. When I was a young man, I, too, felt the beneficial influence of his example and, as a student, I was impressed by the force of his testimony."

> —Adapted from the official USA website for Blessed Pier Giorgio Frassati

- Reflect: Blessed Pier Giorgio Frassati came to see Christ in the poor and needy.
- How could his vision change your attitude and behavior toward people?
- How could it help you grow as a person of the Beatitudes?

SHARE FAITH WITH FAMILY AND FRIENDS

- How have you benefited from the gifts of family members, friends, teachers or coaches, or members of your parish, who are living the Gospel as single people?
- How might you offer your support to other single young people or join with them as they strive to live the Gospel?

REFLECT AND DECIDE

- Reflect: Single people often have more time to give to works of justice and compassion.
- Think of a single person whom you might join with to live the gospel call to justice and compassion.
- How might you work together?

JOURNAL EXERCISE

- Reflect: The single life is a beautiful way of life through which some people choose to strive for holiness, fulfillment and loving service of others.
- Might the committed single life be the vocation to which God is calling you? Describe what makes you think one way or the other.

LEARN BY HEART

"There is no one who has left house or wife or brothers or parents or children, for the sake of the kingdom of God, who will not get back very much more in this age, and in the age to come eternal life."

LUKE 18:29—30

PRAYER REFLECTION

Pray the Sign of the Cross together.

LEADER
Loving God, Creator and Father of all,
thank you for this conversation
which has helped us to appreciate and respect
the single way of life.
Send your Spirit upon us today
that we may live with the same love and integrity
as did your Son, Jesus.

ALL
Amen.

READER
A reading from the First Letter of St. Paul to the
Corinthians.
Proclaim 1 Corinthians 13:4–8a, 13.
The word of the Lord.

ALL
Thanks be to God.

LEADER
Let us reflect together on St. Paul's description
of love and ask: How does this Apostle challenge
every Christian to live as an authentic disciple of
Jesus Christ?
Pause and allow time for reflection.

LEADER
Spirit of the living God,
you invite your people to live their Baptism in a
variety of ways.
We now pray for those lay people in our Church
who choose to live the single life.
We present our prayers of gratitude to you for
the many gifts these single people render to your
Church.

ALL
*In the silence of your hearts or aloud, pray for single
people who serve you and the Church. After a brief
time of prayer, all respond, "Thank you, loving
God."*

LEADER
Lord God,
we thank and praise you for the gifts you give to
all single people.
We thank you for all those who faithfully use
those gifts to advance God's reign in the world.
May the example of their lives encourage and
inspire us.
In gratitude, praise and hope, we join our voices
in prayer:

ALL
Gracious God, Creator and giver of life,
you have gifted me in many ways.
Through Baptism you have sent me to continue
the mission of Jesus by sharing my love
generously and selflessly with others.
Open my heart to listen to your call.
Strengthen me to respond to that call each day.
Give me the wisdom and courage to become all
you desire of me.
Inspire me to make a difference in others' lives.

Fill us all with your Holy Spirit.
Enkindle in our hearts the desire to make the
world a better place by working with others to
bring about your reign of justice and love.
Amen.

*All share a sign of peace and pray the Sign of the
Cross together.*

CATHOLIC PRAYERS, DEVOTIONS AND PRACTICES

SIGN OF THE CROSS

In the name of the Father,
and of the Son,
and of the Holy Spirit. Amen.

OUR FATHER (LORD'S PRAYER)

Our Father who art in heaven,
hallowed be thy name;
thy kingdom come,
thy will be done
on earth as it is in heaven.
Give us this day our daily bread,
and forgive us our trespasses,
as we forgive those who trespass against us;
and lead us not into temptation,
but deliver us from evil. Amen.

GLORY PRAYER (DOXOLOGY)

Glory be to the Father,
and to the Son,
and to the Holy Spirit;
as it was in the beginning
is now, and ever shall be,
world without end. Amen.

PRAYER TO THE HOLY SPIRIT

Come, Holy Spirit, fill the hearts of your faithful.
Enkindle in them the fire of your love.
Send forth your Spirit and they shall be created.
And you shall renew the face of the earth.

O God, by the light of the Holy Spirit you have
    taught the hearts of your faithful.
In the same Spirit, help us to know what is truly
    right and always to rejoice in your consolation.
We ask this through Christ, our Lord. Amen.

HAIL MARY

Hail Mary, full of grace,
the Lord is with thee.
Blessed art thou among women
and blessed is the fruit of thy womb, Jesus.
Holy Mary, Mother of God,
pray for us sinners,
now and at the hour of our death. Amen.

APOSTLES' CREED

I believe in God,
the Father almighty,
Creator of heaven and earth,
and in Jesus Christ, his only Son, our Lord,
who was conceived by the Holy Spirit,
born of the Virgin Mary,
suffered under Pontius Pilate,
was crucified, died, and was buried;
he descended into hell;
on the third day he rose again from the dead;
he ascended into heaven,
and is seated at the right hand of God the Father
    almighty,
from there he will come to judge the living and
    the dead.

I believe in the Holy Spirit,
the holy catholic Church,
the communion of saints,
the forgiveness of sins,
the resurrection of the body,
and life everlasting. Amen.

NICENE CREED

I believe in one God,
the Father almighty,
maker of heaven and earth,
of all things visible and invisible.

I believe in one Lord Jesus Christ,
the Only Begotten Son of God,
born of the Father before all ages.
God from God, Light from Light,
true God from true God,
begotten, not made, consubstantial with the
    Father;
through him all things were made.
For us men and for our salvation
he came down from heaven,

and by the Holy Spirit was incarnate of the Virgin
Mary,
and became man.

For our sake he was crucified under Pontius Pilate,
he suffered death and was buried,
and rose again on the third day
in accordance with the Scriptures.
He ascended into heaven
and is seated at the right hand of the Father.
He will come again in glory
to judge the living and the dead,
and his kingdom will have no end.

I believe in the Holy Spirit, the Lord, the giver of life,
who proceeds from the Father and the Son,
who with the Father and the Son is adored and
glorified,
who has spoken through the prophets.

I believe in one, holy, catholic and apostolic
Church.
I confess one Baptism for the forgiveness of sins
and I look forward to the resurrection of the dead
and the life of the world to come. Amen.

JESUS PRAYER
Lord Jesus Christ, Son of God, have mercy on me,
a sinner. Amen.

ACT OF FAITH
O my God, I firmly believe that you are one God
in three divine Persons, Father, Son, and Holy
Spirit. I believe that your divine Son became man
and died for our sins and that he will come to
judge the living and the dead. I believe these and
all the truths which the Holy Catholic Church
teaches because you have revealed them, who
are eternal truth and wisdom, who can neither
deceive nor be deceived. In this faith I intend to
live and die. Amen.

ACT OF HOPE
O Lord God, I hope by your grace for the pardon
of all my sins and after life here to gain eternal
happiness because you have promised it, who are
infinitely powerful, faithful, kind, and merciful. In
this hope I intend to live and die. Amen.

ACT OF LOVE
O Lord God, I love you above all things and I love
my neighbor for your sake because you are the
highest, infinite and perfect good, worthy of all
my love. In this love I intend to live and die. Amen.

PRAYER FOR VOCATIONS
Loving Mother, Our Lady of Guadalupe,
you asked Juan Diego to help build a Church that
would serve a new people in a new land.
You left your image upon his cloak as a visible
sign of your love for us,
so that we may come to believe in your Son, Jesus
the Christ.
Our Lady of Guadalupe and St. Juan Diego,
help us respond to God's call to build your Son's
Church today.
Help us recognize our personal vocation to serve
God as married or single persons or priests,
brothers or sisters as our way to help extend
the Reign of God here on earth.
Help us pay attention to the promptings of the
Holy Spirit.
May all of us have the courage of Juan Diego to
say "Yes" to our personal call!
May we encourage one another to follow Jesus,
no matter where that path takes us. Amen.

Daily Prayers

Morning Prayer
CANTICLE OF ZECHARIAH (THE BENEDICTUS)
(based on Luke 1:67–79)
Blessed be the Lord, the God of Israel;
for he has come to his people and set them free.
He has raised up for us a mighty Savior,
born of the House of his servant David.
Through his prophets he promised of old
that he would save us from our enemies,
from the hands of all who hate us.
He promised to show mercy to our fathers
and to remember his holy covenant.
This was the oath he swore to our father Abraham:
to set us free from the hand of our enemies,
free to worship him without fear,
holy and righteous in his sight
all the days of our life.

You, my child, shall be called the prophet of the
    Most High,
for you will go before the Lord to prepare his way,
to give his people knowledge of salvation
by the forgiveness of their sins.
In the tender compassion of our God
the dawn from on high shall break upon us,
to shine on those who dwell in darkness and the
    shadow of death,
and to guide our feet into the way of peace.
Amen.

MORNING OFFERING
O Jesus, through the Immaculate Heart of Mary,
I offer you my prayers, works, joys and sufferings
    of this day
for all the intentions of your Sacred Heart,
in union with the Holy Sacrifice of the Mass
    throughout the world,
for the salvation of souls, the reparation for sins,
    the reunion of all Christians,
and in particular for the intentions of the Holy
    Father this month. Amen.

Evening Prayer
CANTICLE OF MARY (THE *MAGNIFICAT*)
My soul proclaims the greatness of the Lord;
my spirit rejoices in God my savior
for he has looked with favor on his lowly servant.
From this day all generations will call me blessed:
the Almighty has done great things for me
and holy is his name.
He has mercy on those who fear him
in every generation.
He has shown the strength of his arm,
and has scattered the proud in their conceit.
He has cast down the mighty from their thrones,
and has lifted up the lowly.
He has filled the hungry with good things,
and the rich he has sent away empty.
He has come to the help of his servant Israel
for he has remembered his promise of mercy,
the promise he made to our fathers,
to Abraham and his children forever. Amen.

GRACE BEFORE MEALS
Bless us, O Lord, and these your gifts,
which we are about to receive from your bounty,
through Christ our Lord. Amen.

GRACE AFTER MEALS
We give you thanks for all your benefits, almighty
    God, who lives and reigns forever.
And may the souls of the faithful departed,
    through the mercy of God, rest in peace.
    Amen.

PRAYER OF ST. FRANCIS (PEACE PRAYER)
Lord, make me an instrument of your peace:
where there is hatred, let me sow love;
where there is injury, pardon;
where there is doubt, faith;
where there is despair, hope;
where there is darkness, light;
where there is sadness, joy.

O divine Master, grant that I may not so much seek
to be consoled as to console,
to be understood, as to understand,
to be loved as to love.

For it is in giving that we receive,
it is in pardoning that we are pardoned,
it is in dying that we are born to eternal life.
Amen.

Contrition and Sorrow
CONFITEOR
I confess to almighty God
and to you, my brothers and sisters,
that I have greatly sinned,
in my thoughts and in my words,
in what I have done and in what I have failed to
    do,
through my fault, through my fault,
through my most grievous fault;
therefore I ask blessed Mary ever-Virgin,
all the Angels and Saints,
and you, my brothers and sisters,
to pray for me to the Lord our God. Amen.

ACT OF CONTRITION
O my God, I am heartily sorry for having offended
you, and I detest all my sins because of your
just punishments, but most of all because
they offend you, my God, who are all good and
deserving of all my love. I firmly resolve with the
help of your grace to sin no more and to avoid
the near occasion of sin. Amen.

Prayers before the Holy Eucharist

THE DIVINE PRAISES

Blessed be God.
Blessed be his holy name.
Blessed be Jesus Christ, true God and true man.
Blessed be the name of Jesus.
Blessed be his most Sacred Heart.
Blessed be his most precious Blood.
Blessed be Jesus in the most holy Sacrament of the altar.
Blessed be the Holy Spirit, the Paraclete.
Blessed be the great Mother of God, Mary most holy.
Blessed be her holy and Immaculate Conception.
Blessed be her glorious Assumption.
Blessed be the name of Mary, Virgin and Mother.
Blessed be St. Joseph, her most chaste spouse.
Blessed be God in his angels and in his saints.

ANIMA CHRISTI (SOUL OF CHRIST)

Soul of Christ, sanctify me.
Body of Christ, save me.
Blood of Christ, inebriate me.
Water from the side of Christ, wash me.
Passion of Christ, strengthen me.
O good Jesus, hear me.
Within your wounds hide me.
Permit me not to be separated from you.
From the malicious enemy defend me.
In the hour of my death call me.
And bid me come to you,
that with your saints I may praise you
forever and ever. Amen.

AN ACT OF SPIRITUAL COMMUNION

My Jesus, I believe that you are present in the Most Blessed Sacrament.
I love you above all things, and I desire to receive you into my soul.
Since I cannot at this moment receive you sacramentally, come at least spiritually into my heart.
I embrace you as if you were already there and unite myself wholly to you.
Never permit me to be separated from you. Amen.

Prayers to Mary, Mother of God

ANGELUS

Verse:	The Angel of the Lord declared unto Mary.
Response:	And she conceived of the Holy Spirit. Hail Mary, full of grace, the Lord is with thee. Blessed art thou among women and blessed is the fruit of thy womb, Jesus. Holy Mary, Mother of God, pray for us sinners, now and at the hour of our death. Amen.
Verse:	Behold the handmaid of the Lord.
Response:	Be it done unto me according to your Word. Hail Mary. . . .
Verse:	And the Word was made flesh,
Response:	And dwelt among us. Hail Mary. . . .
Verse:	Pray for us, O holy Mother of God,
Response:	That we may be made worthy of the promises of Christ.

Let us pray. Pour forth, we beseech you, O Lord, your grace into our hearts: that we, to whom the Incarnation of Christ your Son was made known by the message of an Angel, may by his Passion and Cross be brought to the glory of his Resurrection. Through the same Christ our Lord. Amen.

MEMORARE

Remember, O most gracious Virgin Mary, that never was it known that anyone who fled to your protection, implored your help, or sought your intercession, was left unaided. Inspired by this confidence, I fly unto you, O Virgin of virgins, my mother; to you do I come, before you I stand, sinful and sorrowful. O Mother of the Word Incarnate, despise not my petitions, but in your mercy hear and answer me. Amen.

REGINA CAELI (QUEEN OF HEAVEN)

Queen of Heaven, rejoice, alleluia:
for the Son you were privileged to bear, alleluia,
is risen as he said, alleluia.
Pray for us to God, alleluia.

Verse: Rejoice and be glad, O Virgin Mary, Alleluia!
Response: For the Lord is truly risen, Alleluia.

Let us pray. O God, who gave joy to the world through the resurrection of your Son, our Lord Jesus Christ, grant, we beseech you, that through the intercession of the Virgin Mary, his Mother, we may obtain the joys of everlasting life. Through the same Christ our Lord. Amen.

SALVE, REGINA (HAIL, HOLY QUEEN)

Hail, holy Queen, Mother of mercy: Hail, our life, our sweetness and our hope. To you do we cry, poor banished children of Eve. To you do we send up our sighs, mourning and weeping in this valley of tears. Turn then, most gracious advocate, your eyes of mercy toward us; and after this our exile show unto us the blessed fruit of your womb, Jesus. O clement, O loving, O sweet Virgin Mary. Amen.

PRAYER TO OUR LADY OF GUADALUPE

God of power and mercy,
you blessed the Americas at Tepeyac
with the presence of the Virgin Mary of
  Guadalupe.
May her prayers help all men and women
to accept each other as brothers and sisters.
Through your justice present in our hearts
may your peace reign in the world. Amen.

THE ROSARY

THE JOYFUL MYSTERIES: Traditionally prayed on Mondays and Saturdays and on Sundays of the Christmas Season.

1. The Annunciation (Luke 1:26–38)
2. The Visitation (Luke 2:39–56)
3. The Nativity (Luke 2:1–20)
4. The Presentation in the Temple (Luke 2:22–38)
5. The Finding of Jesus after Three Days in the Temple (Luke 2:41–50)

THE LUMINOUS MYSTERIES: Traditionally prayed on Thursdays.

1. The Baptism at the Jordan (Matthew 3:13–17)
2. The Miracle at Cana (John 2:1–11)
3. The Proclamation of the Kingdom and the Call to Conversion (Mark 1:14–15)
4. The Transfiguration (Matthew 17:1–13)
5. The Institution of the Eucharist (Matthew 26:26–28)

THE SORROWFUL MYSTERIES: Traditionally prayed on Tuesdays and Fridays and on the Sundays of Lent.

1. The Agony in the Garden (Matthew 26:36–56)
2. The Scourging at the Pillar (John 18:28—19:1)
3. The Crowning with Thorns (John 19:2–3)
4. The Carrying of the Cross (John 19:17)
5. The Crucifixion and Death (John 19:18–30)

THE GLORIOUS MYSTERIES: Traditionally prayed on Wednesdays and Sundays, except on the Sundays of Christmas and Lent.

1. The Resurrection (Matthew 28:1–8)
2. The Ascension (Matthew 28:16–20/Acts 1:1–11)
3. The Descent of the Holy Spirit at Pentecost (Acts 2:1–13)
4. The Assumption of Mary (See CCC, no. 966)
5. The Crowning of the Blessed Virgin as Queen of Heaven and Earth (See CCC, no. 966)

How to pray the Rosary

1. Pray the *Sign of the Cross* and pray the *Apostles' Creed* while holding the crucifix.
2. Touch the first bead after the crucifix and pray the *Our Father*, pray the *Hail Mary* on each of the next three beads, and pray the *Glory Prayer* on the next bead.
3. Go to the main part of your rosary. Say the name of the Mystery and quietly reflect on the meaning of the events of that Mystery. Pray the *Our Father*, and then, fingering each of the ten beads, pray ten *Hail Marys*. Then touch the next bead and pray the *Glory Prayer*. (Repeat the process for the next four decades.)
4. Pray the *Salve Regina (Hail, Holy Queen)* and conclude by praying:
   Verse: Pray for us, O holy Mother of God.
   Response: That we may be made worthy of the promises of Christ.
   Let us pray. O God, whose only-begotten

Son, by his life, death and Resurrection, has purchased for us the rewards of eternal life, grant, we beseech you, that meditating on these mysteries of the most holy rosary of the Blessed Virgin Mary, we may imitate what they contain and obtain what they promise, through the same Christ our Lord. Amen.

5. Conclude by praying the *Sign of the Cross*.

STATIONS, OR WAY, OF THE CROSS

The tradition of praying the Stations, or Way, of the Cross dates from the fourteenth century. The tradition, which is attributed to the Franciscans, came about to satisfy the desire of Christians who were unable to make a pilgrimage to Jerusalem. The traditional Stations of the Cross are:

FIRST STATION: Jesus is condemned to death
SECOND STATION: Jesus is made to carry his Cross
THIRD STATION: Jesus falls the first time
FOURTH STATION: Jesus meets his mother
FIFTH STATION: Simon helps Jesus to carry his Cross
SIXTH STATION: Veronica wipes the face of Jesus
SEVENTH STATION: Jesus falls the second time
EIGHTH STATION: Jesus meets the women of Jerusalem
NINTH STATION: Jesus falls the third time
TENTH STATION: Jesus is stripped of his garments
ELEVENTH STATION: Jesus is nailed to the Cross
TWELFTH STATION: Jesus dies on the Cross
THIRTEENTH STATION: Jesus is taken down from the Cross
FOURTEENTH STATION: Jesus is laid in the tomb.

In 1991 St. John Paul II gave the Church a scriptural version of the Stations. The individual names given to these stations are:

FIRST STATION: Jesus in the Garden of Gethsemane—Matthew 25:36–41
SECOND STATION: Jesus, Betrayed by Judas, Is Arrested—Mark 14:43–46
THIRD STATION: Jesus Is Condemned by the Sanhedrin—Luke 22:66–71
FOURTH STATION: Jesus Is Denied by Peter—Matthew 26:69–75

FIFTH STATION: Jesus Is Judged by Pilate—Mark 15:1–5, 15
SIXTH STATION: Jesus Is Scourged and Crowned with Thorns—John 19:1–3
SEVENTH STATION: Jesus Bears the Cross—John 19:6, 15–17
EIGHTH STATION: Jesus Is Helped by Simon the Cyrenian to Carry the Cross—Mark 15:21
NINTH STATION: Jesus Meets the Women of Jerusalem—Luke 23:27–31
TENTH STATION: Jesus Is Crucified—Luke 23:33–34
ELEVENTH STATION: Jesus Promises His Kingdom to the Good Thief—Luke 23:39–43
TWELFTH STATION: Jesus Speaks to His Mother and the Disciple—John 19:25–27
THIRTEENTH STATION: Jesus Dies on the Cross—Luke 23:44–46
FOURTEENTH STATION: Jesus Is Placed in the Tomb—Matthew 27:57–60

Some parishes conclude the Stations with a prayerful meditation on the Resurrection.

The Way of Jesus: Catholic Practices

THE SEVEN SACRAMENTS

Sacraments of Christian Initiation

BAPTISM: The sacrament by which we are freed from all sin and are endowed with the gift of divine life, are made members of the Church, and are called to holiness and mission.

CONFIRMATION: The sacrament that completes the grace of Baptism by a special outpouring of the gifts of the Holy Spirit, which seals and confirms the baptized in union with Christ and calls them to a greater participation in the worship and apostolic life of the Church.

EUCHARIST: The ritual, sacramental action of thanksgiving to God which constitutes the principal Christian liturgical celebration of and communion in the Paschal Mystery of Christ. This liturgical action is also traditionally known as the Holy Sacrifice of the Mass.

Sacraments of Healing

PENANCE AND RECONCILIATION: The sacrament in which sins committed after Baptism are forgiven, which results in reconciliation with God and the Church. This sacrament is also called the Sacrament of Confession.

ANOINTING OF THE SICK: This sacrament is given to a person who is seriously ill or in danger of death or old age which strengthens the person with the special graces of healing and comfort and courage.

Sacraments at the Service of Communion

MARRIAGE (MATRIMONY): The sacrament in which a baptized man and a baptized woman enter the covenant partnership of the whole of life that by its nature is ordered toward the good of the spouses and the procreation and education of offspring.

HOLY ORDERS: The sacrament in which a bishop ordains a baptized man to be conformed to Jesus Christ by grace, to service and leadership in the Church as a bishop, priest, or deacon.

GIFTS OF THE HOLY SPIRIT

The seven gifts of the Holy Spirit are permanent dispositions which move us to respond to the guidance of the Spirit. The traditional list of these gifts is derived from Isaiah 11:1–3.

WISDOM: A spiritual gift which enables one to know the purpose and plan of God.

UNDERSTANDING: This gift stimulates us to work on knowing ourselves as part of our growth in knowing God.

COUNSEL (RIGHT JUDGMENT): This gift guides us to follow the teaching the Holy Spirit gives us about our moral life and the training of our conscience.

FORTITUDE (COURAGE): This gift strengthens us to choose courageously and firmly the good, despite difficulty, and also to persevere in doing what is right, despite temptation, fear or persecution.

KNOWLEDGE: This gift directs us to a contemplation, or thoughtful reflection, on the mystery of God and the mysteries of the Catholic faith.

PIETY (REVERENCE): This gift strengthens us to grow in respect for the Holy Trinity, for the Father who created us, for Jesus who saved us, and for the Holy Spirit who is sanctifying us.

FEAR OF THE LORD (WONDER AND AWE): This gift infuses honesty into our relationship with God.

FRUITS OF THE HOLY SPIRIT

The fruits of the Holy Spirit are the perfections that the Holy Spirit forms in us as the "first fruits" of eternal glory. The Tradition of the Church lists twelve fruits of the Holy Spirit. They are: love, joy, peace, patience, kindness, goodness, generosity, gentleness, faithfulness, modesty, self-control and chastity.

VIRTUES

The Theological Virtues

Gifts from God that enable us to choose to and to live in right relationship with the Holy Trinity.

FAITH: The virtue by which the believer gives personal adherence to God (who invites his or her response) and freely assents to the whole truth that God revealed.

HOPE: The virtue through which a person both desires and expects the fulfillment of God's promises of things to come.

CHARITY (LOVE): The virtue by which we give love to God for his own sake and love to our neighbor on account of God.

The Cardinal Moral Virtues

The four moral virtues on which all other human virtues hinge.

FORTITUDE: The virtue by which one courageously and firmly chooses the good despite difficulty and also perseveres in doing what is right despite temptation.

JUSTICE: The virtue by which one is able to give God and neighbor what is due to them.

PRUDENCE: The virtue by which one knows the true good in every circumstance and chooses the right means to reach that end.

TEMPERANCE: The virtue by which one moderates the desire for the attainment of and pleasure in earthly goods.

THE NEW LAW

The Great, or Greatest, Commandment

"You shall love the Lord your God with all your heart, and with all your soul, and with all your mind. . . . You shall love your neighbor as yourself."

—Matthew 22:37, 39, based on Deuteronomy 6:5 and Leviticus 19:18

THE NEW COMMANDMENT OF JESUS

"Love one another. Just as I have loved you, you also should love one another." John 13:34

THE BEATITUDES

Blessed are the poor in spirit, for theirs is the kingdom of heaven.

Blessed are those who mourn, for they will be comforted.

Blessed are the meek, for they will inherit the earth.

Blessed are those who hunger and thirst for righteousness, for they will be filled.

Blessed are the merciful, for they will receive mercy.

Blessed are the pure in heart, for they will see God.

Blessed are the peacemakers, for they shall be called children of God.

Blessed are those who are persecuted for righteousness' sake, for theirs is the kingdom of heaven.

Blessed are you when people revile you and persecute you and utter all kinds of evil against you falsely on my account. Rejoice and be glad, for your reward is great in heaven, for in the same way they persecuted the prophets who were before you.

—Matthew 5:3–11

SPIRITUAL WORKS OF MERCY

Admonish and help those who sin.
Teach those who are ignorant.
Advise those who have doubts.
Comfort those who suffer.
Be patient with all people.
Forgive those who trespass against you.
Pray for the living and the dead.

CORPORAL WORKS OF MERCY

Feed the hungry.
Give drink to the thirsty.
Shelter the homeless.
Clothe the naked.
Visit the sick and those in prison.
Bury the dead.
Give alms to the poor.

THE TEN COMMANDMENTS, OR THE DECALOGUE

Traditional Catechetical Formula

FIRST: I am the LORD your God: you shall not have strange gods before me.

SECOND: You shall not take the name of the LORD your God in vain.

THIRD: Remember to keep holy the LORD'S Day.

FOURTH: Honor your father and mother.

FIFTH: You shall not kill.

SIXTH: You shall not commit adultery.

SEVENTH: You shall not steal.

EIGHTH: You shall not bear false witness against your neighbor.

NINTH: You shall not covet your neighbor's wife.

TENTH: You shall not covet your neighbor's goods.

Scriptural Formula

FIRST: I am the LORD your God, who brought you out of the land of Egypt, out of the house of slavery; you shall have no other gods before me.

SECOND: You shall not make wrongful use of the name of the LORD your God, for the LORD will not acquit anyone who misuses his name.

THIRD: Observe the sabbath day to keep it holy. . . .

FOURTH: Honor your father and your mother. . . .

FIFTH: You shall not murder.

SIXTH: Neither shall you commit adultery.

SEVENTH: Neither shall you steal.

EIGHTH: Neither shall you bear false witness against your neighbour.

NINTH: Neither shall you covet your neighbor's wife.

TENTH: Neither shall you desire . . . anything that belongs to your neighbor.

—From Deuteronomy 5:6–21

PRECEPTS OF THE CHURCH

The precepts of the Church are positive laws made by the Church that name the minimum in prayer and moral effort for the growth of the faithful in their love of God and neighbor.

FIRST PRECEPT: Participate in Mass on Sundays and on holy days of obligation and rest from work that impedes keeping these days holy.

SECOND PRECEPT: Confess serious sins at least once a year.

THIRD PRECEPT: Receive the Sacrament of the Eucharist at least during the Easter Season.
FOURTH PRECEPT: Fast and abstain on the days established by the Church.
FIFTH PRECEPT: Provide for the materials of the Church according to one's ability.

SOCIAL DOCTRINE OF THE CHURCH

These seven key principles are at the foundation of the social doctrine, or social teaching, of the Catholic Church:

1. *Life and dignity of the human person.* Human life is sacred and the dignity of the human person is the foundation of the moral life of individuals and of society.
2. *Call to family, community and participation.* The human person is social by nature and has the right to participate in family life and in the life of society.
3. *Rights and responsibilities.* The human person has the fundamental right to life and to the basic necessities that support life and human decency.
4. *Option for the poor and the vulnerable.* The Gospel commands us "to put the needs of the poor and the vulnerable first."
5. *Dignity of work and workers.* Work is a form of participating in God's work of creation. "The economy must serve people and not the other way around."
6. *Solidarity.* God is the Creator of all people. "We are one human family whatever our national, racial, ethnic, economic and ideological differences."
7. *Care for God's creation.* Care of the environment is a divine command and a requirement of our faith.

FAITH GLOSSARY

Abbreviations: CCC = *Catechism of the Catholic Church;* Compendium = *Compendium of the Catechism of the Catholic Church;* USCCA = *United States Catholic Catechism for Adults*

A–B

abstinence: The term "abstinence" is used in two ways. (1) "*Abstinence* is refraining from eating meat. The Church identifies specific days and times of fasting and abstinence to prepare the faithful for certain special feasts; such actions of sacrifice can also help us to grow in self-discipline and in holiness" (USCCA, 335). (2) Abstinence is also related to the virtue of chastity. In this instance, it is refraining from sexual intercourse and other inappropriate expressions of intimacy until one marries.

agape: In 1 John 4:8, 16 we read: "God is love." The Greek word used here for "love" is *agapē.* The word *agape* describes God's total "self-gift" of unconditional and infinite love, both among the Persons of the Blessed Trinity and for each and every one of us.

annulment (declaration of nullity of a marriage): The consent of the spouses entering into marriage must be a free act of the will, devoid of external or internal invalidating factors. If this freedom is absent, the marriage is invalid. For this reason, the Church, after an examination of the situation by a competent Church court, can declare the nullity of a marriage, i.e., that the sacramental marriage never existed. In this case, the contracting parties are free to marry, provided the natural obligations of the previous union are discharged (see CCC, 1628–1629; CIC, canons 1095–1107; CCEO, canons 1431–1449). (USCCA, Glossary, 503–04)

Apostle(s): "The title traditionally given to those specially chosen by Jesus to preach the Gospel and to whom he entrusted responsibility for guiding the early Church" (USCCA, Glossary, 504). The names of the first Apostles, also called the Twelve, are Peter, Andrew, James, John, Thomas, James, Philip, Bartholomew (also known as Nathaniel), Matthew, Judas, Simon, and Jude (also known as Thaddeus). After the Ascension of Jesus, Matthias, who replaced Judas Iscariot, and Paul were also called to be Apostles.

apostolate: The activity of the Christian which fulfills the apostolic nature of the whole Church by working to extend the reign of Christ to the entire world. (CCC, Glossary)

Apostolic Succession: The passing on of the office of bishop from the Apostles to bishops, and from them to other bishops down each generation, by means of ordination. (USCCA, Glossary, 504)

Apostolic Tradition: Jesus entrusted his revelation and teachings to his Apostles. They passed it on by their preaching and witness. Along with others, they began writing the message down in what became the New Testament. (USCCA, Glossary, 504)

archbishop: A bishop of a diocese whom the pope appoints to preside over an ecclesiastical province or another jurisdiction. An archbishop, who has the title Metropolitan, has limited authority specified by Church law over the bishops who serve the dioceses in the Province. The bishops are called suffragan bishops.

archdiocese: A diocese which is governed by an archbishop. It is called an archdiocese usually because of its size or historical significance. An archdiocese is established to foster collegial pastoral action within the Province. An archdiocese is also called a metropolitan.

artificial contraception: The use of mechanical, chemical, or medical procedures to prevent conception from taking place as a result of sexual intercourse; contraception offends against the openness to procreation required of marriage and also the inner truth of conjugal love. (CCC, Glossary)

ascesis: The practice of penance, mortification, and self-denial to promote greater self-mastery and to foster the way of perfection by embracing the way of the cross. (CCC, Glossary)

asceticism: *see* **ascesis**.

Baptism: The first Sacrament of Initiation by which we are freed from all sin and are endowed with the gift of divine life, are made members of the Church, and are called to holiness and mission. (USCCA, Glossary, 505)

bishop: The highest of the three degrees of Holy Orders; a bishop is normally ordained to teach, to sanctify, and to govern a diocese or local church; a bishop is a successor of the Apostles. (USCCA, Glossary, 505)

Blessed Trinity: *see* **Trinity**.

Body of Christ: A name for the Holy Eucharist. . . . It is also a title for the Church, with Christ as her head, sometimes referred to as the Mystical Body of Christ. The Holy Spirit provides the members with the gifts needed to live as Christ's Body. (USCCA, Glossary, 505)

C

cardinal: Usually an archbishop or bishop, named by the pope in recognition of their service to the Church. A bishop (and sometimes a priest) does not become a cardinal through receiving the Sacrament of Holy Orders. The pope names and appoints cardinals to serve as his senior counselors and assist him in governing the Church. Cardinals become members of the

Sacred College of Cardinals who have the honor and responsibility to elect the pope.

cardinal virtues: Four pivotal human virtues (from the Latin *cardo*, meaning "pivot"): prudence, justice, fortitude, and temperance. (CCC, Glossary) *See also* **temperance**.

catechesis: The act of handing on the Word of God intended to inform the faith community and candidates for initiation into the Church about the teachings of Christ, transmitted by the Apostles to the Church. It also involves the lifelong effort of forming people into witnesses to Christ and opening their hearts to the spiritual transformation given by the Holy Spirit. (USCCA, Glossary, 506)

celibacy: "The state or condition of those who have chosen to remain unmarried for the sake of the kingdom of heaven in order to give themselves entirely to God and to the service of his people" (CCC, Glossary). Celibacy should not be confused with the virtue of chastity. *See also* **chastity; virginity**.

charism(s): Special graces of the Holy Spirit given to the Church and the baptized for the building up of the Church.

chastity: Connected to purity of heart, this is a virtue that moves us to love others with generous regards for them. It excludes lust and any wish to exploit them sexually. It helps us see and put into practice God's plan for the body, person, and sexuality. All people are called to pursue and live the virtue of chastity according to one's state in life. (USCCA, Glossary, 506) *See also* **celibacy; virginity**.

Chrism: "Perfumed oil consecrated by a bishop at the annual Mass of the Chrism during Holy Week; it is used in those Sacraments which confer a permanent mark or character—Baptism, Confirmation, and Holy Orders" (USCCA, Glossary, 506). Being anointed with Sacred Chrism signifies that we have been consecrated, or set aside, to represent Christ to the world by what we say and do.

Chrismation: The term used for anointing with Chrism and for Confirmation in the Eastern Churches.

Christian discernment: The spiritual practice of looking out for the presence and the workings of the Spirit in our life. It includes trying to understand the promptings of the Spirit in our life and deciding to act in cooperation with the grace of the Holy Spirit. This process includes seeking to know the path to holiness of life as "collaborators and cooperators in continuing the redemptive work of Jesus Christ, which is the Church's essential mission" (USCCA, 452).

Church: The name given the "convocation" or "assembly" of the People God has called together from "the ends of the earth." In Christian usage, the word "Church" has three inseparable meanings: the People that God gathers in the whole world; the particular or local church (diocese); and the liturgical (above all Eucharistic) assembly. The Church draws her life from the Word and the Body of Christ, and so herself becomes Christ's Body. In the Creed, the sole Church of Christ is professed to be one, holy, catholic, and apostolic. (CCC, Glossary)

clergy: Those who receive the Sacrament of Holy Orders to serve the whole communion of the Church.

cloister: A place where nuns or monks live. *See also* **monasticism/monastic life**.

cohabitation: An unmarried couple living together. *See also* **free unions**.

college of bishops: All bishops, with the Pope as their head, form a single college [an organized body of persons], which succeeds in every generation the college of the Twelve Apostles, with Peter at their head. Christ instituted this college as the foundation of the Church. The college of bishops, together with—but never without—the pope, has the supreme and full authority over the universal Church. (USCCA, Glossary, 507)

collegiality: *see* **college of bishops**.

committed single life: A permanent chaste and celibate way of living the Gospel that a baptized woman or man freely chooses and promises to live. *See also* **celibacy; chastity; single life**.

common priesthood of the faithful: *See* **priesthood of the faithful**.

concupiscence: The disorder in our human appetites and desires as a result of Original Sin. These effects remain even after Baptism and produce an inclination to sin. (USCCA, Glossary, 507)

consecrated life: A permanent state of life recognized by the Church, entered freely in response to the call of Christ to perfection, and characterized by the profession of the evangelical counsels of poverty, chastity, and obedience. (CCC, Glossary)

contemplation: "Wordless prayer in which a person focuses the whole person in loving adoration on God and his very presence" (USCCA, Glossary, 508). Contemplation is one of the three forms of Christian prayer.

covenant: A covenant is a solemn agreement made between human beings or between God and a human being involving mutual commitments or guarantees. The Bible speaks of covenants that God made with Noah and, through him, 'with every living creature' (Genesis 9:10). Then God made the special covenant with Abraham and renewed it with Moses. The prophets constantly pointed to a new covenant that God would establish with all humankind through the promised Messiah—Jesus Christ.

D-E

deacons: Men ordained by the bishop to serve. They receive the Sacrament of Holy Orders but not the ministerial priesthood. Through ordination, the deacon is conformed to Christ who said he came to serve, not to be served. Deacons in the Latin Church may baptize, read the Gospel, preach the homily, assist the bishop or priest in the celebration of the Eucharist, assist at and bless marriages, and preside at funerals. They dedicate themselves to charitable endeavors, which was their ministerial role in New Testament times. (USCCA, Glossary, 509)

declaration of nullity of a marriage: *see* **annulment**.

detachment: The virtue of not attaching oneself to material possessions or other created things. The Tenth Commandment mandates that we live a life of gospel simplicity and detachment. *See also* **poverty, voluntary**.

diocese: A "particular Church," a community of the faithful in communion of faith and sacraments whose bishop has been ordained in apostolic succession. A diocese is usually a determined geographical area; sometimes it may be constituted as a group of people of the same rite or language. In Eastern Churches, an eparchy. (CCC, Glossary) *See also* **particular Church**.

discernment: *see* **Christian discernment**.

disparity of cult: A marriage with disparity of cult is a marriage between a Catholic and a non-Christian, or an interfaith marriage. The law of the Catholic Church requires specific permission for a Catholic to marry a non-Christian. The process involved highlights the unique challenges the Catholic partner will face.

dispensation: According to canon law, a mixed marriage must receive the express permission of ecclesiastical authority for the marriage to be lawful. "In case of disparity of cult an *express dispensation . . .* is required for the validity of the marriage (see can. 1086). This permission or dispensation presupposes that both parties know and do not exclude the essential ends and properties of marriage; and furthermore that the Catholic party confirms the obligations, which have been made known to the non-Catholic party, of preserving his or her own faith and ensuring the baptism and education of the children in the Catholic Church (see can. 1125)" (CCC, no. 1635).

divine providence: God's loving care and concern for all he has made; he continues to watch over creation, sustaining its existence and presiding over its development and destiny. (USCCA, Glossary, 510)

divorce: The claim that the indissoluble marriage bond validly entered into between a man and a woman is broken. A civil dissolution of the marriage contract (divorce) does not free persons from a valid marriage before God; remarriage would not be morally licit. (CCC, Glossary)

domestic church: Term meaning "Church of the home." "The Christian home is the place where children receive the first proclamation of the faith. For this reason the family home is rightly called 'the domestic church,' a community of grace and prayer, a school of human virtues and of Christian charity" (CCC, no. 1666).

Donatism: A heresy that teaches that the effectiveness of the sacraments depends on the holiness of the bishop or priest; that is, if the minister of the sacrament was not in the state of grace, then the graces of the sacrament would not be available to its recipient. This heresy is contrary to the Church's teaching that Christ is the one who works in and through the minister of the sacraments, and he is not prevented from doing so by the moral condition of the one who administers the sacraments.

Eastern Catholic Churches: *see* **Eastern Churches and Western Churches**.

Eastern Churches and Western Churches: The Eastern Churches originated in that region of the world that was at one time part of the Eastern Roman Empire. These churches possess their own distinctive traditions that may be seen in their liturgy, theology, and law. The Western Church, focused in Rome, is sometimes called the Latin Church. All individual churches, Eastern or Western, that are in communion with the Apostolic See (Rome) are part of the Catholic Church. (USCCA, Glossary, 510–11)

episcopacy: *see* **bishop**.

eremitical life: The life of a hermit, separate from the world in praise of God and for the salvation of the world, in the silence of solitude, assiduous prayer, and penance. (CCC, Glossary)

eschatology: From the Greek word *eschaton*, meaning "last." Eschatology refers to the area of Christian faith which is concerned about "the last things," and the coming of Jesus on "the last day": our human destiny, death, judgment, resurrection of the body, heaven, purgatory, and hell—all of which are contained in the final articles of the Creed. (CCC, Glossary)

evangelical counsels: Those vows taken by men or women who enter the religious life; there are three vows: poverty, chastity, and obedience. (USCCA, Glossary, 511)

evangelization: "This is the ministry and mission of proclaiming and witnessing Christ and his Gospel with the intention of deepening the faith of believers and inviting others to be baptized and initiated into the Church" (USCCA, Glossary, 512). Evangelization is the primary work of the Church.

extraordinary minister of Holy Communion: A non-ordained member of a religious community of brothers or sisters or a lay person commissioned by the local ordinary, the bishop of a diocese, to distribute Holy Communion.

F-G-H

family: "A man and a woman united in marriage, together with their children, form a family. This institution is prior to any recognition by public authority, which has an obligation to recognize it. It should be considered the normal reference point by which the different [authentic] forms of family relationship are to be [recognized]" (CCC, no. 2202).

freedom: "Freedom characterizes properly human acts. It makes the human being responsible for acts of which he is the voluntary agent. His deliberate acts properly belong to him" (CCC, no. 1745). "The more one does what is good, the freer one becomes. Freedom attains its proper perfection when it is directed toward God, the highest good and our beatitude. Freedom implies also the possibility of choosing between good and evil. The choice of evil is an abuse of freedom and leads to the slavery of sin" (*Compendium*, no. 363).

free unions: The term "free unions" refers to several types of intimate relationships between a man and a woman. These include trial marriages, cohabitation and concubinage. All these relationships have one thing in common: the partners have chosen to live together without being married and they remain "free" from entering a full marriage commitment. The partners do not commit themselves to all or some of the indispensable elements that make a marriage a marriage.

fruits of the Holy Spirit: The Tradition of the Church lists twelve fruits of the Holy Spirit: love, joy, peace, patience, kindness, goodness, generosity, gentleness, faithfulness, modesty, self-control and chastity. (USCCA, Glossary, 513)

gifts of the Holy Spirit: These gifts are permanent dispositions that move us to respond to the guidance of the Spirit. The traditional list of these gifts is derived from Isaiah 11:1–3: wisdom, understanding, knowledge, counsel [right judgment], fortitude [courage], reverence (piety), and wonder and awe in God's presence (fear of the Lord). (USCCA, Glossary, 513)

grace: The word "grace" comes from the Latin word *gratia*, which means "free." Grace is the "free and undeserved gift that God gives us to respond to our vocation to become his adopted children. As sanctifying grace, God shares his divine life and friendship with us in a habitual gift, a stable and supernatural disposition that enables the soul to live with God, to act by his love. As actual grace, God gives us the help to conform our lives to his will. Sacramental grace and special graces (charisms, the grace of one's state of life) are gifts of the Holy Spirit to help us live out our Christian vocation" (CCC, Glossary). *See also* **charism(s); sacramental graces.**

hermit: *see* eremitical life.

hierarchy: The Apostles and their successors, the college of bishops, to whom Christ gave the authority to teach, sanctify, and rule the Church in his name. (CCC, Glossary)

holiness: "A state of goodness in which a person—with the help of God's grace, the action of the Holy Spirit, and a life of prayer—is freed from sin and evil" (USCCA, Glossary, 514). A person in the state of holiness lives in communion with God, who is Father, Son and Holy Spirit.

Holy Orders: The Sacrament in which a bishop ordains a [baptized] man to be conformed to Jesus Christ by grace, to service and leadership in the Church. A man can be ordained a deacon, priest, or bishop. Through this Sacrament, the mission entrusted by Christ to his Apostles continues to be exercised in the Church. The Sacrament confers a permanent mark or character on the one who receives it. (USCCA, Glossary, 515–16)

Holy Trinity: *see* Trinity.

I-J-K

image of God: God has made us in his image by giving us the capacity for intelligence, love, freedom, and conscience. By Baptism, our bodies are made temples of the Holy Spirit. (USCCA, Glossary, 515)

Incarnation: By the Incarnation, the Second Person of the Holy Trinity assumed our human nature, taking flesh in the womb of the Virgin Mary. There is one Person in Jesus and that is the divine Person of the Son of God. Jesus has two natures, a human one and a divine one. (USCCA, Glossary, 515)

inculturation: A two-way process whereby the Gospel is woven into the various dimensions of human culture and experience, both personal and social, and authentic cultural values are in turn integrated into the Christian life. *See*

also evangelization, Kingdom (Reign) of God/ Kingdom of Heaven.

infallibility: This is the gift of the Holy Spirit to the Church whereby the pastors of the Church— the pope, and bishops in communion with him— can definitively proclaim a doctrine of faith and morals, which is divinely revealed for the belief of the faithful. This gift flows from the grace of the whole body of the faithful not to err in matters of faith and morals. The pope teaches infallibly when he declares that his teaching is *ex cathedra* (literally, "from the throne"); that is, he teaches as supreme pastor of the Church. (USCCA, Glossary, 516)

joy: One of the twelve fruits of the Holy Spirit that flows from living a life of faith, hope and love as revealed by Jesus. Joy is the happiness, or blessedness, we experience when we follow the way of Christ and keep God first in our life above all else. Such joy gives us a taste of the happiness of heaven, living in eternal communion with God.

Kingdom [Reign] of God/[Kingdom of Heaven]: The actualization of God's will for human beings proclaimed by Jesus Christ as a community of justice, peace, mercy, and love, the seed of which is the Church on earth, and the fulfillment of which is in eternity. (USCCA, Glossary, 517)

L–M

laity: Members of the Church, distinguished from the clergy and those in consecrated life, who have been incorporated into the People of God through the Sacrament of Baptism. (USCCA, Glossary, 517)

Latin Church: *see* Eastern Churches and Western Churches.

lay ecclesial ministers: The men and women of every race and culture who serve in parishes, schools, diocesan agencies and Church institutions. Lay ecclesial ministers are lay people who give their lives in a full- or part-time capacity to carrying out the ministries of the Church.

lay ecclesial movements: Groups, associations and communities that have arisen within and are approved by the Church that support the laity to achieve holiness of life and work toward a specific mission, to "announce the power of God's love which in overcoming divisions and barriers of every kind, renews the face of the earth to build the civilization of love" (St. John Paul II, Homily, Mass for Pentecost, May 31, 2000). Membership in ecclesial movements is not limited to lay people. The ordained, religious and other members of the consecrated life are also members of ecclesial movements.

laying on of hands: The laying on, or imposition, of hands signifies the bestowing of the gift of the Holy Spirit. This ritual finds its roots in both the Old Testament and the New Testament and has been part of the Tradition of the Church from the time of the Apostles. The laying on of hands, or extending of hands over, is used by the Catholic Church both in the celebration of the sacraments and in the celebration of her sacramentals, for example, in the blessing of people and objects.

local ordinary: *see* **ordinary, local.**

Magisterium: The living, teaching office of the Church, whose task it is to give authentic interpretation to the word of God, whether in its written form (Sacred Scripture) or in the form of Tradition. The Magisterium ensures the Church's fidelity to the teaching of the Apostles in matters of faith and morals. (CCC, Glossary).

Marriage, Sacrament of: "The marriage covenant, by which a man and a woman form with each other an intimate communion of life and love, has been founded and endowed with its own special laws by the Creator. By its very nature it is ordered to the good of the couple, as well as to the generation and education of children. Christ the Lord raised marriage between the baptized to the dignity of a sacrament" (CCC, no. 1660).

Matrimony: Another name for the Sacrament of Marriage. *See also* **Marriage, Sacrament of.**

ministerial priesthood: This priesthood, received in the Sacrament of Holy Orders, differs in essence from the priesthood of the faithful. The ministerial priesthood serves the priesthood of the faithful by building up the Church in the name of Christ, who is head of the Body, by offering prayers and sacrifices to God on behalf of people. A priest is given the power to consecrate the Eucharist, forgive sins, and administer the other Sacraments, except Holy Orders. (USCCA, 519–20). *See also* **priest; Priesthood of Christ; priesthood of the faithful.**

miracle(s): Miracles are signs of the presence of God at work among us. "The miracles and other deeds of Jesus are acts of compassion and signs of the Kingdom and salvation" (USCCA, 80).

mixed marriage: A marriage between a Catholic and a non-Catholic baptized person. The law of the Catholic Church requires specific permission from the local ordinary (bishop) for the celebration of a sacramental mixed marriage. The process involved highlights the unique challenges the Catholic partner will face.

modesty: A virtue and fruit of the Holy Spirit connected with the virtues of respect and reverence. "A modest person dresses, speaks, and acts in a manner that supports and encourages purity and chastity and not in a manner that would tempt or encourage sinful sexual behavior" (USCCA, Glossary, 520).

monastery: A place where monks live.

monasticism/monastic life: Consecrated life marked by the public profession of religious vows of poverty, chastity, and obedience, and by a stable community life (in a monastery) with the celebration of the Liturgy of the Hours in choir. (CCC, Glossary)

moral virtues: *see* **virtue.**

O–P

obedience: "The submission to the authority of God which requires everyone to obey the divine law. Obedience to the Church is required in those things which pertain to our salvation; ... In imitation of [the] obedience of Jesus, as an evangelical counsel, the faithful may profess a vow of obedience; a public vow of obedience, accepted by Church authority, is one element that characterizes the consecrated life" (CCC, Glossary). Obedience is also due to parents and to legitimate civil authority.

ordinary, local: The bishop of a diocese. In general the term "ordinary" also applies to all who, even for a time only, have been given authority to preside over and serve a particular Church or other church community.

ordination: The rite of the Sacrament of Holy Orders by which the bishop, through the imposition of hands and the prayer of consecration, confers the order of bishop, priest, or deacon to exercise a sacred power which comes from Christ on behalf of the Church. (CCC, Glossary)

parables: A characteristic feature of the teaching of Jesus. Parables are simple images or comparisons which confront the hearer or reader with a radical choice about his invitation to enter the Kingdom of God. (CCC, Glossary)

parish: A stable community of the faithful within a particular church or diocese, whose pastoral care is confided by the bishop to a priest as pastor. (CCC, Glossary)

particular Church: The Church in a local community, or in a diocese or archdiocese in the Latin Church and in eparchies in the Eastern Churches. *See also* **diocese**.

Paschal Mystery: In speaking of the Paschal Mystery we present Christ's death and Resurrection as one, inseparable event. It is *paschal* because it is Christ's passing into death and passing over it into new life. It is a *mystery* because it is a visible sign of an invisible act of God. (USCCA, Glossary, 522–23)

passions, moral: The emotions or dispositions which incline us to good or evil actions, such as love and hate, hope and fear, joy and sadness, and anger. (CCC, Glossary)

pastor/pastoral office: The ministry of shepherding the faithful in the name of Christ. The pope and bishops receive the pastoral office which they are to exercise with Christ the Good Shepherd as their model; they share their pastoral ministry with priests, to whom they give responsibility over a portion of the flock as pastors of parishes. (CCC, Glossary)

pastoral associate: A lay ecclesial minister appointed to the bishop to assist a pastor in his administration of a parish, except in the administration of the sacraments.

pastoral life director: A lay ecclesial minister appointed to the bishop to lead a parish that does not have a priest to serve as its pastor; a pastoral life director can perform all pastoral duties, except the administration of the sacraments.

People of God: God calls the Church into existence as his people centered in Christ and sustained by the Holy Spirit. The visible structure of the People of God as the Church is the means intended by Christ to help guarantee the life of grace for the whole. (USCCA, Glossary, 523)

polygamy: The practice of having more than one wife at the same time, which is contrary to the unity of marriage between one man and one woman, and which offends against the dignity of woman. (CCC, Glossary)

pope: The successor to St. Peter who serves as the Bishop of Rome and as the visible and juridical head of the Catholic Church. (USCCA, Glossary, 523)

poverty (voluntary): One of the three evangelical counsels whose public profession in the Church is a constitutive element of consecrated life. Poverty of spirit signifies detachment from worldly things and voluntary humility. (CCC, Glossary)

prayer: "The raising of one's mind and heart to God in thanksgiving and in praise of his glory. It can also include the requesting of good things from God. It is an act by which one enters into an awareness of a loving communion with God" (USCCA, Glossary, 523–24). "Prayer is the response of faith to the free promise of salvation and also a response of love to the thirst of the only Son of God" (CCC, no. 2561).

presbyter: Another name for an ordained priest. "An 'elder' or priest, a member of the order of priesthood; the presbyterate is one of the three degrees of the Sacrament of Holy Orders. Presbyters or priests are co-workers with their bishops and form a unique sacerdotal [priestly] college or 'presbyterium' dedicated to assist their bishops in priestly service to the People of God. Through the ministry of priests, the unique sacrifice of Christ on the cross is made present in the Eucharistic sacrifice of the Church" (CCC, Glossary). *See also* **priest; priesthood, ordained/ ministerial**.

presbyterate/presbyterium: *see* **presbyter**.

priest: A baptized man ordained through the Sacrament of Holy Orders. "Priests are united with the bishops in priestly dignity and at the same time depend on them in the exercise of their pastoral functions; they are called to be the bishops' prudent co-workers" (CCC, no. 1595). With the bishop, priests form a presbyteral (priestly) community and assume with him the pastoral mission for a particular parish. They serve God's People in the work of sanctification by their preaching, teaching, and offering the Sacraments, especially the Eucharist and the forgiving of sins. (USCCA, Glossary, 524) *See also* **ministerial priesthood; priesthood of the faithful**.

priesthood: *see* **ministerial priesthood; priesthood of Christ; priesthood of the faithful**.

priesthood of Christ: The unique high priest, according to the order of Melchizedek. Christ fulfilled everything that the priesthood of the Old Covenant prefigured. (See Hebrews 5:10,

6:20.) He offered himself once and for all (see Hebrews 10:14), in a perfect sacrifice upon the cross. His priesthood is made present in a special way in the Church through the ministerial priesthood, conferred through the Sacrament of Holy Orders. (CCC, Glossary).

priesthood of the faithful: Christ gives the faithful a share in his priesthood through the Sacraments of Baptism and Confirmation. This means that all baptized and confirmed members of the Church share in offering prayer and sacrifice to God. The priesthood of the faithful differs in essence from the ministerial priesthood. (USCCA, Glossary, 524)

providence: *see* **divine providence**.

purity of heart: "Purity of heart is the precondition of the vision of God. Even now it enables us to see *according* to God, to accept others as 'neighbors'; it lets us perceive the human body—ours and our neighbor's—as a temple of the Holy Spirit, a manifestation of divine beauty" (CCC, no. 2519). This attitude and virtue strengthens us to resist inordinate desires that are a consequence of concupiscence, one of the effects of Original Sin. *See also* **concupiscence**.

R–S

rabbi: Jewish religious leader, recognized as a teacher and interpreters of the Law and of Jewish tradition. Jesus' disciples, leading Pharisees and others acknowledged and respected Jesus as a rabbi.

sacramental grace(s): Gifts of the Holy Spirit received in the sacraments to help us live out our Christian vocation. (See CCC, Glossary, "Grace") *See also* **grace**.

Sacraments, Seven: The seven "efficacious sign[s] of grace, instituted by Christ and entrusted to the Church, by which divine life is dispensed to us by the work of the Holy Spirit" (USCCA, Glossary, 526; *see also* CCC, Glossary). The Seven Sacraments are the three Sacraments of Christian Initiation (Baptism, Confirmation, and Eucharist), the two Sacraments of Healing (Penance and Reconciliation, and Anointing of the Sick), and the two Sacraments at the Service of Communion (Marriage and Holy Orders).

Sacraments at the Service of Communion: The term *communion* refers to the Community of the Church. Holy Orders and Matrimony are the Sacraments at the Service of Communion (the community of the Church). This means they are primarily directed toward the salvation of others. If they benefit the personal salvation of the ordained or married person, it is through service to others that this happens. (USCCA, Glossary, 527)

Sacred Chrism: *see* **Chrism**.

sanctifying grace: The word "sanctifying" means "that which makes holy." "Sanctifying grace is a habitual gift of God's own divine life, a stable and supernatural disposition that enables us to live with God and to act by his love" (USCCA, Glossary, "Grace," 514). *See also* **grace**.

Sanhedrin: The Sanhedrin was the highest governing and judicial body of the Jewish religious community in Jesus' time.

scandal: An attitude or behavior which leads another to do evil. (CCC, Glossary)

scribe: The Jewish scribe in Jesus' times is the scholar and the intellectual of Judaism, who receives the title rabbi. His scholarship was the knowledge of the law, which he regarded as the sum of wisdom and the only true learning. (John L. McKenzie, SJ, *Dictionary of the Bible*)

secular institutes: " 'A secular institute is an institute of consecrated life in which the Christian faithful living in the world strive for the perfection of charity and work for the sanctification of the world especially from within.' . . . [T]he members of these institutes share in the Church's task of evangelization, 'in the world and from within the world,' where their presence acts as 'leaven in the world.'

'Their witness of a Christian life' aims 'to order temporal things according to God and inform the world with the power of the gospel.' They commit themselves to the evangelical counsels by sacred bonds and observe among themselves the communion and fellowship appropriate to their 'particular secular way of life' " (CCC, no. 928; see also CIC, canons 710, 713 § 2).

seminary: A place of study and formation for men, seminarians, preparing for the priesthood. Seminaries address the human, spiritual, academic (intellectual) and pastoral education and formation of future priests.

separation (of married couples): "[T]here are some situations in which living together becomes practically impossible for a variety of reasons. In such cases the Church permits the physical *separation* of the couple and their living apart. The spouses do not cease to be husband and wife before God and so are not free to contract a new union. In this difficult situation, the best solution would be, if possible, reconciliation. The Christian community is called to help these persons live out their situation in a Christian manner and in fidelity to their marriage bond which remains indissoluble" (CCC, no. 1649).

single life: A temporary or permanent choice by a lay person to live out their faith and give witness to Christ. *See also* **committed single life**.

societies of apostolic life: "Alongside the different forms of consecrated life are 'societies of apostolic life whose members without religious vows pursue the particular apostolic purpose of their society, and lead a life as brothers or sisters in common according to a particular manner of life, strive for the perfection of charity through the observance of the constitutions. Among these there are societies in which the members embrace the evangelical counsels' according to their constitutions" (CCC, no. 930; see also CIC, canon 731 §§ 1,2).

Son of Man: The title used by our Lord of himself in the Gospel. This title connotes a relationship with the eschatological figure of the "Son of man appearing in clouds and glory" in the prophecy of Daniel (see Mark 13:26; Daniel 7:13). (CCC, Glossary)

states of life: The term "states of life" refers to the ordained ministry, the consecrated life, and the married life.

T–Z

temperance: The Cardinal Virtue by which one moderates the desire for the attainment of and pleasure in earthly goods. (USCCA, Glossary, 530) *See also* **cardinal virtues**.

temptation: An attraction, either from outside oneself or from within, to act contrary to right reason and the commandments of God. (CCC, Glossary)

theological virtues: Gifts "infused by God into the souls of the faithful to make them capable of acting as his children and of meriting eternal life" (CCC, no. 1813). The theological virtues are faith, hope and charity (love).

Theology of the Body: The teachings of St. John Paul II about the goodness and sacredness of the human body and its role in our expressing and sharing our truest and most intimate self. God is the giver of spiritual and bodily life. God creates us body and soul. Our spiritual and immortal soul is the source of our unity as a person. All our desires for what is good, including our sexual desires, are rooted in and connected inseparably with our desire for life with and in God.

Trinity: One God in three Persons—Father, Son, Holy Spirit. (USCCA, Glossary, 530)

virginity: A perfection of the virtue of chastity and celibacy; voluntary and complete chastity and celibacy; abstinence from sexual intercourse and pleasure throughout the course of one's life. *See also* **celibacy; chastity**.

virtue: A habitual and firm disposition to do the good. The moral virtues are acquired through human effort aided by God's grace; the theological virtues are gifts of God. (CCC, Glossary)

vocation: The term given to the call to each person from God; everyone has been called to holiness and eternal life, especially in Baptism. Each person can also be called more specifically to the priesthood or to religious life, to married life, and to single life, as well as to a particular profession or service. (USCCA, Glossary, 531)

Western Church: *see* **Eastern Churches and Western Churches**.

wisdom: A spiritual gift which enables one to know the purpose and plan of God; one of the seven gifts of the Holy Spirit. Wisdom is also the name of one of the books of the Old Testament. (CCC, Glossary)

works of mercy: Charitable actions by which we come to the aid of our neighbors in their bodily and spiritual needs. The spiritual works of mercy include instructing, advising, consoling, comforting, forgiving, and patiently forbearing. Corporal works of mercy include feeding the hungry, clothing the naked, visiting the sick and imprisoned, sheltering the homeless, and burying the dead. (CCC, Glossary)

Acknowledgments

Scripture quotations taken from or adapted from *New Revised Standard Version Bible: Catholic Edition*, copyright © 1989, 1993, Division of Christian Education of the National Council of Churches of Christ in the USA; all rights reserved.

Excerpts from the English translation of the *Catechism of the Catholic Church* for use in the United States, second edition, copyright © 1997, United States Catholic Conference, Inc., Libreria Editrice Vaticana; all rights reserved.

Excerpts from *Compendium of the Catechism of the Catholic Church*, copyright © 2005 Libreria Editrice Vaticana; all rights reserved.

Excerpts from documents of Vatican II from A. Flannery (ed.), *Vatican Council II: Constitutions, Decrees, Declarations* (New York/Dublin: Costello Publishing/Dominican Publications, 1996).

Excerpts from *Sons and Daughters of the Light: A Pastoral Plan for Ministry with Young Adults* (1996); *Lay Ecclesial Ministry: The State of the Questions* (2000); *Co-Workers in the Vineyard of the Lord* (2005); *United States Catholic Catechism for Adults* (2006); *Catholic Household Blessings & Prayers*, Revised Edition (2007); *Marriage: Love and Life in the Divine Plan* (2009); and from the website of United States Conference of Catholic Bishops (*www.usccb.org*); all copyright United States Conference of Catholic Bishops, Washington DC; all rights reserved.

Excerpts from Paul VI, *Perfectae Caritatis* (1965) and *Humanae Vitae* (1968). John Paul II, *Familiaris Consortio* (1981); Homily, November 30, 1986; *Mulieris Dignitatem* (1988); *Pastores Dabo Vobis* (1992); Letter to Families, February 2, 1994; *Vita Consecrata* (1996); *Christifideles Laici* (1998); *Ecclesia in America* (1999); *Novo Millennio Ineunte* (2000). Pope Francis, *Evangelii Gaudium* (2013); homily at World Youth Day, Rio de Janeiro, 2013; Sermon, September 16, 2013; Letter to Families, February 2, 2014; *Rejoice! A Letter to Consecrated Men and Women* (2014); *Amoris Laetitia* (2016). Excerpts from New American Bible [NAB]. All copyright © Libreria Editrice Vaticana.

Excerpts from the English translation *of Rite of Baptism for Children* © 1969, International Commission on English in the Liturgy Corporation (ICEL); excerpts from the English translation of *Rite of Marriage* © 1969, ICEL; excerpts from the English translation of *Rite of Consecration to a Life of Virginity* © 1975, ICEL; excerpts from the English translation of *Rites of Ordination of a Bishop, of Priests, and of Deacons* © 2000, 2002, ICEL; excerpts from the English translation of *The Roman Missal* © 2010, ICEL. All rights reserved.

"Fall in Love," p. 6, attributed to Fr. Pedro Arrupe, S.J., from *Finding God in All Things: A Marquette Prayer Book* (Milwaukee, MI: Marquette University, 2009); used with permission.

Quotation from C.S. Lewis, p. 9, from *Mere Christianity* (HarperCollins, 2001).

Mission statement of the Society of Our Mother of Peace, p. 209, from *www.marythefont.org*.

Mission statement of Catholic Relief Services (CRS), p. 227, from *www.crs.org*.

Prayer to Our Lady of Guadalupe, pp. 245, copyright the National Coalition for Church Vocations (NRVC).

Image credits:

COVER: *Main image:* Detail from *Supper at Emmaus*, 1606 by Michelangelo Merisi da Caravaggio. Oil on canvas, 141 x 175 cm. Brera Fine Arts Academy, Milan, Italy. © akg-images / Mondadori Portfolio / Mauro Magliani.

p. 15. Photo: Daderot

p. 19: Photo: Buda Mendes/Thinkstock

p. 28: Wellcome Collection

p. 33: Photo: Marcio Antonio de Castro Campos/Thinkstock

p. 44: J. Paul Getty Museum

p. 49: J. Paul Getty Museum

p. 52: Photo: Cabealva/Thinkstock

p. 55: Photo: Nheyob

p. 66: Photo: Vignaccia76

p. 67: Walters Art Museum, Baltimore, Maryland

p. 68: Universität-und Landesbibliothek Darmstadt

p. 73: Wellcome Collection

p. 76: Photo: Franco Origlia/Thinkstock

p. 78: Photo: WMPearl

p. 79: Wellcome Collection

p. 87: Photo: Andreas Praefcke

p. 89: Photo: Anagoria

p. 91: Photo: Nheyob

p. 105: Photo: © 2010 H. Michael Miley

p. 108: *Don't Marry a Catholic* by Rev. Daniel A. Lord, SJ (CTSI, 1955); artwork by John Henry. © Veritas

p. 121: Photo: Ambrosius007 at English Wikipedia

p. 153: Photo: G Freihalter

p. 158: Photo: Miguel Hermoso Cuesta

p. 159: Photo: Alejo2083

p. 163: Photo courtesy of Susan Kehoe (http://adeaconswife.com)

p. 164: Photo: P. Vasiliadis

p. 165: Photo: Geoffroy Blanc

p. 171: Photo: Nheyob

p. 172: Photo: Sailko

p. 173: Photo courtesy of Dieter Philippi, Philippi Collection, http://philippi-collection.blogspot.com

p. 175: Photo: Chris McGrath/Thinkstock

p. 177: Photo: Marcio Antonio de Castro Campos/Thinkstock

p. 178: Photo: Marcio Antonio de Castro Campos/Thinkstock

p. 181: Photo: John Stephen Dwyer (Boston at en.wikipedia)

p. 182: Photo: Bill Wittman

p. 185: Photo: Farragutful

p. 186: Photo: Daderot

p. 190: Photo: Nheyob

p. 191: Photo: Bachrach/Getty Images

p. 199: Andrey Mironov

p. 203: Photo: Florestan

p. 205: Wellcome Collection

p. 209: Photo: Paula Bronstein/Thinkstock

p. 210: Photo: Spencer Platt/Thinkstock

p. 211: Wellcome Collection

p. 227: Photo: Lane Hartill/Catholic Relief Services

p. 230: Library of Congress

p. 232: Photo: Judge Florentino Floro

p. 234: Photo: Bill Wittman

Index

Page numbers set in **bold italics**
indicate definitions in Faith
Glossary

Printed in the USA
CPSIA information can be obtained
www.ICGtesting.com
W061836100823
0JS00003BA/4